Library of
Davidson College

The Bayonets of the Republic

Publication of this work was supported in part
by grants from the National Endowment for the Humanities
and the Andrew W. Mellon Foundation.

© 1984 by the Board of Trustees of the University of Illinois
Manufactured in the United States of America

This book is printed on acid-free paper.

Library of Congress Cataloging in Publication Data

Lynn, John A. (John Albert), 1943–
　　The bayonets of the Republic.

Bibliography: p.
Includes index.
1. France. Armée—History—18th century.
2. Tactics—History—18th century. 3. Military art and
science—France—History—18th century. I. Title.
UA702.L95 1984　　355′.00944　　83-9093
ISBN 0-252-01091-4

The Bayonets of the Republic

Motivation and Tactics in the Army of Revolutionary France, 1791–94

John A. Lynn

University of Illinois Press

URBANA AND CHICAGO

*To Andrea Lynn,
who has had to wait
far too long for
this dedication*

Contents

Introduction   xi

SECTION ONE:
Victory in the North

Chapter 1:   The Armée du Nord on Campaign   3

Chapter 2:   The Elements of Victory: A Theory of Combat Effectiveness   21

SECTION TWO:
Composition, Control, and Motivation

Chapter 3:   The New Soldier: Composition and Character of the Rank and File   43

Chapter 4:   The New Officer Corps: Social Composition, Political Surveillance, and Military Leadership   67

Chapter 5:   Discipline in an Army of Citizen-Soldiers   97

Chapter 6:   The Political Education of the Armée du Nord   119

Chapter 7:   The *Ordinaire* and Motivation   163

SECTION THREE:
Doctrine, Training, and Tactics

Chapter 8:   The Cult of the Bayonet: Enthusiasm and Tactics   185

Chapter 9:   Cavalry and Artillery in an Infantry Army   194

Chapter 10:   Training an Evolving Infantry   216

Chapter 11:	Line and Column on the Battlefield	241
Chapter 12:	The Dimensions of Open Order Combat in the Armée du Nord	261
Conclusion:	Motivation and Tactics: The Experience of the Armée du Nord in Context	278
Appendix:	Tables Concerning Tactical Practice	287
Notes		301
Bibliography		329
Index		341

Acknowledgments

I hope the reader will understand if I take this opportunity to pay my bills in public. In a very real sense *Bayonets of the Republic* has been twenty years in the writing, since I first broached the subject when still an undergraduate at the University of Illinois. Over such a long period I have benefited from the advice, aid, and comfort of many individuals.

Let me express my debt to those who guided my studies and shaped my standards in historical work, Charles Nowell, Richard Schwab, Peter Paret, Andrew Lossky, and the late B. H. Liddell Hart. Among the mentors who have helped me so much I must single out Isser Woloch, now of Columbia University and once of UCLA. He has been both my strongest critic and staunchest supporter for fifteen years.

The staff of the Archives de la guerre at Vincennes were of the greatest possible service to my research. I also enjoyed the kind assistance of personnel at the Bibliothèque Nationale, the Archives Nationales, and the municipal library of Valenciennes.

My thanks as well to Paddy Griffith, whose graduate paper on infantry attacks gave me important methodological insights which aided my research.

I have been assisted in the preparation of this manuscript by the counsel of Samuel F. Scott and Jean-Paul Bertaud. They have been the best of friends, both to me and to my scholarship. In fact, without the constant assistance of Jean-Paul it is hard to see how my book would have ever been completed. Others I must thank for their suggestions concerning the manuscript are Morris Janowitz, Theodore Ropp, Blair Kling, and Paul Schroeder. For his investment of time and energy far beyond the call of duty, I want to acknowledge my dear friend and colleague Frederic Jaher.

I also must recognize the financial support of the National Endowment for the Humanities, which awarded me a grant to study the political education of the revolutionary army.

The years devoted to this project have been made richer by the very real support and kindness of some other fine people: Adelle S. Lynn, Judd and Jean Lynn, Susan Sackett, Ralph and Janice Rosenfeld, Vicki Berger, Harry and Helyn Kramer, and Richard and Sharon White. Thanks as well to Robert and Monique Auger of Montreuil and Amponville who have done so much to help me understand the strong character of the *sans-culottes*.

And, lastly, thanks upon thanks to my wife Andrea and my sons Daniel and Nathanael, who have had to travel the ups and downs of the path that led to *The Bayonets of the Republic*.

Introduction

THE VICTORIES won by the armies of revolutionary France claim a significance in history rivaled by few battlefield triumphs. If not for the success of republican arms, foreign enemies who threatened to reimpose the ancien régime upon France would have set back the great political and social work of the Revolution. At the same time as they secured the Revolution, these forces also transformed the character of war in Europe. The unprecedented commitment and effort of the French people brought to an end the age of dynastic war and ushered in the era of national war.

My study examines the motivation and tactics of the troops who stood in defense of their Patrie during the crucial first years of the war. It concentrates on combat or, more exactly, on combat effectiveness. It is first a history of detail, scrutinizing the composition, command, discipline, education, doctrine, training, and combat style of an army. Second, it is an analysis of the nature of troop motivation and the relationship between that motivation and the tactics of battalions in the field.

Since the ultimate concern here is traditional—how troops performed in battle—many of the questions asked have been asked before, but I have sought answers by new means. Theories of unit cohesion and combat effectiveness borrowed from the social sciences shape the discussion. They emphasize such seldom considered factors as the sense of individual worth, shared beliefs, and group-enforced standards. The rich production of the "new military history" provides fresh information and insights. Over the last decade several fine works have appeared that have examined the French army from a social, political, or institutional perspective. I have benefited from them, and I hope my own work complements them. It has been my goal to integrate their findings with the study of troops under fire. When reconstructing the tactical system itself, my research followed a quantitative approach designed to transcend the narrow experience and impressionistic judgments of individual partisans of one point of view or another.

To keep my project within manageable bounds, I have focused primarily on only one of the several republican armies that guarded the French frontiers, the Armée du Nord. The time period covered runs from mid-1791 through mid-1794. In 1791 the French geared up for war. Regular regiments began to rebuild after two years of disintegration; volunteer battalions mobilized to join the regulars at the front. Troops along the borders of France organized into armies, and the Armée du Nord came into existence. Important breaks in continuity dictate the cutoff point in 1794. First, the Armée du Nord changed form radically in June 1794, when much of it split off to merge with the Armée de la Moselle to create the Sambre et Meuse. Second, the government's important political policies directed toward the army shifted abruptly with the end of the Terror. Third, by the victories of May and June 1794 the Nord accomplished its defensive task. In the future it became a secondary offensive army and eventually atrophied. To concentrate on the Armée du Nord 1791–94 is to concentrate on essentials—the most critical theater of war at revolutionary high tide.

When dealing with composition, control, and motivation, my discussion necessarily reaches beyond the Nord, although the Nord exemplifies the broad issues covered. I am confident that conclusions reached in this section can be reasonably extended to French field forces as a whole. However, concerning training and tactics, it is more difficult to generalize from the experience of the Nord. Each of the Republic's armies evolved its own tactical style, influenced by the particular circumstances of leadership, opposition, and geography unique to that army. Here, revolutionary flux and improvisation produced variety.

The results of my study challenge the textbook wisdom that revolutionary soldiers, unskilled but driven by patriotic enthusiasm, won by simply overwhelming their enemies with the ragged horde tactics of the bayonet assault. Of course, every new interpretation tilts at its own straw man. On occasion more moderate views have found their way into print, and some of the most expert criticisms have denied the stereotype to insist that the French fought only as light infantry or in line alone during the early years of the war. However, for the last two centuries, the great majority of commentators exclusively stressed the charge *en masse*. To the contrary, the reality presented in this volume is a story of complexity. Combat motivation involved more than patriotism, and tactics consisted of more than frenzied charges. Only a thorough and varied analysis can truly explain why victory crowned the bayonets of the Republic.

SECTION ONE

Victory in the North

Chapter 1

The Armée du Nord on Campaign

Few readers can be expected to know the history of the Armée du Nord. For most, its triumphs merge into the broad flow of revolutionary events, and its victories belong not to one army but to France. Commanders of the Nord are more likely to stir memories—the comte de Rochambeau, the marquis de Lafayette, Charles François Dumouriez, and Jean Baptiste Jourdan—yet they too are but seldom associated with the army they led. Since analysis requires context, the following narrative history of the Nord introduces the names and events discussed throughout this volume. It joins together in proper sequence elements that will later be dissected for detailed study. It also suggests that the explanation of French victory in the North lies in the citizen-soldiers who made up the Armée du Nord.

Prelude to War

By 1791 the French feared armed intervention by the monarchs of Europe, and after Louis XVI attempted to flee the country in June of that year, war seemed all but inevitable. Yet, in fact, Austria, Prussia, and Russia were far from agreeing on any joint course of action toward revolutionary France. Mutual distrust and the lingering question of Poland's fate precluded them from forming a common front. Despite the lack of a real threat, the French edged toward war, since the most powerful factions in Paris saw war as a servant of their own political aims. But had the French politicians truly understood the weakness of their armed forces, they might not have so lustily voted to declare war against the Hapsburgs on 20 April 1792.

The first two years of the Revolution had greatly weakened the French army. Egalitarian ideas corroded discipline, while the turbulent confusion of the times resulted in a high rate of desertion. A rapid turnover in command, occasioned by the emigration of nearly 60 percent of all officers, struck the army still harder. On 1 January 1791 the National Assembly authorized a peacetime army of 157,000 men, yet the real strength of French forces did not exceed 130,000. After much debate the Assembly voted to shore up the defenses of France by calling up National Guard volunteers. The old regular, or line, army of the ancien régime did not enjoy the full confidence of the legislators. The new volunteer battalions seemed more politically reliable. At first these volunteer battalions constituted only a kind of inactive reserve force, but in the heated session of 21 June 1791, when the Legislative Assembly learned of Louis's flight, they were mobilized to stand alongside the understrength regular army. Volunteers and regulars alike were in need of discipline and training.

Troops moved up to the frontiers during the summer of 1791, but only in December did the government set up three major armies along France's eastern boarder. Entrusted with the frontier from Landau to Huningue, the Armée du Rhin numbered about 49,000 troops under the command of Marshal Nicolas, baron Luckner. From Montmedy to Bitche stood the Armée du Centre with about 30,000 men under the marquis de Lafayette. And from the Meuse to the sea the Armée du Nord stretched its nearly 53,000 soldiers commanded by Marshal Jean-Baptiste de Vimeur, comte de Rochambeau, possibly the ablest officer in the French high command. As the war expanded, enveloping ever more of the French frontier and claiming ever more manpower, the French Republic by mid-1794 would be defended by eleven armies totaling roughly 750,000 men. Throughout the period 1792–94, however, the Nord remained the largest single assemblage of French fighting men.

Early Trials and Setbacks

As soon as war was declared, the government in Paris, pressed by its foreign minister Charles François Dumouriez, ordered Rochambeau to send his ill-trained and inexperienced battalions against a numerically smaller Austrian force in the Austrian Netherlands. The Marshal wisely objected to this unreasonable demand on the basis that even his line units needed more training before they could face the excellent Hapsburg troops, but his objections were overruled. On 28 April General Théobald Dillon led a column of some 2,300 troops from Lille toward Tournai. Meeting a small force of Austrians just across the border, he decided to withdraw the next day, but an orderly retreat proved too much for his soldiers, and they panicked. On 29 April 1792 General Dillon met his death at the hands of his own troops who shouted, "We are betrayed!" and "Every man for himself!" as they fled in utter rout. The same day saw Armand-Louis de Gontaut, duc de Biron, depart Valenciennes with some 15,000 men in an

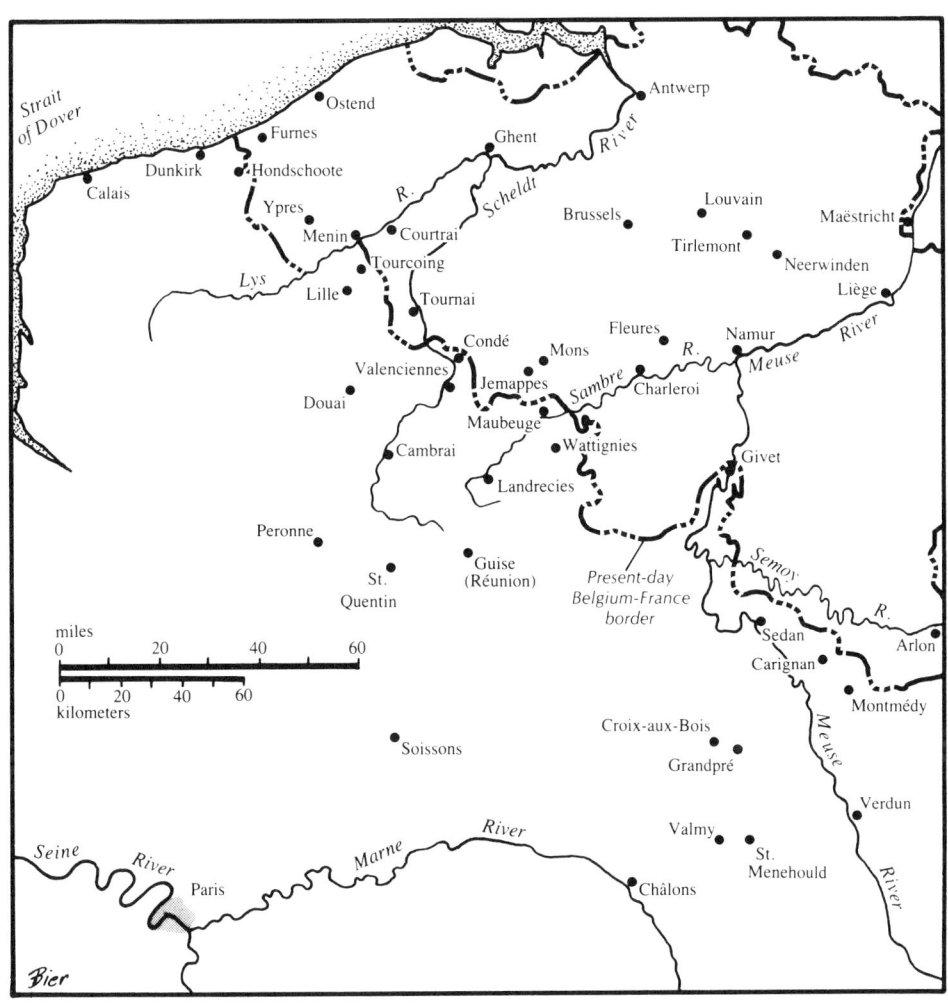

MAP 1. *The Campaigns of the Armée du Nord, 1792–94.*

attempt to take the fortress of Mons. His command never reached Mons but instead turned back before it got as far as Jemappes. Panic seized Biron's retreating troops just as it had gripped Dillon's, but, fortunately, Biron escaped with his life. These defeats stimulated the Assembly to call for a new levy of volunteers, the Volunteers of 1792. Circumstances confirmed Rochambeau's judgment, but, since the government was reluctant to let him exercise command as he saw fit, he submitted his resignation.

Dumouriez, who virtually ran the Ministry of War as well as foreign affairs, now chose Marshal Luckner, commander of the Armée du Rhin, to replace Rochambeau. The interim command of the Rhin went to General Alexis Magallon, comte de La Morlière. Luckner for some inexplicable reason enjoyed considerable favor with the revolutionaries at this time. The marvelous "Chant de guerre pour l'Armée du Rhin," known later simply as "La Marseillaise," was even composed in his honor. Yet the fact remained that he possessed only the most mediocre of skills. His military reputation rested on his feats as a daring leader of Hanoverian light cavalry against the French in the Seven Years' War. He arrived at Valenciennes on 15 May, and after less than a month with the Nord, this bumbling septuagenarian led 20,000 troops of his army from the Camp de Famars near Valenciennes on a futile invasion of Flanders. Marching first to Lille, he finally took both Menin and Courtrai on 19 June. But Luckner's timidity in command of an army exceeded his temerity in command of a squadron, and without good reason he withdrew from both towns on 30 June and returned to Lille.

Now occurred a most strange maneuver, the *chassé-croisé*. Lafayette, first and always a political general, desired to play a greater role in the affairs of government. He reasoned that if his troops were closer to Paris he might rise to become the arbiter of French politics. Consequently, he conspired to switch commands with Luckner, since Luckner's Nord lay closer to Paris than did Lafayette's Centre. Yet while he wished to exchange commands, Lafayette was unwilling to part with the battalions serving under him, because he believed they bore him special loyalty. Consequently, Lafayette proposed that not only the commanders trade places but also that their entire armies switch names and positions. Incredible as it may seem, this insane maneuver received the ministry's approval. The government forced Lafayette to accept only one alteration in his plans. The fallen Dumouriez, who had joined the Armée du Nord on 1 July, used what influence he still had in Paris to win the right to remain with the troops he commanded on the northeast frontier. In charge of the entrenched Camp de Maude, he would cover the frontier while the two armies changed places. In mid-July the actual exchange took place without serious incident.

The turn of events now intervened to give the Nord still another commander-in-chief and to provide revolutionary France with a new hero. The threatened Prussian invasion under Karl-Wilhelm-Ferdinand, duke of Brunswick, charged the Parisian air with fear and determination. On 11 July 1792 the Legislative Assembly proclaimed, "Citoyens, la Patrie est en danger." Then on 1 August Paris heard of Brunswick's ill-considered and ill-timed manifesto threatening to destroy Paris should any harm befall Louis XVI. The revolutionary crowd answered this challenge to its bravery and integrity with the revolution of 10 August 1792. Lafayette, a man of the Revolution perhaps, but always a royalist as well, now labored to invest the political capital he had acquired in the *chassé-croisé*. On 15 August he tried to get his troops at Sedan to take an oath to the king, but he no longer commanded their loyalty. With his army unwilling to march on Paris to restore the king, Lafayette on 19 August crossed the frontier and surrendered himself to the Allies, who imprisoned him for the next five years. Two days before he fled, the Assembly had voted the command of the Nord to Dumouriez.

Dumouriez's Fall Campaigns

Dumouriez could not have been more pleased; he had long advocated an invasion of the Austrian Netherlands, which he could now undertake. He proposed that the best way to stop the Prussian advance would be by an offensive in the north, but the wary Paris government ordered him to bring his army south to defend the capital. This he reluctantly agreed to do, and on 1 September Dumouriez led the majority of the Nord south from Sedan. At this point begins a rather confusing problem with names. Dumouriez chose to christen the battalions now moving south toward the Argonne the Armée des Ardennes, though in actuality they were only part of the Armée du Nord and not a separate army. The Ardennes was to the Nord as a task force is to a fleet. From September 1792 until June 1794 the Ardennes existed as a separate unit, but it would always be subordinate to the Nord's commander. So closely connected were the two that historians often refer to the Armée du Nord et des Ardennes. The coming months witnessed the creation of two other task force armies, the Armée de la Belgique and the Armée de la Hollande; like the Ardennes they constituted mere subdivisions of the Nord, although unlike the Ardennes they were both defunct by mid-1793.

Dumouriez threw the Armée des Ardennes into the wooded hills of the Argonne in an attempt to bar the Prussian advance on Paris. The Armée des Ardennes displayed unexpected determination and ability for several days, which bought valuable time for the French. But owing to a nearly

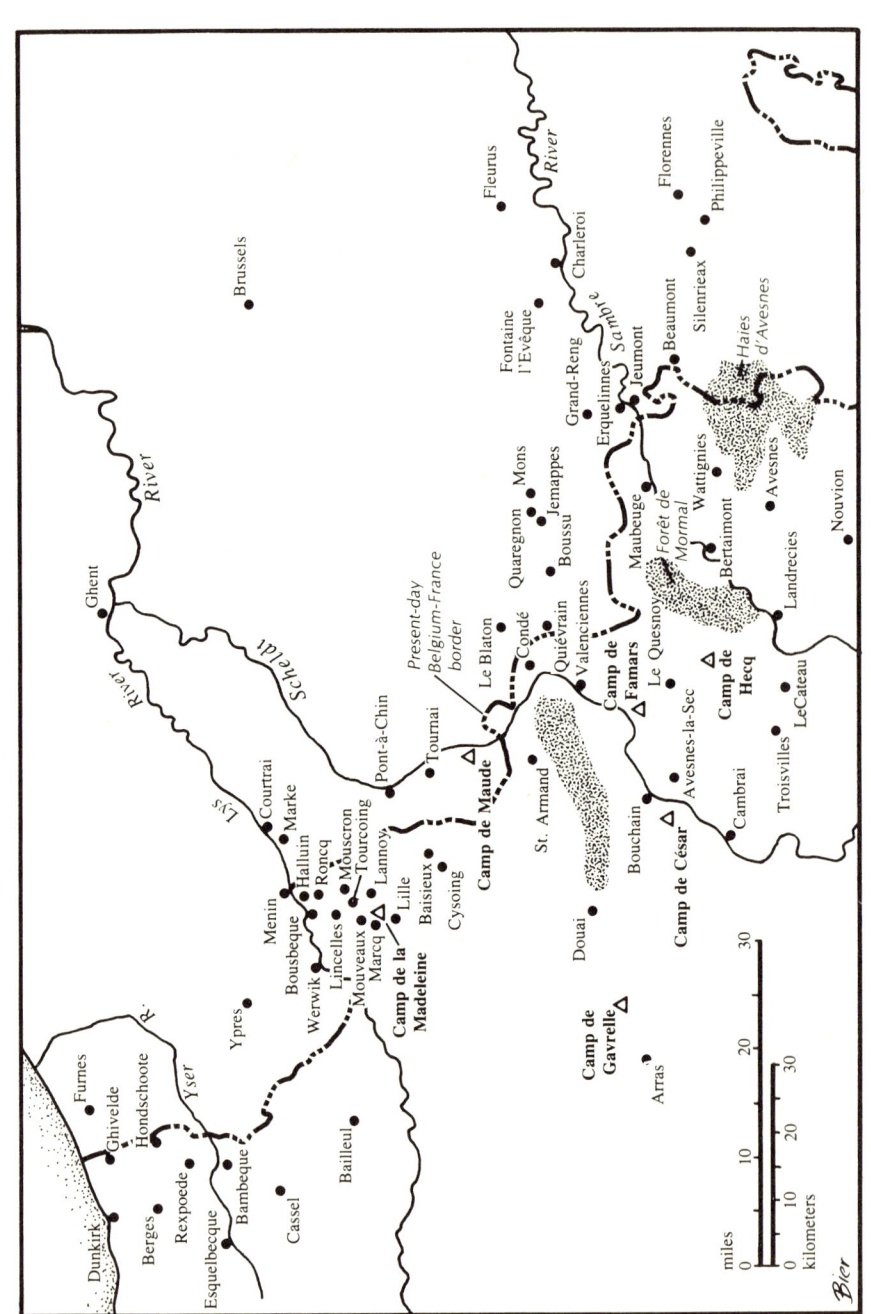

MAP 2. *The Main Battleground of the Armée du Nord.*

fatal instance of confusion, the pass at Croix-aux-bois was left unguarded, and Brunswick's troops were able to seize it on 12 July. The Armée des Ardennes then withdrew toward St. Menehould and a rendezvous with the Armée de Centre, now under the command of General François-Etienne Kellermann. Units of the Ardennes did the best they could, marching and fighting their way south. Combats took place at Grand-Pré on the 15th, at Clermont on the 17th, and elsewhere until Kellermann and Dumouriez finally joined forces on 19 September 1792. The next day Kellermann's troops faced Brunswick's army; Dumouriez's harried and tired battalions stood in reserve. More cannonade than battle, the battle of Valmy stopped the Prussian advance, and, although Brunswick's army was not destroyed, Kellermann gave the Republic a complete strategic victory that day. After more than a week of inactivity, Brunswick began his retreat on 30 September. Dumouriez and the Ardennes had greatly aided in the task so well completed by the Centre. Now he could turn his attention once more to the Low Countries.

Dumouriez confided the command of the Armée des Ardennes to General Jean-Baptiste de Timbrune, comte de Valence, and it began its march back to the north. Dumouriez detoured to Paris in order to win support for his plans. He was authorized to attack the Austrian Netherlands, which the French already called Belgium, with the 88–95,000 troops grouped together in his command. To oppose this invasion the Austrians could muster only perhps half that number. No longer the inexperienced and panicky troops of April, these French soldiers who massed along the border displayed a new confidence gained through training and on the battlefield. The men suffered the matériel shortages that would plague the Nord for years, but they were eager to fight. On 3 November Dumouriez set his troops in motion from Valenciennes toward Mons, while he ordered the rest of his command in Lille, Maubeuge, and elsewhere to carry out diversions to occupy Austrian attention. After preliminary skirmishes at Boussu on the 3rd and Quaregnon on the 5th, on the 6th Dumouriez's main body of 30,000 joined by 10,000 Volunteers of 1792 under the command of General Louis -Auguste des Ursins, comte d'Harville, formed in order of battle below the town of Jemappes, situated a short distance from Mons. At noon Dumouriez launched his main assault against the 14,000 Austrians holding the heights. In tightly packed columns his battalions marched directly at the enemy. The outcome could not long be in doubt; by two o'clock the Austrians were in retreat, although they had put up an admirable fight. That same day, to the north, other French forces defeated an Austrian detachment at Le Blaton, and on the 7th still other units of the Nord clashed with the Austrians at Halluin. Further victories, however, were unnecessary to establish French control of Belgium—the battle of Jemappes decided the issue.

The Hard Winter and Bitter Spring

French troops now poured into Belgium. Dumouriez himself led what he called the Armée de la Belgique; he delegated the command of the Armée des Ardennes to Valence and the small Armée du Nord first to Anne-François, comte de La Bourdonnaye, and later to Francisco de Miranda. By the end of December the French held Brussels and Liege. But this success had in fact seriously weakened French forces in the Low Countries. Men who had flocked to the tricolor in support of "la Patrie en danger" reasoned that victory, delivering the Republic from its foes, gave them the right to return to their homes. For those who remained with their battalions there was no time for rest, reorganization, and reequipping. Training proved impossible, since the soldiers dispersed into small groups to survive the worst of the winter months as best they could. Had the home government more faithfully and efficiently supplied its victorious troops, perhaps they could have been assembled in large camps where training exercises could have been conducted. For this tired and disorganized army, the worst trials were yet to come. On 1 February 1793 the Convention declared war on England and on the Dutch Netherlands. Dumouriez then received orders to invade Holland. To undertake this ill-considered attack he assembled a force of some 23,000, new recruits in the main. This army, christened the Armée de la Hollande, advanced toward Antwerp on 16 February. Meanwhile its sister armies were engaged in the siege of Maestricht. All told, the various armies under Dumouriez boasted a paper strength of over 122,000, but in reality this total must be discounted.

On 24 February 1793, the representatives sitting in the National Convention in Paris declared the levy of 300,000 men, but these new recruits would not be assembled and trained in time to help stay the tide of Austrian victories that would soon sweep the French out of Belgium. While the republican troops busied themselves with the siege of Maestricht and the invasion of Holland, the prince of Coburg gathered together an Austrian army of 40,000. On 1 March 1793 this formidable array crossed the Roer River, catching the French by surprise. Dumouriez rushed south, leaving the Armée de la Hollande under General Louis-Charles de La Motte-Ango, marquis de Flers. The French abandoned Maestricht and recoiled back on Louvain. With about 40,000 infantry and 4,500 cavalry Dumouriez resolved to attack Coburg's 30,000 infantry and 9,000 cavalry. On 18 March, at Neerwinden, occurred the great battle Dumouriez desired. Considering the poor condition of the French troops, they performed well. On the center and right they fought the Austrians to a bloody standstill, but the troops under General Miranda on the French left broke and retreated on Tirlemont. After the defeat of Neerwinden, Dumouriez attempted to stand again at Louvain on the 22nd, but by then it was hopeless. To spare the fruitless loss of additional lives and to insure the retreat of his widely scattered forces, Dumouriez negotiated a convention with the enemy. By not contesting the Austrian advance his troops would themselves be unmolested in their withdrawal to the French border. Dumouriez's negotiations, however, had a treasonable goal, since he proposed using his army to reestablish the monarchy in Paris. Unhappy with the defeat Dumouriez had just suffered and fearful of his secret negotiations, the Convention wisely dispatched commissioners to arrest him. On 1 April these commissioners found him at his headquarters, but he turned the tables on them and had them arrested. Later they were handed over to Coburg. In only four more days, however, Dumouriez found his situation untenable, and like Lafayette he went over to the Austrians. The treason of Dumouriez filled the Convention with an excessive fear of its own generals. From then on the shadow of the guillotine followed the footsteps of even the most successful officers.

The next commander of the Armée du Nord et des Ardennes, General Auguste Picot, marquis de Dampierre, seemed dwarfed by the tasks set before him. The disheartened and disorganized battalions under his command had been eroded by desertion during the long retreat, and Dampierre could only bring them back to strength by rapidly incorporating raw levies into their ranks. From an objective military standpoint, this was the Revolution's darkest hour; all that stood between Paris and the fine Austrian troops in Coburg's army were defeated battalions and a few poorly defended fortresses. In addition to the crisis in the north, the comte de Custine's Armée du Rhin was in retreat, and rebellion shook the Vendée. Luckily, the Allies forswore a major invasion of France in 1793. The Paris government mirrored the seriousness of this situation by passing a great deal of revolutionary legislation. Committees of Surveillance were to be established in every commune. A new revolutionary Tribunal was created in Paris. The famous and feared Representatives on Mission received almost unlimited power to perform their civil and military tasks. And to direct the entire war effort, the Committee of Public Safety, created in April 1793, rose to heights of executive power that even Louis XIV could not have rivaled.

Coburg decided to besiege Valenciennes, gateway on the road to Paris. Near that fortress, in the Camp de Famars, Dampierre mustered what force he could to keep the Austrians from realizing their goal. Mercifully for the tormented Dampierre, his trials were not to last long, for on 8 May 1793 he received a mortal wound in battle outside the Camp de Famars. That attempt to meet the Austrians in battle ended only in one more French defeat. To General François Joseph Drouet, known as General Lamarche, fell the unenviable task of carrying on the defense of Valenciennes as interim commander of the Armée du Nord. On 23 May the Austrians attacked again, this time assisted by English troops under the duke of York. Bottled up in the Camp de Famars, the main body of Lamarche's command awaited the onslaught, and it was defeated by the Austrian and English forces. That night, Lamarche left General Jean-Henri-Becays Ferrand to defend the fortress of Valenciennes itself and withdrew the main force to the Camp de César, some fifteen miles to the southwest of Valenciennes. Valenciennes and Condé were both besieged by the end of the month.

The Regeneration of the Nord

On 27 May 1793 General Adam Philippe, comte de Custine, arrived at Cambrai to take permanent command of the Armée du Nord. Although the victim of serious defeats earlier in the spring, Custine still enjoyed a considerable reputation. Throughout the months of June and July, while the Austrians and English busied themselves with sieges, Custine labored to reorganize and train the troops of the Nord. At Cambrai he set up a training camp for men picked from every battalion in the Nord and Ardennes for the purpose of giving them a crash course in infantry drill and then sending them back to their battalions to teach what they had just learned. A strict disciplinarian, Custine possessed an autocratic and independent character, which brought him into controversy with the Ministry of War. He was still popular with his men, since they apparently thought him able to turn the Nord into a more creditable fighting force. Custine fought no battles with the Nord; rather, he devoted the two months to better pursuits; but unfortunately he suffered defeats without risking battles. On 12 July 1793 Condé fell to the Austrians. Four days later Custine obeyed a summons from the Committee of Public Safety and journeyed to Paris. He was arrested on 22 July, and his fate was sealed by the fall of Valenciennes on the 28th.

General Charles-Edouard Jennings de Kilmaine, of Irish ancestry, then became the interim commander of the Nord. His only military act of any significance while in command of the Nord took place when he ordered his troops to abandon the Camp de César in the face of an imminent attack by Coburg. When the attack came on 8 August, it fell on empty space. The Nord had moved to the Camp de Gavrelle. Kilmaine shortly thereafter handed over command to General Jean-Nicolas Houchard, who possessed only one advantage over Kilmaine—he was French. The Armée du Nord and the Armée des Ardennes now in Houchard's hands mustered a total strength of over 175,000 men. Houchard seemed hardly the man to command such a force. Significantly, he was the first permanent commander of the Nord who had no claim to nobility. He was the *sans-culotte* general demanded by the radicals. Yet he could boast only the mediocre talents of a dragoon with scant intelligence or force of character. Luckily for the brave but dull Houchard, although the road to Paris now lay open to the Allies, they refused to march down it. The rules of eighteenth-century warfare forbade Coburg to leave his lines of communication exposed to an enemy army. The duke of York also determined that the English must have Dunkirk to serve as a base for further operations. While the English marched north to besiege Dunkirk, Coburg besieged Le Quesnoy. During the English march, there were some minor brushes with the French. At Linselles on 18 August, for example, a small force of English under Colonel Lake routed a larger force of French troops under Generals Jean-Baptiste Jourdan and Antoine Lecourt de Béru.

At the insistence of the Committee of Public Safety, Houchard and the Representatives on Mission with the Armée du Nord resolved to thwart the English siege as best they could; they had little choice. In late August Houchard marshaled his forces for an attack on the Hanoverian and English troops covering the siege. On the 24th General Théodore-François Leclaire drove the Allies out of Esquelbecque, only to see them retake it. On the 27th the French won the towns of Roncq, Lannoy, and Tourcoing, thus clearing the way for an advance against the Hanoverian army covering the siege of Dunkirk. After suffering a mild setback at Rexpoede on the night of 6–7 September, Houchard and 22,000 French troops confronted General Johan Ludwig von Walmoden's 14,600 Hanoverians across the marshes and hedges of Hondschoote on the 8th. Advocates of mass shock action, Houchard and his chief of staff General Etienne-Ambroise Berthélemy disapproved of this particular battlefield, since it hampered confrontation with the bayonet. Early in the battle the French dispersed into small bands, finding cover where they could and firing into the Hanoverian defenses. Only with great effort and some threat was Houchard able to rally his soldiers for a final onslaught, which carried the day for the French. Complete victory eluded the Republicans, however, since Walmoden withdrew his troops with little difficulty. There was no pursuit, a failure that was to cost Houchard his life. The English did give up the siege, but instead of crushing the enemy, Houchard had only caused them to draw back. Few permanent gains flowed from this victory. Le Quesnoy surrendered to the Austrians on 11 September, and, although the French had success in some serious engagements on the 12th at Werwik and Avesnes-le-sec and on the 13th at Menin, by 15 September Menin was again in Allied hands. The Committee of Public Safety then relieved Houchard of his command on 22 September, the first day of the momentous Year II in the new revolutionary calendar. The day after he lost his command he was arrested. On 16 November he became the third commander of the Nord to lose his head; Luckner and Custine had preceded him to the guillotine. Mercifully, he also was the last of the Nord's commanding generals to suffer this fate.

The next man to take over the Nord kept his head and gained a great reputation. General Jourdan, a future Napoleonic marshal, received the responsibilities of the Nord after only a little more than a week as the subordinate commander of the Armée des Ardennes. He chose General Jean-Augustin, baron Ernouf, for his chief of staff, and they did not have to wait long to test their skills. After the fall of Le Quesnoy, Coburg concentrated his attention on Maubeuge. The timidity of the Allies may seem astounding; with a gap in the frontier defenses made by the Austrian occupation of Valenciennes, Condé, and Le Quesnoy, the Allies still refused to strike at Paris. Still, it was late in the year, and, encumbered by necessary supply lines, Coburg could hardly leave 175,000 armed Frenchmen in his rear. Maubeuge and the adjoining camp contained 20,000 men of the Armée des Ardennes. Seizure of the town and the destruction of its garrison would bode well for the next campaign. Jourdan sought to strike the covering force at Wattignies and by destroying it end the siege. Lazare Carnot, the Organizer of Victory, joined the Armée du Nord in the field as a Representative on Mission.

The battle of Wattignies lasted for two days, 15 and 16 October 1793. Although the Austrian General Charles de Croix, count von Clairfayt, had 37,000 men, during the battle he could resist Jourdan's 45,000 with only 21,000. Still Coburg, in supreme command, remained so confident of victory that he promised to become a *sans-culotte* should the French win. The events of the 15th almost proved Coburg right. The splendid Austrian battalions beat back wave after wave of the numerically superior French forces. Meanwhile, a small contingent of Allied troops stopped and later scattered an attempted flanking maneuver by General Jacob-Job Elie and 3,500 troops from Philippeville. Elie's battalions broke and fled at Beaumont on the 16th. The night of 15–16 October saw Carnot and Jourdan change their basic plan. On the 15th the French had attacked all along the Austrian line; on the 16th the great bulk of Jourdan's army would concentrate against the Austrian left wing. Though massively outnumbered, the Austrian left fought well and hard, but after two unsuccessful attacks the third carried away the Austrian defenders. As at Hondschoote, pursuit was out of the question, and the Austrian and Dutch forces around Maubeuge retreated without serious challenge. Shortly after the battle of Wattignies, General Jean-Baptiste Davaine launched an attack on the Allies in Flanders, but this tardy effort came to nothing. Combats at Cysoing on 20 October, Tilleul on 23 October, and elsewhere led to no real alteration of the frontier. Menin once again fell to the French only to be evacuated as before on 27 October. General-in-Chief Jourdan himself received orders to pursue the enemy down the Sambre, but, at the risk of his life, he refused. On 6 January 1794 the Minister of War ordered the reluctant Jourdan and his chief of staff to come to Paris, where both men were relieved of command.

The Nord in Triumph

Upon Jourdan's departure, the interim command of the Nord devolved upon Ferrand, a veteran soldier of France. Then, on 8 February 1794, General Jean Charles Pichegru arrived to take charge of the Nord for the rest of its combat career. Previously a commander of the Armée du Rhin, he was a man of experience. The army, or rather armies, he now led numbered about 207,000 for the Nord and 36,000 for the Ardennes. Although this strength could only be achieved through incorporating large numbers of new recruits, the Nord would not take the field in 1794 as undisciplined and unmaneuverable units. Commanders used the time purchased by Jourdan to train their men. Since the majority of the battalions were grouped together in major camps instead of dispersed over the countryside, the possibility existed for serious mass drill. The Armée du Nord that took the field in the spring of 1794 would be a superior force to that of either 1792 or 1793.

The crucial campaign of 1794 revolved around two river axes, the Sambre to the south and the Scheldt and Lys to the north. Pichegru possessed an uncanny ability to be absent whenever any major battle occurred on either front. The spring combat began when Pichegru ordered the divisions of Generals Antoine Balland, Jacques-Gilles Goguet, and Jacques-Pierre Fromentin along the Sambre axis to attack Cateau-Cambrésis on 29 March 1794. This attack ended in failure, French casualties numbering over 1,000. The republicans would not again take up the offensive for about a month. The initiative passed to the Austrians who began a siege of Landrecies in mid-April. An attempt by the troops of Goguet's and Balland's divisions to relieve Landrecies on 21 April resulted only in another defeat.

Pichegru attempted to rectify a nearly impossible command situation by conferring the command of the entire right wing of the Nord on Ferrand. The Nord had always been too large for one man to control, and, although the Ardennes had always had a separate chief, this still left the man in charge of the Nord with too great a responsibility. Technically now, Pichegru would directly supervise the troops between the Scheldt and the Lys, while Ferrand would take charge, under Pichegru, of all troops along the Sambre. In reality, the command structure still left much to be desired. Ferrand, his subordinate commanders, and the Representatives on Mission vied for authority. Only the arrival of Jourdan with troops from the Armée de la Moselle in June would truly give the French right wing the unity and independence it required. (Jourdan received command of the Moselle after a short retirement.)

Ferrand resolved upon a new attempt to relieve Landrecies, and to this end he planned a massive advance by several divisions along a broad front. The beginning of the advance on 24 April was attended by some brushes with the enemy as at Silenrieux, but the real confrontation took place on the 26th. Balland's division from Maubeuge was routed; Chapuis's ill-fated division was crushed at Troisvilles. Some limited success came to troops led by General Jean-Baptiste, baron Cacault, at Boussu, but the defeat of other parts of the advance eventually made his position untenable. Once again the Allies failed to exploit their victory, and the only fruit they harvested for all their labor was the fall of Landrecies on 30 April 1794. The French at least took the opportunity to dismiss some incompetent division commanders. General Jacques-Philippe Bonnaud took over the division of General Réné-Bernard Chapuis, who had fallen prisoner during the disaster of the Troisvilles. His own troops assassinated General Goguet; his division went to General Paul-Alexis Dubois, recently brought up from the Armée de la Moselle. The excellent General Jean-Baptiste Kléber replaced General Balland.

To aid in the relief of Landrecies, Pichegru decided to launch an attack in the north, where he chose to exercise personal command. To this end he marshaled the divisions of Generals Joseph Souham, Jean-Victor Moreau, and Pierre-Antoine Michaud. Numbered among the brigade commanders of these northern divisions were two generals destined to become distinguished Napoleonic military figures, Etienne-Jacques MacDonald and Dominique-Joseph Vandamme. Pichegru, after having set up an advance in West Flanders, went off to attend to other duties; he left General Souham in charge of the entire operation. Souham aimed at the seizure of Menin and Courtrai, which promised to be soft targets, since the Allies had concentrated further south. On 27 April all went well as the French took Werwik and crossed into Austrian territory. The next day, however, Clairfayt brought up an Austrian and Hanoverian force to strike the French right at Mouscron. Clairfayt drove the French out of Mouscron, but Souham refused to let even a day pass before turning in greater numbers on Clairfayt himself. The day of 28 April was not to bring any of the tragedy brought by the 26th. Souham himself led the attack that afternoon, using the brigades of Generals MacDonald, Henry-Antoine Jardon, Nicolas Bertin, and Hermann-Wilhelm, comte Daendels. Souham turned Mouscron into a considerable French victory, boding well for the subsequent campaign. Meanwhile other troops in his command had surrounded and besieged Menin. Much of the garrison escaped on the morning of 29 April, but the remainder surrendered later that day. Courtrai also soon fell into French hands.

With the capitulation of Landrecies, the main body of the Allied army now marched north to concentrate against the French occupying Menin and Courtrai. Action flamed high during the second week of May. On the 10th, Bonnaud's division met defeat at the hands of the English near Baisieux. The same day Souham struck west from Courtrai, but when the town had been weakened by his withdrawal Clairfayt attacked it. Only quick action and hard fighting by the brigades of Vandamme and Daendels drove off the Austrians. The stage was now set for a great French victory. With the Allied troops gathering in the neighborhood of Courtrai, Coburg and the duke of York adopted a plan by the much-vaunted General Karl Leiberich, baron Mack, for a gigantic envelopment of the entire force under Souham's command. By employing six widely separated columns, Mack hoped to cut off and annihilate the invading French. This plan, however, required a high degree of coordination and timing, while at the same time it allowed the French to concentrate their resistance on isolated elements of the Allied army.

As the Allied net tightened around the divisions of Souham and Moreau, an objective observer might have given the French very little chance of success. Seventy-three thousand Allied troops menaced a force of only 60,000 French. In the past the French had required a significant numerical advantage even to fight the Allies to a draw; what chance had they now? But Souham rose to the occasion. Out of the doomsday reports coming in to his headquarters at Courtrai, he learned that in reality only three of the six columns posed a serious immediate threat and that by throwing Moreau's division against one of the three threatening columns he could concentrate his own division and that of Bonnaud at Lille against the other two. With a cool head, Souham thus massed 40,000 French against only 20,000 Allies. The several resultant engagements fought on 18 August within the triangle, Courtrai-Lannoy-Werwik, are all covered by the same title, the battle of Tourcoing.

On the morning of the 18th Vandamme's brigade of Moreau's division suffered heavily at the hands of Clairfayt's large force of nearly 20,000. But these French troops possessed a new confidence and ability; Vandamme rallied them, and in an admirable feat his brigade alone stopped Clairfayt's advance and threw his troops out of Linselles and Bousbecque. At Lannoy and Mouveaux the combined forces of Souham and Bonnaud caught the columns led by the duke of York and General Rudolph Otto off guard and unsupported. In the fighting to the south of Tourcoing the Allies lost over 5,500 men, killed, wounded, or captured. The French did not pursue the defeated Allies. After the battle of Tourcoing, Souham began an advance north toward Ypres and east toward the Scheldt. On 22 May 1794 the roughly equal forces of 50,000 clashed at Tournai. The drawn battle halted the French advance, but only temporarily. The Austrians concentrated around Tournai, drawing troops away from Ypres, which the French then besieged.

After Tourcoing the center of attention shifted down to the Sambre. Throughout the month of May and for half of June the French south of the Sambre constantly and unsuccessfully battered against the Austrians facing them just across the river. The confused command structure, the intervention of inept Representatives on Mission, and the poor behavior of the soldiers jeopardized the chances of victory. Small Austrian forces beat back attack after attack by the French. At Grand-Reng on 12 and 13 May and again on the 20th and 21st and at Erquelinnes on the 24th the story was always the same. Even the fine performance of some brigades, such as the light infantry commanded by General Philibert-Guillaume Duhesmes, could not rescue the French from repeated setbacks. However, help arrived early in June. By a difficult march, Jourdan brought about 40,000 troops of his Armée de la Moselle north to the banks of the Sambre. This not only doubled the number of men available but also placed all the troops under a single general, since Jourdan received supreme command over the 20,000 men of the Nord and the 21,000 men of the Ardennes fighting on this front. In mid-June the French again crossed the Sambre, this time with the intention of besieging Charleroi. They invested the town, but on 16 June the Austrians again defeated them and drove them back across the river. It would be the last time.

On 18 June Jourdan's troops began the siege of Charleroi again; that very day, to the north, Ypres fell into French hands. The Austrians had now concentrated their forces to the south; as of 23 June Coburg himself commanded the Austrians facing Charleroi. He lost heart after Tourcoing and regarded the large French forces before him with foreboding. Nevertheless obligated to relieve the siege, on 26 June 1794 he attacked the over 70,000 French troops entrenched around Fleurus. The French enjoyed a substantial, but not overwhelming numerical advantage, since Coburg had only about 52,000 soldiers. Coburg fell liable to much the same error he committed at Tourcoing; instead of concentrating his army for one great attack, he split it into five columns in an attempt to envelop the entire French position. Standing on the defensive, Jourdan successfully resisted all Austrian attacks and won a great triumph for the Republic. Austrian, English, and Dutch troops retreated, and the towns of Belgium fell again as they had in 1792. Some hard fighting remained, but victory was inevitable. The Austrian Netherlands was in French hands by the end of the year, and in 1795 Holland fell to the French.

The history of the Armée du Nord et des Ardennes came to a close in June 1794. On 29 June the Convention officially reconstituted Jourdan's ad hoc assemblage of divisions from the Nord, Ardennes, and Moselle as a new army, the Armée de Sambre et Meuse. With this stroke, the Ardennes ceased to exist and the Nord remained only as an ever-shrinking portion of its formal self. The main job of dealing with the Austrians fell to the Sambre et Meuse, which grew accordingly, while a victorious but now secondary Nord drove back the Dutch and English.

During its existence, 1791–94, the Armée du Nord et des Ardennes lost many battles but held the frontier largely intact and eventually defeated the armies sent against it. To what can the ultimately victorious career of the Nord be attributed? Certainly not to logistics. The French did not win in the northeast by virtue of a miracle of production and supply. Despite heroic efforts by the Committee of Public Safety, their troops suffered crippling shortages of food, equipment, and arms. The Nord subsisted on a much more meager diet of matériel than would have been considered acceptable by other contemporary forces. It is tempting to ascribe victory to the numerical superiority of the French; however, while this advantage unquestionably contributed to their success, it does not explain it. In the context of the entire theater the Nord outnumbered its opponents by a considerable margin. But examined battle by battle, the numerical differences were less outstanding. Consider in particular the three largest battles of 1794; the French were outnumbered at Tourcoing, equaled their foes at Tournai, and blessed with only a 7:5 edge at Fleurus. Due to the lack of equipment and training, a high percentage of the Nord was not with the field forces. It is also possible to sidestep the whole debate by citing the obvious truth that God does not always favor the biggest battalions and by noting that military history is full of examples in which an artful and determined few have defeated an unskilled or wavering multitude.

Turning to generalship, here again the French could boast of no clear advantage. Of the supreme commanders of the Nord, only Rochambeau, Dumouriez, and Jourdan stand up to scrutiny. The first two met defeat, and, although Jourdan won the battles of Wattignies and Fleurus, neither victory bears witness to any real military genius. Souham, who never commanded the entire Nord during these years, deserves the greatest praise for his leadership at Tourcoing, but this is the only battle of the Nord that demonstrated timing and finesse. If French generalship rarely rose above the mediocre, that of their enemies was not so debased as to account for Allied defeat. Granted, the strategic situation of the Allies was hardly to be envied. Divided command, divergent goals, and only partial commitment to victory in Belgium hampered them. The Austrians, chief among the forces arrayed against the Nord, had Polish affairs very much on their minds. But if Allied leadership may have made great strategic success unlikely, it was not abysmal enough to make French victory inevitable.

The best explanation for triumph along the Belgian frontier lies in the combat effectiveness of French troops. There is reason to argue that by 1794, the Allied troops who faced the Nord had deteriorated to a degree, but this only highlights the importance of the growing fighting quality of republican battalions. A combination of high motivation plus effective tactics resulted in superior French performance. Troops were committed and spirited, possessed of both endurance and energy. The flexible combinations of infantry formations, ably supported by artillery, allowed them to adjust tactics to terrain and circumstance. As a consequence, an analysis of victory in the north must be an analysis of the combat effectiveness of the Armée du Nord.

Chapter 2

The Elements of Victory: A Theory of Combat Effectiveness

A DISCUSSION of the elements that made the Armée du Nord victorious on the battlefield ought to proceed from an informed understanding of combat effectiveness. Far too many histories are founded upon simplistic or vague assumptions concerning troop performance under fire. Rarely do authors even bother to elaborate the underpinnings of their analyses. Distortion and confusion can result from such methodological carelessness. To avoid these pitfalls, this study begins with an attempt to identify the factors that determine the quality of performance in combat and to define the relationships among them.

The theory presented in the succeeding pages grew out of the body of literature on combat effectiveness that has appeared since the mid-1940s. Sociologists, psychologists, political scientists, and military critics have explored the motivational and technical dimensions of effectiveness. Through extensive use of interviews and questionnaires their research has built up an impressive body of data that few historians can match. Their studies of contemporary armies provide insights that aid in understanding past warfare. The benefits promised by such an interdisciplinary approach are great, although it requires a detour from the smooth paths of historical narrative. The model of combat effectiveness proposed here can be reduced to graphic form, as it is in Figure 1. However, the full complexity of the model lacks such aesthetic simplicity, but so does the subject. Some critics might accuse me of using a heavy theoretical sledgehammer to swat a rather puny methodological fly, but the results justify the effort.

The model argues that the soldier's concept of his interest determines the type of motivation and control that will be most effective. Citizen-soldiers of the French Revolution identified their interests with those of the nation; consequently, obedience within the army rested primarily on the soldier's willing agreement rather than on force or material rewards.

THE MILITARY SYSTEM
  Disciplinary System
    Coercion
    Standards
    Justification

  Tactical System
    Weapons
    Doctrine
    Training
    Experience
    Tactics

  Administrative System
    Logistics
    Services
    Maintenance
    Manpower policy

  Organizational System

  Command System
    Officer/NCO Selection
      and Promotion
    Command Structure
    Communications
    Political Officers

INTEREST
  Compliance
    Coercive
    Remunerative
    Normative

  Self-Interest
    Well-Being
    Survival

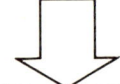

THE MOTIVATIONAL SYSTEM

Morale
  Basic Class and Societal Attitudes
  Indoctrination
  Wartime Opinions/Appreciation
  Reactions to Conditions of Service
  Esprit de Corps

Primary Group Cohesion
  Group Dynamics
  Conduit of Shared Values and
    Attitudes

Motivation
  Initial Motivation
  Sustaining Motivation
  Combat Motivation

EFFECTIVENESS

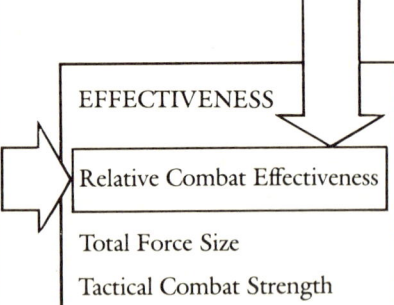

Relative Combat Effectiveness

Total Force Size

Tactical Combat Strength

FIGURE 1.
A Model of Combat Effectiveness

Such normative compliance dictated a pattern, or system, of motivation common to armed forces today. Morale, the complex culmination of an army's attitudes and opinions, is a combination of those shared by society as a whole and those common only to the troops. Morale acts upon and through the small group of comrades surrounding the individual. The bonds that unite the members of this primary group have been shown to exert tremendous influence upon the combat soldier. Motivation itself involves different factors when men are under fire than when they are out of combat, and both situations must be understood. Most of this chapter deals with interest and motivation, since they are complicated subjects that have absorbed the greater share of theoretical discussion for decades and since they are of great relevance to the study of the Revolution.

The more technical elements of the military system contribute to motivation, but need to be examined separately. They constitute the mechanisms of the army, not the motive force that drives it. Military justice, administration, organization, tactics, and command all define a particular military system. In turn, these technical aspects of the military system combine with the psychological dimensions of the motivational system to determine combat effectiveness—the quality of performance in combat. Finally, the tactical strength of a unit in the field is a product of both its combat effectiveness and its size. Quantity as well as quality must be placed on the scales.

Interest

This hypothesis must begin with a discussion of the concept of interest, which is central to troop motivation and, therefore, to combat effectiveness. The soldier who follows an order to hold out on the defensive or to strike out on the offensive essentially chooses to obey that order. He may do so to avoid punishment, to gain some reward, to protect himself and his friends, or because he believes that he ought to obey, but in some sense he fights because it is in accord with his sense of his own interests. Interest is a word with several meanings. It can mean a profit or benefit from something, a share or participation in something, or a concern with something. In each of these three senses, it can influence an individual's actions. On the modern battlefield, interest can wear both a "selfless" and a "selfish" face. A soldier is supposed to obey willingly a command that puts his life in jeopardy. At the same time his drive to defend his own life in battle is expected to make him fight all the harder. To understand combat motivation, it is necessary to consider both dimensions of interest.

Compliance Theory

For an army to operate properly, for battles to occur, soldiers must do what they are told to do, no matter how unpleasant or dangerous the task. Throughout history compliance with orders has been gained from soldiers by applying three kinds of leverage: coercive, remunerative, and normative.[1] Coercion involves the use or threat of direct physical punishment for the disobedient and the hesitant. Remuneration is based upon authority's control of material resources and rewards, such as land, pay, or booty. Normative factors consist of giving or withholding symbolic and psychological rewards and punishments, such as acceptance, commendation, or condemnation. This third type of leverage is more subtle than the first two. For it to be effective, the soldier must have an interest in, that is, he must be psychologically invested in, the community around him enough to value its praise.

Over the centuries European armed forces have relied upon different combinations of these three forms of leverage to gain compliance. The feudal knight fought both to retain his fief, to increase his holdings or obtain booty, and to uphold his honor; he was moved by remunerative and normative rewards. The brutal mercenaries of the sixteenth century fought mostly for material gain, so remunerative leverage was most effective. In the seventeenth and especially in the eighteenth centuries harsh coercive force was regarded as the most effective means to gain the soldier's compliance. It was Frederick the Great who insisted that the soldier "must be more afraid of his officers than of the dangers to which he is exposed."[2]

The French Revolution fundamentally and permanently altered the pattern of compliance. The prime motivation of volunteers and conscripts was perceived to be their concern for the nation's welfare. Harsh and degrading punishments were not consistent with the soldier's new status as a free and equal citizen. Military punishments remained, but they became more a matter of justice than of compulsion. And although the men certainly needed remuneration, salary was considered as subsistence not as incentive. Normative control became the primary influence over the conduct of the rank and file. Discipline was expected to be mainly self-imposed, and obedience an act of self-will. It would require decades before all European armies operated on these same principles. The dispersal required by modern tactics has also made normative compliance technically necessary, since these tactics rely on the obedience and initiative of soldiers who cannot be closely observed and controlled.

Since the soldier has nothing material to gain from risking his life in battle, to justify following a dangerous order, the soldier must value the interests or the approval of some collectivity beyond himself. The three types of collectivities that evoke loyalty in a modern military environment are the national sociopolitical system, the military unit, and the primary group. An interest in each of these collectivities carries with it a particular level of motivation. In an appeal to the national sociopolitical system, the source of connection is large and remote: e.g., an ideal notion of a people, a political ideology, or a social system. It is expressed in certain creeds or convictions, such as nationalism or Marxism. Concern with the military unit, a regiment, for example, is best summed up by the term esprit de corps. The primary group, that small group of men the soldier lives and fights with, brings out intense personal loyalties expressed as primary group cohesion. These three levels of attachment need not be mutually exclusive: ideally one would wish to tap all three.

The strength of the bonds essential to normative compliance reflects the depth of commitment felt by the soldier. Should these bonds weaken, authorities may be tempted to fall back on coercive or remunerative compliance. Either alternative is dangerous. Coercion seems to be a necessary part of all modern military systems, but discipline that is seen by the troops as unreasonable and brutal can undermine whatever loyalty the men still feel to their government or their cause. It may result in resistance rather than in obedience. Remunerative rewards may encourage the men to place self-interest above all other criteria, again further weakening the force of the normative principle.

Self-Interest

The soldier's concern for his own self-interest and survival can never be read out of the story of men in battle. In a force like the U.S. Army, composed of individualistic and self-centered troops, self-interest seems to be a particularly potent and unavoidable influence, but it is almost certainly a factor in all armies.

The soldier's concern for his own well-being makes the punishments associated with military discipline necessary and effective. An army based on normative compliance ought not to overemphasize punishment or the threat of punishment. However, the disciplinary system can shape the soldier's concept of his self-interest, even leading some men to prefer the risk of injury in combat to the certainty of punishment should they refuse to obey orders.

Even though military codes of conduct tend to deny individual self-interest, it is not necessarily destructive of proper military behavior. Self-interest can reinforce collective bonds when the individual sees his security as dependent upon the group. It can also strengthen the soldier's acceptance of the military system, if he believes that his own survival or success requires that acceptance. Under fire, self-preservation can motivate a man to fight back, though it is probably not the most important factor in causing resistance to the enemy.

The Motivational System

Troop motivation is an important and highly complex subject. It results from a pattern of attitudes, relationships, and structures linked together in a system. The principle of compliance operative in a particular armed force goes a long way toward defining that motivational system. The system described in this chapter is appropriate to an army relying predominantly on normative compliance. For this case, morale, defined in broad terms, is one basis of motivation, and small group cohesion is another. A complex and only partially understood interaction between the two, modified by interest, results in motivation. Motivation itself will be divided into three types, in order to clarify some of the confusion associated with this crucial concept.

Morale

Morale is clearly vital to troop motivation and combat performance. As Napoleon testified, "In war, morale counts for three quarters, the balance of material force only makes up the remaining quarter." At the same time, though morale is crucial, it is poorly understood, to some extent because the term itself is usually ill-defined. S. L. A. Marshall defined morale as "the whole complex of an army's thought."[3] This is about the best definition available. It is, of course, extremely broad, but its breadth emphasizes the illusive complexity of morale. There is a difference, however, between Marshall's use of the term and the way it will be defined in these pages. He included the relations between soldiers within the small group as an element of morale, but here morale is separated from the small group. The rationale for this separation will become apparent later.

For convenience, the climate of opinion within an army can be divided into five categories: (1) basic societal and group attitudes, (2) opinions and codes from army indoctrination, (3) wartime opinions, (4) reactions to service conditions, and (5) esprit de corps.

Basic societal and group attitudes are those fundamental opinions and values held in civil society or in a segment of it. They include the most basic beliefs that an individual comes to share at an early age, before entering military service. These attitudes can vary significantly between different economic, racial, ethnic, or religious groups within the same society. They are normally stable, changing very slowly.

Consider, for example, the views of the individual and of the self held in a society. Although there is variety in the definition of the individual held by soldiers of similar origin, the society or group itself basically defines how far a person can and should willingly submerge himself in some greater body or cause. Whether the soldier conceives of the individual as an active being capable of all things or as a passive instrument of fate is also largely a reflection of societal attitudes. The army may try to influence these views, but they are part of the basic mentality a new soldier brings with him to the service. Attitudes toward the individual and the self can also be subcategorized into group attitudes. A group despised by the rest of society, or believing itself to be despised, may react by forming a negative view of its own members. This negative view of self can lead members of that group to expect less from themselves and their comrades in military life. There is a direct correlation between low expectations and low performance.[4]

Other important societal and group attitudes include the definition of manly behavior,[5] the concept of citizenship, the image of the soldier as seen from the civilian community, the degree of satisfaction with the economic or social system, and patriotism. This list does not exhaust the possibilities; it only suggests the range.

Indoctrination is the effort made by the army or the government to mold the values and opinions of its troops, not just to teach skills. Soldiers must be indoctrinated to a certain extent, because a modern army is structured in hierarchies far more sharply defined than those of civilian society, and because the army operates on principles that differ significantly from those governing life outside the military. Men in uniform must come to accept, or at least comply with, military values and standards. Part of the function of early training and of military discipline is to instill these values.

In addition, indoctrination can go further by attempting to affect political attitudes, as was done rigorously in the Chinese Communist Army. Political indoctrination carried out within an army can exploit the soldiers' position as a captive audience. Political education can be directed toward deepening the soldier's commitment or toward guaranteeing his loyalty to the civilian authorities. Another form of indoctrination works in the opposite direction by urging the soldier to identify with the army, thus creating an esprit de corps. Indoctrination for esprit de corps involves fostering not only military values but also intense reverence for a particular regiment or division. The British regimental system was particularly good at building such strong loyalties.

Wartime opinion has considerable influence on morale, but probably not in the sense usually expected. By wartime opinion is meant both opinion expressed by the civilian community and that held within the army concerning the character and value of a particular war and of the soldiers fighting in it. Since it deals with reactions to current events, the feelings are not of distant origin, though they are related to long-term basic values. Should the momentum of the war shift direction or should the war drag on without result, opinion can change. Wartime opinion includes such elements as hatred of the enemy, support for the war's perceived purpose, and approval of government policy in pursuit of war aims.

It can be argued that war aims and political creeds are far more important to the civilian sector than to the military. Wartime orators tend to overestimate the importance of war aims as motivation for the common soldier in the field. Studies of several twentieth-century armies in the West indicate that front-line soldiers are not much concerned with politics or ideology, although some specially politicized units, such as the Lincoln battalion in the Spanish Civil War, are exceptions to this rule. Even troops in the politically self-conscious Communist forces of the East may not be as intensely ideological as many believe.[6]

Most soldiers in most armies have at best only a partial understanding of the causes and goals of the war they are fighting, but they do have a sense of whether or not their efforts are valued. The most crucial wartime opinion is this appreciation of soldiers' sacrifices and triumphs. Appreciation is the focal point for the elements of morale already discussed. It is the most potent transmitter of values and opinions from the homefront to the front line. Appreciation is the recognition of value. A strong-minded soldier may be able to appreciate his own efforts and be satisfied at that. But for the average man, value is usually determined by the opinions of those immediately around him or by society as a whole. The climate of opinion among the troops is important, but this will most frequently mirror societal opinion as they see it. If the whole concept of normative rewards is to be taken seriously, then societal appreciation rates as a most basic influence.

American troops in World War II definitely felt that their efforts were appreciated. Of 3,754 troops who were surveyed in the European theater, 82 percent answered that one half or more of the American people appreciated the soldiers' efforts.[7] The last word has yet to be written concerning the American experience in Vietnam, but it is clear that the young men who fought in its jungles and rice paddies felt no such confidence in the folks back home. Some of the troops even went so far as to express their disillusionment by chalking "UUUU" on their helmets, that is "the unwilling led by the unqualified, doing the unnecessary for the ungrateful."[8] There are indications that the young American in Vietnam was no less patriotic, tough, and capable than was his father in World War II. The great difference was that by the late 1960s a profoundly divided America could not applaud the soldier's actions.[9] War resistance may have affected combat troops not so much by winning them over as political converts but by telling them that their suffering, endurance, and bravery would go unappreciated and unrewarded. The soldier could be left with the conviction that no one cared about him. He was a victim or sucker, fighting the war no one wanted.

Another aspect of wartime opinion is the status awarded to the wartime soldier. A nation that holds the peacetime soldier in contempt may glorify him at war. Perhaps it is only because an army swelled to wartime proportions contains a broad cross-section of society, so to look down on men in uniform is to look down on your own neighbors and sons. A last element of wartime opinion worth mention is the respect and aid given to soldiers' families. The knowledge that those at home are being honored and cared for not only frees a soldier's mind, but also tells him that he is respected and valued.

Reactions to conditions of service include opinions and feelings generated by the realities of the soldier's daily life. Some observers go so far as to say that good food, sufficient rest, efficient equipment, proper medical care, and frequent mail guarantee high morale. Experience does not always bear out this view, but such conditions are unquestionably important. Without doubt, good weapons give troops confidence while poor weapons sap it. Conditions of service also include less tangible, but very important elements, such as the character of discipline, the concern shown by company grade officers, and the competence of commanders. The momentum of victory or defeat is also a determinant of morale. An army marching from success to success has fewer morale problems than does the army it is defeating. Ultimately, troop reactions to all the elements of what will be called the military system become part of morale.

For the combat soldier, the most essential condition of service is danger and the fear it engenders. This point cannot be overstressed. Experience—time on the line—can teach a man to learn how to fight effectively, how to depend on his fellows, and how to deal with fear. Yet at the same time studies have demonstrated that courage has its season; men can only bear the burden of fear for a given amount of time before they collapse under its weight.[10] But fear is not the only condition that undermines morale after long periods at the front; boredom, too, takes its toll.[11]

Reactions to service conditions arise from the circumstances themselves and from the state of mind that soldiers bring to these circumstances. The same conditions can produce different reactions. On the most obvious level, soldiers of one culture may be satisfied with less or poorer quality food, shelter, and medical care than are soldiers of another culture. On a more complex level, it is probable that the way in which conditions are perceived may be determined by the extent to which the soldier sees his actions as valuable and appreciated. Enduring danger, discomfort, and privation may, within limits, strengthen resolve if that endurance is applauded. But should either the soldier or the society reject the value of the soldier's efforts, then hard conditions may breed dissatisfaction and defiance. The soldier who feels ignored or condemned by society, however, may still consider his efforts worthwhile if he sees them as justified and appreciated by his military unit, i.e., if esprit de corps is high.

Esprit de corps in its fundamental form is identification of the individual soldier with his military unit, most commonly on the regimental to the corps level. Unit identification can also give rise to self-confidence, pride, and elitism. Unit self-confidence grows as either training or experience leads the soldier to see his unit as capable of performing its tasks. Unit pride can come from proven ability, but it can also come from pride in the unit's traditions and history. Elitism—the conviction that one's unit ranks above all others in character and ability—usually results from selection, training, and performance in battle that justify claims of superiority. Since esprit de corps stresses that the man in uniform is first a soldier with loyalty to the army, rather than a citizen with loyalty to the nation, some regimes regard esprit de corps as dangerous.

It is important to note that morale need not be uniform throughout an entire army. Morale can differ from unit to unit, or different kinds of soldiers within the same unit can have various levels of morale. John Helmer argues that the latter was true of U.S. troops in Vietnam, whom he separated into "heads" and "juicers."[12]

Primary Group Cohesion

For several decades social scientists have pointed to the crucial role of primary group cohesiveness in explaining combat effectiveness. The primary group is that small number of comrades who constantly deal with one another on a face-to-face basis. Its size is determined by the organizational structure that establishes the number of men who will live and fight together as a team and by the number of men the individual soldier can know and depend upon in a combat environment. To the extent that the men composing a primary group materially and psychologically aid one another, particularly in achieving a common goal, that group can be called cohesive. From this cohesiveness comes the most effective support and compulsion that keep the soldier at his task.

Our understanding of the primary group dates from World War II, although some observers, notably Ardant du Picq, had described elements of its character before the 1940s. Three crucial studies based on World War II experience appeared in 1947–49, and their findings so convinced social scientists and soldiers that they remained unchallenged for twenty years.[13] Each deemphasized patriotic and ideological motivation for the combat soldier. American troops were pictured as being particularly apolitical. The typical attitude toward great causes was expressed by one combat veteran: "You're fighting for your skin on the line. When I enlisted I was patriotic as hell. There's no patriotism on the line. A boy up there 60 days in the line is in danger every minute. He ain't fighting for patriotism."[14] Later studies generalized this feeling, even to armies that paid considerable attention to political indoctrination.

If a sense of cause could not explain combat motivation, what could?

The same answer was offered by all three works—primary group cohesion. In *American Soldier,* M. B. Smith supplied the classic definition of the group's functions: "It *set and enforced group standards* of behavior, and it *supported and sustained the individual* in stresses he would otherwise not have been able to withstand."[15] Military historian and critic S. L. A. Marshall emphasized fear and personal isolation on the modern battlefield. A sense of union with his comrades assured the common soldier that he did not face the enemy alone and that he could count upon the weapons and the care of his fellows. Although the utilitarian advantages of group bonds are not denied, these works stress the brotherly, caring nature of the ties between soldiers. There are, however, group standards to be met if an individual is to retain the respect of the group. Standards of manliness, responsibility, and proficiency, inherited from the civil society and military environs, are enforced by the group.

Put to the test of combat, the same men who would fight effectively alongside men they knew and had come to trust would not fight when placed among strangers. Marshall observed and reported this phenomenon in the paratroop phase of the Normandy invasion and in the combat around Bastogne. In a similar vein Shils and Janowitz demonstrated that German units, which had once fought well, became ineffective when their cohesion dissolved. Rout can occur when the moral force of the group is broken because someone displays or seems to display cowardice.[16] Should someone violate the code, it can release the others from their obligations to honor it, and cohesion dissipates.

No tough and ruthless warrior character emerged from these studies. Marshall argued that the qualities that allow a man to face battle bravely are the same that allow him to face life bravely, "friendship, loyalty to responsibility, and knowledge that he is the repository of the faith and confidence of others."[17] The more a soldier believes that his task is important to his fellows, the more he is likely to do it well. Hatred of the enemy may have helped combat performance to some small degree among American troops, but seemed to have had little effect with the British.[18]

Small group cohesion dominated the opinions of soldiers and social scientists alike through the late 1960s. At the most extreme, there was almost a one-to-one correlation between primary group cohesion and combat effectiveness. However, the decline of morale and performance among American troops in Vietnam brought on a serious revision of the original argument. The role of self-interest and the importance of political consciousness were reexplored, and the equivalence between cohesion and combat effectiveness was ultimately redefined.

The rotation system and the pattern of friendship in Vietnam made it clear that self-interest and survival play a big part in combat motivation. Under the rotation system a soldier spent only twelve months in Vietnam, and the personal goal of the soldier was not to win the war but to survive his tour. Self-interest encouraged the soldier to pursue a goal different from the official organizational goal. Another question was whether or not the bonds between men in the small group were really based on affection or on self-interest. Roger Little had asked this question in the Korean War and concluded that the group was largely utilitarian and that the strongest personal bonding occurred between two buddies and not among the entire group. Judging from the Vietnam experience, Charles Moskos argued that "rather than viewing soldier's primary groups as some kind of semi-mystical bond of comradeship, they can be better understood as pragmatic and situational responses."[19]

Moskos went further in his revision of accepted theory. He felt that unless troops basically accepted and approved of their government and society, they would not perform well in combat. Their support need not be obvious; it could be latent, present but not expressed. "Put most simply, I argue that combat motivation arises out of the linkages between individual self-concern, primary-group processes, and the shared beliefs of soldiers." In a sense, for Moskos there is a threshold level of commitment that gives direction to the group. Below that level, the group functions, but it may very likely support the soldier in resisting or avoiding orders. Helmer, a more outspoken writer, fundamentally concurred. He saw American soldiers as split into those who agreed with policy and those who did not. Those in disagreement used the primary group as a source of resistance.[20]

Forty years of research into primary group cohesion and debate over its character and significance make possible a synthesis that may come closer to the truth. Within soldier groups, cohesiveness seems to be a natural, even unavoidable, response to the conditions of army life. Shared labor, shared discomfort, and shared danger unite men when it is clear that they can achieve their goals better through association. Proximity alone is an important influence. Self-interest undoubtedly plays a major part, since the individual sees his chances of comfort and survival dependent upon his membership in the group. But the soldier probably *feels* these needs rather than *calculates* them. Camaraderie cannot be put aside; the very psychological needs of the soldier under stress can be met only by friendship, at least with one or two buddies. Self-interest can reinforce camaraderie within a cohesive group, just as self-interest can reinforce love within a good marriage. The "mystical" sacrifice of individual interest for the benefit of group interest is too much to expect, but friendship is still an important factor, even if it fades when men return home.

Primary group cohesion is probably a universal military phenomenon; however, it is crucial to consider the pattern of the group formed in a specific army at a specific time. The character, intensity, and significance of primary group cohesion are to a large degree determined by the group's structures, practices, relationships, and standards.

The structures of primary groups vary; they can be set down in detail by official regulations or allowed to take shape on their own within the body of residential or combat units. The first extreme is represented by the three-by-three organization of the Chinese Communist Army, and the second by the U.S. Army. It seems reasonable to suppose that, all other things being equal, groups that are carefully and intelligently structured are more likely to become strongly cohesive. Of course, the soldier from a society intolerant of regimentation may consider a closely structured small group as confining and frustrating. The practices followed within the structure of the group could also influence cohesion. Men who prepare their food together, eat together, and sleep together will probably be more cohesive than soldiers who live in a more individualistic style, only coming together for training or combat. The more duties are shared, and shared equitably, the stronger the group is likely to become.

Relationships between men are at the same time defined by the group's structure and practices and shaped by the religious, ethnic, class, and other societal attributes typical of the men themselves. Men from a more individualistic society may find it harder to merge themselves into a group of fellows and may continue to relate to each other as isolated individuals rather than as parts of a whole. Cohesion will ultimately be founded upon the relationships the men forge within the group, upon the quality and strength of the bonds between them.

As already stated, a basic function of the group is to set standards. The importance of these standards is immense, since they most directly translate into effectiveness or ineffectiveness. Yet it is not easy to describe the way they are formed because they are the sum total of different influences. These standards may be situational responses to field duty or combat, or they may be the combined values and opinions that the men brought with them into the army. In any case, it seems certain that men who are themselves responsible, who see their fellows as worthy, who identify with their nation, the army, and their comrades, who do not see the purpose of the war as repugnant, who feel that their efforts are appreciated at home and by their comrades, and who believe group performance to be a key to personal survival will set and live up to high standards.

Just as standards vary, so do the mechanisms by which they are enforced. They could be as formal as a self-criticism session among soldiers of the Viet Cong or as informal as an insult from an outraged G.I. Penalties could range from denial of respect, to personal isolation, to beating at the hands of fellow soldiers, to sanctions imposed from outside the group.

Beyond defining the pattern of the small group in a particular army, there is the larger question of the relative significance of the group as an influence upon motivation. This question will be dealt with later in this chapter, but a few words concerning the subject are in order now. Debate over whether primary group cohesion or ideology exerts the most influence on motivation is complicated by the very nature of the primary group. The small group is both a body of men, with its own group dynamics, and a conduit for shared attitudes and beliefs. Stating it in these words still simplifies the complexity, because even the relationships between the men are to an important extent determined by a set of attitudes they have translated from society to their group life. To carry it one step further, the ties between men are probably affected by the extent to which they are like-minded, or appear to be, on a wide range of issues.

Consider, for example, the group's function of setting and enforcing standards of behavior. Those standards derive from at least three sources. First, that the soldiers face problems and dangers together creates a common interest and a sense of comradeship that helps define standards of conduct. Second, should the army have instilled certain military habits and values, these become part of the group's standards. Third, values and opinions carried over from civilian life, such as definitions of manly behavior, are fundamental to the entire system of standards. The extent to which political opinion is fostered or ridiculed by the group can vary a great deal. The U.S. Army may, indeed, have been apolitical in World War II, but for modern revolutionary armies political ideals can be important.[21]

The group is both the repository and the agent of a broad range of values and attitudes, and, as a corollary, without the group those beliefs would have only limited effect. Rare individuals may be motivated by principle regardless of the group's shared beliefs and standards, but for the average man the belief must be shared to be a significant factor in compelling his actions. As Moskos insisted, "The ideological and primary group explanations are not contradictory."[22]

Lastly, if strong primary group cohesion is an essential element of high combat effectiveness, it does not follow that high cohesiveness in itself guarantees effectiveness. In certain circumstances strong small group cohesion lowers combat effectiveness. Should a man stop to aid a wounded comrade in spite of orders to press the attack, cohesion works against effectiveness. In a more important case, if the group regards a war as pointless or stupidly directed, it may see its commanders as the real enemies, since it is these commanders and their orders who expose the men to danger. It is reasonable to argue that troops in Vietnam who did their best to avoid the enemy on patrol or who fragged their officers could be very cohesive. Group desertions can be evidence of small group cohesion, and so can mutiny. Should morale, the thinking of an army, be such that it rejects the war effort or the leadership, the normative principle can work against the goals set by the army or the state.[23] One of the reasons that it is helpful to see group cohesion as something distinct from morale is that cohesion can be "high" when morale is "low." Even if it is agreed that an army cannot fight effectively should small group cohesion be absent or decay, cohesiveness in itself does not inevitably translate into combat motivation and combat effectiveness.

Troop Motivation

This brings us to a definition of motivation, the final stage in our discussion of the motivational system. Motivation is the set of reasons, both rational and emotional, which leads a person to decide to act or to do nothing. There is a complexity to the term when it is used in a military context, since it must be divided into the categories of initial motivation, sustaining motivation, and combat motivation, based upon the circumstances in which decisions and actions are taken.

Initial motivation concerns the decision to become a soldier, to enlist or at least to comply with conscription. At the time of making such a decision a young man is usually surrounded by civilian friends and family, and he is liable to legal and informal sanctions from the civil community. In most cases he has time to weigh his decision, if he is in doubt. How much the young man is in accord with normative compliance will have serious impact. Small group pressure can be very influential, but the group in question is a civilian small group. Patriotism and ideology can strongly influence the young man as well. Initial motivation can lead him to adopt one of a number of courses of action from draft resistance, or even rebellion, to wholehearted volunteering.

Sustaining motivation applies to military life, but not to combat. The soldier must exercise, train, march, and endure, but there is still time to talk things over. There may be danger, but even close to the front the greatest enemies may be discomfort and boredom. Although the soldier maintains contact with his civilian world through letters, his real family has become the small group of comrades around him. They are his ultimate judge and support. If a formula existed for sustaining motivation, besides primary group cohesion, it would include harmony with the compliance system, individual self-interest, as modified by the system of discipline, and much of the agenda of morale, particularly a sense of value and appreciation, as channeled through the primary group.

It has been said that some of the problems troubling the discussion of troop motivation come from studying it only in the context of combat. If so, a more explicit consideration of sustaining motivation may aid our understanding as a whole. How well a unit performs in combat will depend heavily on how well it performed its duties before combat. Passively or actively, it is sustaining motivation that brings a soldier to battle. Moreover, it is most often units out of combat that either resist army authority or simply disintegrate.[24] The range of behavior influenced by sustaining motivation runs from cheerful and energetic acceptance of duty to surrender, desertion, or mutiny.

Combat motivation stands out as unique because of the overwhelming presence of fear. Death is near; decision and action must come fast, if they come at all. The flesh and blood soldier seeks security in the support of the comrades around him, and out of loyalty to them he plays his part in the struggle. Primary group dynamics are paramount. The individual, however, is not driven by group interest alone. Self-interest, in particular the desire to survive, motivates the soldier to defend himself and to adhere to the group as a way of bettering his chances. Such elevated concerns as patriotism and ideology cannot be entirely read out of the combat picture for all armies in all circumstances; however, for most soldiers, and certainly for U.S. soldiers, it seems that patriotism and the like are far from their minds. The effects of combat motivation cover a spectrum from abject surrender, to the nonuse of weapons, to aggressive initiative.

The Military System

The elements of the military system are easier to set out briefly than are the complexities of the motivational system. This does not mean that the military system is less important, only that it can be delineated in fewer words. This system includes the basic tools, techniques, procedures, and structures of the army on campaign and in battle. All these can and do effect motivation, but they make up the framework in which men act, not the commitment behind that action. For analysis, the whole can be subdivided into five subsystems: disciplinary, tactical, administrative, organizational, and command. Each subsystem is bound up with the others, so any attempt to separate them is to a degree artificial, even if it is conceptually convenient.

Though clearly part of the military system, the disciplinary system is intrinsically related to morale and motivation. As already stated, discipline and the punishments associated with it help determine the soldier's judgments concerning his own self-interest. Military discipline and justice have several dimensions. Punishment for common criminal offenses committed in uniform have little bearing on combat effectiveness, but penalties against specifically military offenses do. There must be a certain coercive dimension, even in a normative system. The soldier's natural concern for his own welfare gives coercion its value, and, of course, there are always individuals who care little for normative rewards and who are misfits in the normative system. However, the overuse of military justice as coercion can create resistance and outrage that may destroy support and corrode morale. The laws and regulations of military justice also set standards for military conduct. It is not expected that the penalty will have to be frequently enforced, but it must exist. Along with training, discipline is influential in indoctrinating the soldier with military standards and habits. In a strange way the disciplinary system can offer the soldier an "excuse" to do what he feels he ought to do anyway. It can serve him as good reason to overcome fear or reluctance to break a group code. For a disciplinary sysytem to augment sustaining and combat motivation, it must be consistent with the soldier's standards of justice, severity, and honor. A good system will reinforce the soldier's resolve to do as he is told. The agents of the disciplinary system can be either military or civil or both. The distinction can at times be crucial. Revolutionary armies, for example, may require civil agents of discipline, since military officers may reflect authoritarian and hierarchical images of an unwanted past.

When surveying a tactical system, it is vital to take into account weapons, doctrine, training, and experience as foundations for the tactics themselves. The value of effective weapons is obvious. Weapons technology even in primitive technologies, usually offers soldiers a range of possible tools of war. Tactical doctrine is limited by this range, but doctrine makes choices within it concerning the weapons themselves and how to use those selected. Doctrine defines a tactical ideal that training is intended to transform into reality. In fact, if training is inappropriate or insufficient, the tactics employed may differ from those envisioned by doctrine. Experience must be taken into account as well. By experience is meant: (1) the backlog of conception and habit carried by the men who teach and lead, i.e., the experience of the commanders; (2) the concurrent feedback from success or failure of tactics in the field; and (3) the experience that seasons troops, turning unsteady recruits into reliable veterans. Especially when a system is evolving rapidly, the first two types of experience play an important role in inhibiting or promoting innovation. A tactical system that is tailored to the mentality and ability of the troops who are to employ it will be more efficient.

The administrative system includes both the personnel in charge of it and the services they perform. Administrators can be either military or civil or both. The nature of their authority can influence their effectiveness. The functions they perform include logistics, human services (such as medical aid), and maintenance of war matériel and equipment. In today's armies the list can go on and on. Administrative policy and its implementation can have great effect on morale, because they put food, weapons, and ammunition into the soldier's hands. One administrative topic that has enjoyed particular importance in the twentieth century is manpower policy. This does not mean recruitment policy, deciding who will be a soldier, but certain technical decisions that set the soldier's terms of service. For example, how often will units be pulled back into reserve, and will men serve on the line for the duration of a war or be rotated out of the line after a set period?

The organizational system runs from the major units, armies and corps, through mid-level units, divisions, brigades, and regiments down to small groups, such as companies, platoons, and squads. A proper organization should be consistent with the tactical, administrative, and command system. Organization may even have to reflect the national, regional, or ethnic origins of the troops. Unquestionably, organization can influence efficiency of the entire military system and can also effect motivation. Esprit de corps is, after all, dependent upon organization. Realizing that the small group is the cornerstone of combat motivation, some armies place great emphasis on small group organization down to the level of three-man teams.

The command system includes both the selection, promotion, and competence of officers and the command structure they staff. Noncommissioned officers also make up a crucial level of command, especially because of the importance of the small groups they lead. In any army communications between the different levels of the command structure unify and coordinate action; cripple them and the command system stumbles. Particularly in the current era of computerized command, communications occupy center stage. Some armies number political officers within their command system. Being party members, they keep an eye on political opinion and attempt to insure the purity and reliability of the army.

There is no separate category for combat leadership in my model of the military system, because when observed on an army-wide basis, the quality of leadership itself derives from a number of other factors.[25] The selection and promotion of officers, the command structure, the way the officer's role is defined in doctrine and tactics, and the training of officers account for leadership. Leadership by and large is like skill in weapons handling; it is the product of a number of influences, not something complete in itself. Granted, genius in battlefield leadership may not be a product of the military system, but it is also rare and can only be a significant factor if possessed by someone who commands an entire army.

All these major subdivisions of the military system have an impact on one another. In combination the elements become a whole, and as a whole they contribute to combat effectiveness.

Tactical Combat Strength and Effectiveness

The entire model proposed in this paper converges in tactical combat strength: the inherent ability of a military force to overcome its enemy in battle. Strategic considerations, such as the diplomacy and economics, that often determine the course of war are specifically excluded from this definition, which concentrates on the battlefield. Weighing combat effectiveness is not simply chalking up victory or defeat, since in *unusual* circumstances chance or the genius of a great commander can tilt the scales in favor of an armed force that is in fact not as strong as its enemy. Such was the case in the battle of Midway.

Tactical combat strength can be regarded as the product of relative combat effectiveness multiplied by total force size. Relative combat effectiveness is the result of both the motivational system and the military system—the coming together of wills and weapons. Effectiveness, as defined here, is a measure of the quality of a force's combat performance, man for man, unit for unit, and system for system. Combat effectiveness must always be evaluated in context; it is not absolute. What is effective in one technological, geographical, climatic, or political environment may not be acceptable in another. Even theaters of the same war can differ sharply. For this reason, the term used here is relative combat effectiveness. Obviously combat effectiveness in a counterinsurgency operation requires a very different set of capabilities than did the drive across northern France in 1944.

Force size is a measure of quantity, not quality. Since a small efficient army could be overwhelmed by a less efficient but much larger one, effectiveness and combat strength are not interchangeable terms. Certain analysts are confusing on this point. Numbers must be considered. Some elements of combat effectiveness can result in larger numbers of men and equipment being put into battle. Proper maintenance of modern combat vehicles, for example, pays off in more usable equipment. To keep this aspect of relative combat effectiveness distinct, the term total force size is used here to signify the maximum potential numbers of men and equipment that *could* be committed to battle by a particular force. Combat effectiveness will determine what percentage of that sum will *actually* be available.

Once achieved, the degree of tactical combat strength as demonstrated in victory or defeat exerts its own influence on the motivational system and the military system. Through this feedback, victory boosts morale, and defeat brings down generals and discredits tactics.

Since models are abstractions that simplify a complex reality, they by nature distort. Unquestionably, the theory presented in this chapter is flawed and incomplete; however, it also says a good deal. It is not just a more complicated or jargon-laden way of stating common knowledge. One great value of a model such as this is that it provides a conceptual matrix that both classifies existing knowledge and generates questions for further research. To respect the matrix, the inquirer must pursue the questions it dictates, not those that are easily answered. In historical research, where the puzzle always lacks certain pieces, there is a temptation to let the availability of sources determine the questions. The approach adopted here

resists such temptation and adheres to the pattern of the model, exploring pivotal issues to the extent that evidence allows.

The organization of the remainder of this book parallels the structure of the model. Section Two deals with motivation, including certain technical subjects, such as discipline and officer selection, which bear on motivation. The section's five chapters climax in a description of primary group cohesion in the revolutionary army. Section Three focuses on that component of the military system that best explains the combat effectiveness of the Armée du Nord—its tactical system. Since this book is a portrait of an army in combat, as well as an analysis of its success, a great deal of detail colors the outlines of the argument. It is hoped that each adds to the other so that neither dominates nor disappears.

SECTION TWO
Composition, Control, and Motivation

Chapter 3

The New Soldier: Composition and Character of the Rank and File

THE COMPOSITION and character of the rank and file lie at the very foundation of an army's combat effectiveness. Although personnel from the old royal regiments contributed a great deal to the creation of the new revolutionary army, the troops of the Republic profoundly differed from those of Louis XV. This transformation came not at once but in stages, or rather in waves, as new levies of volunteers or conscripts joined the battalions already in the field. Each influx of troops was separate and different from those that had preceded it. As they arrived and eventually merged, the army evolved into a force both unprecedented and unequaled by the Year II of the revolutionary calendar.

An analysis of this revolution in personnel ought to be both quantitative and qualitative. Research published over the last two decades provides an excellent set of figures that details the demography and social composition of the French army from 1716 through the revolutionary era. This basic quantitative profile traces the outlines of an army that had become far more representative of French society by 1794. Even more dramatic than the change revealed by these figures was the fundamental turnabout in the way the French people honored the common soldier. This reversal of opinion reflected the altered relationship of the army to the people, the undeniable necessity for defense of revolutionary France, and the new spirit of the young men who found themselves in uniform. Reduced to its essentials, the army of revolutionary France, 1791–94, became an army of citizen-soldiers, that is, men who fought to fulfill their duties and to preserve their rights as citizens. They were not what soldiers had been before 1789—men who turned to military service because the society and the economy offered them little other alternative.

The Revolution raised the citizen-soldier as a demanding but attainable ideal. Eighteenth-century political philosophers had discussed the concept of the citizen-soldier before 1789; baron de Montesquieu and Jean Jacques Rousseau gave it serious attention. Military *philosophes,* such as Jacques Guibert, focused on it, and its most developed treatment appeared in Joseph Servan's *Le soldat citoyen,* a publication of 1780. In these prerevolutionary works the citizen-soldier often seemed a lamentably unattainable goal. The more hard-minded reformers reluctantly set it aside and turned to thorough-going professionalism. The realization of the ideal after 1789 owed something to the eighteenth-century discussion but more to the political revolution and war pressures. Faced by the onset of armed conflict, the National Assembly first relied on volunteer battalions to supplement the line army. These volunteers were citizen-soldiers, to be sure, but the Assembly had yet to proclaim military service as a duty for all citizens able to bear arms. This decision came only in 1793, when the Convention abandoned voluntary enlistment and adopted conscription in order to meet the manpower needs of an urgent defense. When the state demanded obligatory service, it took the final step in reshaping the composition and character of its army, creating the new soldier.

The Line Army, 1716–93

The preservation of personnel records of the French army during the eighteenth century makes it possible to sketch a statistical profile of its rank and file. Such records, called *contrôles,* when complete, listed each soldier's date of birth, birthplace, profession, and date of enlistment. In addition, the *contrôle* recorded his promotions and eventual discharge, desertion, or death. Not every *contrôle* provides all this data, but as a whole they constitute an incredibly rich source. André Corvisier was the first to demonstrate the value of the *contrôles* for a social study of the army. His essential *L'armée française* covered the period 1716–63. Samuel F. Scott later filled in the years 1787–93. Together, the works of these scholars both describe the line army over eight decades and provide a benchmark by which to measure the transformation of French fighting forces during the revolutionary era.[1]

Between 1716 and 1789 the size of the line army remained at figures established during the late seventeenth century, with a peacetime level of 130,000 to 150,000 and wartime peaks approaching 400,000, at least on paper. The best estimates for 1789 peg strength at about 112,000 infantry, 33,000 cavalry, and 6,400 artillery.[2] This totaled roughly 150,000 troops, excluding the royal household and the new light infantry battalions, which were not as yet fully assembled in early 1789.

Under the ancien régime the line army relied fundamentally upon volunteer enlistments. During peacetime manpower needs could be met with willing volunteers from the towns of France and from the landed estates of aristocratic officers. Certain border provinces along the northern and eastern frontiers, between Switzerland and the Channel, always supplied far more recruits than did other areas of France. The presence of garrisons along these borders made recruitment more efficient, and the experience of repeated campaigns over their territory may have made military service more acceptable. During wartime high enlistment bounties plus some force and trickery helped fill the ranks. Another, but highly unpopular, means of meeting the needs of war was through use of the *milice*. The *milice* provided a pool of available manpower to be incorporated into the regular army in wartime; it changed its form, even its name, during the century but its function remained the same. Militia service fell almost exclusively on peasants, who were chosen by lot. The peasantry detested the militia as unfair and burdensome.

Corvisier and Scott have shown that military service of any kind was not a particularly popular vocation for peasants. In a country that was upward of 80 percent peasant in population, the line infantry only included about 42 percent peasants in 1716 and 1763. By 1789 this percentage had fallen off to roughly 15 percent of those whose social origins can be determined. Scott explains this sharp drop by the fact that the militia had not been incorporated into line units for some time, and without this forced infusion of peasants, their numbers declined.[3] While it is clear that peasants were grossly underrepresented in the line army as a whole, those who did serve showed a marked preference for cavalry and artillery over infantry, but even in these branches their numbers did not approach what they were in the civilian population. For ease of comparison, Table 1 presents social and demographic data concerning French infantry, 1716–94. Figures for the army as a whole, as well as for other branches, usually differ slightly from those for infantry. Note that the proportion of men with backgrounds as artisans or shopkeepers climbed from 45 percent of the infantry in 1716 to 63 percent in 1789. Those who claimed social origins in the middle classes were roughly stable at just under 9 percent in 1716 to just under 10 percent in 1789.

Just as the peasantry in particular was underrepresented in the army, so too, understandably, was the entire rural population regardless of occupation, although the figures here are not as lopsided as for the peasantry alone. Assuming that towns of 2,000 or more inhabitants constituted urban settings, the most respected estimates put the town population at 15 to 20 percent and the rural at 80 to 85 percent of the estimated 26,000,000 who inhabited France in 1789.[4] In 1763 the infantry numbered only about 65 percent men from rural backgrounds, a figure which by 1789 had risen slightly to 67 percent. Although the cavalry and artillery boasted higher

TABLE 1.
Selected Characteristics of Infantry Rank and File

Troops	Social Composition	Origins	Age	Height	Years of Service
1716 Line	9% bourgeois 45% artisans & shopkeepers 42% peasants	40% urban 60% rural	3% 18 and below 36% 25 and below	16% 1.67 m and less	
1763 Line	4% bourgeois 50% artisans & shopkeepers 42% peasants	35% urban 65% rural	5% 18 and below 46% 25 and below (all branches)	19% 1.67 m and less	
1789 Line	10% bourgeois* 63% artisans & shopkeepers 13% day laborers* 15% peasants (* sample; all branches)	37% urban 63% rural	4% 17 and below 50% 25 and below	18% 1.67 m and less	9% less than 1 year 21% 1–3 years 27% 4–6 years
1791 Volunteers	5% bourgeois 90% artisans & shopkeepers 5% day laborers (sample: Paris, section Bonconseil)	85% urban 15% rural	10% 17 and below 79% 25 and below	52% 1.67 m and less	
1792 Volunteers	23% artisans 68% peasants (26% of peasants were domestics or agricultural laborers)	31% urban 69% rural	15% 17 and below 75% 25 and below	64% 1.67 m and less	

Levy of 300,000	65% peasants (half of these peasants were domestics and agricultural laborers) (sample: Département de la Manche) (sample: Département de Seine-et-Oise)		66% 18–25 years of age	66% 1.67 m and less
1793 Line	11% bourgeois* 48% artisans & shopkeepers 35% peasants (* sample: all branches)	33% urban 67% rural	4% 17 and below 56% 25 and below	37% 1.67 m and less	33% less than 1 year 24% 1–3 years 11% 4–6 years
Levée en masse	Insufficient data, but sampling indicates a close mirror of regional social composition	16% urban 84% rural	2% 17 and below 89% 25 and below	65% 1.67 m and less	
Early 1794 army (all branches)	No data available	25% urban 84% rural	77% 25 and below		37% new recruits 62% had seen some service 18% from Line 5% from Volunteers of 1791 23% from Volunteers of 1792 15% from 1793 levies prior to *levée en masse* 39% from *levée en masse*

percentages of rural men, the figure for the army as a whole did not top 69 percent on the eve of the Revolution. Towns were overrepresented, probably because it was more efficient for recruiters to operate in towns, and because village peasants did not welcome recruiters.

The royal army was young: 46 percent of the soldiers in 1763 were age twenty-five or less; by 1789 this percentage had climbed by two points.[5] In the latter year 5 percent of the men were below age eighteen; 14 percent were age thirty-six or older. Cavalry and artillery, both services with more prestige for the rank and file and higher pay for enlistment bounties, had a slightly older body of troops. The average height of an infantryman in 1789 was 1.7 m; that for cavalry and artillery was about 7 cm. taller. In 1789 the army could rely on a good proportion of experienced men. About 70 percent of the common soldiers had served four years or more, while only 10 percent had less than a year in the ranks.

Before war came again to France in April 1792, the line army had undergone considerable turmoil. When called upon to suppress revolutionary crowds in 1789, regiments were more likely to resist than to obey. Throughout 1789 and 1790 the army suffered from extensive desertion and mutinies. Mass emigration of officers robbed the line army of its command structure. Noncommissioned officers found themselves elevated to commissioned rank in order to fill the great number of vacant slots. Numbering 150,000 in 1789, the line army was already short of its authorized strength; by the close of 1790 it had slipped to approximately 130,000, and that may be a generous estimate.[6]

In 1791 the regular army began to rebuild as war approached. An average of 332 enlistments per infantry regiment helped restore the line army to about 150,000 troops by December. The regulars continued to grow through 1792, despite the outbreak of war and its attendant losses. A law of 12 July 1792 called for recruiting an additional 50,000 men into the line regiments. By early 1793 the line had reached nearly 180,000, and its regiments constituted the most numerous and reliable segment of French field forces.[7] However, in February 1793, for administrative and political reasons the line army ceased to exist as a separate entity. Through the policy of *amalgame*, it was to be merged with volunteers and conscripts to form a new unified national force.

Before turning away from the regulars, it should be recognized that although they embodied many French military traditions, the troops who wore the uniform of the line army in 1793 were different from those who wore it in 1789. Most important, by 1793 the line army had become more socially representative of France. Rank and file with origins as artisans and shopkeepers still predominated, but their percentage fell to 48 percent, while the number of peasants doubled from 19 percent of the entire army in 1789 to 38 percent in 1793. True, the countryside was still underrepresented in the ranks by much the same percentages that it had been before. The continued practice of volunteer enlistment may explain this. Frontier provinces continued to send a disproportionate number of their sons. One-half of the cavalry and one-third of the infantry came from the north and northeast. However, the private soldiers were now younger. Nearly 63 percent were age twenty-five or younger as opposed to 55 percent in 1789. They were also shorter; 38 percent of infantry privates measured 1.67 m. or less in 1793 as opposed to 19 percent in 1789. Crucially, most of the private soldiers had come into the army since 1789. Nearly 65 percent had served less than four years, and over 38 percent had less than one year. Noncommissioned officers unsurprisingly claimed more experience, to be sure; 86 percent of corporals in all branches had spent over six years in the army; and 92 percent of sergeants boasted such long service. Still by February 1793 the line army was not, in the main, composed of experienced professionals, but of men much like the Volunteers of 1791 or 1792. In the summer of 1792 Dumouriez said that his line and volunteer soldiers were "all equally new and inexperienced."[8]

From Volunteers to Conscripts, 1791–93

As war first threatened and then engulfed France, she sent wave after wave of new levies to join the line army at the front. For its first levy in the summer and fall of 1791, the Legislative Assembly relied only upon the patriotic enthusiasm of its young men to supply adequate numbers of volunteers, but with every new call the French moved closer and closer to universl conscription, ultimately expressed in the *levée en masse* of August 1793. At the outset new recruits did not serve as replacements, but as entire battalions fighting alongside the old regiments. It was as if revolutionary France chose to defend itself by creating whole new armies. Each levy had its own character and composition, so each must be considered individually—for the men it contained as well as for the method in which they were raised. This is possible because of the remarkable research of Jean-Paul Bertaud, who has examined the *contrôles* of revolutionary volunteers and conscripts.

First to be summoned to the defense of the new France were the Volunteers of 1791. The decision to call them up rested on a belief that the National Guard constituted a reserve for the defense of the frontiers. Crisis had given birth to the Guard in July and August 1789. Worried both by the possibility of counterrevolutionary intervention by the king's army and by the reality of armed crowds in their streets, the electors of Paris created a civic militia for the capital on 13 July 1789. In the next few weeks a kind of mass hysteria, known as the Great Fear, swept over France. As a response to the threat of imagined brigands, and to preserve order in the midst of paranoia, town after town created their own National Guard units in imitation of Paris. By the fall the National Guard was a virtually universal institution, but the National Assembly made no move to regularize the recruitment and organization of Guard forces for the next two years.

The decay of the line army and the mounting threat of war finally forced the National Assembly to turn its attention toward the Guard. In January 1791 the Assembly heard that the line army had shrunk to 120,000 men. The speaker proposed not only bringing the line regiments up to strength but also enacting a voluntary inscription of National Guardsmen to create a reserve force of 300,000 men. The Assembly shelved this latter proposal until April, when the military committee of the Assembly proposed the nationwide organization of the Guard into battalions.[9] Only "active" citizens were to be allowed to enroll. "Active" meant only those who paid yearly taxes equal to three days labor. In other words, the very poor would be barred from membership since they paid no such tax. In practice the very poor had usually been barred since the creation of the Guard.[10] After bitter debate, in which Maximillien de Robespierre argued that *all* citizens should serve, the original proposal was adopted.

On 11 June the Assembly went a step further. The diplomatic and military committees feared that revolutionary France might soon be attacked by foreign enemies "in hate of the liberty which she has given." They then proposed that one-twentieth of the Guard volunteer for active duty, to be actually mobilized only when the Assembly decided it was necessary. This was essentially a return to the January proposal. Before the Assembly could act, Louis XVI attempted to flee France. Before he was even apprehended at Varennes, the Assembly met during the day of 21 June and took measures to form a reserve of 300,000 to 400,000 Guards. The Assembly declared the National Guard "put into activity" and ordered that it be assembled in battalions of 357 men. On 3 July, 26,000 men were ordered to immediate active duty on the northeast frontier; it was anticipated that 60,000 to 80,000 Guards of the reserve would eventually take the field. On the 22nd, the figure of National Guard volunteers to be mobilized climbed to 97,000, apportioned in fifteen divisions. On 4 August their battalions were to be reorganized to include 571 men, and on 17 August the total number of men to be mobilized reached 101,000.

Those volunteers called up in 1791 differed profoundly from the line army they joined in the field. Bertaud has gone so far as to call these Volunteers of 1791 another army, a "bourgeois" army.[11] The volunteers were much younger; 79 percent were aged twenty-five or less. They were shorter in stature; 52 percent stood 1.67 m. or less. They were overwhelmingly urban in origin, with only 15 percent coming from countryside villages of less than 2,000 inhabitants. The social composition of these town-based battalions varied, but since they were supposed to be active citizens of the National Guard, men of artisan and middle-class background predominated. In one representative battalion from Paris, artisans and shopkeepers constituted 90 percent of the manpower; today such men would be termed upper working class and lower middle class. To be sure, not all battalions followed this pattern.[12] Rarely had the privates and noncommissioned officers served in the line army before enrolling in volunteer battalions; however, nearly one-third of the company grade officers and two-thirds of battalion commanders had such service. The experience of their superiors reflected well on the judgment of the rank and file, since they elected their own officers.

These volunteer battalions came on line with the Armée du Nord during the fall and winter of 1791–92. They played their greatest role in the fall of 1792. Over the next winter many or most of the men left their battalions. Volunteering for only one campaign, they were legally free to go home two months after notifying their officers. Some who chose to leave returned to the army later as volunteers or conscripts.

When war broke out in April 1792, the government responded by calling for more volunteers. On 5 and 14 May the Assembly augmented the levy of 1791. To the original 183 battalions of 574 men, the Assembly added 31 more battalions and ordered that all battalions be brought up to a strength of 800. On paper these two acts increased the volunteer force from 101,000 to 171,000. In February the height restriction had been abolished, so shorter men could serve, but they were still to be active citizens and volunteers. June witnessed a further, and minor, adjustment in the levies. As an additional force to police and defend Paris, whose line and volunteer battalions were leaving for the front, the Assembly summoned five National Guardsmen from each canton of France to come to the capital, take part in the celebration of 14 July, and camp near Paris for a few months.[13] Twenty thousand *fédérés*, as they were known, thus marched to Paris. They were not asked to make any long-term commitment, and they came to fulfill a mission that was political as well as military; therefore, they constituted a special group: highly politicized, weakly disciplined, and poorly equipped. Eventually they were marshaled into eighteen battalions.

The men who came to be known as the Volunteers of 1792 were not called upon to form their battalions until July. During the first months of the war, the failures of French troops in the field sank to the level of farce. At the same time, a very serious invasion force gathered across the border. With an understandable sense of urgency, the Legislative Assembly declared that "la Patrie est en danger" on 12 July. That very day it resolved to raise an additional 50,000 recruits for the line army and forty-two more battalions of volunteers. Legislation of 20 July spelled out the details of the new levy. The term "active citizen" disappeared; all "National Guardsmen and other citizens capable of bearing arms" were to assemble to choose volunteers. Instead of forming entire battalions, companies were to be raised by quota throughout the eighty-three departments and then assembled into polyglot battalions later on. Only Paris and two other departments were to raise enough companies to form their own battalions. Once enrollment began, the response overwhelmed expectations. The Department of Haute-Saône, charged with assembling one company of 100 men, mustered eight battalions totaling roughly 6,400 men.[14] Paris assembled thirty-one battalions instead of two. Calvados offered seven battalions, not the three companies assigned to it.

Valiant young men did not rush to volunteer in all corners of France. In Maine-et-Loire the authorities offered recruitment bounties to attract volunteers. Since the legislation demanded quotas and stipulated that men were to be "chosen by their brothers in arms," some compulsion might be used. Even at this, enrollments on occasion came up short. A Lieutenant Serrat told how his department sent only eleven men, not the 500 of the quota.[15] Motivated by patriotism or bounties, the overwhelming majority of the 1792 levy were volunteers, and they still felt that they had not committed themselves for indefinite service. Louis Bricard volunteered for the 5th Paris on 5 September. On 17 September shoes were distributed to the men, but Bricard reported, "I did not want to take them, having as my reason that if I took some equipment from the Nation, I would be like a man who had enlisted for regular service [*comme engagé*], and as a consequence, I could not go home at the end of the campaign."[16] Even if some quotas went unfilled and some unwilling "volunteers" hired substitutes, as a whole the Volunteers of 1792 marched off in numbers far greater than had been set down in statute. In place of the forty-two battalions legislated, over 275 were formed—a force that at full strength could have exceeded 220,000 men.

In composition, the Volunteers of 1792 were more like the new recruits of the line army than they were like the town-based Volunteers of 1791.[17] The rural-urban breakdown was 69 percent to 31 percent, only slightly different from what it was for line infantry in 1793. However, peasants now appeared in numbers something more like their true percentage of the population. In a representative levy from the Department of La Manche, 68 percent were peasants, while 23 percent were artisans. Bertaud characterized the Volunteers of 1792 as an army of *sans-culottes,* in contrast to the bourgeois Volunteers of 1791. Some units of 1792 volunteers did not fit his pattern. Paul Charles Thiébault testified that his grenadier company contained young men "almost all in the most elevated social position."[18] The men of 1792 were a bit older than those who volunteered in 1791, but they were still much younger than the line soldiers below commissioned rank. Since height restrictions had been waived, it is not surprising that the men were shorter, and 64 percent stood less than 1.67 m. The men who rallied to the defense of revolutionary France were approaching a representative slice of the French population. They would come to reflect French society even more closely in 1793.

In February 1793 the Convention learned that its troops, which totaled perhaps 450,000 in November 1792, had shrunk to about 290,000. In early 1793 the Convention believed it had to maintain an army of over 500,000 men and perhaps as many as 800,000.[19] The remedy adopted was a new levy of 300,000 recruits, which the Convention decreed on 24 February 1793. By a complicated piece of mathematics, the Convention assigned each department a quota based on 17 percent of its male population less the troops raised in the 1791 and 1792 volunteer levies and still serving at the front. Thus a department that had contributed less in the past would be called on to do more now.

The levy aimed at men aged eighteen to forty who were unmarried or widowers without children. Voluntary enlistments were to be preferred, so once again the Convention pulled up short of universal conscription. However, should insufficient numbers of willing volunteers step forward, the law provided for compulsory enlistment to complete the quota. The local group of those liable for service was to decide on a method of choosing some of their number for compulsory service, basically by election or by drawing lots. In the Département du Nord tickets were drawn from a hat to select the last five men for one canton's levy.[20] After the men were selected, cries of "Vive la nation" and "Vive la République" rang out. To many men the choosing of lots, *tirage au sort,* however, smacked of the old and hated *milice.*

The Convention also authorized the hiring of replacements by the chosen who wished not to serve. Replacements had been allowed by the legislation of 20 July 1792 as well, but the vast majority of that levy had volunteered. Bertaud estimates that 11 percent of the men supplied by the February levy were hired replacements, but in some contingents the proportion climbed to one-fourth or one-third. The prevalence of replacements scandalized contemporaries. Lazare Carnot wrote: "In the sacred land of liberty, in that very country where the rights of man have just been sanctioned, a commerce in human beings is carried on. . . . An infamous agent approaches a young peasant or worker and says to him: 'Do you want to sell yourself for the contingent?' Suddenly there is 300 livres. The deal is made." Communities took up collections or sold church bells and communal lands to hire men. Comments from the field suggest that the men they bought were not quality goods. Sergeant Alexandre Brault sneered at the yield from this levy, "Those dogs that were led about with blows from a stick are never any good."[21] Also the inequities seemed obvious; the rich could escape service, but the poor could not.

The fruit of the Levy of 300,000 belied its name. By mid-May only about 97,000 men raised by this levy had marched off for the front, and an additional 37,500 were ready to go. In the end about 150,000 joined the army as a consequence of the February legislation.[22] The levy lagged behind expectations, but the problems created by it exceeded the worst fears. Reaction against the Levy of 300,000 provoked the counterrevolutionary revolt of the Vendée in mid-March 1793.

In composition, the Levy of 300,000 was young and poor. From a sample of men from five departments, Bertaud concludes that two-thirds of the men were eighteen to twenty-five years of age. He found as well that these recruits came from social levels lower than those which typified the men of 1792. The liberal professions played only a small part in this levy. On the contrary, the greatest share seems to have been made up of peasant society. In Seine-et-Oise, for example, 65 percent were peasants, more than half of them of the meanest sort, domestics and agricultural laborers. In some ways the February levy represented the nadir of the volunteer system.

With the exception of the 12 July 1792 levy of 50,000 men for the line army, all the special levies discussed thus far were earmarked for the infantry. French cavalry decayed considerably during the winter of 1792–93 and fell behind the expansion of the infantry. To redress this balance, on 16 April, the Convention decreed a levy of 30,000 men for the cavalry. This decree stipulated that the recruits would enter old units and that no new cavalry regiments would be formed. On 27 June the Convention apportioned quotas among the departments at a tenth of the levels set for the February levy. The mechanisms used in recruiting these men were presumably to be those employed in raising the Levy of 300,000. A further piece of legislation, passed 12 July 1793, set down the proportion of the new cavalrymen to be distributed to the various armies. The Armée du Nord et des Ardennes was to receive 8,770 men, or just shy of 30 percent of the levy.

In squaring off against the Vendée rebels, the Convention moved one step closer to universal conscription. Hatred against the Vendée "fanatics" exceeded that harbored against any other internal threat to the Revolution. As early as 19 April the Convention demanded that the Committee of Public Safety report on what had been done to crush the rebellion. On 27 April Georges Jacques Danton moved, and the Convention decreed, that 20,000 recruits be sent to the Vendée.

In the same session that Danton made his motion, Joseph Cambon, speaking for the Committee of Public Safety, read the Convention a letter from officials of Hérault, a department on the Mediterranean. In this note they described their frustration with past recruitment: "This department has just furnished a considerable body of recruits; and while one would like to flatter oneself that these recruits . . . will maintain the glory of the

Nation, one ought not to hide the composition of these recruits . . . ; the majority . . . are replacements, who by the lure of a substantial bounty, have decided to leave their homes." Hérault had recently been charged with assembling another 5,000 men for a special levy to aid in the defense of southern France against the Spanish. The administration adopted a new method to assemble this quota. A local Committee of Public Safety was formed and charged with drawing up the list of draftees. This was direct, selective conscription rather than volunteer enlistment, *tirage au sort,* or election. The principles of selection included family situation, physical suitability, and patriotism of the young men. Theoretically such a method guaranteed a levy of sound, able, and public-spirited youths. The expenses incurred by raising and equipping these 5,000 were to be handled through a forced loan imposed on the well-to-do. The Convention so approved of the actions taken in Hérault that they awarded the plan honorable mention in the *Bulletin of the Convention*. Three days later the minister of the interior reported that he had arranged to print and distribute throughout France "a great quantity" of the Hérault order.

The Hérault pattern of recruitment stimulated debate, at least in Paris. *Père Duchesne,* a radical journal, approved. Others fretted over the loss of liberty outright conscription implied. Despite some opposition, the General Council of the Commune of Paris voted on 1 May to follow the Hérault example in raising 12,000 for the Vendée, and in each section of Paris a committee prepared a list of conscripts.[23] Notwithstanding this turn toward conscription, the Vendée levy continued a practice dear to volunteers. Before the Convention on 6 May, Representative Prieur of the Marne took the floor to propose "that the citizens who form battalions to rush to the aid of the Vendée and its neighboring departments prey to the revolt, will be able to return to their homes as soon as the National Convention will declare that these departments are no longer in danger."

In 1791–94 France was a nation of patriots, but even in that nation of patriots the voluntary principle proved inadequate. Consequently, in the summer of 1793, the theory of the citizen-soldier became an imperative, not a choice; military service became a duty rather than a privilege. Bertaud argues that the necessity for some form of universal military conscription became obvious to Representatives on Mission with the armies before it was accepted by the Convention. The experience of the Armée du Nord bears out this judgment. On 1 August Representatives Élie Lacoste and J.-P.-C. Peyssard with the Nord declared a local levy, by virtue of their extraordinary powers. "A war of tactics will not suffice to drive off our enemies; it is necessary that all citizens capable of bearing arms, . . . that the entire body of the people rise in mass to crush them."[24] This *levée en masse* called up all men ages sixteen to fifty who were not fathers of families. It was a more extensive levy than that declared in Paris three weeks later.

Not only did such precedent indicate the path the Convention must follow, but petitions from the sections and Jacobin Club of Paris also pointed the way. On 16 August delegates from the sections appeared before the Convention to call for a *levée en masse*. That day the Convention declared, "The French people . . . is going to rise as a whole in defense of its liberty, of its Constitution, and in order to finally deliver its territory from its enemies." This decree left the form of this national rising to the Committee of Public Safety. Through Bertrand Barère, the Committee made its first proposals on 20 August, but the matter was sent back to the Committee. On 23 August the great Committee came forward again. This time the Convention enthusiastically accepted the Committee's work. The first article of its decree has become the classic statement of a nation at arms:

> From this moment until the enemy has been chased from the territory of the Republic, all the French are in permanent requisition for the service of the armies.
>
> Young men will go to battle; married men will forge arms and transport supplies; women will make tents, uniforms, and serve in the hospitals; children will pick rags; old men will have themselves carried to public squares, to inspire the courage of the warriors, and to preach the hatred of kings and the unity of the Republic.

The poetic exaggeration of the first article became clear and demanding prose in the body of the decress. All men ages eighteen to twenty-five, unmarried or widowers without children, were to go to the front. Exceptions were rare, and no replacements were allowed. Should this age group not yield enough men, the upper age limit would be increased to thirty, then thirty-five, on up to fifty if need be. However, as Barère explained, the Committee expected to raise as many as 500,000 from the levy for eighteen to twenty-five year olds, and this would suffice. To supply arms for the growing number of troops, the decree ordered the creation of arms factories in public parks and wherever practicable. "Aux armes, citoyens!" became a reality.

By putting the defense of the Patrie before the convenience and liberty of the individual, the *levée en masse* testified to the patriotism of the nation. Yet paradoxically it also recognized that patriotic devotion was not so intense among young men that it alone could overcome all reluctance to abandon the civilian life for military service. Compulsory service tested the patriotism of those drafted into the army. Desertion among conscripts was a serious problem. A cynical observer could argue that the *levée en masse* diluted the concentrated patriotism of the volunteer forces. In reply it can be shown that despite desertions the *levée en masse* produced roughly 300,000 men, built the army up to the unprecedented strength of 750,000 troops, and supplied military manpower needs for the next several years.[25] Ultimately, it made the army a people's army fighting a people's war.

Just how much the *levée en masse* reflected the population of France is shown by Bertaud's research. Eighty-four percent of the levy came from the rural villages and 16 percent from towns and cities—the same breakdown of rural-urban population that typified France as a whole. In age, 87 percent were between eighteen and twenty-five, as stipulated in the legislation, and in height 65 percent of those requisitioned as infantrymen measured 1.67 m. or less. The levy was socially representative of the population from which it was drawn. Although the records are sparse, Bertaud's samples indicate that the middle classes, for example, were now tapped by the levy in roughly the same percentages as their civilian numbers: "In certain departments," he writes, "holy equality was respected. No more rich, no more poor; the blood of the indigent was as pure as that of man at ease."

The Emergence of a United Army

The flow of new levies into the armies of revolutionary France posed a serious problem. Levies differed considerably one from the other, yet the French had to find a way of welding these disparate elements into a single united force. For cavalry and artillery regiments, this was a fairly straightforward task of feeding new recruits into established units. Volunteers formed few independent cavalry squadrons, and, although a considerable number of volunteer artillery companies came to the front, they generally served the light cannon attached to infantry battalions and did not merge with the line artillery. The real question was posed by the infantry, which swelled to unprecedented proportions. Here the French employed three methods of integrating new levies; ad hoc brigading, incorporation, and amalgamation. The Nord provides an excellent case study in all three procedures. This process took over three years, but by the summer of 1794 a new French army was emerging from the crucible of crisis.

Ad hoc brigading, or *embrigadement*, applied to the influx of volunteers from the 1791 and 1792 levies. In general, these men arrived at the Nord in complete battalions, which maintained their integrity. In late 1791 and the first half of 1792 line infantry formed its own brigades in the Nord and the Volunteers of 1791 stood apart. This practice changed permanently during the marquis de Lafayette's brief tenure as commander of the Nord. He combined line and volunteer battalions in the same brigades, with the expectation that this would steady the volunteers.[26] Heavy infantry brigades included one battalion of line infantry and two of volunteers. This three-battalion brigade was itself a switch, since before Lafayette a brigade had consisted of four battalions in the Nord. These new brigades were temporary creations of convenience, made to fit circumstances.

Ad hoc brigading took care of some difficulties, but others remained.

Volunteers enjoyed better conditions of service and higher rates of pay than did regulars, giving line troops a legitimate grievance. Meanwhile, the volunteers suspected the line of holding lukewarm sentiments toward the Revolution. At times mutual resentment burst out in physical violence. Administrative confusion only made things worse. As a consequence, the National Convention could no longer tolerate the continued existence of two bodies of soldiers. On 7 February 1793 Edmond Louis Dubois-Crancé rose before his fellow representatives to present a report by the *comité de la guerre,* which now proposed the elimination of all distinctions between volunteers and regulars. When this proposal was adopted on 21 February, it spelled the official end of the line army.

The report went on to argue that the expedient of ad hoc *embrigadement* be generalized throughout the armies and transformed into a permanent organization. One battalion of line infantry would join with two of volunteers to create a new permanent unit of three battalions, called a demibrigade. Controversy over the political implications of this organization marred the debate, and when the proposal was adopted by the Convention it postponed the actual implementation of *embrigadement* until the end of the 1793 campaign.[27] By then, amalgamation, and not simple brigading, would be the answer adopted. Ad hoc brigading of line and Volunteer battalions continued in the Armée du Nord throughout 1793.

Whereas the volunteers of 1791 and 1792 formed battalions that remained on army rosters, the recruits and conscripts of the 1793 levies generally did not. A decree of 18 April stated that the men raised in the February levy would be incorporated into existing units until these had reached full strength, and legislation of 22 November 1793 ordered all conscripts raised by the *levée en masse* to be incorporated as well. So although they arrived at the front in battalions, these units dissolved and the men served as replacements. In the Armée du Nord the numbers of battalions increased only slightly after March 1793. Situation reports of 1 March 1793 listed 283 battalions and a total of 150,000 troops in the Nord and Ardennes. A year later when the number of troops had climbed to 243,000, only 300 battalions appeared on the situation reports. The added increase of manpower came almost wholly from incorporation. Tracing the size of the Nord and the strength of a sample of its battalions through this period demonstrates when this incorporation occurred. The Levy of 300,000 was incorporated between 1 May and 30 July 1793. The *levée en masse* was incorporated primarily from mid-December 1793 to mid-February 1794. Although the original volunteer battalions bore the names of the departments in which they were raised and had a strong regional identity, the replacements fed into these battalions usually were not from the same departments as their new comrades, but simply men from a convenient replacement depot. So incorporation eroded some of the regionalism that had typified the volunteers at the outset.

By the time incorporation of the *levée en masse* had begun, the process of amalgamation had also gotten under way. The *amalgame* was an extension of ad hoc brigading, but it differed in two senses. First, just as in Dubois-Crancé's earlier proposal, the *amalgame* would create permanent demi-brigades of three battalions each. Second, the *amalgame* would thoroughly mix the battalions together. They would be broken down into companies, which would be combined in such a manner as to produce three entirely new battalions. Legislation of 12 August 1793 picked up and developed the proposals put forward by Dubois-Crancé in the previous February. The August law set the organization of the new amalgamated demi-brigades, and a further decree of 10 January 1794 detailed the thorough process of review, evaluation, and inspection that was to precede the actual amalgamation of three battalions.

From the moment when Dubois-Crancé first broached the subject before the Convention on 7 February 1793, until the last decree eleven months later, permanent *embrigadement* stirred vigorous debate. The conflict centered on the political impact of this reorganization, while the technical arguments in its favor were never seriously questioned. Authorities agreed on the utility, perhaps the necessity, of tactical units larger than the battalion. Even the foes of the *amalgame* conceded the continued ad hoc brigading of line with volunteer battalions. There also seemed to be little debate over the supposed superiority of the former line infantry in drill and discipline, and the consequent benefit of buttressing less skilled units by welding them together with line troops. However, the ghost of Charles François Dumouriez haunted the Convention. Some representatives feared that a treasonous officer might be able "to profit, to the detriment of the public interest, from large units and the esprit de corps which dominates them." There were also questions concerning the choice and promotion of officers. In response, Dubois-Crancé repeatedly insisted that the political affects of the *amalgame* would be "to generalize the republican spirit" of the army by submerging one battalion of former line infantry in two of patriotic volunteers.[28] Eventually the technical logic and the belief that volunteers would guarantee the reliability of the new demi-brigades won acceptance.

To speed amalgamation, the Convention dispatched Representatives on Mission to direct the process. Even with such encouragement the *amalgame* took time. Units were first brought up to strength through incorporation. Before being combined with others, the state of each battalion's manpower, training, equipment, and finances had to be ascertained. Its officers were also evaluated, one by one. Only after this complete inspection were battalions brought together for the ceremony of amalgamation. The Armée du Nord carried on this work at a better pace than did any of the Republic's other armies. By April 1794 one-third of the demi-brigades assigned it had already been formed, and by the end of the year 90 percent were constituted. The pattern of amalgamation did not always follow that prescribed by the Convention. Bertaud states that at least one-quarter of the demi-brigades formed in this *amalgame* joined together only volunteer battalions, with no former line troops involved. After the completion of the first *amalgame,* another would be ordered in 1796 to consolidate and combine under-strength units. The first *amalgame* resulted in the formation of over 230 demi-brigades of heavy and light infantry. The 1796 *amalgame* trimmed the number down to 140.[29]

As the republican army worked toward the new fusion of the *amalgame,* it reached a strength of 750,000 men by mid-summer of 1794, according to the best estimates.[30] On paper the numbers were even greater. Situation reports for June list the strength of the Nord and Ardennes at 260,000.

Studying all branches of the army, Bertaud has revealed that as the good weather returned in 1794, 37 percent of the soldiers present under arms were green conscripts who had yet to serve in their first campaign, and 62 percent could boast some experience under fire.[31] Fifteen percent were recruits of 1793 who had arrived at the front early enough to take part in the fall and winter fighting of that year. About 23 percent were Volunteers of 1792, and 5 percent were Volunteers of 1791. Soldiers of the old line army accounted for 18 percent of the rank and file. As an aggregate, only 5 percent of the common soldiers under arms in 1794 had seen service before 1789, meaning that 94 percent had become soldiers during the revolutionary era.

Statistically, the army of the Republic was more representative of French society than had been the troops of the monarchy. The rank and file was more rural; the urban percentage would seem to have fallen to about one-quarter by 1794. There is not enough information available to support any definitive statements concerning the social mix of the army in 1794, but all indications are that it, too, was more in accord with the civilian population. On the whole, these citizen-soldiers were young; 77 percent were age twenty-five or less. By comparison, this figure had been only about 48 percent in 1789. They were also short; most stood less than 1.67 m., while only 18 percent of infantrymen had been of such slight stature in 1789. This simply means that recruiting was no longer so selective, a function of the tremendous expansion of the armed forces.

Bertaud's examination reveals that the cavalry and artillery maintained more demanding standards than did the infantry. Neither service had been inundated by volunteers as had the infantry. Thirty-four percent of cavalrymen had served in the line army. The artillery contained 56 percent of men who could trace their army careers back to the line, although the majority of these men had only enlisted after 1789.[32] Cavalrymen also stood taller than infantrymen; men who fought on horseback had to be tall to be able to mount horses with ease and command an adequate reach with their weapons during the charge. The tallest men served in the artillery, where 90 percent of the men were 1.70 m. or more in height. Just as in the ancien régime, it took big men to manhandle cannon on the field of battle. The artillery also boasted more men over the age of thirty than did the other branches.

The eleven armies that the Republic maintained differed somewhat one from another in the make-up of their troops, e.g., the Armée du Nord contained men who were more experienced and slightly older than the Armée des Pyrenées. With good reason the Nord also had a certain regional character. The majority of its troops came from that area of northern France bordered by the Channel, the Seine, and the Meuse.

Attitudes and the Definition of the New Soldier

Statistical profiles of the various levies and of the army they combined to form reveal much, but a full definition of the republican soldier demands more. Quantifiable factors such as age, birthplace, and profession tell only part of the story; a notation on a *contrôle* that a man was an artisan, for example, leaves much unsaid. It does not say whether the man was successful or marginal at his trade. It does not answer the question of whether or not his people regarded him as economically and socially expendable when he entered the service. Statistics also remain mute concerning whether French society admired or despised the soldier after he had left his civilian occupation to march in the ranks. To come to grips with such matters requires a comparison of the kind of men who became soldiers before and after 1789 and a consideration of the attitudes held toward the troops under the ancien régime and during the crisis period 1791–94. The contrasts demonstrate that through much of the century, the rank and file were largely regarded as outcasts, but the Revolution transformed them into honored citizen-soldiers.

Those who found themselves in the ranks before 1789 were men who had little place else to go. Recruiting was more effective in the towns and cities because these population centers were reservoirs of the unemployed. Consider the case of Claude Le Roy, who was born in the village of Talmay, but who was driven out of the village by his family's limited wealth.[33] After a youthful adventure at sea, he returned to Talmay, learned the trade of hatter, and went to Paris to practice that trade. Unable to find employment, he enlisted in 1784. The *contrôle* would have shown only a young man of rural origins, born in 1767, who claimed to be an artisan. Young men in Le Roy's straits must have been prime targets for eager recruiting sergeants.

Despite the numberless horror stories about eighteenth-century recruiters, Corvisier's research shows that most French recruits were willing enough. In peacetime the French army relied on legitimate practices in the towns and on seigneurial recruitment in the countryside. This latter way of filling the ranks was more paternalistic than town recruitment. French officers were granted extended leaves, called *semestres*. Officers, or more commonly their families, would canvas the countryside surrounding the family home to find young peasants who were willing to enlist. Such men would almost always be the younger sons of peasant or artisan households with limited or no land. Their presence in the family cottage was more an embarrassment than a blessing. If they enlisted to serve under a local noble, there was some assurance that they would not be abused. Their families had one fewer mouth to feed, and perhaps some of the new soldier's meager income would help his family.

The worse abuses of the recruiter were reserved for wartime, when true volunteers were not abundant enough to satisfy the army's growing hunger for manpower. The French were not guilty of the same level of deceit and brutality in filling their quotas of new recruits as were the Prussians or the English, but French recruiters did use "ruses, liquor, trickery, and bad faith" when the demand for new men was high.[34] Even then the heavy-handed recruiting sergeant was more a phenomenon of the towns than of the countryside.

During the eighteenth century the French also employed a system of conscription to form the *milice,* as already mentioned. The organization and function of the *milice* varied from decade to decade, but it was always recruited by *tirage au sort* among those young men not lucky enough to enjoy some sort of exemption. These exemptions were so plentiful that the only class left unprotected was the middling and poorer peasantry. The *milice* was a hated institution; to be chosen to serve in it was regarded as an unfair curse. Anne-Robert-Jacques Turgot, the reforming minister of Louis XVI, once wrote, "Each *tirage* was the signal for the greatest disorders in the conutryside."[35]

Certainly some young men chose military service because of a taste for arms and adventure, and service seems to have been less objectionable to young men from border provinces. The overwhelming majority of the rank and file, however, seems to have been men who had "lost" in the civilian world. They were marginal, expendable. Once in service they had little hope for advancement beyond the rank of sergeant. Only a few men rose from the ranks to become lower grade officers after long years of service. Such officers were burdened with the more unpleasant tasks, such as drilling recruits, and were never fully accepted by their brother officers.

In short, the soldier's career was dangerous and undesirable. Speaking of the army of his day, the French war minister, 1775–77, the comte de Saint Germain stated, "In the present state of things, armies can only be composed of the slime [*bourbe*] of the nation and of all that is useless to society."[36]

Even though officers enjoyed elite status in French society, that society regarded its rank-and-file soldiers with contempt and fear. Soldiers who were cast-offs of the French economy were seen as moral outcasts as well. The great military philosopher Guibert lamented that common soldiers were "unfortunate and deprived." Memories of the seventeenth century branded them as men who lived by robbery and pillage. Dubois-Crancé encapsuled the French attitude toward soldiers when he argued, "Is there a father who does not tremble to abandon his son, not to the hazards of war, but to a mob of unknown brigands, a thousand times more dangerous?"[37] The average French recruit probably shared this opinion of his new profession.

It is possible to build an army with high morale out of society's refuse—the British did it in the era immediately prior to World War I. But to do this successfully, the soldier ought to be entirely cut off from the civilian community and so immersed in his military unit and its values that he comes to accept the unit's definition of him as good and useful, regardless of the disdain of society at large. But the French soldier was never as isolated from the French populace at large as was the British soldier of a century later. The construction of regular barracks for French troops had made real progress by the late eighteenth century, but for most of that era troops were usually quartered among the local population. Even in garrisons the meager salaries of French troops often required them to work as craftsmen or laborers alongside civilians during off-duty hours. The soldier could not help but be offended or wounded by his low status. He must have felt a mixture of shame and fury to read the sign that stood at the entrance of public places, "No dogs, prostitutes, or soldiers."[38] It is impossible to determine how much this societal opinion remained part of the individual soldier's attitude after he had enrolled. But it seems reasonable to assume that it corroded individual self-respect and mutual respect among soldiers. Most French troops probably saw themselves, justly or unjustly, as losers, surrounded by other losers.

With astonishing rapidity the Revolution redefined the man in the ranks. He became a citizen-in-arms, a defender of his people, and a paragon of revolutionary morality. Some early praise of the soldier in the summer of 1789 smacks of seduction. The revolutionary bourgeoisie and the crowd feared suppression by troops loyal to Louis XVI. Had not the soldiers of the French Guards deserted in droves to the Parisian crowds, the events of July 1789 might not have led to a popular triumph. It is no surprise, then, that the publicist and politician Camille Desmoulins could write in a publication of 17 July 1789: "Brave soldiers, mingle with your brothers, receive their embraces. You are no longer satellites of the despot, the jailers of your brothers. You are our friends, our fellows, citizens, and soldiers of the Patrie."[39] Praise here was, in fact, an appeal to the soldiers to join in the revolutionary movement.

But something more basic than an appeal for allies had occurred. A transformation of the nature of the government had instantly redefined the relationship of the soldier to the people. Under the ancien régime the soldier was a servant of the king, who could use the army to impose the royal will upon his subjects. As veterans of the Revolution attested, "[Before 1789] we were regarded merely as vile instruments for the oppression of the people." Now that the government was responsible to the people, the soldier was their servant—no longer an enemy, but an ally. No one put it more plainly than Dubois-Crancé when he argued, "It is an honor to be a soldier, when this title is that of defender of the Constitution of his country." The man wearing the uniform of the regular army could claim to be sacrificing "his individual liberty and even his life for the liberty of all, for the security of their days and of their property, and for the glory of the Patrie."[40] Those who wore the colors of the new National Guard were even closer to the ideal of the citizen-in-arms.

From the first days of the Revolution its leaders insisted that "every citizen ought to be a soldier and every soldier a citizen." The idea, the very words come right out of Rousseau. Although the Revolution did not always read Rousseau with understanding, here it did. This demand forced the citizen to identify with the soldier and granted to the soldier the responsibilities and rights of a citizen. Robespierre addressed his colleagues in April 1790, "I ask the Assembly to not forget the principle that soldiers are citizens." Dumouriez, future minister and commanding general of the Nord, insisted repeatedly that "the man who binds for a time his liberty, in order to defend the public liberty, loses none of his rights as a citizen."[41] This insistence upon the full citizenship of Frenchmen in uniform defined the soldier not as something alien to civil society but rather as an embodiment of a duty required of all citizens.

The outbreak of war in 1792 gave substance to theories and ideals expressed during the preceding three years. With foreign armies threatening France, the French soldier stood as the actual defender of the property, lives, and liberties of his people. Those line troops and volunteers who defeated the Prussians at Valmy were more than a symbolic barrier against oppression. In addition, war made real the theoretical obligation of all citizens to become soldiers in defense of the Patrie.

Expansion of the army to the gargantuan size it attained in the summer of 1794 meant that young Frenchmen from all walks of life were called upon to serve. The soldier was no longer remote: he was a son, a brother, a husband, or a father. As is often the case for a large wartime army, the sacrifices and suffering demanded of its soldiers now became immediate, personal, and comprehensible to the civilian population at home, while battlefield victories became the personal triumphs of all the families of the troops involved. The shirker, not the soldier, became the outcast.

Volunteers and conscripts made the army a representative cross-section of the French population. The troops were now composed of the respectable and hard-working sons of its peasantry, artisans, and bourgeoisie. This change in composition alone, which can be seen in the statistics, had immense significance. In the past those who suffered economic hardship, social inequity, or plain hard luck marched behind the regimental flags; they had reason to be reluctant or dispirited; they were certainly alienated. But by 1792–94 those young men who possessed the full talent, confidence, and élan of the French people rallied around the banners of the revolutionary battalions; these men had good reason to be proud of themselves and their deeds. It is impossible to read their letters without being struck by the intense pride of these soldiers who fought in defense of their homes and families and who expressed enthusiastic support for the revolutionary political and social order.

The soldiers of the Republic were honored by a grateful people. In hundreds of the songs that so typified the Revolution, they were lauded as the heroes who protected their people and their revolution:

> Glory to the republican soldiers!
> Glory to their leaders, and their valor!
> More triumphant than Greeks or Romans,
> They are the saviors of France.
> Liberty, you create valor,
> Virtue, wealth, and happiness.

The dangers and suffering they endured were memorialized, "What laurels crown your heads, soldiers of liberty." The state could not take official note of the death of every soldier, but some were enshrined. At St. Quentin the town council renamed "rue Ste. Catherine" "rue Grenadier Malfuson" in honor of a brave volunteer from St. Quentin who died fighting before Lille in November 1792. Such recognition may not seem unusual to a modern reader, but Europe was not in the habit of memorializing its common soldiers in the eighteenth century. In a way that both honored the troops and expressed the unity between the nation and its army, soldiers participated in civic celebrations and in civic acts. Every municipal celebration included soldiers. Contemporary taste for the symbolic and allegorical meant that this participation was more than just bands and bayonets. Some deeper meaning was worked into the soldiers' presence. In one procession, which involved citizens of all ages, a detachment of infantry marched behind a banner reading "We Die for the Republic, One and Indivisible."[42] Even baptisms and marriages under the laws of the Republic often included a soldier as part of the ceremony.

The contrast between the status of the new soldier and that of the ancien régime trooper could hardly have been greater, and the difference was made clear at the time. One theme put before the troops was that under the ancien régime the soldier was despised and exploited. One song of 1789 ran:

> In olden days a machine,
> The poor soldier,
> Under discipline
> Was a convict.

Men of the Armée du Nord could read in a July 1792 issue of the *Argus* that "every good soldier ought to remember that no one was more of an unfortunate victim of despotism than the soldier who served in the ancien régime." This had now changed, and the soldier was valued. A Jacobin placard meant to discourage draft resistance stated simply, "The profession of arms used to be considered as dishonorable, today it is an honored profession."[43]

The administrators responsible for the army's welfare shared the new attitude toward the soldier. As Representative on Mission Gillet wrote in April 1794, "The soldiers are like the people, they are good." The same phrase occurs repeatedly in the correspondence of Minister of War Jean-Baptiste Bouchotte, "The soldiers are good."[44] They had come to define the new soldier in a way far from St. Germain's "slime."

A new soldier of 1794 was authentically representative of revolutionary France. The social composition of the Republic's army much more faithfully mirrored French society than had the army of the ancien régime. When the Convention abandoned volunteer enlistment and adopted conscription, the *levée en masse* came closest to mirroring the male population of military age. The common soldier had stepped forward as the best young manhood France could put on the line. By 1794 the rank and file represented not only the social composition but also the ideals of the French people. A citizen-soldier stood for civic responsibility, self-sacrifice, and defense of the public welfare. He appeared as the *sans-culotte* in arms.

Chapter 4

The New Officer Corps: Social Composition, Political Surveillance, and Military Leadership

THE REVOLUTION transformed the French officer corps in both composition and outlook. Measured by statistics considered important by social historians, this transformation exceeded changes in the rank and file. By 1794 the aristocracy, which once treated commissioned rank as a privileged preserve, constituted a mere 2 to 3 percent of the cadre. Before the Revolution an abyss of class and wealth had separated the leaders from the led, but it disappeared as men from the ranks rose to exercise command.

The emigration of aristocratic officers, followed by the desertion of Lafayette and the treason of Dumouriez, shook government trust in its officer corps. Anxious authorities faced a dilemma: a choice between professional competence and political reliability. Recognizing the need to maintain a sufficient level of technical capacity, Paris opted to retain skilled personnel but kept an ever watchful eye on the political opinions and actions of its officers. Generals, whose dreaded treachery had first fueled the mechanisms of suspicion, suffered frequent suspension and arrest. At the height of this fear, the Committee of Public Safety purged remaining nobles from the cadre.

The quality of leadership displayed by revolutionary officers depended upon their mastery of the military art and upon their relationships with their men. Suspensions and purges, undertaken at a time of massive military expansion, exacerbated an already difficult problem of inexperience. Although the French built their new officer corps on a foundation of long service noncommissioned officers (NCOs) and enlisted men, the army suffered from officers ill-prepared for their posts. Despite technical deficiencies, French officers benefited from a new set of relationships between themselves and their men. This advantage resulted from the social innovation of an army whose officers and men shared common backgrounds and from the conscientious application of revolutionary equality and fraternity in the military environment. The French officer knew that he must suffer privation, endure labor, and risk death beside his men. He no longer lived in a world apart, governed by standards of its own.

The Composition of the Officer Corps

Officers of the Line Army to 1793

In the mid-eighteenth century the system by which officers received commissions and promotions favored the well-to-do and the well-born. Captaincies and colonelcies legally went for a price, and appointments to other commissioned ranks might also, though illegally, involve the exchange of money. An officer did not have to climb the ladder of promotion by mounting each rung in the proper order. The powerful and rich rose quickly: first perhaps a brief apprenticeship as a gentleman volunteer, then the purchase of a suitable captain's billet, followed by investment of more funds in a colonel's commission. Full colonels in their twenties and thirties were not unusual. The impecunious noble who chose a military career, however, could be stuck as a company grade officer until he retired. With some luck he might rise to major, a largely administrative post, or to lieutenant-colonel, acting as de facto commander in place of an inexperienced or absent colonel. The gradual phasing out of the purchase system after St. Germain's reforms of 1776 curbed the worst abuses, but money still played a role. Influence mattered, too. By a decree of 1760 only nobles who had been presented at court could rise above the rank of colonel; a decree of 1788 recognized that only they could aspire to the rank of colonel as well.

The receipt of a direct commission was an aristocratic prerogative after 1715. About 10 to 13 percent of officers throughout the army were nonnobles, or *roturiers,* who rose from the ranks, the officers of fortune.[1] In the infantry they could aspire to no rank higher than captain of grenadiers, an officer forced to perform much of the battalion's dirty work. In some ways officers of fortune are better seen as senior NCOs than as true officers. Excluding officers of fortune, *roturiers* constituted only about 5 percent of the officer corps.[2] Throughout the century commissions were effectively denied to the sons of the middle class. The upper reaches of the officer corps contained aristocratic families endowed with great prestige. In 1789 only nine of 196 lieutenant-generals and only six of 200 infantry colonels lacked titles.[3] See Table 2 for a comparison of infantry officers from the ancien régime through 1794.

The prestige and composition of the officer corps varied in different branches of the army. Generally speaking, a cavalry commission carried the most status and burdened its recipient with the greatest expenses. Infantry came next, followed by the technical branches, artillery and engineers, which required more bourgeois education and training than did the cavalry or infantry. In an odd paradox the artillery demanded an elite rank and file, who were known both for physical strength and for skill, but bestowed little prestige on its officers, who were dismissed by fellow aristocrats as mechanics. Poor nobles and some men with no aristocratic lineage went to the artillery schools.

Beginning in the 1750s, the French attempted to professionalize their officer corps. Reformers did not equate professionalism with education or intelligence but with a commitment evidenced by long years of service. According to their logic, the ultimate officer was the poor but dedicated provincial noble who devoted his entire life to the army. Money ran contrary to professionalism. Rich young officers, often from families who had only recently bought patents of nobility, were seen as frivolous by their less affluent colleagues mired in the lower ranks. Critics charged that dedication could not be purchased in the way that a title could. From midcentury on, these essentially conservative reformers moved in the direction of restricting entry to all but nobles from long-established families. The pinnacle of the reform movement was the Ségur decree of 1781, which required four generations of nobility in order to qualify for a direct commission.[4] Limited exceptions were made only for men from families with a proven dedication to military service. After 1781 nobles with short pedigrees, as well as *roturiers,* found the door closed to them.

Revolution transformed the line cadre. The Constituent Assembly laid the basis for a new officer corps in 1790. In February it abolished the last vestiges of venality and opened all ranks to all citizens. July brought a substantial boost in officers' pay, which finally made it possible for an officer to live on his own salary. In the fall the Assembly decreed that three-quarters of entering sub-lieutenants were to receive their commissions on the basis of examinations and one-quarter would be supplied by NCOs.[5] Promotion to lieutenant and captain would follow seniority alone. Two-thirds of the commissions awarded to lieutenant-colonels and colonels would be based on longevity of service, with one-third left to the king's discretion.

The orderly process of selection and promotion embodied in the reforms of 1790 gave way to rapid turnover and promotion in 1791–92. In mid-summer 1791 French officers began to resign from the service in large numbers. The event that prompted these mass resignations and eventually drove thousands of officers to emigrate from France was the attempted flight of Louis XVI in June. From that moment until the overthrow of the monarchy on 10 August 1792, the king was a prisoner in his own palace.

TABLE 2.
Selected Characteristics of Infantry Officers to 1794

Troop	Social Composition				Origins			Age		Service	
1790 Line	Titled gens. and cols. 85% nobles 5% *roturier*, direct commission 10% soldiers of fortune							Young cols. Older lts.			
1791 Volunteers		lt.-cols.	capts. & lts.	sous-lts.		ur-ban	ru-ral		median age		having previous service
	nobles	48%	2%	1%	lt. cols.	69%	31%	lt. cols.	40–44	lt. cols.	66%
	bourgeois	41%	52%	43%	capts.	58%	42%	capts.	25–29	capts.	37%
	artisans and shopkeepers	5%	24%	28%	lts.	52%	48%	lts.	25–29	lts.	29%
	peasants	4%	14%	20%	sous-lts.	49%	51%	sous-lts.	25–29	sous-lts.	26%
1792 Volunteers			capts. & lts.	sous-lts.					median age		having previous service
	nobles		1%	0%				lt. cols.	40–44	lt. cols.	51%
	bourgeios		43%	33%				capts.	25–29	capts.	41%
	artisans and shopkeepers		30%	40%				lts.	25–29	lts.	29%
	peasants		16%	18%				sous-lts.	25–29	sous-lts.	15%
1793		cols. & lt.-cols.	capts. & lts.			ur-ban	ru-ral		median age		
	nobles	40%	9%		cols.	68%	32%	cols.	51–55	cols.—88% more than 24 yrs.	
	bourgeois	36%	34%		lt. cols.	44%	56%	lt. cols.	51–55	lt. cols.—64% more than 24 yrs.	
	artisans and shopkeepers	—	19%		capts.	44%	56%	capts.	41–45	capts.—52% more than 24 yrs.	
	peasants (all branches)	4%	17%		lts.	53%	47%	lts.	31–35		

Mid-1794 Army (*all branches)

	capts.	lts.	sous-lts.
nobles	2–3%		
bourgeois	44%	37%	37%
artisans	25%	34%	35%
peasants	22%	24%	27%

cols.* 58%—age 45 or less
capts. 50%—age 30 or less

lts.—49% more than 16 yrs.
gens.* 23% were NCOs in 1789; 43% were officers in 1789
cols.* 87% had served in 1789; 46% had 13 yrs. service in 1789
lt. cols.* 73% had served in 1789; 43% had 13 yrs. service in 1789
capts. 60% had served in 1789; 50% had 9 yrs. service in 1789
lts. 46% had served in 1789
sous-lts. 44% had served in 1789

Officers disenchanted with the course of events and unwilling to take a new oath that made no mention of the monarch left the service in great numbers. Just between late June 1791 and early August 1792, about 5,000 officers resigned or abandoned their posts. Captain Bodinier's research sets the final tally of officers who resigned or abandoned their commissions by April 1794 at 6,693, with 2,692 more leaving the service in some other manner, and death accounting for an additional 637. Eighty-seven percent of the officers who were on active duty in the summer of 1789 had left the service in one way or another by April 1794.[6]

The pressure to replace absent officers in the line army overwhelmed the procedures outlined in the 1790 legislation. On 24 June 1791 generals received authorization to nominate whomever they thought best to vacant sous-lieutenancies. One-half of their nominees were to be NCOs from the units in which vacancies occurred. The Legislative Assembly repeatedly considered the matter of replacement and examinations from August through November. Finally the decree of 29 November 1791 settled the question for the line army.[7] Examinations for infantry and cavalry were suspended and replaced by nomination; examinations continued only in artillery and engineers. One-half of vacant sous-lieutenancies would go to NCOs, and the remaining half to National Guards. Promotions beyond that rested essentially on seniority. As it stood on the books, this legislation could have resulted in an influx of sous-lieutenants with little if any military experience, but this did not happen. By February 1793 over 70 percent of captains and lieutenants in the army had served as enlisted men in the line before their promotions, and less than 12 percent of line officers came from National Guard or volunteer battalions.[8]

In early 1793 the line officer corps looked very different than it had before the Revolution. Only 10 percent were of noble birth, although 40 percent of colonels and lieutenant-colonels claimed an aristocratic background. The middle classes, from manufacturers to students, accounted for 34 percent. Artisans and shopkeepers totaled 18 percent, and peasants another 16 percent. The rural-urban mix depended on the branch of service and the rank. Lieutenants of infantry came from 47 percent rural origins and 53 percent urban; the percentages were exactly the reverse for cavalry lieutenants. Infantry colonels were 32 percent rural and 68 percent urban by birth. As a group the officers were men of age and experience. The median age for colonels (*chefs de brigade*) was between fifty-one and fifty-five. Eighty-eight percent of infantry colonels had already logged twenty-four or more years in the service. The median age for infantry captains was between forty-one and forty-five, and over 52 percent of these captains boasted at least twenty-four years in the army. Even lieutenants were old, with a median age of thirty-one to thirty-five, and nearly half of them had served over sixteen years. Cavalry officers were somewhat older, with more years of service, and artillery officers were even older and more experienced. The median age for artillery lieutenants was forty-one to forty-five with twenty-one to twenty-four years in the army.

By a route hardly to the taste of prerevolutionary military reformers, the army had reached one of the goals for which it had fought. Long-term professionals dominated the officer corps of the line army. This had not been achieved by reserving commissions for serious nobles of modest means, but by flooding the commissioned ranks with able and proven noncommissioned officers of *roturier* background.

Officers of Volunteers, 1791–93

The volunteer battalions of 1791 and 1792 elected their officers according to practices laid down in a decree of 4 August 1791. This legislation stipulated that all company-grade officers and NCOs were to be chosen from among those men who had some previous service, either in the line army or in the National Guard. Each battalion was to elect two lieutenant-colonels, one of whom must have commanded a company in a line regiment. The law reserved the choice of an adjutant-major for the local commanding general. The adjutant-major was to be selected among currently serving line officers and was to bear responsibility for instruction in the battalion.

An analysis of the officers commanding the Volunteers of 1791 reveals that only 4 percent were of noble and 48 percent of middle-class origins; an additional 24 percent were artisans and 15 percent were peasants.[9] Surprisingly, nearly half the lieutenant-colonels were noble; that is probably explained by the requirement that one-half the lieutenant-colonels were required to have prior service as captains in the line army. The median age of lieutenant-colonels was forty to forty-four, and twenty-five to twenty-nine for captains. Lieutenants and sous-lieutenants were somewhat younger than captains. Volunteer officers could boast nothing like the experience of line officers. Although the law dictated that all volunteer officers have some military experience, only about 31 percent of company-grade officers had served in the line. Among volunteer lieutenant-colonels, only about 13 percent had over twenty-four years' service; a comparable figure for line infantry lieutenant-colonels was almost 64 percent in 1793.

The Volunteers of 1792 elected even less experienced men to command.[10] Again, about one-third of their officers had some experience in the line; however, on closer inspection, there was a difference. Officers of volunteer battalions of the 1791 levy had in most cases been sergeants, or at least corporals in the line, but the men who claimed line experience and who now commanded the Volunteers of 1792 had only been corporals or common soldiers. The officers of 1792 were a trifle younger than those of 1791; 33 percent of lieutenants in 1792 battalions were aged twenty-four or less, and this percentage stood at 29 percent for 1791 battalions. Officers chosen by the Volunteers of 1792 were socially more like the men they led, whereas officers of 1791 battalions tended to be notables. For example, sous-lieutenants from artisan backgrounds constituted nearly 40 percent of the men who bore that rank in 1792 battalions, but only 28 percent in 1791 battalions.

The levies of 1793 did not contribute immediately to the pool of officers. In decreeing the Levy of 300,000, the National Convention forestalled election and ordered the minister of war to dispatch the number of commissioned and noncommissioned officers necessary to take charge of the new recruits.[11] Battalions raised by the *levée en masse* were allowed to choose their officers according to the decree of 4 August 1791, but these appointments were temporary. The law of 22 November 1793, which declared that all conscripts would be incorporated into existing units at the front, also stripped the new elected officers of their rank.

Laws on Selection and Promotion, 1793–94

The law of 21 February 1793 eliminated official distinctions between line and volunteer troops. One pay scale, one organization, and one system of officer selection and promotion would now apply across the board. All ranks from sergeant through lieutenant-colonel, now termed *chef de bataillon,* would be chosen by two methods. One-third of the vacancies would be filled on the basis of seniority from among those of the next lower rank. The law was open to some confusion but was interpreted to mean longevity of total service, not just time in grade.[12] This interpretation favored applicants from the old line army. The other two-thirds of all vacancies would be filled through an election, which picked three nominees. The final choice was to be made by all men of the battalion currently serving in the rank to which the candidates aspired. Promotion to full colonel, retitled *chef de brigade,* was to fall on one of the lieutenant-colonels, based alternatively on seniority in grade and on longevity of service. Election presented serious inconveniences, since polling units took time, especially if a battalion was quartered in several places. The emphasis on seniority caused even greater potential hazards. Young officers disliked the practice, since it promoted old war horses "grown grey in the harness, but unskilled and inept."[13]

The revolutionary government altered this system by the decree of 22 November 1793 and the law of 19 July 1794. One-third of the vacancies were now to be filled by the choice of the Convention, which would make its selection from three nominees submitted to it by the *conseil d'administration* of the unit involved. This amendment allowed the promotion of men of talent, regardless of their length of service. Of the remaining two-thirds of promotions, one-third would be based on seniority, and one-third by election, as set down in the February decree. According to the organizational decree of 12 August 1793, the important *conseils d'adminis-*

tration consisted of seventeen men, eleven of whom were selected for duty because they were the most senior men in each of the ranks from private to captain. The National Convention soon revamped the *conseils d'administration* in a decree of 9 March 1794. On the battalion level, the lieutenant-colonel was joined by one each of every commissioned and noncommissioned rank and five privates, all elected by their peers in that particular rank. Thus reconstituted, the *conseil d'administration* became a democratic institution composed of only four officers and eight enlisted men. There was to be a *conseil* on the demi-brigade level for organized demi-brigades, and it took precedence over the battalion *conseil*. The new *conseil* could be expected to pay less attention to seniority than had the original one. Further modifications of practice included a December 1793 authorization for Representatives on Mission to make promotions they deemed necessary and a law of 15 February 1794 barring from promotion to commissioned and noncommissioned rank those who could not read and write.[14]

The Officer Corps in 1794

By the summer of 1794 years of turnover and promotions, capped by the merging of line troops with volunteers and conscripts, had produced a new and unique officer corps. Twenty-one percent of the officers on duty then had joined the army with the Volunteers of 1791; 28 percent were Volunteers of 1792.[15] About half the republican officers of 1794 were men of long service, who had been in the army before 1789. The number of years in service that officers could point to depended on rank and branch. Eighty-seven percent of generals were already soldiers before the Revolution, and 43 percent of them had been officers in 1789. Eighty-seven percent of colonels and 73 percent of lieutenant-colonels were in the army before 1789; 46 percent of the colonels and 43 percent of lieutenant-colonels already had put thirteen years or more of service behind them by 1789. A closer look at the colonels reveals that 40 percent of them wore officers' epaulettes before the Revolution, while 31 percent led men as NCOs. In the heavy infantry 60 percent of captains, 46 percent of lieutenants, and 44 percent of sous-lieutenants had military experience before 1789. Clearly, company grade officers owed their rank to the Revolution. If 5 percent of heavy infantry captains had been officers in 1789, 55 percent had been corporals. Cavalry officers had more years of service than did their counterparts in the infantry. Eighty percent of cavalry captains had already been in the army by 1789, and 60 percent of them had more than thirteen years of service at that point. Even more experienced officers led the artillery. There, 84 percent of captains, 74 percent of lieutenants, and 81 percent of sous-lieutenants had already worn the king's uniform by 1789. The military engineers boasted the highest percentage of experienced officers.

Taken as a whole, by mid-1794 the officer corps was young; in fact, they were noticeably younger than the line officers of a year before. More than half the generals of 1794 had yet to reach their forty-fifth birthday. Thirty percent of colonels in 1794 were under thirty-five, and 58 percent were under forty-five. Half the heavy infantry captains of 1794 were in their twenties; only 14 percent of line infantry captains had been under thirty in 1793. The tremendous expansion of the French army and its officer corps to unprecedented levels and the turnover associated with combat allowed for comparatively rapid promotions. It must be kept in mind, however, that the system of promotion emphasized seniority and proven talent. Nevertheless, some reached the top with meteoric speed. In 1793 thirty-two officers were promoted directly from lieutenant or captain to major-general or *maréchal de camp*.[16] Napoleon Bonaparte climbed from a twenty-year-old artillery lieutenant in 1789 to the command of an entire army at twenty-six. However, such rapid ascents were not the usual route of advance for the vast majority of officers. One factor that resulted in a low average age, even in a system which put a premium on seniority, is that the veterans with long years of service had enlisted at an early age. Later, a 1795 law requiring four years service in grade to be promoted to the next higher pushed average ages to a higher level, so in 1797, 36 percent of infantry sous-lieutenants were thirty-five or older, while in 1794 this figure had been only 25 percent.[17] The officer corps of the Year II came from a broad cross-section of French society. Men of middle-class origins constituted roughly one-third of all company grade officers—a strong representation to be sure, but it did not render the officer corps a preserve of the new elite. Among heavy infantry 44 percent of captains and 37 percent of lieutenants and sous-lieutenants had bourgeois backgrounds. Artisans accounted for 26 percent of captains, 34 percent of lieutenants, and 35 percent of sous-lieutenants. Peasants made up 22 percent of heavy infantry captains, 24 percent of lieutenants, and 27 percent of sous-lieutenants. Jean-Paul Bertaud's research suggests that the peasants who saw their sons rise to commissioned rank were not restricted to the better-off segment of the agricultural class. Over 60 percent of peasant captains listed their origins as *cultivateurs,* a group described as "more needy than rich." As might be suspected, the peasantry contributed comparatively more to the cavalry than the infantry. Thirty-four percent of cavalry captains and 33 percent of lieutenants and sous-lieutenants came from peasant stock. Those who commanded troopers were twice as likely as infantry officers to be the better-off peasants or *laboureurs.* The artisan contribution sank to only about 23 percent of all grades of cavalry officers. Middle-class families supplied 38 percent of cavalry captains, 39 percent of lieutenants, and 36 percent of sous-lieutenants. The artillery, which demanded so much education and training of its officers, surprisingly drew only 24 percent of its captains from the middle classes. The once dominant aristocracy contributed no more than 2 to 3 percent of the officers in all branches.

The educational standards of French officers in the Year II were respectable by contemporary standards. In the heavy infantry 85 percent of captains, 81 percent of lieutenants, and 79 percent of sous-lieutenants knew how to read and write.[18] Skill at mathematics was less common. In the Armée du Nord 54 percent of infantry officers could do their figures.

By 1794 the French army was led by an officer corps that was already surprisingly experienced, though not always as officers. The old social disparity between officers and men was gone. In the ancien régime the army had contained elite officers while the rank and file were cast-offs if not outcasts. Both officers and men now came from all levels, even if the officer corps, more than the rank and file, represented the literate middle classes. The officer corps was patriotic as well. Forty-nine percent volunteered with the levies of 1791 and 1792. Moreover, an inquiry carried out by the Committee of Public Safety described the majority of officers as "experienced patriots."[19] The government had great interest in the patriotism of its officers, as will be seen.

Surveillance and Purge

The revolutionary government never felt completely at ease with its officer corps. In a sense each held the other hostage. Survival of the Revolution and its institutions demanded success on the field of battle, which rested upon the quality of leadership the troops received. On the other hand, an officer's fate, his promotion or dismissal, depended upon the will of the government.

Publicly and privately, revolutionary authorities placed their ultimate confidence in the common soldier. The conviction that "the soldier is good" permeated so much of the discussion of victory and defeat that it rose to the level of dogma. A Parisian left-wing political club, the Cordeliers, argued that "the virtue of the soldier always surpasses that of the officers."[20] Such an assertion had technical, political, and moral meaning. Soldiers fought well if led well, remained loyal to the Revolution, and served as a personal sacrifice for the public welfare. By this logic defeat resulted from the incompetence, cowardice, or disloyalty of officers. "I say to you with the truthfulness of a true republican, . . . the soldiers are good, but the cowardice and crass ignorance of the officer has taught them cowardice."[21] This characteristic criticism came from the pen of General Houchard, soon to suffer death for his own failures.

Clearly the government required skilled officers, but it feared that treason might go hand in hand with talent. As one orator stated before the

Convention, "We stand between two dangers, treason and ignorance."²² It was a dilemma common to revolutionary regimes—a choice between technical competence and political dedication. By and large, technical necessity prevailed, and laws of promotion favored seniority and skill. However, the government placed those chosen to command under careful surveillance and did not hesitate to suspend or arrest officers who provoked its suspicion. Vigilance became the price for competence. Generals were subject to the closest scrutiny, since they held great power. Heightened insecurity finally forced a purge of nobles from all commissioned ranks, but even the *roturier* entrusted with no more than modest rank was not immune from the watchful agents of central and local authorities.

Generals and the Fear of Treason

Government suspicion of its military officers began at the top. Unreliable generals posed a particularly serious threat to the Republic. Only at the highest level of command could treason turn an entire army against the Revolution, or incompetence cost battles and fortresses. In the popular mind four generals best represented the desertion, treason, arrogance, and incompetence that menaced the Republic. All four commanded the Nord—Lafayette, Dumouriez, Custine, and Houchard. Their actions and fates marked the stages in an escalating, and sometimes paranoid, campaign against suspect officers of all ranks.

The marquis de Lafayette, once the hero of two worlds, fell out of step with the Revolution in 1792. As previously described, in a maneuver he hoped would give him more political leverage in Paris, he exchanged command over the Armée du Centre for that of the Nord on 11 July 1792. Upon learning of the storming of the Tuilleries on 10 August, he publicly opposed the overthrow of the monarchy and tried to play the Nord as a trump card in the political game. At Sedan he asked his troops to renew their oath to the deposed monarch, but they balked. To forestall a coup, the Assembly suspended his authority and quickly dispatched commissioners to guarantee the loyalty of the army. On 19 August Lafayette and a band of supporters crossed over to the Austrians. The immediate consequences for officers on the morrow of Lafayette's desertion were surprisingly small. It would take the addition of Dumouriez's treason to suggest, or to confirm, that treachery by generals was widespread and dangerous to the Republic.

By his attempt to lead the Nord on Paris in the first days of April 1793, Dumouriez set off a profound government reaction against its generals and its officer corps. After defeats at Neerwinden and Louvain, he concluded a tacit armistice with the enemy, who allowed him to withdraw French forces unmolested. At a dinner with the Austrian, General Mack, on 25 March, Dumouriez announced his intentions to move on Paris to restore the monarchy and asked the prince of Coburg's word of honor not to attack during the coup. In exchange Dumouriez surrendered all of the Low Countries to Coburg. Confronted by agents of the Convention and the minister of war himself, Dumouriez arrested them and turned them over to the Austrians. However, Dumouriez's troops soon turned against his designs, while from Valenciennes representatives of the Convention rallied his battalions to the Republic. On 5 April a bitter Dumouriez crossed the frontier. That very day a young Volunteer of 1791 wrote this disheartened note: "The idols of nations, are they therefore only deceivers? To whom is he now faithful, this Dumouriez who the French Republic regarded as its savior . . . ? [A]ll our misfortunes have been caused only by him; he is a hundred times more guilty than Lafayette."[23]

The Convention wasted no time before it took steps to protect itself from Dumouriez and his subordinates. Even before Dumouriez fled, the Convention decreed on 3 April: "The fathers and mothers, the wives and children of the officers of the army which was commanded by Dumouriez, from the rank of sous-lieutenant to that of lieutenant-general, will be watched carefully as hostages by each municipality." Two weeks later the Convention nullified all promotions granted to officers under Dumouriez's command after 5 February 1793. As part of this order, the minister of war received temporary authorization to replace these officers with his own nominees; however, the Convention was not yet so alarmed as to abandon its laws on promotion or to grant too much discretion to the minister of war.

The National Convention also appealed directly to the troops through proclamations and placards. They charged that Dumouriez had always planned to betray France and compared him to Oliver Cromwell and to Lafayette: "From this moment on, renounce all idols."[24] Continuing in this vein, the Committee of Public Safety and the Ministry of War began an extensive campaign of political education among the troops—which included the purchase and distribution of over seven million copies of political journals. The campaign hammered at the need for troops to be suspicious of their officers.

Later in April the Committee of Public Safety directed its attention toward the top generals to determine those fit to lead armies; in that month only five generals were suspended.[25] Charges against aristocratic officers of all ranks multiplied in the political clubs and in the Convention, but a true purge was still months in the future. Although Dumouriez's actions had set in motion the mechanisms of suspicion and surveillance, only the reaction against comte de Custine exposed the officer corps to the full force of the government machinery.

Custine fell victim not to outright treason but to his arrogance, born of a concept of authority inconsistent with the new Republic. He had shone with a kind of brilliance during the fall campaign of 1792. When he eventually left the Armée du Rhin to assume command of the Armée du Nord, in May 1793, the Nord was in a poor state, and he did a great deal to put it back on its feet. Less than two months after his arrival, however, the government judged his sins to be greater than his virtues. He left the Nord on 16 July to face charges in Paris, was condemned, and mounted the scaffold on 28 August.

Some charges that he wished to make himself a dictator surfaced before he left the Rhin. He arrived at the Nord with a well-deserved reputation as a strict disciplinarian. In 1792 he had ordered three men shot for pillage, without giving them the privilege of a court martial. Ample testimony establishes that he maintained his rigorous standards in the Nord, yet Custine retained the respect and affection of his troops.[26] His severity struck Parisian radicals as unrepublican, and his popularity struck them as subversive. Their fears that he harbored unacceptable political views were justified in their eyes by Custine's resistance to the distribution of revolutionary journals sent to the front as part of the government's efforts in political education. He systematically frustrated deliveries of the *Père Duchesne* and the *Journal de la Montagne*. Custine gave further evidence of his reactionary attitudes by backing the wrong candidate for the disputed command of Lille. His man, Lamarlière, was criticized by his enemies as aristocratic and allied with suspect individuals.

Through it all, Custine fought a running battle with Minister of War Bouchotte. Custine dared to write: "And I too, Citizen Minister, see only the Republic; but when the success of its armies requires that I criticize a minister for his ignorance, or his ineptitude in the difficult functions that have been confided to him, I do not believe that I have failed the Republic in speaking out against him strongly." A month later, on 1 July, Custine insisted, in a note to the Committee of Public Safety, "It is finally time . . . that you give us a Minister of War. There is no other man as stupid and as incapable in that position as Bouchotte."[27] Here Custine challenged the supremacy of civil authority precisely at a time when that authority had resolved to curb its generals, when all generals remained suspect until proven loyal. The logic of civil-military relations in the Jacobin Republic demanded his removal from command; the extremes of accusation and action typical of intense revolutionary eras sent him to the guillotine.

Custine's fall from grace was followed by an extensive purge of generals. In 1792 twenty-one generals were suspended from their functions. The first half of 1793 added another forty-five to this list. In the last six months of the year 230 were suspected. On 28 July the National Convention voted to set aside the laws of promotion as they applied to general officers and their immediate staffs. As Barère stated when proposing this measure, the Convention wanted "to place a good *sans-culotte* at the head of our armies." The minister of war received tremendous leeway to nominate new generals and staff officers as he pleased.[28] Generals were removed from the rolls in August and September for little other reason than their noble birth. Self-consciously, the government turned to *roturiers* to fill the vacancies. Enter Houchard.

There was nothing aristocratic about Houchard. He rose from the ranks as an officer of fortune, reaching the rank of captain in 1779, after twenty-four years of service.[29] When war broke out in 1792, Captain Houchard climbed the ladder of promotion rapidly and followed Custine as chief of the Nord on 1 August. Unfortunately, Houchard soon revealed himself to be a man of limited capacity. Although he won the confused fight at Hondschoote, 6–8 September, he so bungled the subsequent operations that an enemy who might have been destroyed escaped with relatively minor losses. Houchard paid for failure with his life. Arrested on 23 September, he went to the scaffold in November not for treachery but for incompetence. By his arrest and execution the Convention made clear that it demanded ability as well as loyalty from its officers.

The final toll from the purge of generals mounted to a considerable number. During the entire revolutionary era 1792–99, the army listed 1,378 generals; 994 sanctions, from suspension to execution, were applied against them. In particular, noble generals fell from the rolls. In April 1792 the army contained 135 generals of aristocratic birth and only eighteen *roturiers;* by January 1794 the nobles numbered only sixty-two and the *roturiers* 275.[30] All this resulted in tremendous turnover at the top. In the Armée du Nord, of eighteen generals commanding the major field forces on 24 October 1792, not a single one still led troops a year later.[31] High rank obviously brought with it high risk, and many men refused promotions. Paul Charles Thiébault reported that "brevets to generals were soon called brevets to the guillotine."[32]

The Purge of Aristocratic Officers

As alarm and suspicion continued to mount in the late summer and fall of 1793, the Committee of Public Safety ordered the suspension of all former nobles. This suspension accompanied a new law of suspects and other measures that intensified the Terror. The assault on the nobility in uniform followed the logic of the times. The fear of an aristocratic conspiracy against the Revolution troubled the *sans-culottes* even before they stormed the Bastille, and revolutionary journalists had been quick to turn this fear against aristocratic officers. Emigration by thousands of officers and their attachment to counterrevolutionary forces across the border called into question the loyalties of those who remained. The treason or suspected treason of prominent generals further justified the fears and expectations of those already convinced that born aristocrats only served the Revolution to betray it.

Publicists and politicians had begun to attack aristocratic officers as a group before Dumouriez crossed over to the Austrians, and his treason accelerated the assault, since the left read the treachery of generals as a barometer of the nobles' true sympathies. "Only give me the name of a single noble, from Layafette to Custine, who has not finished by being a conspirator and a traitor." The radical press continued its attack throughout the summer. Nobles had denied France an easy victory, they charged. Jacques René Hébert answered, "No more nobles, I will not cease to tell you, no more nobles. All of them are enemies of the people."[33] Points of view expressed in the journals were heard in the political clubs. On 9 June Billaud-Varenne argued before the Jacobins for the dismissal of all nobles. The number-two man at the Ministry of War, a radical named Vincent, made the most extreme statements at the Cordelier Club. "In order to save France, there is only one means: exterminate the nobles and priests without a single exception."[34] Bouchotte himself believed in the exclusion of all nobles, which by mid-summer had taken on very much the tone of a *sans-culotte* crusade. It is not surprising that the city government of Paris, the Commune, publicly ordered that "no ex-noble or recalcitrant priest will fill the functions of an officer or public official."[35]

An outcry for action besieged the Convention and the Committee of Public Safety in August and September. Petitions from popular societies all over France poured into the Convention, and for political reasons alone something had to be done. In many ways September 1793 was a time of decision and extremes in Paris. On 5 September the Convention declared that Terror was "the order of the day." It recast its revolutionary tribunals and initiated a series of actions to protect the Revolution from suspects. That very day, it received a delegation from the Jacobins and the sections of Paris, who again demanded, "Before all things, bannish from every army that insolent caste, always the enemy of liberty and of equality." On 15 September the momentum of fears, demands, and actions finally drove the Committee of Public Safety to order that "all *ci-devant* nobles who have positions in the armies of the Republic are dismissed."[36] Discharged officers, now suspects, had to set up residence at least twenty leagues from the armies, the frontiers, and from Paris.

The actions following the decree were neither as immediate nor as sweeping as the order commanded. Authorities did not banish every officer. Many who had pressed for exclusion recognized that it would cost the Republic the services of good and talented men. In some areas this cost was too high. Lazare Carnot, a military engineer himself and long aware of the shortages of skilled officers in artillery and engineers, insisted on the maintenance of professional standards.[37] The Committee of Public Safety mirrored his concern by reinstating ex-nobles to their posts in these technical branches on 13 January 1794.³⁸ In other cases the purge moved selectively and slowly. Comte Jean Baptiste Jourdan, a *ci-devant,* took command of the Nord on 22 September 1793. He was only removed from command on 6 January 1794. A poster of 25 January 1794 issued by Representative E. D. Duquesnoy with the Nord announced the dismissal of ex-nobles as if it were a policy new to the Nord.³⁹ Although many purged officers found themselves reinstated after a time, for some the purge meant an end to their careers, or at least an extended hiatus until Thermidor changed the political climate of France.

The Vulnerability of All Officers

While generals inspired the most serious concern, and *ci-devant* aristocrats fell victim to blanket suspension, *roturier* officers, even in minor positions, did not enjoy immunity from revolutionary surveillance. The *roturier* might not be assumed guilty until proven innocent, as was the case for the aristocrat, but he must still measure up to revolutionary standards.

Even a hint of disloyalty propelled authorities into action against a suspected officer. A law of 24 June 1791 authorized generals to suspend any officer "whose conduct appeared suspect." Later, the minister of war ordered his agents, the *commissaires du conseil exécutif,* to keep a close watch on individuals including "officers . . . who manifest opinions contrary to liberty, equality, and the unity and indivisibility of the Republic."⁴⁰ "Incivic" remarks could bring prison or death to the disloyal or the unlucky. Association with someone pronounced a traitor, particularly a traitor of high rank, could condemn an officer to close scrutiny, if not to suspension or arrest. Confronted with the charge of disloyalty, the threatened officer could produce "certificates of civism" and hope they would shield him.

Officers of line regiments seemed particularly open to suspicion, at least through 1793. A revolutionary catechism of 1792 asked the question, "What is an officer of the line?" The answer: "He is an aristocrat by birth, estate, and taste."⁴¹ The actual aristocratic composition of the line officer corps diminished to only 10 percent by early 1793, yet the supposedly conservative complexion of the line still called its officers into question. The *amalgame* was, in fact, intended to lessen their influence. In May 1793 the Convention commanded line infantry officers to lay aside their white uniforms and don the blue coats of the volunteers, the national uniform as it was called.⁴² Wearing the blue uniform had become a test of loyalties and should an officer put off the change, he fell suspect.

Officers could rarely look to their own soldiers for support against accusations of treason. The rank and file believed what the government told them, and their loyalty went to the state not to the generals. Even before the repeated arrests, troops feared treason; witness their cries of "We are betrayed!" during the first months of the war. Arrests and revolutionary propaganda only confirmed suspicions that probably had their roots in the fear of an aristocratic conspiracy in 1789. The events of 1793 made soldiers all the more wary of their officers. As Louis Bricard wrote of his comrades' reaction to the removal of Houchard, "We were so accustomed to the treason of the highest generals that we learned of this news without any surprise."[43]

Agents and Agencies of Surveillance

The variety of agents and agencies involved in the surveillance of officers reflected the common recognition that only intense vigilance could protect the Revolution from betrayal. Widespread alarm created a national campaign that enlisted the full apparatus of central and local government to insure that those entrusted with the defense of the Republic would not turn on her.

The Ministry of War was central to the scrutiny and purge of officers. Between April 1793 and April 1794, Jean-Baptiste Bouchotte held the post of minister. He had held the rank of captain of cavalry before the Revolution and had risen to colonel since 1789. Although not a political radical, he owed his political survival to the influence of prominent radicals on his staff, most notably his assistant, François-Nicolas Vincent. Until the arrest of Vincent and the journalist Hébert, the Ministry remained a stronghold of the Hébertists, extreme democrats who wielded considerable influence among the *sans-culottes* and municipal government of Paris. It came as no surprise, then, that the Ministry adopted Hébertist points of view, attacking Custine and urging the purge of ex-nobles.[44]

In addition to its obvious administrative duties, the Ministry of War assumed important political functions. More than any other organ of government, it bore the responsibility for political education of the army, and it put great energy into rooting out suspect officers. The primary agents of the Ministry in these tasks were the *commissaires du conseil exécutif*. An instruction sent by Bouchotte to one of these *commissaires* defined their role with great clarity.

> I send you, citizen, your new commission of agent of the Executive Council; you ought to be thoroughly convinced of the importance of your mission, on which can depend the safety of the Republic. The agent of the Council is the eye of the minister with the armies in order to discover all treasons, intrigues, and abuses.
>
> The agent of the Council ought especially to devote himself to knowing the spirit and principles of the generals . . . if they have been public or private partisans of the tyranny and of the factions which have succeeded it, and that the people have overthrown.

Equally, he ought to find out if there exist in the headquarters staff or among the officers of particular units former nobles, men who had been attached to the service of tyrants or the creatures of *Lafayette, Dumouriez, Custine, Houchard, Biron, Brunet,* and other generals, officers, and employees of the administration, with the armies, who manifest opinions contrary to liberty, equality, and the unity and indivisibility of the Republic.[45]

Celliez provides an interesting example of the *commissaires* at work. He was most prominent during the summer of 1793, when he fought constantly against Custine. Celliez gave his political allegiance to Hébert; in fact, the Archives de la guerre has a letter that he wrote to Hébert on 19 July 1793. In it he expressed extreme, indeed paranoid, fears of treachery. "The majority of officers as you know are . . . enemies of the Revolution." He argued, "Here as in Paris the aristocrats are raising their heads, it is necessary to join together to exterminate without pity all those scoundrels who threaten liberty, and then the Republic will triumph." In this letter Celliez repeatedly praised the *Père Duchesne,* which he personally distributed to the troops. Antoine-Anatole Jarry, an adjutant-general under Dampierre and Custine, once charged that Celliez was "sent to the Armée du Nord to watch over the generals and spy on the Representatives on Mission." Jarry was close to the truth. Celliez did keep notes on officers he suspected, as did other *commissaires,* since reporting on the political opinions of officers was part of his job. Spying may not be the word for it, but Celliez did report on the political acts and even the amours of Representatives to the Ministry and to the press.[46]

Representatives on Mission also involved themselves in the cycle of surveillance, denunciation, suspension, and prosecution. Their efforts could not be as extensive as those of the *commissaires* because Representatives on Mission, being regular members of the Convention, did not generally stay with the armies for long periods, and when they were with the armies, they usually shouldered a great number of pressing responsibilities. The efforts of Representatives could complement or even duplicate those of *commissaires*. As early as November 1792 General Anne-François La Bourdonnaye, serving in Belgium with the Nord, requested that the Convention send four or six Representatives to "oversee the conduct of the generals." They frequently suspended and arrested officers. In one case Representative Jacques Isoré suspended nine officers of a light infantry battalion because they "had manifested some sentiments contrary to the Revolution" and had "been denounced several times in the popular societies." As late as 24 March 1794, Representative Letourneur purged *ci-devant* officers from the first cavalry and sixty-eighth infantry and suspended officers "by reason of principles of incivism for which they were reproached." Representatives also suspended officers for incompetence, as when Antoine-Louis St. Just cashiered the lieutenant-colonel and all the captains of the 2nd Vienne for the poor showing of that battalion.[47]

The authorities directing and conducting the surveillance and purge could count on the assistance of individual officers and soldiers. Officers might denounce their brother officers, since the army contained men of differing political convictions. A supporter of Robespierre, such as Adjutant-General Calandini, might condemn men he suspected of politically unacceptable sentiments. Soldiers accused their officers, sometimes in an open format, such as a political club, and sometimes when interviewed by *commissaires* or Representatives. In a circular of 31 August 1793, Bouchotte reminded his *commissaires:* "One of the most important objects of the mission of agents of the council is to take information, especially from soldiers, concerning officers who do not merit public confidence and on those who have patriotism and capacity." The survey of officer competence ordered by the Committee of Public Safety on 28 July 1794 required that enlisted men evaluate officers. Denunciations by soldiers led to some problems, and the Committee of Public Safety, with its concern for competence, became aware that some soldiers might accuse their officers just to settle old scores.[48]

Popular societies enthusiastically assisted by reporting on units stationed in their district. The clubs issued a stream of denunciations, particularly in the fall and winter of 1793–94. *Commissaires,* Representatives, and even the institutions of central government turned to the popular societies. In extreme cases popular societies might receive from the hands of Representatives on Mission the power to do more than denounce. An order of 18 September 1793, signed by Representatives Élie Lacoste and J.-P.-C. Peyssard read: "Ordered: that the commissioners named by the popular societies of the major towns of the departments of the north, are authorized to bring before them the officers and employees of the different administrations of the Armée du Nord, to remove from command and to have arrested all those who seem suspect to them." The popular societies also provided a platform for denunciations, or even served as a sponsor for denunciations, by common soldiers. The particularly radical club of Lille issued an order encouraging "the soldier citizens to assemble peaceably and without arms, in order to judge the civism of their officers."[49]

Committees of surveillance also played a role, although one not as great as that played by the popular societies. These committees first sprang up spontaneously in 1792 to name and keep track of suspects. Legislation of 21 March 1793 regularized their structure and power, subsequently extended by a new law of suspects in September. Since they formally investigated suspects, their concern with suspect officers grew out of their normal duties. Local municipal governments, of which the committees of surveillance formed a part, might also be called upon in the effort to weed out the unreliable.

The last institution involved in the prosecution of officers believed guilty of treason or disloyalty was the court system. Here, the purge of officers overlaps with the system of military justice, to be explored in the next chapter. The military tribunals established during this period had several goals, but in a directive to these tribunals the Committee of Public Safety made it clear that traitors were primary targets, after which came cowards and war profiteers.[50]

The officer unjustly charged with noble ancestry, dangerous opinions, disloyalty, or treason had few ways to defend himself. Of real use were certificates of civism, which might be obtained from a friendly popular society or a hometown municipal government attesting to the proper revolutionary sentiments of the man in question. An aspiring young volunteer with the Nord, François Mireur, described the utility of a certificate testifying that he was not a noble. "They wanted to make me pass for a noble, but I silenced those who denounced me by showing my certificate to the Representative of the People, who likes me very much. The man who made the denunciation is now under arrest." Such a certificate also paved the way for advancement, as the following promotion demonstrates: "Considering the state of service of Citizen Pierre Housset, lieutenant . . . considering the diploma accorded to him by the . . . revolutionary society of Gravelines, . . . which demonstrates that the said Pierre Housset enjoys the esteem of his fellow citizens, and that he is of the highest principles and a good republican. . . .the constituted authorities request that Citizen Housset fill the position of adjutant.[51]

Two Aspects of Leadership

In discussing the revolutionary officer to understand morale and effectiveness better, the fundamental issue is leadership. I approach this question in awe of its difficulty. So complex and so controversial is the phenomenon of military leadership that it often defies analysis. To try to piece it together for an army that fought two hundred years ago smacks of the brash. Tales of the daring-do of brave republican officers cannot substitute for an examination of leadership. Bravery does not equal leadership: brave men can be incompetent in their craft and despised by their men. Besides this, leadership's contribution to morale and motivation must be seen in a context broader than the battlefield, bravery's theater. What follows are general considerations of two aspects of leadership, which by no means exhaust the subject. The first is technical competence and the second, officer-soldier relationships. Together they help explain the tactical rough edges but high morale and effectiveness that typified the French army by 1794.

Officer Competence

To a degree, the quality of leadership depends upon the officers' skills as technicians. The term "professional" accurately described the majority of French officers in 1793–94, if professionalism is equated with years of service alone. The technical competence of these officers, however, remains a separate question, which cannot be settled by counting the years of service listed on *contrôles*.

In the summer of 1794 a large portion of the French officer corps could not justly claim to have mastered the art of war at the level on which they exercised their commands. Providing technically competent officers for an army that leaped from 150,000 in 1792 to 750,000 in 1794 exceeded the range of the possible for any government of the time. The problems of this Herculean challenge were exacerbated by the flight or purge of qualified officers. In reporting their mission of early 1793 Georges Jacques Danton and his colleagues explained the crisis: "After 10 August the army was purged as much as possible of all whose civism was suspect, but . . . this beneficial operation forced the admission into important and difficult posts of new men, whose patriotism was proven but whose talents were not yet aided by experience."[52] The particular weaknesses of the French officer corps flowed from the system, or systems, of promotion developed to meet the challenge of this extraordinary era.

The promotion of NCOs into the commissioned ranks, and the emphasis upon seniority as a criterion for further steps up the ladder, guaranteed that men in command would have experience, but it is worth asking whether long years as an NCO provided the best preparation for a junior officer. For one thing, many junior officers produced by this system were old. This problem was most acute in 1793. In the line army of early 1793, which at that time comprised the majority of French troops, the median age for cavalry lieutenants was thirty-six to forty. Cavalry captains, meant to ride hard at the head of their companies, were usually middle-aged men; their median age stood at forty-six to fifty. If it is true that leading small groups in combat is a young man's job, many of the lieutenants and captains of 1793 were not well suited to their duties. By 1794 officers were much younger on the average, but there were still many who were older than they ought to have been. In another far more subjective sense, the ex-sergeant may not have made an ideal officer. Long years as a sergeant carrying out the minutiae of eighteenth-century warfare hardly trained a man to take the initiative and show the imagination of a first-rate officer. Of course, this assertion is open to debate. The criticisms expressed here were voiced by observers at the time. Representatives with the Rhin complained in despair, "Old corporals pass from grade to grade up to the highest rank, and heaven only knows how they will turn out. We ask you to bring about some prompt remedy." Representatives Delbrel and Letourneur wrote from their post with the Armée du Nord in August 1793 to recommend that the Committee of Public Safety alter the principle of seniority: "The officers named by seniority in grade could be good honest men, but they could also be in no condition to command and are often timid and inept; for a long time you have been sent observations of this type."[53] Seniority was also flawed at the top levels of command. It assured promotion to a man like Nicolas Berthel, who was raised to general at age seventy-four in 1793.

Election of officers stood poles apart from the principle of seniority, but it, too, led to serious problems. In many cases the men of new volunteer battalions did elect those among them who possessed some military experience; Bertaud has established that roughly one-third of company grade officers in volunteer battalions claimed some experience in the line army. But if one-third had line experience, two-thirds did not. Although National Guard service provided some familiarity with drill to those without regular service, the new officers were hardly old hands. Many owed their election to their popularity or to the respect they commanded in civilian life. Some found themselves at the heads of units because they had been efficient at the peacetime drills of part-time soldiers. Thiébault tells of the story of his captain, an engraver by trade, who broke down when he faced an enemy attack for the first time. "Oh misery!" he cried, "What a fire! Ah! My faith, this is it. . . . But are they crazy to fire like that? Can't they see there are people here?"[54]

Inexperience was not the worst problem imposed by elections; more of a threat to performance was the corroding effect that they could have on discipline. Men might well see themselves as the masters of the officers they chose. General Armand-Louis de Gontaut, duc de Biron objected to volunteer practice in these terms: "It is rare that these officers enjoy some consideration from their troops and are obeyed." Ambitious individuals could try to win favor in the eyes of their comrades. When he was questioned, one sergeant of the 1st Sarthe replied bitterly: "I say, therefore, that the method of promotion dooms [perde] our armies by giving soldiers the right to choose those who command them; it results in a lack of discipline because the soldiers choose only men who flatter them, who buy them drinks, and who thus sanction vice." An article from the *Argus du Département et de l'armée du Nord,* dated 20 December 1792, not only criticizes the drinks and food that sometimes accompanied elections, but the factionalism they engendered.[55] These "dreadful cabals," as another soldier called them, could only erode the unity and mutual confidence essential to a combat unit. Officers ought to command a certain respect; debased politicking could only undermine that respect.

Neither did appointments by government officials always lead to the selection of competent officers. By the law of 28 July 1793, Bouchotte held the power to appoint highly placed officers without regard to the laws of promotion. Power to appoint officers directly also rested in the hands of Representatives on Mission, the Committee of Public Safety, and the Convention. Each had to weigh both technical and political considerations. Bouchotte was known to insist on intense patriotism as a sine qua non for high command. To General Etienne-Ambroise Berthélemy he stated that such officers "ought to have zeal and above all patriotism, which often makes up for talent." A frustrated Berthélemy wrote back a month later, "It is a great deal to be a patriot, it is the first thing, but it is not all." As already stated, there was always a tension between skill on the one hand and political belief on the other. Comte Jean Baptiste Jourdan complained of one of his generals: "Fromentin, a citizen devoted to his Patrie and full of courage, ignored the first elements of the art of war and literally believed what is ceaselessly repeated from the podium of the Convention and the Jacobins—that all the talent of a general consists of charging at the head of his troops against the enemy whereever he may be found."[56] If Bouchotte stood for a political bias, Carnot was far more the technocrat. Eventually the ascendance of the Committee of Public Safety, the eradication of the Ministry of War, and the emphasis on seniority brought what Bertaud has termed a "revenge of talent." But the highly charged political atmosphere of the times made it inevitable that promotion would come to some incompetents, like another brave but inept *sans-culotte,* Louis Charbonnier, who replaced the politically suspect former noble Michel-François de Sistrières as chief of the Armée des Ardennes in February 1794.[57]

In the long run many of the problems were self-correcting. Older men often gave way under the pressure of campaigns and commands. The venerable General Berthel, for example, was put out to pasture in 1794, where he survived to the age of ninety-four. Elected officers unsuited to command fell by the wayside. Thiébault's comical captain left the battalion soon after his first action and made way for a man of tougher spirit. The Republic removed from command even good *sans-culottes* when their capacities did not match their principles. Charbonnier lost his command of the Ardennes in June 1794 and quietly retired. Throughout 1793 and 1794 the military justice system ferreted out cowardice and proven incompetence. Of course, all this took time, as the winds of war separated the wheat from the chaff.

The National Convention and the Committee of Public Safety made some attempt to discover the abilities of their officers. The instruction to Representatives dispatched to expedite the *amalgame* ordered them to evaluate briefly the technical capacities of the officers and to point out those who "merit distinction." Carnot apparently bears the responsibility for instituting an army-wide inspection in July 1794. The Council of Administration in every unit was to report on "the service and personal qualities of all the officers" and to recommend for promotion those who united "unusual talents or aptitudes with true sentiments of patriotism and high standards of conduct [*conduite soutenue*]." The result of government study showed that most officers knew their jobs well, but the margin was narrow. For example, 61 percent of captains in the heavy infantry had mastered the military art at their level of command; this meant that nearly 40 percent fell short.[58]

The Republic labored to maintain standards, particularly in the technical branches, artillery and engineers. They retained requirements for qualifying examinations, which had been suspended for new officers of infantry and cavalry. Carnot made efforts to train and keep skilled men in the technical services. Schools were established for both branches, and skilled nobles allowed to remain at their posts. There were even field examinations for the officers and NCOs who led the small artillery units attached to infantry battalions.

Certainly the French transformed the social composition of their officer corps after 1789, but to argue that they had brought off a miracle of command by 1794 is unjustified. Battlefield brilliance was neither omnipresent nor completely lacking among revolutionary officers. Yet the particular character of the new commissioned ranks may have bestowed certain valuable advantages on the unorthodox armies of the Republic. The sergeant-like quality of so many of its leaders may have aided the French in forging able soldiers out of green recruits. That so many of the new and inexperienced officers were not committed to maintain the tactics of the ancien régime, plus the influence of the revolutionary atmosphere, probably aided in the creation of a new tactical system. Lastly, only a radically transformed officer corps could effectively lead the new citizen-soldiers of the Revolution. The common soldier was the true heart of the new army; the officers must be judged not only on the basis of technical capacity but also on how well they suited the men who rallied to defend a new government, a new society, and a new set of principles.

Relationships between Officers and Men before 1789

Effective leadership is built upon the relationships established between officers and men, and the Revolution profoundly altered these relationships. Under the ancien régime, officers came from the social elite, while the men they commanded were society's cast-offs. This great gap between the social origins of officers and men closed after 1789. Even if the officer corps was more heavily weighted to the middle classes than were the rank and file, the virtual exclusion of the aristocracy from command, plus the promotion of countless NCOs to commissioned rank, eliminated the old distinctions and barriers.

Relationships between officers and men derive not only from the social distance or proximity of the two groups but also from expectations and attitudes. Case studies of different armies and different time periods suggest that the leader is most effective who most closely matches the ideals of leadership held by his men. The Revolution precipitated a conflict between habits of deference and ideals of equality, between discipline based on authority and discipline based on voluntary compliance. Traditional patterns of relationships between officers and men had to give way in an army of citizen-soldiers. By conscious direction and by trial and error, officers and men evolved a new way of dealing with one another. The new pattern of relationships between them probably contributed greatly to success on the battlefield, despite the technical weakness of many officers.

Before 1789 few officers bridged the social chasm that separated them from their men. Their aristocratic values and style of life removed them even from physical proximity to the rank and file. Generally they had little to do with their soldiers and delegated the day-to-day chores of leadership to sergeants. Only rarely did officers take part in drill and training. Moreover, they enjoyed regular leaves of seven and a half months duration every two years, and other special leaves were also available. It would not be unheard of for an officer to spend more time away than with his unit. In a very real sense French officers had more in common with the aristocratic officers of enemy armies than they did with their own troops.

A modern reader might hastily judge an army like this, which drew its commanders from a privileged elite and its men from the lower classes, as prone to poor performance and to possible disintegration, all due to an intrinsic antagonism between the leaders and the led. But this does not necessarily follow. Consider the army of Great Britain, immediately prior to World War I. The common soldier came from the dregs of society while the officers were men of independent wealth. Yet instead of tension, this combination of social extremes produced regiments of superb fighting quality. The men firmly felt it was best to be commanded by a proper gentleman and even felt some pride in the bearing and status of their officers. The question to ask of the French army before 1789, then, is whether or not the structures and patterns of conduct established between officers and men satisfied the soldiers as well as their commanders?

There is reason to believe they did not. Common soldiers of the period have left little evidence of their reactions to their officers. In a rare memoir one man who served as a corporal in the old army wrote that in the West Indies where he served "the officer corps did not have the esteem of the soldier, and, on the contrary, far from regarding their chiefs as their protectors, the rank and file saw them only as tyrants and as men without decency."[59] On a broader scale the whole question of corporal punishment with the flat of the sword sheds some light on troop attitudes toward authority. One of the reforms instituted by the comte de Saint Germain in 1776 was the assigning of a regulated number of blows with the flat of a sword as a punishment for certain crimes and breaches of discipline. This will be discussed at greater length in the chapter on discipline and military justice. The troops despised this punishment, because they saw it as degrading. Desertion increased, and it became harder to find recruits. The flat of the sword immediately became a cause célèbre and remained highly controversial until its abolition in 1790. The opposition to the flat of the sword suggests that by the late ancien régime the French soldier already had turned against unquestioning deference to authority and had developed a sense of his own dignity. Proclamations issued under the Revolution would later ask troops to remember the demeaning conditions they had been forced to accept and the frustration and humiliation they had felt at the time. Other pieces of evidence also point to growing dissatisfaction with a system that increasingly cut off nobles from *roturiers* and officers from their men.

Relationships, 1789–94

Whether or not the principles of separation, subordination, and subjugation institutionalized during the ancien régime ceased to make good sense before 1789, they became clearly irrelevant with the onset of the Revolution. Flux and confusion muddied the waters through 1789, 1790, and 1791. Desertion, insubordination, and mutiny plagued an army uncertain of the proper relationship between officers and men. The definition of the soldiers changed from subjects to citizens, and they were attracted by the patriotic rhetoric in praise of liberty and equality. Meanwhile, many officers denounced a national army as a utopia and tried to continue on much as they had before 1789.[60]

New principles governing the relationship between officers and men made considerable headway before war struck in April 1792; however, during the first year of the war vestiges of the old abuses remained. Revolutionary orators and journalists were quicker to understand and express the full implication of equality than was the army. For example, absenteeism among officers continued to plague units. Even some volunteer officers were guilty of this abuse inherited from the royal army. In 1793 there was talk of numerous women at the headquarters of the Armée du Nord. More important, the official definition of officer-soldier relationships often came close to mimicking the docile subordination demanded under the ancien régime. The adoption of new patterns of behavior may have been slowed by the continued dominance of the army, at its highest level, by men of aristocratic birth who had risen to major rank before 1789. When the war began, 89 percent of the generals on the army list were of noble birth.⁶¹

The full tide of change did not sweep over the army until the spring of 1793, when Dumouriez's treason cast its shadow of suspicion over the entire officer corps. The appointment of Bouchotte as minister of war in mid-April brought to that office a man tied to the revolutionary left-wing. Less than a month before Bouchotte took over, Pierre de Riel, marquis de Beurnonville, then minister of war, wrote an illuminating letter to the Convention. It spoke of the need for discipline and subordination and complained that "as long as the soldier believes himself equal in intelligence and knowledge to his commanders, he will not obey."⁶² Bouchotte could never have written such a note. His ideal was equality and fraternity between officers and men. Discipline and obedience were necessary, no doubt, but compliance was owed more to the law than to men. This point of view was not original with Bouchotte, but it now rose to the level of official and insistent policy.

The duties and responsibilities of leaders differed from those they led, but all men in uniform were equal as citizens. As the *Père Duchesne* put it, "Now that the time of the *sans-culottes* has arrived, those who command and those who obey are equal." Brotherhood marched step for step with equality, and neither was thought to conflict with reasonable discipline. A Ministry circular insisted, "It is necessary that the despots tremble in seeing a most severe discipline reign in our camps, which ought to be composed only of brothers." As a symbol of the new familiarity between officers and men, Bouchotte went so far as to encourage the use of the familiar "tu" in place of the formal "vous" in all conversation. In October 1793 a delegation from the popular societies of Paris presented a petition to the National Convention suggesting this practice for all Frenchmen; the Convention gave the petition honorable mention and ordered that it be printed in the *Bulletin*. Bouchotte picked up this symbolic issue. He ordered the petition reprinted and distributed to the armies and sent a cover note with it. "This manner of speaking will be easily adopted by the *sans-culottes* because it is familiar to them; it is also suitable to principles of equality. Therefore, brothers and friends, I invite you to make use of 'tu' when you talk to an individual. Whatever the power is that he bears, he cannot use the formal tone without avowing that he is not a *sans-culotte*. I invite the friends of equality to post up my letter."⁶³ Bouchotte's insistence on the familiar "tu" met with a mixed reception.⁶⁴

Equality and fraternity had to be more than symbolic, if they were to result in unity and mutual understanding. As late as the summer of 1793 officers who did not stay constantly by their men still posed significant problems. Bouchotte now required officers to live in the field with their men and share the full rigors of life on campaign. He directed "that officers and NCOs learn all the details of service and especially to live constantly with their brothers in arms." This was a sound order and it was seconded by field commanders. In one case General Nicolas Bertin discovered two officers not with their battalion following a day of combat action outside Bailleul. Entering the town, the general searched the inns and found the captain in question, "sleeping peacefully in a good bed while his company was camped out in the field; I put him in prison."[65] He found the battalion commander drunk in town and locked him up as well.

Equal standards of discipline and justice were enforced. When the government cracked down on the number of women with the army, the Ministry sent commanding generals a circular that stated "that the wives of general officers and of all other officers were subject to the exclusion." The law was to be enforced even more rigorously concerning officers than men, since officers had "to set the example."[66] When it was a matter of punishment for incompetence or cowardice, if anything, officers were judged by harsher standards and punished more severely. If condemned to be shot, generals suffered this fate before their troops, according to the law of 1 January 1794.[67]

As government policy insisted on more equitable relationships between officers and men, the rank and file would have been satisfied with nothing less. It is beyond the reach of historians to establish with certainty the expectations and attitudes of common soldiers in 1794; however, their letters and diaries plus the journals, songs, proclamations, and circulars sent to the front by the government provide a basis for a brief and tentative outline. By 1794 the republican soldier rejected the notion of special privilege, in his society and in the army. Certainly the officer exercised power beyond that of the common soldier, but the officer should receive no special exemptions from disciplinary measures, and he should endure the same campaign conditions imposed on his men. The rank and file fiercely rejected petty tyranny on the part of an officer and the humiliation of demeaning punishments. Whatever smacked of servitude and deference met with ridicule or resistance.

The republican soldier expected to look across to, more than up at, his officer. A certain amount of paternalism on the part of the officer would be welcomed, if it was expressed as concern for his men's welfare. Yet if the soldier could respect fatherly consideration, he would be put off by lordly behavior or bearing. Recognizing this, General Jean-Baptiste Kléber counseled his subordinates, "Generals will talk with the troops, encourage them, and cheer them by joking with them; generals will seek to gain the confidence of their men and inspire their energy."[68]

After the first panics and the unjustified cries of treason had been put behind them, the rank and file recognized that victory demanded obedience to legitimate authority. French troops were not enemies of discipline, but of unquestioning and uncritical obedience. By 1794 the common soldier looked on his generals with a suspicious eye, and he was constantly encouraged to evaluate all officers around him. Officially and in their private correspondence, republican troops exercised a right of judgement never granted under the monarchy and that would be limited under the empire. In addition, the ambitious private of the revolutionary army could expect to rise through the ranks and hold a commission. Everywhere he looked, he saw men who had done just that. Officers occupied a less lofty plane and had to be all the more approachable in the eyes of a man who saw himself as a future officer.

Measured by this set of attitudes and expectations, the style of command practiced by officers of the ancien régime could not have served the army of the Republic. The officers of 1794, however, measured up very well. In social origins and in attitudes they were a great deal like the men they led. The government's programs and policies not only informed the enlisted man of what he was to expect of his officers, but they also reeducated officers on the limits of authority and privilege granted to commissioned rank. In a technical sense many of those who commanded companies and battalions may not have fully mastered their art by 1794; but in the crucial matter of relationships, and the unit cohesion and morale that depended upon them, the officers were an excellent match for the men they led into battle. Since the tactical system that emerged by the summer of 1794 put a premium on commitment and individual initiative, the problems resulting from technical flaws were probably more than compensated for by putting citizen-officers at the head of citizen-soldiers. Viewed in this light, Bouchotte's insistence that *sans-culottes* in arms be led by *sans-culottes* in command makes sense.

Chapter 5

Discipline in an Army of Citizen-Soldiers

IN MANY WAYS the army forged by the Revolution was unique, yet the trilogy of *liberté, egalité, fraternité* could not obscure its need for discipline and even coercion. Discipline maintains the moral sinews that bind an army together. Obedience makes it possible to control and coordinate bodies of men that might otherwise dissolve in confusion. To accomplish its purposes, an army, even a highly motivated one, must set and enforce standards of conduct and compliance.

The unprecedented expansion of French forces in a time of revolutionary crisis presented the army with a serious enough challenge as it struggled to impose discipline upon its troops; however, the government had to confront additional paradoxes. First, it had to reconcile the discipline of the soldier with the liberty of the citizen. The men who fought to defend a revolution made in the name of freedom were required to limit or relinquish many of their basic liberties, yet they were supposed to maintain their constitutional rights. Second, the government had to insist that soldiers obey their officers, while at the same time it feared the power of these commanders whom it considered politically suspect. The government felt itself simultaneously compelled both to promote and to attack the authority of the officer corps.

The French reconciled these conflicts by insisting that obedience was owed to the law and not to the officer. Only so long as the officer stayed within the definitions of his legal authority ought he to be obeyed. The government also injected more and more civilian influence into the process of military justice. Men accused of serious disciplinary infractions eventually stood before civilian judges, not before their own officers. The highest authority at the front became the Representative on Mission, not the commanding general.

The Evolution of Discipline in the Nord

The evolution of discipline and military justice never succeeded in eliminating the disorder or misconduct of French forces. In the Armée du Nord the changing state of discipline went from weak, to terrible, to tolerable between 1791 and 1794. During the first year of its existence the Nord was no stranger to disobedience and disorder. Regulars and volunteers did not always mix well. Sometimes tension gave way to open violence. *Fédérés* were a disciplinary disaster from the moment they appeared at the front. Disobedience and chaos embarrassed the Nord during its April and May offensives; the murder of General Théobald Dillon stands out as a supreme act of disobedience. However, if desertion took place, it did not wither battalions, and pillage, while it occurred, did not soar to such proportions that it entailed great disorder or lost battles. Over the months the Nord improved in its conduct and performance to the point that it fought a respectable and victorious campaign in the fall of 1792.

The period from December 1792 through April 1793 came close to destroying the Nord. Mass desertion by volunteers stripped the army of its veteran manpower. Logistics collapsed in Belgium, and men without food or clothing turned to pillage. Troops dispersed to survive, but scattered soldiers were more likely to maraud and less likely to obey. Women filled the encampments and barracks, sometimes outnumbering the soldiers. Defeat at Neerwinden and Louvain forced the Nord to retreat, and this retreat only exacerbated its already severe problems. All observers concur, the Nord sunk to a nadir of disorder and indiscipline.

From May on the Nord began to mend, although the influx of new recruits in the spring probably weakened its actual combat effectiveness for a time, until they had been integrated and sufficiently trained. Better weather, improved supply, and assembly of troops in camps lessened the worst problems of the preceding months. Comte Adam Philippe de Custine imposed strict disciplinary standards upon his arrival. Civil authority stepped in to play an ever greater role in enforcing discipline. Yet, while the guillotine and firing squad took their toll, disobedience, desertion, and pillage still troubled the Nord. Continued pillage posed the worst problem. Yet the return of cold weather in 1793 did not bring with it the disaster of the winter of 1792–93. Units continued to train; Representatives on Mission and military courts vigorously insisted on obedience. By the spring of 1794 the level of discipline was tolerable and the army victorious.

The Discipline of Free Men

The all-too-common disciplinary problems of the republican armies derived not solely from the turmoil of revolutionary crisis, but also from a clash between the conflicting principles of liberty and obedience. At first revolutionary leaders agreed on no single resolution to this important issue. They did concur that the French soldier could no longer be expected to obey blindly. In 1789 Edmund Dubois-Crancé insisted that "the French soldier was not an automaton" and that he would be "all the better soldier since he retained the rights and quality of a citizen."[1] One issue that helped to crystallize opinion in 1790–91 concerned the right of the rank and file to attend the meetings of political clubs, or popular societies, a right guaranteed to civilians. The National Assembly initially feared that attendance might encourage insubordination, so on 6 August 1790 it forbade soldiers to form their own clubs. On 19 September it further banned contacts between the troops and civilian societies. After several months, the Assembly reconsidered its decision. Alexander Beauharnais, representing several of the Assembly's committees, rose and successfully argued for an about-face on 29 April 1791. "In a free State the elements which compose this army are citizens; they alienate a part of their liberty in favor of this subordination; but this sacrifice . . . does not deny that, as soldiers, they still have rights to exercise. . . . In a free State, where the army is not composed of automatons, soldiers ought, therefore, to know the military laws. . . . Your committees have found that, far from fearing that the presence of soldiers at the societies . . . would deny subordination, . . . they believe that it would be very valuable to enlighten all men concerning the duties that they must fulfill." Here the law emerged as the vital link between citizenship and discipline.

The debate in the Assembly continued. When that body turned to adopting a new military penal code in September 1791, it heard General Félix de Wimpffen, reporting for the military committee, express a different point of view. "It is necessary to consider an army as an entity outside of society and to submit this entity to a regime most proper to the purpose for which society intends it without regard to the regime adopted by the social body." In violent contrast to this assertion, Lazare Carnot took the floor on 10 April 1792 to declare, "It is said that soldiers have alienated their liberty, that they ought not to be likened to citizens; the Constitution replies that liberty is inalienable and imprescribable."[2]

When war broke out shortly after Carnot's declaration, the theoretical debates of the assemblies were transported to the front. A new justification of discipline had to be explained to the troops; so much rested on their understanding. The journal of the Armée du Nord, the *Argus,* played a role in this process. In its "Credo of a Good Soldier" it presented a simplified, direct, yet accurate statement of what became the foundation of obedience. Every good soldier should obey "without resistance, every time the law commands him." The law, not the officer, deserved obedience, and if the soldier believed his officer had overstepped the law, the good soldier "ought to denounce the chief who commands him, otherwise he shares in the crime of the man who would mislead him."³ The citizen-soldier retained some right of judgment.

On the practical level, the sensible definition of the citizen's status as a soldier became muddied by reality. The men at the front in 1792 were not astute theoreticians who had followed the debates in the assemblies. They were young men conscious of the Revolution and aware that as citizens they were supposed to enjoy certain liberties. Much of the army was composed of volunteers who saw military service as a brief hiatus in their civilian life. Discipline smacked of deference; they regarded it "as an instrument of slavery created by the aristocrats." Officer selection did not make matters better. That the volunteers elected their commanders only reinforced their notions of independence. Elected officers were often loath to push their authority, for fear of losing the men's support. Inexperience among the newly promoted officers of line regiments almost certainly weakened their authority as well. And so a frustrated adjutant-general from the Armée du Rhin raged: "Ah! If only I could go into details, you would see if it is pariotic in the Assembly . . . to concede like cowards to all the caprices of a mutinous and furious rabble, to cry out against every idea of subordination and discipline, and to declare ceaselessly against every means to bring back order and peace. I would like to see these so-called patriots surrounded by drunken and wild soldiers who threaten anyone who dares to talk to them of the laws."⁴

When the winter of 1792–93 brought physical hardships and precipitated desertion and pillage, this disciplinary crisis had little to do with concepts of soldier as citizen, except that many volunteers took it upon themselves to decide that they had fulfilled the legal obligations of their enlistments and went home.

As the government responded to the treason of Charles François Dumouriez in the spring of 1793, it reasserted the notion that the citizen-soldier served the law and not his officer. Suspicion and purge of officers bore witness to the fact that the government was now even less willing to elevate officers as supreme and unquestioned authorities. In an extensive program of political education, the civil government repeatedly counseled its soldiers to obey the law but to regard their officers with suspicion and to denounce those they believed to be guilty of counterrevolutionary acts or opinions. Officers who remained at their posts had good reason to hesitate before declaring themselves the agents of a rigorous code of discipline, especially after the arrest of Custine demonstrated that the Convention was ill at ease with his concept of strict discipline.

Yet the Ministry of War desired that order and harmony replace confusion and discord in the French camps. It was precisely at this time that the Convention dictated a greater civilian participation in the disciplinary process: in the military courts, now headed by civilian judges, and in the persons of the Representatives on Mission. Bouchotte spoke of the need for well-disciplined troops, "not the discipline of slaves, but that of free men." A circular from the Ministry to commanding generals ordered: "Constantly see to it that there is the most exact observation of the military laws. . . . It is necessary that the despots tremble in seeing the most severe discipline and the sweetest harmony reign in our camps which ought to be composed only of brothers."[5] The discipline of free men consisted of obedience to laws made by the elected representatives of the soldiers. Generals were asked to apply the law as a way of insuring discipline. Discipline did not exclude fraternity, because the brothers, whatever their rank, served the same law.

The pressure for more exacting discipline grew in late 1793 and early 1794, but Representatives on Mission, not military officers, stepped forward as the vocal proponents of strict obedience. As a general order to the Nord in May 1794 declared, "The time for impunity is past: a severe and republican discipline is going to be established in the army. Let the cowards tremble."[6] As agents of the Convention and empowered by it with almost limitless authority, Representatives on Mission were uniquely suited to carry out a disciplinary program. The Convention trusted them with authority they would have denied to any officer. Punishments intensified as a way of combating the most destructive crimes, most notably pillage, and discipline improved under this demanding regime of civil authority.

Military Laws, Courts, and Agents of Justice, 1790–94

A survey of legislation concerning justice reveals an evolving system of councils, courts, and administrative agents. Initial reforms of 1790 were followed by a series of additional changes, leading to legal machinery that accorded officers a continually shrinking role in the judgment of accused offenders. By 1794 military justice, though severe, had become more humane, more democratic, and fairer than it had been under the ancien régime.

The disciplinary codes of the ancien régime invested officers with great and often arbitrary power while subjecting accused soldiers to humiliation, beatings, and death. For the rank and file, disobedience to superiors brought swift and severe penalties; striking an officer or sergeant was a capital offense. At the same time, officers could slap or cane their men at will. Accused of a serious offense, a common soldier came before a court composed of officers. In garrison, in camp, and on campaign he was judged by a *conseil de guerre* of seven officers chosen by the highest ranking commander. While on the march, the soldier's fate was decided by a *prévôt des maréchaux* assisted by officers of the accused man's regiment. In all but rare cases the officer's noble status made him exempt from this disciplinary machinery.

Common soldiers faced a wide range of corporal punishments in addition to the death penalty. From running the gauntlet, to riding the wooden horse, to branding, such beatings and tortures humiliated as well as hurt the men subjected to them. As mentioned in the preceding chapter, the punishment that raised the greatest fury was the flat of the saber, instituted in 1776 by comte de Saint-Germain. For various minor offenses, it subjected common soldiers to a prescribed number of blows with the flat of a saber across the buttocks. The many who objected to this punishment did so more because of the shame it brought than the pain it inflicted. Lafayette wrote of this hated punishment: "The introduction of blows from the flat of the saber by the comte de Saint Germain humiliated, irritated the entire army and became the cause of an implacable hatred of soldiers against the officers . . . who had the weakness or the stupidity to devote themselves . . . to this innovation."[7] The flat of the saber signaled a brutal trend toward "Prussianizing" the French army after it had suffered defeat in the Seven Years' War. Even before the onset of the Revolution, many critics charged that such discipline was foreign to the character of the French soldier.

The Work of the Revolutionary Assemblies

Revolution transformed the codes of the ancien régime. Spurred on by a disciplinary crisis culminating in the mutiny at Nancy, the National Assembly began to reform the system of military justice in 1790. Legislation of 14–15 September replaced corporal punishment with extra work and limited periods of confinement for *fautes contre la discipline,* including disobedience, drunkenness, and failure to report for duty. It was also a *faute* for an officer to strike an enlisted man. Penalties could be assigned by an officer superior to the guilty party, but his decision could be reviewed and additional periods of punishment assigned by a *conseil de discipline* made up of seven officers. Men could also lodge complaints against their officers with the *conseil*.

The Assembly next moved to establish a new high court. In a law passed on 22 September and promulgated on 20 October 1790 it guaranteed soldiers a jury trial in all offenses beyond minor disciplinary *fautes*. Fundamentally, this legislation recognized the soldier's claim to fair and equal justice as promised by the Declaration of the Rights of Man. No longer could he receive major punishment at the whim of officers. If the soldier committed a civil offense, he was to be tried before a civil court. Serious military offenses went before a court-martial. The court-martial system outlined by the law was rather clumsy, with separate juries for accusation and judgment. An involved process of jury selection insured that enlisted men as well as officers would serve on juries and that the accused would have considerable leverage in selecting the final panel. As an example, the jury for the trial of a common soldier would contain four officers, two NCOs, and three soldiers, that is, four officers and five enlisted men. The judges of the court-martial were to be uniformed military administrative officials called *commissaires des guerres*.

A complete new military penal code did not appear until 30 September 1791. It defined which military offenses were punishable by a court-martial and the corresponding penalties. This law was rigorous, perhaps extreme. Death sentences threatened those who failed to take their post or who abandoned it for their own safety in time of war, who slept on guard duty in the face of the enemy, or who gave information to the enemy. Ten or twenty years in irons awaited those convicted of desertion in wartime. Generals could formulate some regulations for their own commands, so pillage was to be punished according to the sentence set down by the general of the army. Many on the political left attacked this code as too severe. Robespierre condemned it as "worthy of the ancien régime."[8] Still, officers received no special privileges or exemptions.

In sessions of 12–16 May 1792 the Legislative Assembly added a third level of tribunal between the court-martial and the *conseil de discipline*. Courts-martial continued for the gravest offenses, those punishable by death, for example. But for lesser offenses, which still exceeded the minor concerns of the *conseils de discipline*, the assembly created *tribunaux de police correctionnelle militaire*, composed of three *commissaires des guerres*. No jury sat in these *tribunaux*. The law also dealt with courts-martial. It modified the composition of the juries and allowed the courts to move from place to place if required. These measures were attempts to afford justice with speed under wartime conditions. An intense battle over this new justice system split the Assembly into those who placed the jury principle over the need for quick justice and those who placed expediency first. The law placed tremendous authority in the hands of the *commissaires de guerres* who were, after all, military officers serving the armies. This also bothered those generally suspicious of the French officer corps.

The overthrow of the monarchy brought further changes. In a measure of 23 August 1792 the Assembly declared invalid all judgments against soldiers "for lack of discipline, insubordination, or threatening words or gestures against superiors" pronounced since 15 September 1791. This grave slight against the officer's authority was followed the next month by a decree recognizing that a new format for courts-martial and *tribunaux de police correctionnelle* was required, one which replaced the *commissaires* as judges.[9] However, a new court system and a revised penal code did not come before the National Convention until May 1793.

The law of 12 May 1793 abolished courts-martial and *tribunaux de police correctionnelles*, replacing them with two *tribunaux criminels militaires* for each army. The three judges of the new *tribunaux* were to be chosen by the Executive Council, a choice then ratified by the Committee of Public Safety. The judges and prosecutor could neither be serving with nor employed by the military. The civil government thus took over the direction of the highest military courts. The juries were to be composed of one superior officer, one captain, one lieutenant, one sous-lieutenant, one sergeant, one corporal, one soldier, and two other men of the same grade as the accused, making a total of nine. Enlisted men would thus always go before a jury composed of a majority of enlisted men. This legislation consequently reasserted the right to trial by one's peers in any but minor disciplinary offenses and removed military officers from a dominant role. The tribunals established by the May law took some time to set up. In the Nord they were still being formed in December 1793.[10] A further step in this direction was taken on 16 August 1793, when the Convention decreed that soldiers stationed behind the lines in depots would be judged in civil courts for military offenses.

Hand in hand with the republican court system went a new wartime penal code of 12 May 1793. The new code covered four categories of offenses: desertion, treason, theft, and insubordination. Georges Michon termed the new code "particularly rigorous, especially in regard to treason and pillage, crimes which seemed to have caused the defeats in Belgium."[11] The authority of the officer was still respected, and it remained a capital offense to assault an officer. However, while the case of a superior striking a subordinate was only a disciplinary *faute* in the legislation of 1790 and 1791, the law of 1793 declared it a serious offense, punishable by loss of rank and three years in prison. This law approached equality, even if it came up short. Generals of armies again had the right to draft their own special regulations, but these ad hoc regulations had to be sent immediately to the Convention if they were to carry the death penalty.

The Terror produced its own alterations of the court structure in the law of 22 January 1794. On the lowest level, the *conseil de discipline* was now to include soldiers as well as officers. Each demi-brigade of infantry was to form a *conseil* of one superior officer, one captain, and lieutenant, one sous-lieutenant, one sergeant, one corporal, and three soldiers. Enlisted men now comprised a majority of the *conseil*. The reconstitution of these *conseils* grows in significance when it is remembered that one of their functions was to hear complaints against officers. An enlisted majority could have made the lodging of complaints all the easier. The January legislation reinstituted a middle grade court, again called a *tribunal de police correctionnelle*. The *tribunal* was to be composed of three men, an *officier de police*, a military man of the same rank as the accused, and a civilian designated by the government of the town in which the tribunal was held. One *officier de police* was to be attached to the headquarters of each army, and, in addition, one *officier* was to be assigned to each division. The Convention itself selected these *officiers* from nominees presented by the Committee of Public Safety. The constitution of the tribunal would be political above all, Jacobin to be sure. At the top of the court structure stood a *tribunal criminel militaire* to be established in each army and charged with those serious cases that could lead to the accused losing his life or liberty. The president, vice-president, and prosecutor of such a court could not be serving military men or those employed by the army. The accused had some role in choosing the jury. Presented with eighteen candidates, he was to pick the final nine: an officer of captain's rank or above, a lieutenant or souslieutenant, a sergeant, a corporal, a soldier, and four civilians from the locality in which the court sat. The verdict rested in the hands of enlisted men and civilians, since commissioned officers held only two of the nine votes. Viewed as a whole, this system gave military officers little role in the machinery of military justice. They retained the ability to set disciplinary penalties, but even in the *conseils de discipline* that reviewed these penalties, enlisted men outnumbered officers. Such a structure is not surprising, since the January legislation was fashioned at a time of maximum suspicion and hostility toward the officer corps.

In a system that so emphasized the law, the men in the ranks had to know the laws under which they lived. The government made every effort to inform and instruct them. Copies of the *Bulletin of the National Convention* were read to them and posted in each camp from January 1793 on. Copies of the law went to the front with orders that they be read aloud. Section five of the 12 May 1793 penal code directed each commander, upon receiving the law, to assemble the troops and "to have it read at the head of each company" and to repeat the reading once every week. Sergeant Alexandre Brault reported one such reading in the Nord on 16 June 1793. "Today, we have just heard read a code of military discipline that we have all sworn to follow, point by point. It is a little rigorous, but those who are sure to conduct themselves always in the path of honor have nothing to fear." A November 1793 circular from the bureau of the Ministry of War charged with distributing copies of military laws to the armies insisted that commanders insure that "the laws which are sent to you be regularly read to the men that you command."[12]

The Codes of the Generals

The military penal codes allowed generals to establish disciplinary regulations beyond those stipulated by the revolutionary assemblies. These regulations, which varied from army to army, must be considered as part of the complex of military justice. Men accused of violating them came up before the councils, commissions, and courts created by the laws and the proclamations of the Representatives on Mission. The guilty faced a number of penalties, including death. Generals used this power to meet the particular needs of their situations. For example, during the first few months of the war, armies had been thrown into panic by terrified soldiers who had raised the cry *"Nous sommes trahis!"* (We are betrayed). In June 1792 Lafayette promulgated a code for his army that declared it a capital offense to yell out this fatal phrase.[13] In the Armée du Nord, where pillage by ill-equipped and ill-fed troops crippled the army at times, generals threatened looters with the death penalty.[14] The creation and enforcement of special codes explains how generals, like Custine, could impose their own disciplinary stamp on an army. As cannoneer Louis Bricard wrote in his journal: "General Custine has just taken over supreme command of the army. He made several proclamations and made known an extraordinary severe military penal code. . . . The twenty-sixth . . . we . . . were at the camp de César. . . . discipline was followed with rigor. If the fault was grave, it was punished by death."[15]

The Work of the Representatives on Mission

Armed with almost limitless powers, the Representatives on Mission influenced the character of discipline and the system of military justice in 1793 and 1794. These officials were elected members of the National Convention, the legislature and supreme authority in revolutionary France during these years. They held temporary commissions from the Convention in order to implement its programs in the departments and with the armies. The Legislative Assembly had dispatched similar agents since 1791, and the Convention picked up the practice as soon as it first met in September 1792. However, the system of Representatives on Mission was regularized and expanded by legislation of 9 and 30 April 1793. Defeat in March followed by Dumouriez's treason called this new wave of Representatives on Mission into existence. Their extraordinary authority provided a means to counteract chaos and demoralization at the front. These laws dispatched a total of sixty Representatives to serve with all the armies; sixteen were sent to the Nord and Ardennes alone. Half of them were to be replaced each month. They reported directly to the Committee of Public Safety, some of whose members went on mission themselves. They were interested in all aspects of the army's administration and effectiveness; high among these interests was a concern with military justice.

These representatives held wide-ranging authority, including the right to appoint military officers, requisition recruits, and decree their own provisional laws. They were much more than judicial officers, but from the outset the powers conferred upon them by the Convention included those to suspend, arrest, and replace individuals they judged guilty of acts contrary to the interests or principles of the Revolution. Their outright authority over the judicial machinery expanded over the months, and they became central to the maintenance of the military discipline and justice. Part of their increased importance is explained by the fact that the Representatives arrived on scene as the rising tide of suspicion and accusation threatened to engulf the officer corps. At a time when commanders labeled as strict disciplinarians risked denunciation—witness Custine—the Representative on Mission legitimized demanding codes of military conduct. Their power stood as an undisputed expression of that civil authority to which the soldiers owed their obedience. As such, their work epitomized the growing and essential role of civilians and civil authority in the process of military justice.

As one of their duties, Representatives observed and reported on the discipline of the troops. As a case in point, during the spring of 1793, Lazare Carnot, serving with the Armée du Nord wrote back letter after letter criticizing the poor conduct he saw at the front; pillage especially distressed him. He personally exerted himself to arrest and try soldiers guilty of this offense. Representatives also concerned themselves with the implementation of the laws establishing military courts.[16]

Beyond their roles as reporters and advisors to the Committee of Public Safety, they issued their own proclamations and regulations concerning discipline. Their declarations of the spring of 1794 were among the most harsh. Notable for their energy and extremism were the Representatives on Mission Louis St.-Just and Philippe Le Bas. In mid-May they issued the following proclamation to troops of the Nord: "Soldiers, We call you back to the rigorous discipline which alone can cause you to win and which spares your blood. Some abuses have slipped in among you; we have resolved to repress them. Those who provoke the infantry to disband in the face of enemy cavalry, those who leave the line of battle before or during combat, or during retreats will be arrested immediately and punished by death. . . . Soldiers, we will give you justice, we will punish those who have refused it to you; we will share your work; but whoever abandons his duty will be struck with a prompt death." St.-Just, also a member of the Committee of Public Safety, went so far as to order the publication of 25,000 copies of one of his disciplinary decrees, so that it could be distributed throughout the army.[17]

Representatives gained the right to alter existing courts and to set up new judicial bodies. By a law of 11 January 1794 Representatives could authorize tribunals, civil or military, to deal with counterrevolutionary crimes. Representatives could order such courts to judge "revolutionarily." In the Armée du Nord "revolutionary" judgment meant the elimination of the jury. Joseph Le Bon transformed the criminal tribunal of Arras into such a revolutionary tribunal. In May 1794 St.-Just and Le Bas ordered a similar alteration: "Until new orders, the military tribunal of the *Armée du Nord* will judge without being constrained by the formalities of a jury." Although the juries might disappear, the judges remained civilian. In fact, implementing "revolutionary" judgment eliminated officers and soldiers from the judgment process altogether. Representatives could also set up special military commissions in certain circumstances. In April 1794, for example, Representative Pierre Choudieu authorized generals commanding divisions and brigades of the Nord to establish five-member commissions to judge pillagers and deserters in the field. The Representatives' broad authority here was eventually curtailed. On 8 May 1794 the Convention voted to suppress revolutionary tribunals and commissions established by Representatives that were passing judgment without the assistance of a jury. However, some commissions continued to appear in the Nord as late as June.[18]

The Disciplinary Problems of the Nord

The disciplinary problems that beset the Armée du Nord were not really new; most had troubled other armies in the past. Minor abuses ran a wide gamut from drunkenness to the sale of government-issued equipment. Desertion and pillage stood as the most significant major crimes. Although these infractions were hardly unique to the troops of the Nord, each can be better understood when put in context. In particular, the character and intensity of the measures taken by military and civil authorities remain a bit bewildering without reference to the special circumstances of republican forces during the first years of war.

The Lesser Abuses

Abuses that did not pose an overwhelming threat to the army's effectiveness and that attracted only a small or moderate degree of government concern included drunkenness, the presence of women, disobedience, friction between units, and the sale of equipment. The abuse of liquor seems to go along with a military uniform. Drunkenness comes as no surprise, but the punishment could be unusual. General Jean-Nicolas Houchard declared that in the Nord "all soldiers who will be drunk during combat or on marches will be undressed completely naked and sent back as men unworthy to defend their Patrie." Cabarets or taverns drew soldiers sometimes even when bullets were flying.[19]

The presence of too many women with the armies also dismayed authorities and caused them to react. By regulation, the army included some women in its train. Each battalion was accorded a few washerwomen, who even had their own tent in an encampment. *Vivandiers*, or sutlers, were also expected and tolerated. But beyond these, a veritable flock of women followed the Nord. An act of the Convention, voted on 8 March 1793, gave soldiers the right to marry whom they would. Previously, marriage had required permission from their superiors, but now free men deserved free choice. This decision did not create the problem, but it exaggerated the abuse and frustrated efforts to curb it. Representative Jean-Baptiste Delacroix alerted the Convention to the problem in a letter he wrote from Dunkirk on 22 March: "The National Convention has permitted soldiers to marry without the consent of their chiefs; this law has brought an inconvenience which it is urgent to reform. It is necessary to set the number of women who ought to follow the army; they are in such great numbers that they encumber troops on the march, consume much, and occupy a great number of wagons meant only for the transportation of the army's baggage and provisions." From his mission with the Nord Carnot wrote to condemn "the flock of women and prostitutes" on 16 April. Urged on by Carnot's letter, the Committee of Public Safety resolved to do something about these women in the meeting of 18 April. On 30 April the Convention acted on its suggestion and voted to order the expulsion of all "useless" women from camps and garrisons. Each battalion could have only four laundresses. The wives of officers and men were to be sent off, with five *sous* per league to speed them to their destinations. This did not completely end the problem. In January 1794 the prosecutor of a tribunal in the Armée du Nord still felt it necessary to issue an order warning soldiers of the dangers caused by the numerous prostitutes, whom he labeled as "the plague."[20]

All too often French troops resisted their officers, or worse. On 29 April 1793 General Dillon died at the hands of his own soldiers; almost exactly two years later General Jacques Goguet was also shot by his men, whom he called cowards when they refused to charge.[21] Such attacks on officers represented only the rare extremes, but units did on occasion balk at the appointment of unpopular officers or demand that some be replaced.[22]

A problem peculiar to the army of revolutionary France was the animosity between the different kinds of troops, such as line, volunteers, and *fédérés*. Animosity occasionally flared up into fratricidal fights between units. Marching through Soissons, Thiébault's battalion of Volunteers of 1792 risked being attacked by *fédérés* who wanted the weapons belonging to the volunteers. As late as April and May 1793 bad feeling still separated line and volunteers. Adjutant-General François-Philippe de Latour-Foissac reported to three Representatives on Mission, "Animosity seems to develop between the troops of the line and the National Guards, disciplinary means do not suffice to repress them." Louis Gay de Vernon stated the problem in grim terms, "It was an intestinal war, open and declared, everyone knowing in what ranks and under which tents he could find his enemy." Disagreements could be no more than cabaret quarrels, but they might escalate to brawls and duels. Though a serious problem, it was not universal; many different units got along well enough, especially on the day of battle.²³

A more pervasive and serious problem, the subject of a good deal of official correspondence, was the sale of their arms and equipment by republican soldiers. This abuse resulted mainly from the hardships and short supplies the troops suffered. Complaints against these sales began during March 1793 and continued for months. Deserters sold their weapons, and volunteers sold their own clothes, presumably to buy food. In late April Carnot reported, "Our volunteers are always naked. . . . Hardly does a soldier receive shoes than he goes to sell them; there are those who sell their coats, their fusils." Local authorities issued decrees and laws to stop this traffic, and finally the 12 May 1793 penal code declared such sales a serious crime, punishable by five years in irons. Throughout the remainder of 1793, the problem continued, though on a lesser scale.²⁴

Desertion in the Armée du Nord

Desertion constituted an important breach of military law during the revolutionary era, yet there is still much more to learn about the topic, both in terms of the numbers of men involved and the motivation that drove them from the army. In lieu of a definitive study this section offers only certain observations concerning the subject.

It is important to point out that the significance and impact of desertion varied from time to time and situation to situation. Desertion among disaffected regulars in early 1790, for example, meant something very different than did desertion among reluctant conscripts in late 1793. Closer to home for this study, the problems posed by desertion for the army of the Republic in general were markedly different than those it posed for the Armée du Nord in particular. Viewed from the offices of the Ministry of War, desertion had to be curbed because it threatened to loosen the moral ties that bound others to the service. From the perspective of the Armée du Nord, however, desertion was a threat only when it diminished the combat strength of the units marshaled in that army.

Desertion caused major manpower problems in the battalions of the Nord only during the six months from December 1792 through May 1793. The case of the 1st Aisne was typical.²⁵ It numbered 550 when war began, and a 1 December situation report shows that its first campaign had cut its numbers to 417. The subsequent winter and early spring were disastrous, and by 1 May 1793 only 223 men were left on its rosters. Dumouriez's complaints of March 1793 were exaggerated but justified. "I have not one battalion which numbers more than two hundred men; desertion continues in a frightening manner, especially among the volunteers."²⁶ Those men who left the Nord during this period were especially valuable, because they were trained men who had already served on campaign. Desertion did not again strike the Nord such a blow. Arguing from situation reports, it would be impossible to demonstrate that desertion substantially decreased the battalion size of the Nord after the spring of 1793. Certainly, there was a continual drain of men taking unauthorized leave of the army, but it seems to have had only a minor impact on the combat strength of the army.

After the spring of 1793 desertion continued to be a topic in the correspondence of the Nord, but it was desertion by conscripts not yet incorporated into established units of the Nord. Draft evasion and desertion by *requisitionnaires* only affected the Nord in that a more complete turnout of those required by the law would have swelled the Nord to even larger proportions than it reached. But it is worthwhile considering that the Republic's resources were already stretched to the limit in feeding, equipping, and training the men it did succeed in mustering. The appearance of additional thousands in excess of those who did reach the Nord might have proven an embarrassment rather than a blessing.

This logic partially explains why desertion was not treated very harshly in the military courts of the Nord. Rarely did deserters pay a heavy price for their deeds, except if they joined the enemy and were later captured bearing arms against their former comrades. Then the penalty was death. Antoine Legrand noted that desertion was also treated with indulgence in the Armée du Rhin.[27] Had it posed a greater threat to the survival of these armies, it would certainly have been dealt with more severely.

The causes of desertion in the Nord were many. An important explanation for desertion when it was at its height was that the volunteers who left the army believed they had the right to do so. Volunteers of 1791 were only obligated to serve one campaign; Volunteers of 1792 did not officially enjoy such a privilege, but many felt they did. With victory at Valmy the Convention declared that the Patrie was no longer in danger. After Jemappes many relieved volunteers believed their job to be finished. Technically a volunteer had to give two months' notice before he left, and the earliest date he could leave was 1 December. The formality of advanced notice seems to have been honored mostly in the breach. Authorities appealed to the young men to stay in the ranks, but the pleas obviously made little difference to many soldiers. As reported by Representatives on a December fact-finding trip to the Nord, "We have found . . . the roads covered with volunteers who are returning to Paris . . . the volunteers are convinced that [the Patrie] no longer needs their services."[28]

Over the winter of 1792–93 many volunteers left because of the lack of food and clothing. The shortage of proper provisions left soldiers with only three choices: starve, steal, or desert. Many turned to pillage, and many left. Concerning clothing, one observer commented in January 1793, "The Representative . . . would consider the lack of clothes as one of the principal causes of the desertion of the troops." Just as starving or freezing men may have chosen the road home as a route to survival, so, too, wounded or ill men sought to return to their villages. Inactivity also brought on desertion, or at least that was Dumouriez's opinion. Some line soldiers deserted to sign up in volunteer units for the advantages they afforded.[29]

Desertion during the winter of 1792–93 does not appear to have been a result of flagging patriotism; however, desertion by the conscripts of 1793 may bear witness to failing intensity among the young men of France. Habitually, the charge made by officials against deserters was that they suffered from "*égoisme*," best interpreted as selfishness. Occasionally deserters were attacked as counterrevolutionary, but that rhetoric was rare. Desertion is a complicated affair, and recent studies on desertion in contemporary armies argue that it only rarely reflects a judgment on war aims and that personal motives weigh more heavily. One such possible rationale surfaced in a note to Representative on Mission Jacques Isoré at Lille in October 1793. "The young men of the *levée en masse* . . . leave for their homes in great numbers under the frivolous pretext that they are needed for sowing their land."[30] Pressing business at home, or what they saw as pressing business, played its role in calling men home.

The pattern of desertion within units is difficult to establish, but one rare document may illustrate the way in which men fled their battalions during the months when the problem was most severe. This particularly useful report concerns the 2nd Pas-de-Calais, a battalion of 1791 volunteers serving with the Armée du Nord.[31] This unusual item lists the names of 205 deserters, the company to which they belonged, and the days they deserted, for the period October 1791 through December 1792. Deserters (seventy-two) left as individuals or as pairs before 25 November 1792. The ten cases in which pairs of men from the same company left on the same day suggests that buddy relationships were important. Since the men of the 2nd Pas-de-Calais were Volunteers of 1791, they had enlisted to serve only one campaign and felt free to leave the army as they wished, in December. With little moral pressure against desertion, it soared. In the month between November 24 and December 28 the battalion lost 113 men. All but seven left in groups of from two to sixteen men from the same company. The pattern strongly suggests the formation of small groups within the company structure, which persevered even when the army itself no longer commanded the men's obedience. There also was a regional character to this desertion, in that men from the same district tended to leave their company on the same day.

Without contradicting what has been said, one form of desertion did threaten combat effectiveness after the spring of 1793; this was flight in the face of the enemy. It could amount to sheer cowardice. It was clearly a capital offense, but actual punishment was less severe. Soundings reveal surprising leniency even for this form of desertion in the Nord. The tribunal at Lille returned twenty-four men to their units after they had been accused of insubordination, abandoning their posts, and desertion. Presumably they could then have received less severe punishments before a *conseil de discipline*. At Cambrai twenty-two volunteers who were found guilty of abandoning their weapons and fleeing in the presence of the enemy were set free because the judge took their youth and inexperience into consideration. Yet along a different segment of the line, thirteen men of a Seine-et-Oise battalion faced the firing squad, convicted of fleeing before the enemy.[32] Inconsistency seemed to be a hallmark of judgments on this breach of the code, or perhaps it is closer to the truth to say that extenuating circumstances received a full hearing.

Pillage in the Armée du Nord

Pillage, like death, arrives hand in hand with war. Armed men, taught and prepared to do violence at a time when moral axioms have been distorted, if not discarded, often take what they need or want. Some armies have been worse than others. Judged by contemporary standards, the armies of the Republic were guilty of pillage in the extreme. There was good reason for their excesses. Throughout the revolutionary era, and certainly from 1792 through 1794, the soldiers of France were ill-fed, ill-clothed, and ill-equipped. In this environment of hardship men stole to survive or to better their condition. Poor logistics and the character of outpost warfare along the front forced units to disperse. French battlefield tactics also encouraged dispersion. Soldiers who were spread out in small detachments had more opportunity to loot and less supervision to hold them back. In addition, standards seemed uncertain, as some officers at first tolerated theft.[33]

Pillage threatened to eviscerate the Armée du Nord in a way that desertion never did. It was all the more hideous because it seemed so inevitable. Pillage taught disobedience and consequently eroded discipline, although it is hard to measure the exact impact of pillage in this sense. In more specific terms pillage alienated the peasants and townspeople unlucky enough to fall in the army's path. Soldiers of liberty turned thieves did not win converts to the Revolution. Criticizing the laxness of Lafayette, dragoon François Marquant reported, "I have seen many peasants tell me, with tears of despair in their eyes, that they preferred the ancien régime a thousand times more than our Constitution, since at least then no one carried off their property." Across the borders of France those who welcomed the French one day found that they had become victims the next. During the winter of 1792–93 the brigandage of the Nord in Belgium reached such an extreme that after Neerwinden a distressed Dumouriez complained, "I fear the dreadful consequences of a retreat in a country where we have raised the inhabitants against us by pillage and indiscipline." In fairness to many soldiers, it is worth pointing out that troops in the field could also be upset by the regrettable behavior of their comrades. A good Jacobin wrote to his father from the Dutch border, "This reflects on all of us, and it is hard to share a reputation which is so far from my principles."[34]

What made pillage most disastrous, however, was its impact on the combat effectiveness of the troops. Men did not loot as organized battalions or companies; they searched for food and booty as individuals or in small groups. When a unit gave itself over to pillage, it dissolved as a combat unit and could no longer advance, hold, or retreat in order. All too often, at the height of victory, revolutionary battalions disbanded to sack a town and lost what they had won or were at least unable to exploit their victory. This is what Carnot feared when he wrote of French troops, "Nothing can stand up to the shock of their first assault [*à leur premier choc*]; but at the moment when it is done, they disbanded everywhere, and if the enemy returns, he has only to attack resolutely to butcher our men."[35] At St. Amand, at Furnes, at Le Blaton, at Linselles, at Menin, and at Pont-à-Chin the story was the same.

The case of Furnes on 31 May 1793 provides a particularly illustrative example. The real significance of the Furnes debacle is not in the military importance of the operation, since it involved only about 3,000 French troops. What made it so important was the presence of Lazare Carnot, then a Representative on Mission with the Nord and soon to enter the Committee of Public Safety.[36] Carnot helped plan the operation to seize Furnes, which lay between Dunkirk and Nieuport. The enemy was quickly driven off. On entering the town, some republican troops began to pillage, but these men were bridled and the victorious French massed in the town square, where their officers clearly explained that looters would be shot. As a friendly gesture, the burgomasters offered the assembled troops some beer. After this good-hearted act, the storm broke. Men fired their weapons into the air in celebration, and large numbers began to pillage. The sight of some must have incited others to get what they could. Carnot reported, "We and the generals found it impossible to stop the disorders; the drunken soldiers heard nothing, and the number of the guilty was too great to think of a violent punishment, which moreover, would have been impossible to execute in such a circumstance." Carnot wanted to continue the attack from Furnes to Nieuport. With difficulty the troops were reassembled and the march begun, but the men were not up to it: "They were almost all drunk, more or less. . . . The soldiers' packs were so full of things they had stolen that they could no longer carry them." Wisely, the general abandoned this advance. Carnot left Furnes to return to Bergues, and on his way back he saw that the French had entirely dispersed. Looters staggered under huge sacks of booty. They slung chickens across their shoulders and led along stolen livestock. One village that had given the French some trouble in their advance on Furnes was now in flames. The next day Furnes itself was abandoned. According to his biographer, Marcel Reinhard, this experience was a watershed in Carnot's attitudes toward discipline; once a proponent of reasonable and lenient codes, this bitter taste of reality led him to conclude, "If every soldier who steals a pin is not shot on the spot, you will never accomplish anything."[36]

The intensity of punishment escalated in late 1793 and especially in 1794. Representatives on Mission sanctioned special commissions to try accused looters. An execution of 25 June 1794 noted by Bricard exemplified the brutal severity that awaited the convicted. A young cavalryman was shot in front of his brigade for "having exchanged his battered hat for a new one, at the home of an inhabitant of the countryside."[37] In a sense this trooper died for the sins of an entire army. Pillage met with such severity because it posed an unequaled threat to the real performance of the army in the field, not because it was a greater moral lapse than all others.

Punishment

Punishment in the military tribunals was more than a means to insure justice. As in other courts, punishment was to be a way of deterring crime. On campaign, obedience and good order brought victory, so by encouraging proper conduct, the courts played a role in raising the level of combat performance. Convicted men suffered punishments not only for their own crimes but also to dissuade others from committing similar offenses. The courts, therefore, set out to make examples of those whom they condemned. As Representatives with the Nord stated in a distressed letter of March 1793, "A repressive force sufficient to give prompt examples of a severe justice is indispensable." Carnot was convinced of their value. Describing the improved discipline of the Nord in May 1793, he concluded, "Some severe examples achieved this important work."[38]

Documentation assembled by Legrand during the 1790s provides the basis for some solid judgments concerning these exemplary punishments handed out by military tribunals.[39] His material concerns the tribunal of the first district of the Armée du Rhin from 28 October 1793 to 6 March 1794. During these months the court judged "revolutionarily," by order of Representatives St.-Just and Le Bas. The same order split the court into three sections, thus making three courts out of one and multiplying the number of cases that could be heard. The three sections heard 600 cases; 282 resulted in acquittal and 188 in sending the accused to the interior, where they were to be incorporated into new units, a light punishment indeed. This tribunal cannot be dismissed as a kangaroo court, since so many cases ended in this manner. Additionally, thirty-six men were demoted, thirty-four sentenced to irons, thirty-four sent to prison for various set periods, and twenty-four confined until peace came. The remaining sixty-two received the death penalty.

Officers were more likely to go to the firing squad than were common soldiers; the ratio of officers to men on the death list was 1:5, at a time when an infantry battalion at full strength had an officer-to-men ratio of 1:38. The chief prosecutor of this court counseled his assistant with another section of the court to "especially distinguish the offenses of the commander from those of the soldier. An officer sometimes makes war out of vanity, by ambition, or for his pleasure. But the soldier, the sole true *sans-culotte*, does it only as a sacrifice to the Patrie."[40]

Three crimes accounted for over 70 percent of the death penalties. These were emigration or desertion to the enemy, incivic remarks or actions, and pillage, by far the deadliest crime. Pillage alone accounted for one-third of all death penalties; it was a soldier's, not an officer's crime. The offense most likely to send an officer to his grave was incivic words or actions, in essence a civil crime. This stands to reason, considering that the government harbored such strong suspicions of treason concerning its officer corps. The tribunal sent Pierre de Beril to his death for carrying a white cocade, a symbol of the Bourbon monarchy, in his pocket and for having written "Think of God and the King" in one of his letters. Simple desertion was not punished with death, but two officers and four enlisted men died for having run away during combat. It was safer to desert than to speak ill of the Republic or steal a chicken.

The experience of this court was mirrored in the Armée du Nord. Bricard, who took some care to note executions in his journal during 1794, recorded one for desertion to the enemy, one for fleeing in the face of the enemy, and seven for pillage. He also contrasted the fate of enlisted men and officers guilty of similar offenses. In a court session of 10 May 1794 twenty-two young soldiers who had thrown down their arms and fled in battle received only a reprimand, since the court regarded their "lack of military experience" as an extenuating circumstance. "Everyone was very satisfied with this moderation." A battalion commander who came to trial before the same court that day was ordered shot for leaving his battalion under fire.[41]

Considering the importance of using punishment as edifying example, it is not surprising to learn that authorities made public the punishments handed out to wrong-doers. The names of those convicted and acquitted of crimes were included in the orders of the day that were read aloud to the battalions. On the morning of 5 August 1793 soldiers in Cambrai heard that one Jean-François Chaumont had been sentenced to eight days' confinement for insubordination. In Dunkirk a poster proclaimed that on 2 October the *chasseur à cheval* François Belloque had been condemned to five years in irons for selling his equipment. A decree of 25 April 1794 allowed prosecutors to print and post any judgments they felt proper to make public in this manner.[42] Judgments against generals and war contractors were also published.[43] Beyond their deterrent effects, these last judgments assured the common soldier that none was immune from revolutionary justice and that the government was trying to protect the soldier's interests.

Far more than publication of verdicts, public executions made an impression on the troops. The emotional impact of seeing one's comrade shot by men of his own army must have been overwhelming. One such execution took place on 15 August 1794.[44] Three days before, six drummer-boys entered the home of an old woman and stole some silver rings and other jewelry. When she struggled to stop them, they struck her. They were arrested that night in camp as they fought over dividing the spoils. All were found guilty, and the two oldest sentenced to death. The troops assembled for the execution; normally they formed an open, three-sided square with the firing squad shooting from inside the square toward the open side, where the condemned stood or knelt. The older of the two boys, an eighteen-year-old kept his courage, but the younger cried for his mother. The four youngest, who watched the execution as their punishment, fought back their own cries. "All the soldiers could not witness this spectacle without shedding tears." How effective such executions were remains a conjecture, but contemporaries believed that coercion could buttress courage, as one fear countered another.

Decisive victory in the spring and summer of 1794 demonstrated that the Armée du Nord had achieved adequate levels of obedience and order, but the Nord never reached the faultless discipline that its critics would have preferred. Military historians, who have bemoaned this shortfall, explained French battlefield strength as something attained *in spite of* disciplinary weakness. However, this is not the only way to view the issue.

At the foundation of French tactical success lay the motivation of republican troops. That spirit depended upon the self-respect and commitment of the soldier in a new revolutionary environment. Had the authority of officers been increased and the men forced into a more compliant mold, French troops may well have lost much of what made them so effective by 1794. As it was, military law and discipline did not alienate the rank and file from their officers and jeopardize this critical relationship. Moreover, abundant evidence shows that the soldiers respected reasonable discipline and that they were not likely to reject a demanding code, as long as they thought it just. "On the contrary, they are happy to see punished those who would have the cowardice to despise it," wrote one sergeant in the Nord.[45] Military law and discipline as applied in the Nord demonstrated the government's resolve to enforce fair and equal justice. This system exemplified the positive gains of the Revolution and consequently could only have enhanced the loyalty of the troops to that Revolution. At the Ministry of War the same bureau responsible for military justice managed the campaign of political education directed toward the army.

The tactical system that evolved in the Armée du Nord did not place a premium on mechanistic discipline. Rather, it balanced obedience with enthusiasm and a high standard of combat performance, largely individualized and self-enforced. Discipline mattered, but the French would have suffered by making it a fetish. Ultimately they did well to treat the rank and file as citizens and not as subjects.

Chapter 6

The Political Education of the Armée du Nord

THE CLIMATE of opinion among the citizen-soldiers of France became a primary concern of the central government after Dumouriez attempted to march on Paris in April 1793.[1] Before then, lesser and more diffuse efforts had been made to shape the political attitudes of the troops. But when treason casts doubts upon the reliability of the officer corps, the National Convention, the Committee of Public Safety, and the Ministry of War responded with a campaign of political education designed to insure the loyalty of the rank and file. They employed various means in this persuasive program—most notable were radical newspapers, patriotic songs, public celebrations, and political clubs.

The recruits who joined the ranks of the Nord obviously did not arrive as tabula rasa, upon which publicists might inscribe their own values and opinions. These young men witnessed the great work of the Revolution. Liberty and equality stood above the ruins of privilege and prerogative. Remnants of the feudal system in the countryside had crumbled; dues and serfdom itself were only hated memories. Given time, perhaps some of the fruits of 1789 would turn bitter, but at the moment when new battalions rose to resist foreign armies seeking to reestablish an unwanted past, the accomplishments of the Revolution were still draped in the bright bunting of enthusiasm. The land, the people, the new society, and the new freedom united in the word Patrie. The French citizen-soldier marched to the front primed with patriotism.

Those who designed and directed the campaign of political education knew this soldier. They had confidence in his motivation and good will, but they feared that his officers might deceive and mislead him. Consequently, their uppermost concern was to inform the man in the ranks and to channel his devotion toward legitimate civilian authority and ultimately to the people. This would insulate him from the potential treachery of his commanders. Certainly the campaign reaffirmed the native patriotism of the troops, but this came only as an adjunct to the first goal of reinforcing the army's loyalty.

This chapter describes the campaign of political education in great detail, probably more detail than some readers care to know. However, since a complete account of the campaign has yet to see print, either in French or English, I felt it important to offer here a thorough study of this pathbreaking effort to mold troop opinion.

Influences on Army Opinion before April 1793

Although the central government did not undertake an elaborate program of political education for its troops until the spring of 1793, the armies were hardly isolated from the Revolution before that date. The battalions that came together as the Armée du Nord in late 1791 had lived in a highly charged revolutionary environment for over two years, and it affected them profoundly. Louis XVI attempted to impose his authority by force of arms in 1789, but, when ordered to turn their weapons against their fellow Frenchmen, many of his regiments balked, and their men deserted. From mid-1789 through mid-1791, the line army suffered discord and disarray. Mutinies large and small struck fully one-third of the army, testifying to the breakdown of old patterns of obedience.[2] While the regular army was profoundly shaken, the National Guard came into existence as a huge citizen militia. The part-time soldiers of the Guard differed in many ways from the regulars. A need to establish harmony between these two separate kinds of troops, as well as a desire to form bonds between National Guard units from different districts gave birth to the federation movement. Entire units, or their representatives, came together to fraternize, hearing patriotic addresses and swearing allegiance and fraternity to one another, sometimes before an altar of liberty. The federation movement peaked in 1790, although federations continued through 1792. Scores of local ceremonies, such as those at Amiens, Dunkirk, and Lille, culminated in a great national federation at Paris, on 14 July 1790.

Public ceremonies and celebrations continued to be important in the sixteen months between the formation of the Armée du Nord and the treason of Dumouriez. The national Fête de la Fédération held in Paris on 14 July 1792 ranks as the best known, but all along the northern frontier there occurred smaller, local ceremonies that involved the troops of the Nord.[3] These festivities enshrined the symbolism of the Revolution. Orations and patriotic songs seemed to be obligatory, and often ceremonies climaxed in some sort of oath to the people, their Revolution, and their government.

There were also ceremonies built around military units alone. In some cases a festival atmosphere surrounded the raising of volunteers. Martial music, parading columns, and banners declaring "Citizens, the Patrie is in Danger" added a stirring note to the ceremonies that called young Parisians to sign up in the summer of 1792. Despite the anticlerical thrust of the Revolution, battalions sometimes ceremoniously presented their new flags to be blessed. Once with the army at the front, units from time to time assembled for political ceremonies meant only for the troops, such as occurred at Avesnes on 5 September 1792.[4] Here, too, troops committed themselves to revolutionary principles and rededicated themselves to defend the land, people, and constitution of France.

After the creation of the Armée du Nord, those efforts made to educate and indoctrinate the troops continued to be initiated and controlled locally. The political clubs of towns dotting the northeast borders of France—which often were affiliated with the famous Jacobins of Paris—had reached out to troops since 1790. At first the National Assembly discouraged contacts between these clubs and the line army. In August 1790 it outlawed the formation of political clubs within the army regiments; the next month it forbade contact between civilian clubs and the troops. The ban was never really effective, and in May 1791 the Assembly overturned its earlier decision and allowed men to attend club meetings during off-duty hours. Although soldiers rarely attained membership, they and their officers might attend meetings. In fact, when units moved, as did the 78th Regiment at Bergues, the local Jacobins might recommend them to the club at their destination, urging the men "to attend regularly the meetings of the club there."[5] The intellectual diet of these small provincial clubs consisted heavily of patriotism and civic responsibility.

Some believed that contact with the clubs encouraged insubordination. Soldiers did consider a political club to be a forum in which to denounce their officers. At Bergues a deputation from a regiment soon to be on the roles of the Armée du Nord charged four of their officers with trying to lead their men over to the Austrians on 4 August 1791. Rochambeau never liked the idea of his soldiers attending club meetings, and when he could not forbid attendance he placed the clubs under surveillance. However, the *Argus,* a news journal soon to become a virtual organ of the Nord's high command, encouraged soldiers to attend clubs, and Dumouriez seems not to have been hostile to them.[6]

Once war broke out and the Nord entered its first campaign, troops had less time to invest in club attendance. Town clubs continued to exist over the summer of 1792, but their attendance seems to have fallen off sharply, judging from the fate of the Valenciennes club, where meetings were "almost always deserted."[7] It would be hard to demonstrate that the influence of the town clubs was great in 1792, and, although some military units may have possessed their own clubs, the lack of comment in both official and private correspondence leads one to doubt that they were either common or significant. More will be said concerning clubs later in this chapter.

Before 1793 only rarely did the central government or its agents directly address the troops concerning political matters. Following the panics of April and May 1792, Louis XVI sent his troops a letter expressing his feelings for them and stressing the need for discipline; the Armée du Nord received 1,000 copies of his bland notice. Little more than a month later, Parisian crowds, *fédérés,* and National Guardsmen overthrew the monarchy. Lafayette unsuccessfully appealed to the Nord to march on Paris; it was a dangerous moment for the Revolution. One explanation for his failure was the quick dispatch from Paris of commissioners charged with explaining the events of 10 August and their meaning to the troops.[8] After Lafayette crossed over to the Austrians, generals or agents of the central government occasionally issued proclamations.

The Convention finally established open and direct communication with its troops through distribution of the *Bulletin de la Convention Nationale.* Only days after it met for its first session in September 1792, the Convention decided to publish its own news sheet. Printed on one side only, in a poster format, this *Bulletin* was more of an official news release than a complete transcription of debates. While it presented a Jacobin point of view, it was not overly polemic. Responding to the suggestion of Representatives on Mission with the Armée du Nord, the Convention voted on 15 October to have the *Bulletin* sent to the armies. On 1 January 1793, Jean-Nicolas Pache, then minister of war, sent out a circular announcing that the *Bulletin* would soon arrive at the front and outlining the way in which copies were to be distributed to the troops. After reaching the front in the second week of January, the stream of *Bulletins* was cut off by events late in February and was only reestablished in May and June.[9]

Long before the *Bulletin* reached the Armée du Nord, the Nord possessed a special, and perhaps unique, instrument of political instruction, the *Argus du Département et de l'armée du Nord.* The *Argus* fell within the category of news journals written for or attached to particular armies of revolutionary France. In his work on this subject Marc Martin states that there were six much journals. The Nord actually produced a seventh, the *Trompette de l'armée du Nord,* a short-lived journal published at Lille; the *Argus* came out of Valenciennes. Among army journals the *Argus* claims the record for longevity, lasting for 234 issues from early April 1792 to the first day of February 1793. During its existence the *Argus* appeared under several titles, beginning with *Ami Jacques, L'Argus du Département du Nord.*[10] Throughout its career, François Melletier published and wrote much of the journal. It appeared daily, except Sunday, and shared with other papers the small, pamphlet-like, octavo format. An average issue contained eight pages.

From the outset Melletier aimed at a national, not just local readership. While the *Argus* concentrated on news of the Armée du Nord and the department, it had other civil and military pieces covering a wide range of topics. Martin argues that the *Argus* functioned as an instrument of the Gironde party of moderate republicans, who dominated the central government in the spring of 1792. At that time, newspapers borrowed stories from one another to the point of plagiarism. Through some complicated logic, Martin reasons that the *Argus* was established, probably with some government money, as a kind of press correspondent or wire service for the Girondin press in Paris. Certainly, articles from the *Argus* later reappeared in journals published by Jean-Pierre Brissot, Louis-Stanislas Fréron, Jean-Louis Carra, and Louis-Sebastien Mercier. It is worth noting that the Girondist minister of foreign affairs at the time when Melletier began his venture was Dumouriez, who would be closely bound up with the *Argus* later on. Another cause for the wide circulation of the *Argus* was its close ties with the Valenciennes Jacobin club. Melletier was for a time secretary of its committee of correspondence. Copies of his journal were sent to all clubs affiliated with the Valenciennes group.[11]

The extensive functions of the *Argus* should not obscure that its focus was the Armée du Nord, especially after mid-June. A prospectus of 18 June 1792 announced to the readers that the *Argus* had won the confidence of the high command of the Nord and that Melletier had made arrangements to print the journal himself from the headquarters of the Nord, wherever that might be. Much of the text of the *Argus* was addressed to the officers and men of the Nord. Appeals for greater discipline were common in May, and they reappeared periodically. Martin, in fact, points out that one of the primary functions of all the army journals was to instruct troops in the new concept of discipline. Knowledge was now considered essential to a just military code. Such pieces as "The Credo of the Good Soldier" and "The Comparison of the Austrian Soldiers and the French" were clearly intended for the eyes of the rank and file. The *Argus* also included articles apparently intended for the political education of the troops, such as its general news items and special pieces like "Comparison of Monarchy with Republicanism." It was, in fact, over France's violent transformation from monarchy to republic that Melletier made his most abrupt about-face. After preaching at some length on loyalty to the king, he turned to defend and explain the fall of the monarchy on 10 August.[12]

Melletier promised the troops still another service. Soldiers "and other people attached to the army, who do not have the time to give their family and friends an exact and extended account of such and such an action will have the ability to send them my newsletter, and everyone's desires will be fulfilled." The *Argus* certainly had an inside track for battle reports. Its account of the battle of Jemappes is almost word for word that sent by Dumouriez to the National Convention.[13]

It is not surprising that Dumouriez would use the *Argus* to publish his own account of things, because from the moment that Dumouriez moved up to the command of the Nord, the *Argus* repeatedly printed articles of almost fawning praise to the new chief of the Nord. Melletier vaunted Dumouriez as "this veritable liberator of the Republic." The *Argus* also carried songs and poems that raised hallelujahs to the great Dumouriez.[14] When *Argus* ended its career in February 1793, it had become not only the journal of the Armée du Nord, but also of its commanding general as well.

Political Education after Dumouriez's Treason: The Distribution of Political Journals

The Crisis and the Intent

After Dumouriez had gone over to the Austrians, the government resolved upon a program of political education. Even before Dumouriez's glaring treason, Representatives on Mission with the Armée du Nord had expressed their conviction that "one can never bind men of war too closely to the public interest [*chose publique*], and it is perhaps only to ignorance that we owe most of the success that agitators have achieved."[15] Now the Committee of Public Safety chose the revolutionary press as the primary medium of political education. Describing the rationale for this decision, the Minister of War Bouchotte explained: "The order was given to send journals to the armies after the defection of General Dumouriez, who by his seductions had nearly turned his army against France. In the journals, the names of the Patrie, public interest [*chose publique*], and government were often found repeated. In putting them before the eyes of the soldiers, the troops were reminded, without affectation, of the objects to which they ought to be attached. Such was the only goal."[16]

The arguments presented in this campaign of indoctrination developed along several lines. In the most direct sense soldiers were warned to watch out for traitors, if need be to suspect every officer. The men also had to be informed of events and decisions to protect them from lies. Moreover, they had to see these events and decisions from the perspective of the Convention and the Committee so as to be convinced of the rectitude of government conduct in Paris; in short, the climate of opinion within the army must be harmonized with that in the capital. Most important, soldiers had to be taught to regard the Convention and its committees as the sole source of legitimate authority. A widespread belief existed that patriotic literature might also raise combat motivation, but this was not a primary rationale behind the extensive efforts now taken to shape attitudes among the troops.

The Agents of Political Education

In early April 1793 the Convention dispatched a number of Representatives on Mission, including the famous Lazare Carnot, to the Armée du Nord et des Ardennes. At one of their periodic meetings, held in Douai on 12 May, they decided to order 1,500 copies of the *Journal des hommes libres* to be supplied to troops of the Nord and the Ardennes.[17] Thus began the purchase of private political journals for massive distribution throughout the armies and with it the campaign for political education.

The agencies and agents responsible for this program were parts of a largely ad hoc government, which continually evolved to meet the mounting crisis. The overthrow of the monarchy on 10 August 1792 left France without an executive; to fill this gap, the Legislative Assembly created the Provisional Executive Council on 15 August. This Council brought together the heads of major bureaucratic departments, including the minister of war. In September the Legislative Assembly gave way to the National Convention, whose primary tasks were to draft a new constitution for France and to act as an interim government until that new constitution could be put into effect. Under the Convention the power of the Executive Council eroded steadily until it ceased to exist on 19 April 1794. As the Executive Council declined, real authority for the execution of war and foreign policy shifted to the Committee of Public Safety, created in April 1793 to replace the earlier and weaker Committee of General Defense. After the elimination of the Executive Council, the ministries themselves were replaced by a series of commissions, the most important of which were directed by the Committee of Public Safety. Representatives on Mission functioned as agents of the Convention and of the Committee of Public Safety; in fact, members of the great Committee occasionally served as Representatives on Mission themselves.

The Representatives on Mission who initiated the campaign of political education on 12 May did not manage the details of the new program. Representatives interested themselves in political education from time to time, but they were usually swamped with other chores. Day-to-day operations of the program fell to the left wing Ministry of War and its agents. The decision taken at Douai was translated into an order of the Executive Council. On 22 May it allotted 50,000 livres to the Ministry of War for the purchase of patriotic journals. This Ministry, directed by Bouchotte and his Hébertist assistant Vincent, consisted of six divisions; the fourth division covered a great range of responsibilities, including inspection, discipline, courts-martial, and the collection and distribution of military laws.

In fact, the work of this division was overwhelmingly political. Its chief was Prosper Sijas, a devoted Jacobin. In one order of 24 May Bouchotte commanded the fourth division to contract for 2,000 copies of each issue of the *Journal des hommes libres* and an equal number of the *Journal de la Montagne*. Later the same day, Bouchotte extended the purchase to an additional 3,000 copies of the *Père Duchesne*. Bouchotte stipulated that Sijas was to send out the journals "proportionately among the armies addressed to the *commissaires du conseil exécutif* and distributed to the army by their cares."[18]

The *commissaires*, so important in the surveillance of officers, also played a major role in the entire program of political education. They shouldered little of the mundane responsibility of keeping an army going. Instead, Bouchotte described such *commissaires* as "the eyes of the Minister with the armies." Bouchotte instructed one *commissaire:* "One of the principal objects of your mission is the distribution of patriotic journals and the maintenance among our brothers in arms of the love of liberty which has made them win so many victories, to warn them against the maneuvers of the aristocracy, and to unmask the false patriots who only want to win their confidence in order to betray the Republic."[19]

The Purchase of Journals for Distribution

Bouchotte originally contracted to purchase only modest numbers of journals, but in the fall of 1793 the amount swelled to very substantial figures. (See Table 3 and Figure 2.) In a memoir he composed later in life, Bouchotte stated that he arranged for the regular dispatch of eight journals.[20] At the top of the list stand the three journals Bouchotte ordered on 24 May. Originally the minister ordered 2,000 copies of each issue of Vatar's *Journal des hommes libres,* but on 22 October 1793 this figure climbed to 5,000 and finally reached 6,000 on 21 March 1794.[21] In May Bouchotte asked Jacques Hébert, radical editor of the *Père Duchesne,* to furnish 3,000 copies of his journal daily. Less than four months later, on 17 September, the subscription jumped to 12,000 copies. No other journal would be purchased in such daily numbers. Hébert's arrest on 13 March 1794 ended publication of his journal.[22] The *Journal de la Montagne,* supplied at a rate of 2,000 or 3,000 copies per issue, went to the front for only a few months. Although its editor, Charles Laveaux, had worked at the Ministry of War, his criticism of Vincent brought an end to the Ministry's support for his journal.[23]

Subscriptions to the other five journals Bouchotte mentioned began before October 1793. Audouin's *Journal universel* arrived in lots of 3,000 copies per issue in August. On 22 October that number mounted to 5,000, where it stayed until 21 March 1794, when it climbed to 10,200.[24] On 10 September 1793 the Committee of Public Safety ordered Bouchotte to

TABLE 3.
Costs and Numbers of Journals Purchased

Journal	Expenses for journals to 1 floréal an II (20 Apr. 1794)[a]	Price per copy paid by government	Approximate number of copies purchased to 10 thermidor (28 July 1794)
Journals Listed in Bouchotte's Accounts			
Journal des hommes libres	108,150 livres	1 sous,9d.	1,810,000[b]
Père Duchesne	118,800[c]	2 sous	1,152,000
Journal de la Montagne	20,000	1 sous,6d.[d]	266,700
Publiciste de la Révolution française[e]	3,675	if 1s.,6d.	49,000
Journal universel	77,220		2,550,000[b]
Antifédéraliste	42,000	if. 1s.,6d.[d]	560,000
Rougyff	41,850[f]	1 sous,6d.[d]	558,000
Batave	15,075	if 1s.,6d.	201,000
Journal militaire	8,333	4 sous,2d.	40,000
Journals Associated with the Committee of Public Safety			
Feuille de salut publique	?	?	?
Républicain français	0	?	?
Soirée de camp[g]	0	6 deniers	80,000
	(9,750 total by 10 fructidor, 27 Aug. 1794)		(390,00 by 10 fructidor)
Totals as dated	435,103 livres by 1 floreal		7,266,700 by 10 thermidor

[a] Unless otherwise stated, all figures are from Bouchotte's accounts reproduced in Herlaut, *Bouchotte*, 2:97–110, and Mathiez, "La presse subventionnée," 112–13.

[b] Number of copies given by Delarue, "L'education politique à l'armée du Rhin," 157–60. His figures for the *Journal universel* may be high, since he seems to have estimated the circulation of this journal at 1,800 copies per issue too high after 30 ventôse.

[c] The price shown here includes that of a subscription for ventôse, which was never fully delivered, since Hébert was arrested on 23 ventôse (13 Mar. 1794). The figure given for copies purchased takes into account only three-quarters of the month of ventôse.

[d] Price per copy given by Delarue, "L'education politique à l'armée du Rhin," 162.

[e] Accounts list payment only for "various works"; Herlaut, *Bouchotte*, 2:84, states that it was this journal Marat sent to the armies.

[f] Expenses and number of copies purchased of the *Rougyff* take into account not only the amount shown in Bouchotte's account but also that found in an order of 28 Jan. 1794 in a letter to the Committee of Public Safety. *RACSP*, 10:493.

[g] Figures for the *Soirée de camp* are based on orders contained to the *RACSP*, particularly 15:166.

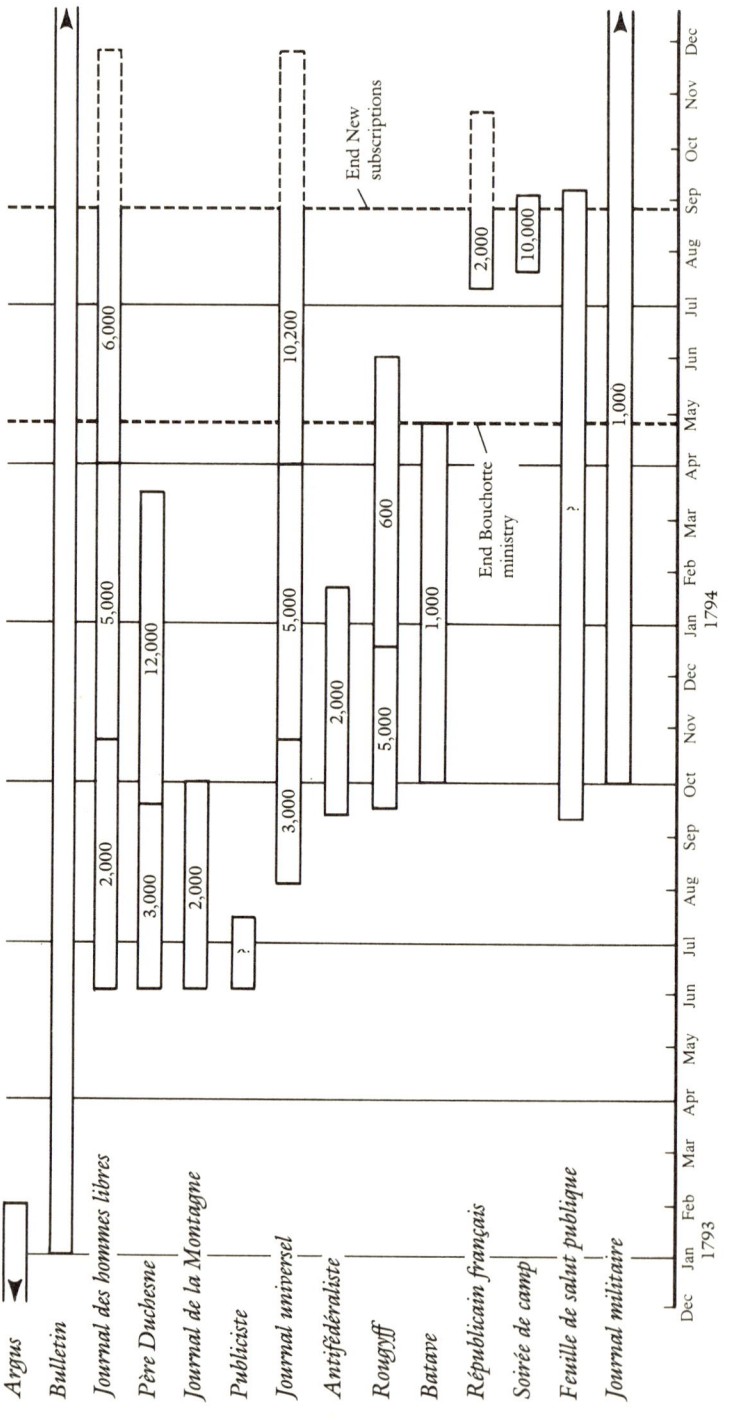

FIGURE 2.
Journals Purchased for Distribution to the Armée du Nord, 1793–94.

contract for copies of the *Antifédéraliste,* by Julian, Claude-François de Payan, and Pascal-Thomas Fourcade.[25] His accounts stated that he carried this subscription of 2,000 copies per day. This rate continued until the journal ceased to appear in January 1794. A journal called *Rougyff,* a playful rearrangement of the letters in the editor's name, Armand Gouffroy, presents a more complicated picture. Bouchotte recorded a payment to Gouffroy for 5,000 copies per issue for three months, but which three months? The answer is probably late September to late December 1793, since copies of the *Rougyff* began to arrive at the Nord during the last week of September. Later, in January 1794, Ernest Duquesnoy, a Representative on Mission serving with the Armée du Nord sent to the Committee of Public Safety an order to pay Gouffroy for a subscription of 600 copies per issue especially for the Armée du Nord. This second subscription probably extended until the journal disappeared on 28 May 1794, when, as Gouffroy explained, they had to close up shop because the army subscriptions had run out.[26] The *Batave,* edited by Naett, received a steady order for 1,000 copies from early October 1793 through mid-April 1794. Perhaps this subscription continued beyond that date, but there is no record that it did. The last journal that Bouchotte discussed in his memoir was the *Journal militaire,* a quasi-official bulletin of military laws, notices, and reports published by Gournay. The Ministry purchased 1,000 copies per issue from 1 October 1793 on.

Bouchotte seems to have been responsible for the distribution of one more journal, Jean Paul Marat's *Publiciste de la Révolution française.* Bouchotte's financial records, submitted in 1794, show that he paid Marat's sister for publications that Marat had supplied the Ministry before his assassination. Apparently these materials were at least in part copies of the *Publiciste.*[27]

With the abolition of the Executive Council and the Ministry of War, the Committee of Public Safety took on the duty of ordering appropriate journals. It continued the current levels for the *Journal des hommes libres,* the *Journal universel*, and the *Journal militaire.* To these three, the Committee added two more in mid-summer 1794. On July 13 it authorized the Commission of Public Instruction to distribute to popular societies and to the armies a total of 2,000 copies per issue of the *Républicain français.* In late July the Committee launched its own journal aimed precisely at the common soldier. This publication, the *Soirée de camp,* was Carnot's brainchild from the start. He alone signed the 14 July 1794 decree that established it under the editorial direction of Valcour and Camille, two employees of the Committee.[28] From 20 July 1794 to 27 August 1794, 10,000 copies of each issue went out to the armies.

There was still one other journal that the Committee may have disseminated to the armies since the summer of 1793. The *Feuille du salut public* came under the clandestine influence of the Committee in August and September 1793, when secret funds found their way to the pockets of the editor. It was supported to carry the Committee's version of the truth to the municipalities and the armies.[29] It must have gone out in only small numbers, since it did not cost the Committee a great deal.

When Robespierre and his companions mounted the scaffold on 28 July, after the coup of 9 thermidor, the urgent drive for revolutionary purity slackened. On 6 August the Committee of Public Safety, now minus its most famous member, voted to renew subscriptions to the *Journal des hommes libres* and the *Journal universel* for three months, but this was the last renewal. No longer compelled to preach the cause of the Revolution and confronting the rising tide of retrenchment and reaction, the Committee declared on 18 August that it would contract for no more journals to go to the army.[30] The final issue of the *Soirée de camp* appeared on 27 August; the *Feuille du salut public,* now called the *Journal de la Républic,* received no more Committee funds after 1 September. If the other journals ran out the course of their existing subscriptions, the last *Républicain français* went to the troops in mid-October, and the last issue of the *Journal des hommes libres* and of the *Journal universel* arrived a month later. Only two publications survived these cuts, the *Bulletin* and the *Journal militaire.* The *Bulletin* remained the Convention's one main avenue of contact with the army. The *Journal militaire,* by its very nature, had always been an administrative convenience directed toward army staffs, not a political medium for mass consumption, and its utility insured its survival.

Before it ebbed in the late summer of 1794, the flood tide of publications deluged the government with over 7.5 million copies of journals meant for the armies, not to mention the steady flow of the *Bulletin*. It also should be noted that on occasion some journals were even reproduced at the front in order to provide more copies for distribution.[31] During the period from 1 October 1793 to 19 January 1794, the government regularly purchased as many as 31,000 journals daily. This high level fell as the *Rougyff,* the *Antifédéraliste,* the *Père Duchesne,* and the *Batave* ceased to be distributed. Another peak in official circulation came with the creation of the *Soirée de camp*. During the *Soirée*'s brief lifetime as many as 29,000 journals were to be shipped to military units in one day.

Distribution of Journals at the Front

Although the government purchased millions of political journals, this did not guarantee that they all reached the front. In fact, arrival of journals to the Armée du Nord seems to have been irregular at best. Probably a significant amount of materials paid for by the Ministry of War never reached the troops.

Orders of the day issued by the general headquarters of the Armée du Nord provide the basis for some statements concerning the rate at which the soldiers of the Nord received the journals meant for them. From the beginning of January 1793 through the first week of the following October, orders of the day listed what issues of the *Bulletin* and of political journals were distributed on that particular day. From mid-October on, the orders only stated that *papiers nouvelles*—newspapers—were distributed, without stipulating which titles or issues were involved.[32] All that can be definitely known after 7 October, then, is the frequency of distribution, that is, how many days per week some sort of political materials were handed out to the soldiers. Judged only by this criterion of days per week that journals were distributed, circulation hit two peaks, one in June-August 1793, and the other in April-July 1794. (See Table 4.) Reception of papers during the fall and winter of 1793–94 became more erratic, probably because of the fall battles and the winter weather. However, the campaigning of spring 1794 did not prohibit frequent dissemination of *Bulletins* and journals. The claim made by some, that journals were distributed even when an army was engaged in combat, is borne out by these later figures.

In the period before 7 October 1793, when journal distribution can be known in detail, the pattern of circulation provides some surprises. After the initial deliveries of the *Bulletin* in January and February, the Austrian reconquest of Belgium, together with the treason of Dumouriez, brought a confused hiatus in distribution. In a letter of 5 May, one week before they ordered copies of the *Journal des hommes libres,* Carnot and his colleagues requested 1,500 copies of the *Bulletin* for the Nord.[33] This communication reads as if they saw themselves as reestablishing the flow of political materials to that army. Journals began to arrive at the Nord during the first week of June, at which time there was also a notable increase in the number of *Bulletins* distributed.

Table 4 shows the number of issues per week of the *Bulletin* and journals that were received before 7 October. The *Journal des hommes libres* appeared in the largest numbers; about ninety-five issues of this journal were distributed before 7 October. The *Journal de la Montagne* showed up as only about twenty-five issues. The much vaunted *Père Duchesne* cannot be traced as accurately because the issues were not dated, only numbered, and the orders never stipulated which issues circulated. The *Père Duchesne* appears to have found its way up to the northeast frontier even less frequently than the *Journal de la Montagne*. A handful of the *Rougyff* and some *Journal universel* complete the list of arrivals from late spring to early fall. Only the *Bulletin* and the moderate Jacobin *Journal des hommes libres* arrived in anything like regular fashion during this period. Over the summer Nord troops received copies of the *Bulletin* five days after the session reported in that

TABLE 4.
Frequency of Distribution of Journals per Week during 1793 and 1794.

Weeks of 1793*	Frequency of Distribution	Bulletin	Journal des hommes libres	Père Duchesne	Journal de la montagne	Publiciste	Journal universel	Antifédéraliste Rougyff	Batave	Weeks of 1794*	Frequency of Distribution
January	0	0	—	—	—	—	—	—	—	January	6
	2	2	—	—	—	—	—	—	—		1
	3	3	—	—	—	—	—	—	—		?
	7	7	—	—	—	—	—	—	—		?
February	4	4	—	—	—	—	—	—	—	February	?
	4	4	—	—	—	—	—	—	—		?
	4	4	—	—	—	—	—	—	—		7
	2	2	—	—	—	—	—	—	—		4
March	?	?	—	—	—	—	—	—	—	March	7
	?	?	—	—	—	—	—	—	—		2
	?	?	—	—	—	—	—	—	—		4
	?	?	—	—	—	—	—	—	—		1
April	?	?	—	—	—	—	—	—	—	April	7
	1	1	—	—	—	—	—	—	—		7
	0	0	—	—	—	—	—	—	—		4
	2	2	—	—	—	—	—	—	—		7
May	1	1	—	—	—	—	—	—	—	May	5
	3	6	0	0	0	—	—	—	—		5
	6	8	5	0	0	0	—	—	—		8
June			7	2	7	0	—	—	—	June	7
											7

July	5	6	6	2	3	0	—	—	—	6
	5	4	4	0	1	0	—	—	—	6
	6	7	7	3	1	0	—	—	—	6 July
	7	7	7	1	5	—	—	—	—	3
	7	7	7	3	1	—	—	—	—	6
August	10	10	10	1	0	—	—	—	—	6
	7	9	7	0	0	0	—	—	—	3 August
	3	6	7	0	0	0	—	—	—	3
	3	6	5	2	2	0	—	—	—	1
	7	10	6	1	0	0	—	—	—	3
September	3	7	4	0	0	0	—	—	—	2
	0	0	0	0	0	0	—	—	—	6 September
	1	1	?	?	?	0	?	—	—	2
	8	8	8	2	3	0	3	—	—	2
October	4	4	4	0	—	0	3	0	—	2
	?								0	0 October
	3									
	5									
November	?									
	3									
	0									
	4									
December	2									
	5									
	3									
	3									

* In this chart months have been divided into exactly four weeks; the last of the four weeks runs from the twenty-second of the month to the final day of the month. After the first week of October 1793, the journals distributed in that year were no longer listed by title or issue in the orders of the day.

issue, and journals reached the soldiers three or four days after the date of the edition. So the news was still hot, or at least warm, when the men read it.

How many copies of each issue arrived cannot be stated with any certainty. Of course, the order that precipitated the first subscription requested 1,500 copies of each for the Nord. There was supposed to be one copy for each company of troops, and, given the size of the Nord during the summer of 1793, 1,500 issues would have provided the proper one copy per company.

Complaints from the field reflect the fact that the *Journal de la Montagne* and the *Père Duchesne* did not arrive or reached the troops only in small numbers during the summer of 1793. *Commissaires* viewed this as especially loathsome, since in their opinion soldiers looked forward to these two journals "with the most avid interest." The *commissaires'* particular desire for more copies of the *Père Duchesne* is quite understandable, given the Hébertist bias of the Ministry. One *commissaire* with the Armée du Nord, Celliez, even corresponded directly with Hébert.[34]

Celliez and his colleague Varin laid the blame for this problem on Custine, who commanded the Nord from late May through mid-July. They accused his staff of intercepting and seizing packets of journals. Military commanders and certain lower echelon administrators originally bore the responsibility for distribution. Custine brushed off charges by claiming that he only received enough copies of the *Montagne* and the *Père Duchesne* to enclose one or two copies with each packet of journals he forwarded to his divisions and garrisons. As a precaution against further interference, Celliez resolved to distribute the radical press himself. While handing out copies of the 29 June issue of the *Montagne,* he was arrested on order of Custine. That issue contained a letter that insisted Custine was "detested by all patriots" and "accused of treachery" in his previous command, the Armée du Rhin. Custine lamely explained that the *commissaire* had simply been placed under protective custody to prevent his being lynched by troops enraged at this attack on their general.[35] Custine paid dearly for his interference, since this obstruction was one of the factors that led to his arrest and execution.

Even after Custine's departure on 16 July orders of the day show no rise in distribution of the two journals. So if the reticence of military officers accounted for the short supply, the reticence infected the command structure at the peripheries as well as at the center. There is good reason to believe this to have been the case, as when the general of the rear guard instigated the burning of copies of the *Père Duchesne*.[36]

It could be reasonably expected that the tremendous increase in the quantities of journals purchased in the fall of 1793 might have solved the distribution problem, but such was not the case. After the Ministry committed itself to 12,000 copies of Hébert's journal, requests for more copies of it stopped. But still, the fall and winter brought more problems. At least three times between 17 September and 20 October, Bouchotte, goaded by complaints, peppered Sijas with demands to find out why the journals were delayed. "The complaints continue from armies which receive neither *Bulletins* nor journals, what are the means that you have taken to discover the reason for this problem?"[37] Sijas finally concluded that the culprits were military commanders and the postal service.

In a circular of 9 November Sijas ordered his *commissaires* to see to the distribution of journals themselves or to place it in the hands of soldiers known for their patriotism. This, he hoped, would circumvent unreliable officers. As far as the *commissaires* with the Nord were concerned, this merely restated an order issued to them by Sijas in July. The 9 November circular also asked popular societies to keep an eye on the personnel of the postal service. Vincent also believed that poor delivery was due to the "malevolence of some employees of the posts." "Malevolence" may have played a role, since some postmasters remained royalists; however, the administration of posts and messengers had such a tremendous task to perform under such obstructive limitations that it is a small wonder deliveries were slow and confused. War crisis, coupled with the torrent of dispatches, circulars, decrees, and laws to be sent, crushed the posts under an incredible avalanche of paper. At the same time the road system suffered, and the horses and men of the postal service fell liable to requisition by the armies.[38]

In February and March 1794 the Ministry dealt with one last series of complaints concerning distribution of journals in the Armée du Nord. Representative on Mission Florent Guiot charged repeatedly that some garrisons still received no journals and that the economy in purchasing journals was a false one.[39] His strongly worded notes were not only to the Ministry of War but to the Committee of Public Safety as well. These letters, together with the cancellation of the *Père Duchesne,* seem to have precipitated the decision to buy more copies of the *Journal des hommes libres* and the *Journal universel*. The absence of further complaints and the regularity of circulation revealed by the orders of the day argue for the conclusion that the flow of journals received along the northeast frontier finally became sufficient in April, just after the increased subscriptions to the *Journal des hommes libres* and the *Journal universel* took effect.

When journals reached front-line encampments and garrisons, they were handed out at the same time as rations, so distribution was orderly and unavoidable. The quantity allotted was supposed to equal one copy of each piece for each company, but, of course, journals often arrived in short supply. When not enough copies were available, companies that received copies might selfishly refuse to pass them around.[40]

The format of the *Bulletin* suited it for public display. An order of 7 May 1793 stated that each battalion should have a billboard, made of two planks on either side of a post, which in encampments "will be placed in the ground at the center of the battalion line [*front de bandière*]. Every day a copy of the *Bulletin de la Convention* will be glued on each side for all soldiers to see." In garrisons the *Bulletin* could be displayed at the *place d'armes* or in the barracks.[41] When journals reached the front in June, they hardly suited posting in the same fashion as did the *Bulletin*, since journals appeared in a small format, printed on both sides of the paper.

Bulletins and journals alike were read aloud by the troops. However, their livelier style must have made the journals greater favorites for public reading. Celliez and Varin reported to Bouchotte how journals were read by the troops of the Nord; "they form groups, one of them reads aloud in such a manner that everyone can hear, and it ends with Bravos."[42] Only by reading journals aloud could the *commissaires* insure that all soldiers were exposed to them. Even the illiterate or uninterested soldier had to listen. Moreover, public reading made journals accessible to all when there were too few copies to pass around. Documentation does not fill in the details as to when public readings were held. Given the eagerness for news, soldiers may have demanded the readings immediately after morning distributions. It is also unclear whether readings took place in a company mess of as many as one hundred men or in the more manageable mess groups (the *ordinaires*). The smaller *ordinaire* would seem a more likely possibility.

The Journals and Their Message

The message carried by the revolutionary press to the armies served the need of the government to insure the loyalty of its troops. Yet the journals also said more, both because they addressed themselves to a broader audience than the armies alone and because soldiers could readily see things in the journals that were only peripheral to the primary intentions of the Convention and the Committee of Public Safety.

Although the political journals were similar, each possessed its own character, so it would be a mistake to lump them together carelessly. The *Bulletin* of the Convention was not a journal, strictly speaking, but it performed much the same function. Begun as an official record, the *Bulletin* became more and more an expression of the government's point of view; still, the *Bulletin* remained relatively matter of fact and straightforward. The folio *Bulletin* appeared daily, and, if warranted, supplements accompanied the first sheet. Government debates and decrees appeared there, as did some letters and even songs that came to the legislators' attention.

Unlike the *Bulletin* or the purely administrative *Journal militaire*, the news journals proper were designed for a specifically Parisian audience.

Such papers included the *Journal des hommes libres,* the *Journal de la Montagne,* and the *Journal universel.* News of the Convention, of the great political clubs, most notably the Jacobins, of the army, and of the Paris Commune regularly filled their quarto and octavo pages. The arts, or at least revolutionary expression in the arts, also received some coverage. Songs, too, occasionally found their way into these journals. Beyond this, short political commentaries by the editors gave their journals a personal and partisan flare. Objective and colorless journalism in a modern sense was neither desired nor achieved. A prospectus for the *Journal des hommes libres* outlined the goals of this and other revolutionary journals: "To propagate the principles of equality, to revive the public spirit everywhere, relentlessly to pursue conspirators and conspiracy, egotism, which so corrupts men, fanaticism, superstition, and error, which makes mankind unhappy, and to enlighten men concerning their duties, without which there are no rights; finally to rouse among all our brothers hatred for tyrants and love for the Patrie."[43]

Although it was also written with an eye to Parisian politics, Hébert's *Père Duchesne* stood apart from the news journals in content, style, and point of view. Strictly speaking, the *Père Duchesne* was not a newspaper. Each of its issues, which appeared twelve times monthly, consisted of a lively and sometimes artful commentary on a particular subject supposedly written by the good *sans-culotte,* Père Duchesne. With rare exceptions, each issue began with the phrase "The Great Fury of Père Duchesne" or "The Great Joy of Père Duchesne" about such and such a topic. Being Hébertist, the Ministry of War favored the *Père Duchesne,* and by subscribing to 12,000 copies of each issue, the Ministry supported Hébert and his faction. With Hébert's fall from grace in March 1794, the Ministry's bias shifted away from the extreme left.

The last paper to make its appearance at the front in 1794, the *Soirée de camp,* claimed a unique status. Carnot created this official paper, issued daily with four pages in octavo, specifically to shape opinion within the armies, making it the first and only journal of its kind. He was particularly concerned with the climate of opinion in the Armée du Nord and to some degree tailored the *Soirée* for that audience. From the defunct *Père Duchesne* it borrowed the form of a relaxed and chatty monologue, this time delivered by a weathered but patriotic veteran, Va-de-bon-coeur. The *Soirée* catered to soldiers' tastes and frequently included songs. However, Carnot's brainchild was also a political weapon wielded against Robespierre.[44] It appeared a week before the coup of 9 thermidor, 27 July 1794, then spent issue after issue in justifying the Convention's action, and finally ceased to exist one month after Robespierre went to the guillotine.

The themes elaborated in the Parisian political press reflected the entire range of concerns of the revolutionary left. All journals lavished praise on the *sans-culotte*—the egalitarian, industrious, and responsible common man, jealous of his liberty and devoted to the Republic. Editors extolled the new values of the Revolution—liberty, equality, and fraternity, to be sure, but also honesty, simplicity, and concern for the public good. Journals urged respect for the Convention, the Committee of Public Safety, and the proposed Constitution. The National Convention in particular received praise as the ultimate expression of the popular will. Revolutionary justice was defended as a response to real threats against the Revolution, although no other journal went so far as the *Père Duchesne* in exalting the "holy guillotine."

The hated elite of the ancien régime topped the enemies list. Journals attacked the institution of monarchy across Europe and reserved special condemnation for the French monarchs. Marie Antoinette would not follow Louis XVI to the scaffold until 16 October 1793, and before her death the papers buried her in invective. The aristocracy came under constant fire. Fear persisted that those nobles still in France were enmeshed in a conspiracy to overthrow the Revolution, so the populace must constantly stay alert against this treachery. Criticism of the Roman Catholic Church and of non-juring priests crept into the papers throughout the era when they were distributed, but anticlericalism was only strident in the fall of 1793. Even Hébert tried to avoid attacking what many soldiers still revered; he went so far as to declare that Jesus was "the model for all Jacobins."[45] Of course, the church and the aristocracy were held responsible for the rebellion in the Vendée. This counterrevolution enraged the Parisian journals. They labeled the insurgents "brigands" and repeatedly urged government and army to suppress them without mercy. Federalism and federalist revolts were also condemned, though without the double measure of vitriol reserved for the Vendée.

The journals also became weapons in the political wars between factions. A heavy note of irony surrounds the journals' assaults on "factionalism," since they were its instruments. Of course, it was important for the journals to make the rise and fall of political cliques comprehensible. The journals were first purchased by Bouchotte immediately on the heels of the 2 June coup, which resulted in the arrest of the once dominant Girondist party. The *Père Duchesne* and the *Montagne* unleashed the most vicious and continued attacks on the Girondist leader Brissot, attacks which did not even end with his execution. Later Hébertists and Dantonists suffered from journalistic barbs, while the *Soirée de camp* owed its creation to the struggle against the Robespierrists.

These partisan stands raise the question as to whether the journals embroiled troops in the fights between factions or in the more subtle but fundamental issue of *sans-culotte* direct democracy versus Jacobin centralism? My reading of both the common soldiers and of the daily concerns that affected them is that such elevated matters were neither understood nor appreciated by the vast majority at the front. The troops were probably confused by or indifferent to the partisan in-fighting of political factions in Paris. Consider the reaction of Louis Bricard's comrades to the execution of Robespierre: "We said to one another, 'They will wind up sending everybody to the guillotine, since each ruling party executes the other and all parties come to rule in turn.'"[46] On the whole, the soldiers of the Nord probably focused on simpler lessons that meant more to their lives of danger and endurance. Revolutionary journals affirmed their sense of purpose, warned them of betrayal, directed their loyalties, and assured them that their sacrifices and triumphs were appreciated by a grateful nation.

"There is no monster more terrible than he who betrays his Patrie." The message of devotion to country and people dominated all the political journals. Today it might be a shop-worn creed; then it was novel and powerful. The people had just come to see themselves as a community; they had just recognized that the nation was theirs and not the exclusive possession of a distant monarch. Patriotism expressed the people's self-confidence and sense of common interest. It became a religion. The *Soirée de camp* could declare, "What ought to be the method of honoring the Supreme Being? It is to love your Patrie and your brothers." War demanded that soldiers bear painful witness to their patriotism, but death was a price worth paying. "It is good to suffer for the Patrie."[47]

Reminded of his obligation to serve his country, the soldier was warned to suspect his officers of treason. This had been a basic rationale for the distribution of journals, and those journals efficiently performed this duty. They castigated Dumouriez and carried out campaigns against Custine and Houchard. They warned that even popular generals might be untrustworthy. Laveaux, editor of the *Journal de la Montagne*, wrote, "I declare that a general, be he the most virtuous of men, seems guilty to me if he is adored by his army and the people." The more extreme journals assumed an ongoing conspiracy of the well-born to subvert the army. "When they have misguided the *sans-culottes* from within, and when they have found the means to have themselves named to all positions, they will betray the *sans-culottes*. It is thus that they will disorganize the armies and bring on civil war."[48]

If factional struggles raged and officers threatened to mislead their men, where should soldiers turn to invest their loyalty? The journals responded, "To the National Convention, to the Committees of Public Safety and General Security. There lays the real center of unity around which the true friends of liberty ought always to rally."[49] The Constitution also seemed to be a worthy focus for the soldiers' devotion, but it was a promise of a system to come, not a real and functioning body, like the Convention.

Never did the journals question the validity of French war aims. The heads of foreign governments were criminals, and their soldiers slaves. They would slaughter women and children if good Frenchmen did not defeat them. Should the struggles against foreign invaders or against internal rebellions be lost, then the ancien régime would return with its kings, aristocrats, and corrupt church.

The men who fought in such a just war could expect the grateful recognition of a thankful nation, and revolutionary journals bestowed it on them. Soldiers were "brave warriors" who "flew to the defense of the *Patrie*." They were models of the selfless and sober sacrifice demanded of true *sans-culottes* in times of crisis. "Above all," said *Père Duchesne,* "we must think of our brave brothers in the armies. There is not a *sans-culotte* who would not reduce himself to bread and water to assure food for those who are defending the country."[50] Officers might mislead their troops, and individual soldiers might be guilty of pillage, but as a whole citizen-soldiers were incorruptible and worthy. They stood between the Republic and destruction. A prime example of the celebration of the soldier appeared in issue 321 of the *Père Duchesne,* entitled: "The Great Joy of Père Duchesne." The article began, "In learning of all the fine actions of our brave guys who fight for the Republic and who will save it despite the rats and traitors and all the crowned thieves who have more chance of biting the moon than they have of laying down the law to us." He invited his readers "to pass in review all our armies" where could be seen "the flower of the Republic. . . . You must see with what courage they endure cold, heat, fatigue and hunger. Days of combat are for them days of celebration, and they march to battle like they go to a ball, singing and dancing. . . . I would not be able to finish if I wanted to tell you of all the fine traits that honor our own brave defenders; still it is right for me to make them known, in order to serve as examples for young citizens." Such overwrought praise probably amused the troops as they heard it read to them in camp, but can it be doubted that such words renewed the listeners' pride in themselves and their mission?

Other Printed Tracts

The *Bulletin* and the journals did not comprise the entire range of printed political tracts sent to the Armée du Nord by the central government. From time to time the government dispatched its own addresses, decrees, instructions, and circulars to the troops. The majority of such mailings came directly from the Convention, but a substantial minority left the office of the minister of war. They did not rival the journals in bulk or in frequency, but they were significant. One scholar counted sixty-two titles of political materials issued from government offices to the armies from 31 May 1793 to 28 July 1794.[51]

Addresses and decrees disseminated to the Nord served a number of purposes. They interpreted and explained the great revolutionary "days," which brought the rise and fall of personalities, factions, and policies. They gave accounts of revolutionary celebrations and triumphs. They outlined the details of new policies, such as the egalitarian practice of discarding the formal *vous* in favor of the informal *tu* in conversation. And some tracts bordered on lectures, such as Robespierre's report of 7 May 1794 concerning moral and religious ideas.

The most important and the most abundantly circulated materials concerned the drafting and adoption of a new constitution. One of the primary tasks of the National Convention was to write a constitution to replace that which died with the monarchy on 10 August 1792. In February 1793 a first proposal was ready for the Convention. The Convention ordered the Executive Council to send copies of it to the troops. After much debate the proposal returned to committee, but when it emerged again the coup of 31 May–2 June cut short renewed debate. A second draft, proposed to the Convention on 10 June, was also dispatched to the armies. On 24 June the Convention adopted the proposed draft and made plans for a referendum. A few days later Celliez wrote from the Nord that "a great number" of copies of the Constitution ought to be distributed to the troops. Bouchotte obliged him and on 7 July sent out circulars announcing that he intended to print enough copies that "everybody can receive and learn it easily." His later rendering of accounts showed that he paid for 400,000 copies. An order issued at the headquarters of the Nord on 29 August 1793 declared that on that day reprints of the Constitution would be handed out.[52] This distribution could very well have had a profound effect, not only by informing the men of the details of their new Constitution and by assuring them that their knowledge and approval mattered, but also by placing in their hands a physical symbol of what they were fighting to establish and protect.

It is worth noting that the Austrians and English, with their émigré allies, made feeble attempts at printing pamphlets and posters of their own to influence soldiers of the Armée du Nord. There is even an account of a counterfeit, and aristocratic, *Père Duchesne* making the rounds along the northeast frontier.[53] These efforts seem only to have met with amused disdain by the men of the Nord.

Song as a Medium of Political Education

The French Love of Song

The government's program of political education utilized songs as well as journals. More money was devoted to the purchase and distribution of journals, and they were sent out in greater numbers than were songbooks.

Yet songs certainly were more popular with the troops and were probably more important in promoting patriotism and revolutionary values. Historians who disregard song ignore a powerful political voice. An understanding of this medium's significance begins with appreciation of the particular French love for song. The government clearly recognized this native penchant and strove to enlist it as a means of patriotic indoctrination.

At every step the French celebrated their Revolution with melody. The best inventory of revolutionary songs lists nearly 3,000 that appeared between 1789 and 1799, but many more existed. Rarely were new songs written to new music; only 150 of those in the inventory were. Often even these could be sung to old airs if desired. The liberal borrowing of familiar tunes made it much easier to introduce and spread new songs. Patriotic street singers were a permanent fixture of the Revolution from the first. Professionals with colorful nicknames such as "Beauchant" and "le Divertissant" entertained Parisian crowds. Ladré, composer of the famous "Ca ira!," was one such street singer. They supported themselves by the sale of printed songsheets, which contained the lyrics of the ditties they sang, with simple notations as to which melody fit the words. Such a prize might cost two sous. These songs moved from the streets into the theaters.[54] Audiences sang before performances, during intermissions, and even joined in when actors sang familiar tunes in the course of a play.

Civic celebrations understandably entailed the singing of revolutionary songs, but serious political meetings also heard them. Political clubs often began or closed their meetings with patriotic songs. The General Council of the Paris Commune regularly heard songs performed before it, and even the National Convention received a steady parade of ardent citizens who came to sing their new odes and hymns. This became such a bother that in March 1794 an irritated Georges Jacques Danton finally felt compelled to ask the Convention to ban such performances.[55]

While Paris always stood at the center, the French passion for revolutionary songs extended across the entire country, even to the smallest villages. Gervais tells how his village in Brie was "inundated with songs each more extravagant than the other. I only had to read them or hear them sung once to learn them. Thus, I sang all day long, and new songs every day." There is no question that, as one patriotic songbook of 1792 asserted, singing was "the pleasure most natural to Frenchmen."[56]

So popular were songs among the republican troops that the authors of the *Soirée de camp* included new songs as a vital part of the text. Va-de-bon-coeur chatted with his readers, "Hey Bluebellies! Have I forgotten to mention the best part, the songs? I promise to give you two or three each decade, all written to easy and well known tunes." Soldiers welcomed song as a constant companion. On the march, singing made bearable monotony, discomfort, and fatigue. One recruit wrote this account of his unit's first march: "We marched without order, in profound silence, each man absorbed in his own thoughts. Suddenly the smallest man in the battalion began to sing. . . . The whole battalion repeated the chorus, and great joy replaced the sadness in our ranks." In camp, when bad weather imprisoned the men in their tents, singing helped to "chase the clouds away." The very act of singing united men by a process easier to recognize than to analyze. This may be the best explanation of why republican troops sang in battle, as they did at Valmy and Jemappes.[57] Singing counteracted fear by breaking down the isolation of the individual, as well as by occupying his mind and giving expression to his resolve.

As a medium of political education in the army, songs enjoyed special advantages. Singing was not limited to any particular time or place, and it required no special materials. Printed lyrics were helpful to propagate new songs, but they could be sung and handed on without the convenience of songbooks. Songs were as portable as the voices and spirits of the troops. This medium required soldiers to memorize the direct and simple messages of the lyrics. Catch phrases and slogans became indelibly printed on men's minds, not just on torn paper. Revolutionaries appreciated the power of the song for the propagation of patriotic idealism within the army; witness Jean-François Chaumette, who in defense of his proposal to print a songbook for distribution among Parisian recruits, declared, "We were born French; we know what a song is worth!"[58]

The Purchase and Distribution of Songbooks for the Armies

The distribution of printed songs was never subject to the same central direction as that of journals. While the Ministry of War and the Committee of Public Safety outstripped other agencies in their expenditures and efforts, they did not exclude other organizations. The Committee on Public Instruction, the General Council of the Paris Commune, the sections of Paris, provincial governments, political clubs, and even Representatives on Mission published or purchased songbooks that reached the troops. So varied are the sources for the flow of song materials to the frontiers that a reliable count of printed songs, songsheets, and songbooks is out of the question. All that can be said is that the numbers were substantial, several hundred thousand at least.

The Ministry of War propagated revolutionary songs in a number of ways. Bouchotte's memos display a real interest in patriotic songs. His rendering of accounts states that he paid 80,000 livres to Thomas Rousseau for songbooks. This was a monumental sum, considering that the same accounts carry a debit of 104,400 livres for 1,044,000 copies of the

Père Duchesne. In November 1793 Rousseau claimed he had already sent nearly 100,000 songbooks to the army. Eighty thousand livres could conceivably have paid for several times that number of booklets. Bouchotte also sent thousands of copies of songs to the front by purchasing and distributing the journals, since patriotic songs often appeared on their pages. In addition, Bouchotte seems to have circulated some individual songsheets or booklets to the army.[59]

The Committee of Public Safety made its major contribution to the distribution of revolutionary songs in 1794. In February it contracted for a monthly issue of large songbooks, one of which would go to each of the 550 districts of France. Then in July the Committee agreed to buy 12,000 songbooks each month for a year. Ten thousand of these would go to the army and 2,000 to the navy. Also, over the brief life of the *Soirée de camp* eleven issues contained songs; at 10,000 copies per issue, this adds up to a total of 110,000 copies of songs circulated through this journal alone. For special celebrations the Committee ordered mass printings of particular songs; the "Bataille de Fleurus" and the "Chant du départ" were each published in editions of 8,000 copies for 14 July 1794.[60]

The Committee of Public Instruction was also actively engaged in the development and dissemination of revolutionary music, though this Committee often played the modest part of loyal assistant to the Committee of Public Safety. The Committee of Public Instruction helped to found and support the National Institute of Music. In the fall of 1794 the Committee distributed 42,000 copies of the "Chant des victoires," the "Chant du départ," and the "Hymne à la fraternité" to the armies.[61]

In one way or another the city of Paris sent off reams of songbooks to the armies. The central government of the city, the Commune, distributed impressive amounts. On 18 September 1793 a young recruit from the Section du Contrat Social took the floor and sang a patriotic song, "and on the demand of Hébert, the Council orders that this republican cantata will be printed in 25,000 copies, with music, and that a copy will be given to every volunteer who will march to the frontiers." A week later the Council voted to print an entire songbook, again in an issue of 25,000 copies to distribute to volunteers who were off to the front. The sections, or wards, of Paris had local assemblies and political clubs of their own. These also chose to publish and circulate songs. For example, the popular society of the Section des picques, on 23 December 1793, ordered the publication and dissemination of 2,000 songbooks.[62] How many of such booklets reached the hands of soldiers is hard to say; certainly some did.

Songs were also published at the front, by order of local town governments and clubs and by order of agents of the central government. So a songbook appeared entitled *Patriotic Songs Sung at Lille*, and in the same city Representative on Mission Joseph Le Bon ordered the publication of a patriotic song.[63]

Writers, Subsidies, and Centralization

The most prolific pens devoted to the composition of patriotic songs belonged to Thomas Rousseau and the musicians of the Parisian National Guard. Rousseau, with nearly a hundred works to his credit, stands out as the most important single composer.[64] He served as a senior clerk in the Fourth Division of the Ministry of War throughout most of 1793. Since the Ministry's program of political education ran through the Fourth Division, Rousseau's concern with propaganda would hardly seem incidental. During the time he worked for the Ministry, he also occupied the position of archivist for the Jacobin Club of Paris and at times wrote accounts of its meetings for the *Journal de la Montagne*. There was obviously no doubt that he was politically in tune with the left-wing Ministry.

Early in the Revolution songwriters had made do by selling their works on the streets, but by 1793 government subsidies to journalists and composers had become indispensable, at least for large-scale publication. As a petition Rousseau presented to the Convention illustrates, private sales could not support his publishing ventures. His songs first appeared in print during 1792, and he continued to write lyrics through 1794, after which time his career as a lyricist ended. Following the practice of his times, he fitted his verses to popular melodies and presented his songs in small songbooks. Rousseau commonly used the same song in several different collections. Perhaps his most important collections appeared as *L'âme du peuple et du soldat*. This was really a series of seven booklets that came out during the time he worked for the Ministry of War.[65] The title and subject matter of the songs suggest that much or all of Bouchotte's 80,000 livres went to purchase copies of *L'âme du peuple et du soldat*.

The musicians of the Parisian National Guard occupied a central position in the writing and publication of revolutionary songs. Toward the end of 1792, Sarette, their commander, formed a music school to train 120 young Parisians, with his bandsmen as the teaching staff. On 8 November 1793 he proposed to the National Convention that it establish a National Institute of Music to teach young people from throughout France. The Convention adopted the proposal, and the final decisions concerning state support were made by the Committee of Public Safety in the spring of 1794. In January and February 1794, while the implementation of the Convention's decision pended, the musicians, with Sarette as spokesman, successfully approached the Committee of Public Safety with a plan to produce a series of booklets containing music suitable for civic ceremonies and celebrations. This Société de musiciens was to be paid 33,000 livres for twelve monthly issues of 550 copies of such music books, one each to go to each of the 550 districts of France.[66]

The success of their first venture encouraged the association to offer its service to the Committee of Public Safety again—this time to prepare and publish a monthly issue of 12,000 songbooks, each to contain four patriotic songs, for distribution to the armed forces. In July the Committee accepted this proposal and agreed to pay 60,000 livres annually for 10,000 copies each month for the army and 2,000 for the navy.[67] Furthermore, it subscribed to about 410 copies for the École de Mars, or military academy, at an additional 2,050 livres.

During the period when the bandsmen of the Parisian National Guard were absorbed in teaching and composing, their work resulted in the creation of new military bands. In October 1793 the Committee of Public Safety charged Sarette with creating a company of musicians for the Armée de l'Ouest. In April 1794 this company was sent off to the Nord, and Sarette was ordered to form another company of musicians expressly for the Armée du Nord. In May still one more band for the Nord appeared in the orders of the Committee of Public Safety.[68]

The musicians of the Parisian National Guard numbered among them some first-rate talents, most notably Etienne-Nicolas Méhul and François Gossec. Marie-Joseph Chénier, too, was closely associated with them and contributed to their publications. They published songs with original melodies. The "Chant du départ," with words by Chénier and music by Méhul, appeared in the sixth number of the association's *Musique à l'usage des fêtes nationales* and in the fourth issue of the *Chansons et romances civiques*, destined for the armies.[69]

The work of the Institute and the association represents a movement toward centralization in the production of propaganda aimed at a military audience. At mid-summer 1794, the climax of this study, the Committee of Public Safety, through its agents, was publishing its own journal for soldiers and its own songbook. There were relatively few titles of political materials going out to the armies, but they were issued in huge numbers. Also, propaganda music was now in the hands of men trained as musicians and composers and who made their livings through the mainstream of music. Rousseau's life as a lyricist was brief, Méhul's and Gossec's were long. The association and its publishing ventures continued throughout the revolutionary years and into the Napoleonic era.

The longevity of the publication and distribution of songs exceeded that of the distribution of political journals. By the end of 1794 only the *Bulletin* and the *Journal militaire* still reached the army on a regular basis; neither was really a political journal. But the *Chansons et romances civiques* continued to be published regularly through two yearly subscriptions.

Perhaps this was so because the songs carried messages that were both simpler and less controversial than those typical of the political journals.

The Message of Patriotic Song

The popularity of song made it inevitable that the government would exploit it as a medium of political education and indoctrination; however, patriotic songs did not carry the same messages as did the political press. Songs did not constitute a major weapon in the struggle against the real or supposed treachery of disloyal generals nor in the battle between political factions. When the Committee of Public Safety and the Ministry of War feared the maneuverings of traitorous generals, they flooded the front lines with copies of the *Père Duchesne* and the *Journal des hommes libres*. When the government sought to explain the necessity for violent purges, it turned to the partisan press.

If songs possessed a strong capacity to seize the soldier's interest, they by nature did not lend themselves to elaborate statements of politics and philosophy. Consequently, their role emerged as inspirational and educational, stripped of subtlety and complexity. Before the National Convention, Representative Pierre Dubouchet proclaimed, "Nothing is more appropriate than hymns and songs to electrify republican souls." In February 1794, as the Committee of Public Safety decided to subsidize the large-scale publication of songbooks, it defined the role as "to improve the public spirit" and "to excite . . . the courage of the defenders of the Patrie." The Committee praised songs for their moral effect. Dealing with the influence of songs on soldiers, the journal *Rougyff* claimed that song could be "an elementary course in politics and war." Bouchotte did not write at length concerning his idea of the function of song; however, his aide Thomas Rousseau did state his own opinion, "The people still sing much more than they read; I think that the best way to instruct them fruitfully is to present them with a lesson in the attractive form of pleasure."[70] Absent from all this logic is the desire to use song as a warning to soldiers to regard their generals as potential traitors to the Republic. Present to an extent beyond any justification of the distribution of journals is the hope that songs will enhance the ardor and commitment of the troops.

Paramount among the themes of the songs is patriotism—a patriotism manifest in a desire to defend the land, its people, and the liberties they just won. Defense and the sacrifices it demands dominate the literature of political songs. The great hymns, such as the "Marseillaise," "Mourir pour la patrie," and the "Chant du départ," burn with pride and defiance. The "Marseillaise" warns that "tyranny has raised its bloody standard against us" and calls, "To arms, Citizens!" to protect your wives, children, and fields. The "Chant du départ" responds:

> Tremble, enemies of France,
> Kings drunk with blood and pride,
> The sovereign people advance,
> Tyrants, descend into the grave!

Lighter but immensely popular, the "Ca ira!" and the "Carmagnole" carried the same message, without the solemnity.

Lesser songs echoed identical sentiments. "Adieux d'un républicain à sa maîtresse" was first sung on the stage of the Théatre de la République in Paris; then it appeared in patriotic songbooks from Paris and elsewhere. It also was transcribed in a handwritten collection of personal favorites by a soldier serving with the Armée du Nord.

> Receive for a time my adieux
> Oh Louise, my sweet friend.
> I must leave this place
> To go to save my Patrie
> She calls me in the name of the law,
> Can I remain deaf to her voice?

Rousseau's *L'âme du peuple et du soldat* rings with similar resolve, nowhere more than in his "Le cri de mort contre les rois." Will a "godless league of cruel potentates" send the Republic to a "dismal tomb"?

> At this barbarous idea,
> Which seizes us with horror,
> Is not the soul possessed
> By a burning fury?
> In the fire which devours me,
> I rush to the danger,
> Of these brigands who I abhore.
> I burn to avenge myself!

What can be called the patriotic death is a recurrent theme. In these songs death is never too great a price to pay for liberty. As a song published in both the *Journal des hommes libres* and the *Journal de la Montagne* claimed, "My friends, one dies without suffering when one dies for the Patrie."[71]

Although the patriotic theme dominates, the songs go beyond it. Hatred for the enemy, the monarchy, and the aristocracy stand behind the more positive love for the Patrie. Sometimes England seems to be singled out for especially strong condemnation. Songs urge foreign peoples to rise against their rulers. "This is the just war of peoples against kings." Enemy soldiers, often dubbed "slaves," do not constitute the real enemy. Aristocrats stand out as prime opponents of the Revolution and its work: "I hate every proud caste whose rights are so many abuses."[72]

In contrast to hatred for the inequities of the ancien régime stood praise for liberty, equality, and fraternity in the new France. At Lille the people sang:

> Liberty! Receive the hommage,
> Of a people worthy of you;
> Their virtues are your work,
> Their happiness is in your law.

Equality, in many ways a more concrete and meaningful term for the common people, meant the end of domination by the rich as well as by the high born. Rousseau phrased it:

> Too long a vile metal,
> Always fatal,
> Under the reign of tyrants,
> Marked the ranks;
> All men are equal,
> And heroes
> Are those whose virtuous [*sainte*] ways
> Charm our hearts.

Equality meant not only the end of prejudice and frustration; it also meant opportunity.

> By his talents, his knowledge,
> Not by his possessions,
> Every mortal ought to elevate himself.

This message must have resonated with the soldiers, who could now hope for advancement. From liberty and equality it was but a small step to fraternity.

> Children, soldiers, old men, wives, daughters, mothers
> The rich citizen, those who live in shacks,
> All swear, united by fraternity,
> To die for Liberty.[73]

The praise of equality did not reach Hébertist extremes. Hébert's resentment and even hatred of the well-to-do did not color their message. My own search through the song literature has uncovered songs that argue that, despite differences in wealth, citizens remain equal in rights and, ideally, in opportunity; they do not demand that the rich relinquish all their goods or that the rich are by nature corrupt. Hébert himself did not include songs in the *Père Duchesne,* but if his taste in song is indicated by his enthusiastic support of one sung at the General Council of the Commune on 18 September 1793, he was partial to a heavy dose of patriotism laced with self-sacrifice.[74]

There were other themes also worthy of mention. Songs reminded the soldier that he was still a citizen. Some verses praised discipline, and some begged him to respect the poor he encountered on campaign. A recurrent tactical theme stressed French skill with the bayonet and the pike. On a more philosophical level, the Supreme Being received praise, as did the cult of reason.[75]

Not all songs sung by the troops dealt with patriotism and civic virtue. Although it is next to impossible to know how frequently patriotic songs were sung, as opposed to songs about wine or women, one soldier's handwritten songbook gives some indication. The soldier's name was Joseph Tondeur, and he fought with the Nord during 1793. Throughout his long years of service, from 1793 to 1801, he kept a *livre de route,* in which he cryptically noted where he was on a particular date. In the back of this *livre* he wrote the verses to songs that pleased him. This valuable songbook provides a perhaps unique glimpse at the popularity of songs at the front. Of the hundred or so songs it contained, about 50 percent were romances, a few were drinking songs, and rest, about 40 percent, were patriotic and military, and some of the military songs had no political content.[76] All that can be stated with certainty from these figures is that soldiers did not exist on a steady diet of undiluted republicanism. Few of the patriotic songs he collected seem to have appeared in any songbook, suggesting the possibility that the men composed their own songs or brought with them little-known songs from home.

Running through the soldiers' songs as a whole is praise for the men's efforts and accomplishments. In the ideal world of songs high standards are set, but the troops meet them. Again the soldier stands as the model *sans-culotte;* in fact, the two images merge. Not just a soldier of France, but the defender of liberty, he is invincible.

> A soldier of Liberty
> When he is exaulted by it,
> Is worth more than a hundred slaves.

The soldier's sacrifices are seen as selfless and ennobling.

> Your blood spilled for the Patrie,
> It spilled for liberty;
> The blow which cut down your life,
> Raised you to immortality.[77]

Even when songs did not address the soldier directly, they justified him. Implied in all rantings against the inequities of the past and the enemies of the present and permeating the patriotic rhetoric is the justice of the Republic's cause and the virtue of those who take up her defense.

Revolutionary Fêtes

In 1793 and 1794 the soldier continued to participate in revolutionary ceremonies and celebrations or *fêtes*. Like song, they appealed to the emotions. *Fêtes* reaffirmed and inspired, rather than considered and convinced. Ceremonies typically involved processions, symbols, and songs, while patriotic orations and oaths often added to the solemn impact. *Fêtes* continued to be part of the raising and departure of troops. Jean-Paul Bertaud suggests that with conscription and the resultant incidence of draft evasion, such ceremonies may have taken on the additional purpose of stating the community's validation of forced recruitment. In any case, "their pattern was well designed to touch popular feelings and to shape collective psychology."[78]

In the camps and garrisons of the Armée du Nord the greatest ceremonies of 1793 came in mid-summer; the first involved the acceptance of the new Constitution; and the second celebrated the Festival of Unity held on the anniversary of the fall of the monarchy. In early July troops of the Armée du Nord assembled in their various camps and quarters to hear the Constitution read, to approve it, and to swear loyalty. The garrison of Cambrai took the oath on 7 July; the commanding general described the ceremony as follows:

> As stipulated by the constitutional authorities, yesterday I ordered all the garrison to present itself at the Place d'armes at 10 A.M. sharp, turned out in their best. I took myself to the city hall where I found the Representatives on Mission . . . , the members of the district directory, and the council of the commune completely assembled. I informed these citizens that the defenders of the Republic awaited with impatience the proclamation of the great work which had established the happiness of the Republic. . . .
>
> It is necessary to be a republican to fully grasp the effect which was produced by the entrance of this cortege into the center of the troops drawn up in a square. One could see that during the reading these brave soldiers could hardly contain themselves from interrupting the reading to applaud. How touching it was to see these warriors hold themselves back out of respect, desiring the moment when they would be able to burst out with their satisfaction. And how happier still it was to be a witness to the shouts and cries of "Vive la République, one and indivisible," "Vive la Constitution" which rang out at the end of this proclamation. On the spot I began to sing the "Marseillaise"; I can think of nothing to compare with the rapidity with which the song could be heard on all sides, with an electrifying effect. All the songs, all the patriotic airs, then followed; and it was only after two hours of republican joy that the troops' enthusiasm gave way.
>
> That evening there were fireworks, and members of the garrison celebrated their own little civic *fêtes*.[79]

These *petites fêtes civiques* of the evening could have been fueled by more than patriotic ecstasy. Bricard reports that at the Camp de César the men were given ten sous each "to drink to the health of the Republic." Celliez in another note filled in one more detail of the ceremony at Cambrai; the Constitution "was proclaimed yesterday to the garrison . . . , and all the soldiers swore to die to defend it."[80] The Constitution was to be the cornerstone of the new Republic, and its establishment became a tangible war aim; therefore, the *fêtes* honoring that document were especially significant.

Only a month later revolutionary France celebrated the Festival of the Unity and Indivisibility of the Republic, the Fête de l'unité. After the Convention decreed this celebration, Bouchotte turned his attention to the form it might take among the troops. "It seems to me that a march, without arms by all the troops of the same camp or garrison, emblems of Liberty and equality, some others which restate our feeling of hatred for tyrants, some music, military and patriotic songs, and revolutionary printed material distributed in large quantities, could put spirits in a proper and happy disposition." The order issued by the headquarters of the Armée du Nord detailing the ceremony stipulated that the troops would swear the following oath after standing at arms in front of their encampments: "We swear to live free or to die; to maintain liberty, equality, and the unity and indivisibility of the Republic; and to defend with all our power, the Constitution which will be accepted by the French Nation." Bricard's memoir states that the celebration in his camp near Vitry followed the pattern laid down in this order. Troops at Carignan heard a *Te Deum* sung by a priest; one citizen Arnould then delivered a patriotic oration in which he declared, "The sentiment which this civic *fête* ought to inspire in us is to make us appreciate the joy of being a free people. Its goal is to inflame our ardor and its result is in making us rush on to victory." In the rear echelon garrison of Abbéville, the day's ceremony united soldiers and citizens who danced the Carmagnole, "forming circles . . . while singing civic songs." That evening brought another and more lively celebration. After singing the "Marseillaise," the crowd, which included the troops, the civil authorities, and the political club, sang and danced in the torchlight.[81]

The central government and the Ministry of War decreed and, to some extent, orchestrated these two great *fêtes* of 1793. But smaller celebrations and ceremonies were undertaken much more by local initiative. At Abbéville, for example, no less than nine civic ceremonies or celebrations took place from October 1793 through July 1794. Town administrations, political clubs, and Representatives on Mission could be involved in proposing and conducting such *fêtes*. Bricard described one such ceremony held at Cambrai on 22 October 1793. "Burned there on the Place d'armes were titles of nobility and feudalism, portraits of members of the royal family, of the cardinals, of the bishops, in a word of all the privileged; three English flags were burned as well. This same day was supposed to have been a day of fraternity between soldiers and townspeople, but different alerts hindered that reunion."[82]

Given that *fêtes* inevitably appealed to fraternity and unity, sectarian symbolism or bitter polemics would have been out of place. Celebrated were those concepts and institutions that already enjoyed nearly universal acceptance or at least were widely palatable. Patriotism was foremost. Defense against foreign invaders, disdain for privilege and monarchy, and reverence for the new Constitution could hardly be called controversial by mid-1793. The structure of the *fêtes* was not only communal, calling for widespread participation, itself a recognition of equality and fraternity, but also hierarchical. *Fêtes* made clear the authority and structure within the new Republic. Men of power played notable roles or were in some way given particular recognition in the *fêtes,* even if only by the special place they occupied in a procession. And oaths to the Constitution, the very principle and statement of government structure, regularly reminded citizen-soldiers that there was order in the new government to come.

The Popular Societies

After the treason of Dumouriez, political clubs appear to have played a lesser role in the politicization of Armée du Nord than did journals, songs, or *fêtes*. Of these four, clubs were the least subject to centralized direction and standards. The government in Paris devoted relatively little attention to the popular societies as media for indoctrination, except when radical clubs threatened to get out of hand. As a rule, the clubs constitute a better measure of political attitudes within the Nord than they provide examples of a conscious campaign of political education.

Some scholars argue that clubs formed within the battalions. Bertaud cites documentary evidence revealing that the 68th Regiment, both of whose battalions served in the Nord, affiliated its club with the Jacobins of Paris.[83] However, a search of the general correspondence of the Armée du Nord and soldiers' letters, journals, and memoirs has provided no evidence concerning such battalion clubs. At best, there could not have been many in the Nord. What clubs did exist did not seem to be worthy of comment.

The town clubs, however, demand attention. Every town of any significance boasted at least one popular society. The most important functions of these clubs vis-à-vis the army were surveillance and political education, and the former seems to have been more important than the latter. The Ministry of War utilized the clubs as patriotic observers. Their condemnation of an officer could lead to that man's being cashiered or arrested;

an endorsement by a club, often formalized in a certificate of civism, was a valuable prerequisite for advancement. During the purges of suspect officers the powers of the popular societies could be awesome. Elie Lacoste, a Representative on Mission at Arras in September 1793, gave commissioners chosen by the popular societies the right to discharge or arrest suspect officers. Soldiers continued to use popular societies as a forum to denounce their commanders.[84]

Bouchotte openly spoke of the clubs as important elements in the patriotic formula. He encouraged his agents to strengthen them, and he felt soldiers ought to attend them. After hearing that public spirit was weak in Landrecies, Bouchotte recommended that the commandant "invite some good patriots to attend meetings of the popular society; go there yourself every time your duties permit; that is the real way to rekindle spirits." Elsewhere he inquired to make sure that *militaires* had free access to meetings. "Write to the popular society in order to make certain if the commandment of the fortress keeps soldiers from going to the society."[85]

There is good cause to argue that Bouchotte's interest in popular societies transcended his concern for the political education of the troops. He was very much a political animal maintained in office by his ties with Jacobins and Cordeliers. As such, he wisely chose to maintain the best relations with the clubs. As one critic charged, "The Minister of War is only a mannequin who does nothing by himself. He takes advice only from the clubs."[86] His sympathy for the popular societies cannot be denied, but did the soldiers attend their sessions?

The best indication is that the life of the clubs involved only a very small percentage of troops along the northeastern frontier. For many soldiers participation in the popular societies would have been impossible. Although the front stabilized during the summer of 1793, training exercises ate up the soldier's time and energy, while campaigning, with its constant movements and skirmishes, made regular club attendance virtually impossible for all but garrison troops. The main body of the Nord changed venue several times between April and October. Not until it went into winter quarters would the Nord enjoy a measure of stability and repose. Even then, much of the army, particularly along the Sambre, engaged in constant small-scale actions.

To the extent that soldiers of the Nord joined or attended clubs, they did so by attaching themselves to the societies already set up in garrison towns. With the exception of one brief period, men in uniform never swamped the civilian membership of a club, even in an important garrison town like Lille. In the period 1790–95 the total membership of the Lille club amounted to 1,092, of which 179 listed their occupation as military officers and seventy-seven as soldiers. Turnover meant that at no one time did membership approach 1,000. Perhaps half that figure would be closer to a realistic estimate for peak membership at any given time.[87] Forces stationed in and around Lille numbered about forty battalions, or upward of 30,000 men by the late winter. The percentage of this total who belonged to the club could only have been minuscule. It is true that soldiers who were not members might attend meetings, but even a handful of participants from each battalion would have cramped a good-sized meeting hall. Those who attended meetings did not always conduct themselves in a decorous manner; to some, it may have just been a good show. An irate letter from General Jean Eblé complained that after he had granted artillerymen time in the evenings to attend club meetings, their behavior at those meetings was unacceptably disrespectful and rowdy.[88]

The popular societies in the departments of the Pas-de-Calais and of the Nord appear to have been fairly quiet and passive until the fall of 1793. In a report delivered to the Executive Council in August Hébertist General Charles-Philippe Ronsin wrote that they were, "with the exception of that in Arras, without the least influence." However, the late fall and winter of 1793–94 witnessed considerable turmoil in the clubs along the frontier defended by the Armée du Nord. At the head of the extremists who brought on this brief but highly charged period of controversy stood prominent military officers. Men in uniform packed several clubs and dominated their executive committees; Cambrai illustrates the phenomenon. The club had been something of a thorn in Custine's side during the summer of 1793, when it was composed primarily of townsmen. But as one official described it, "Since the end of October I saw intrigue at work at Cambrai, without being able to know its authors. Certain military officers assiduously attended the meetings of the popular society, and soon its executive [*bureau*] was in part composed of them."[89]

This movement of military men into the clubs had its greatest impact in Lille. During the summer of 1793 the comte de Lamarlière, the military commander of Lille, had been denounced for having "no relations with the popular society," and he did not remain in command for long. A series of clashes pitted him against another general, a political radical named Louis Lavalette, and his aide Simon Dufresse. After temporary setbacks Lavalette and Dufresse emerged triumphant. Lavalette won command of the garrison, and Dufresse rose in the ranks of the Jacobins. With the support of Representatives on Mission Jacques Isoré and Pierre Châles, they drove out moderates and dominated in the club; "the popular society of Lille has left the torpor in which moderantism had plunged it."[90]

In late October the popular society, now presided over by Dufresse, voted to create an *armée révolutionnaire*. Patterned after the *armée révolutionnaire* of Paris, it was organized and armed much like the army of the Republic, but this revolutionary army had nothing to do with the defense of the frontiers. It was wholly composed of revolutionary militants, and its primary duty centered on securing food for the major towns. In fact, it conducted a kind of political war against moderates. Centered at Lille, the *armée révolutionnaire* also had units at Cambrai, Donai, and Bailleul, where "the club was almost military and directed by a detachment of the revolutionary army of which Lavalette is the head. This detachment practically spoke only of death and of the guillotine, and this without any discretion." When a detachment reached Dunkirk, Brault wrote that he saw "the revolutionary army followed by three guillotines. The doors of the city were closed to all the townspeople. Beware to those who refuse to conform to the law, the guillotine awaits them!"[91]

Officers from the Armée du Nord played a crucial role in the radicalization of clubs at Lille, Cassel, Bailleul, and Cambrai. However, their participation demonstrates the influence of certain army men over the local clubs; it does not really demonstrate an influence of the clubs over the Nord. Richard Cobb, in his classic study of the *armées révolutionnaires,* pointed to the sort of military men who radicalized the clubs and established the revolutionary army. He described the Lille club as "completely dominated by a group of Parisians" and spoke of new leadership as "foreigners" who "colonized" the political life of Lille.[92]

The uniformed militants of the popular societies and of the revolutionary army soon felt the strong and disapproving hand of the Committee of Public Safety, which viewed them as too radical and too chaotic. From the onset, Robespierre had been uneasy about the revolutionary army at Lille and aimed at its elimination. His agents in this affair were Representatives on Mission Florent Guiot and Charles Hentz. On 4 December, only a month after the creation of the revolutionary army at Lille, the Convention abolished revolutionary armies, save that of Paris. On 12 December Guiot and Hentz purged the popular society of Lille. The next day Lavalette and Dufresse were arrested, and the *armée révolutionnaire* was formally disbanded. In February, Guiot could report: "The popular society, which is no longer composed of men of two epaulettes [officers], but of *sans-culottes* and citizens in workers' smocks [*tabliers*], occupies itself with things of importance to the public welfare, notably in helping the defenders of the Patrie, in keeping an eye on the wastefulness of military administration, and in extinguishing ... the last sparks of superstition and fanaticism."[93]

In important towns on the southern flank of the Nord popular societies also came under the influence of soldiers, but did not cause the authorities much concern until after the crisis in Lille. As early as November Etienne Brouard wrote to Sijas claiming that the Maubeuge society was composed primarily of soldiers. Claude Vézu, the local commander, struggled to win influence in this society and apparently succeeded in dominating it by the end of December, but Vézu was no radical in the mold of Lavalette. Vézu would lose his command for a time, though not his head. The popular society of Sedan became a lever by which General Michel-François de Sistrières sought to elevate himself to command of the Armée des Ardennes. Representative on Mission Pierre Gillet reported Sistrières's method of forming his own party; "his chief of staff, his aides de camp, and his adjutants were the first orators in the Committees of Surveillance and the popular societies."[94] Gillet successfully recommended the replacement of Sistrières. As in the case of Maubeuge, the conflict of Sedan seems to have involved ambition and power more than radicalism.

In all this activity of the popular societies, their greatest influence on the troops was probably to reassert that the new state would be based on the active participation of all of its citizens. This is speculation, to be sure, but the clubs constantly reminded soldiers of popular support for and involvement in the Revolution. This reminder could affect the soldier, even if he never set foot in the political club of a garrison town.

Other Media

Beyond the journals, songs, *fêtes,* and clubs lay a miscellany of lesser contributions to the political education of the army. They make the modern reader aware that troops lived in a politically charged environment, in which the ideology, terminology, and symbolism of the Revolution constantly confronted the soldier.

Revolutionary theater employed the arts to instruct and convince. It could be argued that the greatest revolutionary stage performances were the *fêtes*, often operatic in their melding of the visual and musical arts with drama. Revolutionary plays never rivaled song as the ultimate popular art form, but dramas devoted to the work and ideals of the Revolution made their way to the front. Garrison towns along the northeastern frontier boasted theaters that presented plays with republican titles such as *Fraud and Liberty, The Defeated Aristocrat,* and *Democracy.* Those who chose to invest the time and money could attend. Some soldiers certainly did, but the cost kept theater from being a medium for mass consumption. Bouchotte purchased and distributed 6,000 copies of one play to the army. Entitled *The Last Judgement of the Kings,* this one act piece came from the prolific pen of Sylvain Maréchal, a man of letters who wrote almanacs, songs, and plays. The play went out to the armies in December 1793. If and when it was presented in the Nord remains unknown. Representatives on Mission with the Nord encouraged the revolutionary theater. Pierre Bentabole and Réné Levasseur wrote from Lille in August 1793: "The spirit of the towns has attracted our attention. The theater, that school of morals, is an essential branch of that spirit. Lille's theater, finding itself unable to advance the sum of two thousand livres that author of *Gaius Gracchus* demands before his play may be given there, and equally unable to pay a lesser sum which the author of *Robert, Chief of the Brigands* requires, we have authorized the theater to give these two plays, stipulating that the nation pay the indemnities due the authors of these plays, which the public good requires to be performed." At Cambrai, Le Bon surpassed his colleagues in Lille. He brought with him his own actors, which he called the "Revolutionary Troop."[95]

The soldier need not go to a theater to realize that words and speech had taken on a revolutionary aura. Passwords set out in orders of the day reminded him of the great moments and the great heroes of the Revolution; sometimes they consisted of entire revolutionary slogans. Many of the nicknames that so pleased French soldiers in the eighteenth century had changed character during the first years of the Revolution. Troopers still carried such incongruous names as "Belle-Fleur," but they were joined by men called "Liberty" or "Equality."[96]

In a similar manner items of apparel became symbols of considerable magnitude. In so far as physical symbols made the soldiers aware of the new Republic they defended, they were part of their political education. The tricolor cockade was to be worn at all times. Failure to display it brought official reprimand upon privates and officers alike. The matter of dress that most concerned the authorities was the continued wearing of white uniform coats by officers of line infantry. White not only was the traditional color of the French army; it was also the Bourbon color. In this case the color of their coats was thought to mirror the color of their politics. Since the Convention feared royalist officers, it insisted that men in command wear the new national uniform of blue to express their loyalty to the nation. After the coats it came down to the buttons. The old buttons were stamped with the fleur de lys, and some officers sewed them on their new coats. An order of 21 August 1793 expressly commanded line officers to buy new buttons emblazoned with the words *République française*. Of course, flags also were to be altered to eliminate emblems of the ancien régime.[97]

The *amalgame*, too, can be regarded as an aspect of political education, in that it aimed at altering the attitudes of one part of the French armies. Contemporaries generally conceded that line battalions surpassed volunteers in discipline and drill, but at the same time the political reliability of the regulars came into question. It was feared that they retained royalist sympathies, or were at least more likely to follow royalist officers. As one volunteer commented in a letter of 5 April 1792, the day Dumouriez crossed over to the Austrians, "The line troops and cavalry share Dumouriez's opinions, but they will be enlightened." One way to "enlighten" the line would be to submerge it in superior numbers of patriotic volunteers. Edmund Dubois-Crancé, a key legislative figure behind the *amalgame*, listed as one of its prime benefits its potential to "generalize the republican spirit," since the line troops "did not always have patriotism for their guide."[98] The primary goal of political education was to guarantee an army loyal to the new Republic. Other rationales lay behind the *amalgame,* but the promised impact on the climate of opinion among regulars was a strong argument in its favor.

The Impact of Political Education

After describing the mechanism and messages of political education in the Armée du Nord, the ultimate question remains. What was the impact of this campaign? In the absence of modern testing procedures, a true measurement of that impact is impossible. All that can be done is to hazard an estimate based more on insights and impressions than on hard evidence.

The government's program of political indoctrination within the army must be put into context before its effects can be reasonably gauged. In the broadest sense political education of the troops involved far more than the circulation of printed materials by the Ministry of War or the Committee of Public Safety. Conditions and events did much more to form the climate of opinion among French troops than did journals and songs; reality taught with greater authority than did these polemics. In fact, for revolutionary propaganda to exert its maximum impact, it had to reflect, or at least not conflict with, the realities that the soldier already knew. Besides, the campaign of political education exerted its impact on the troops for a relatively short period, in the case of a conscript of 1793, less than nine months. This campaign might sway him, but it could not transform him.

The volunteers and conscripts of the French army came of age in the ancien régime and suffered its inequities. They saw the Revolution change their society, state, and army, and the benefits of this transformation were manifest. The following words of a battalion commander owe their force not to clever persuasion but to their blunt evocation of a hated past. "Born in the villages, we have known the horrors of the feudal regime far better than have the townsmen. We were the serfs [*villains*]. Eh! We have taught our former masters well that the serfs, the *sans-culottes,* will no longer let their harvests be eaten by rabbits and will no longer pay feudal dues [*dimes*]." Revolutionary journals and songs picked up these themes. Materials directed at the army also emphasized the sharp differences between the life of the soldier before and after the Revolution. "French soldiers, with a King comes the aristocracy, and with the aristocracy comes a contempt for the common soldier and the end of promotions; the soldier can become a corporal or a sergeant . . . but nothing more. He has no right to complain; he is created only to obey, never to command."[99] These appeals could convince men because the conditions surrounding them in the new army were in such sharp contrast with a past that they knew firsthand or through the stories of veterans. Promotion by merit from the ranks was a far more compelling lesson in equality and equity than were wall posters. So, too, the purge of suspect officers and the rigor of revolutionary justice were important elements in the political education of the army.

The necessity for self-defense was also obvious before a conscious program of political education focused attention on it. As the French people erected a better and more hopeful society, their crowned enemies invaded the homeland. From the soldier's point of view, war had been forced on France, and he knew he had much to defend. The *Soirée de camp* could justly claim, "Free men fight for themselves, in order to defend their rights, their property, their wives, and their children." Soldiers who observed the brutality of war knew the fate that threatened their families. As Sergeant Alexandre Brault reported: "Before we had arrived here, the enemy had stripped the country, so that we could find nothing, they had beaten the poor peasants whom they had seen wearing tricolor cockades, torn down the liberty tree, taken off the constitutional priests."[100]

There is a temptation to equate the struggle of these French soldiers to throw back their counterrevolutionary enemies with the struggle of present-day guerrillas fighting wars of national liberation. The parallel is a weak one. In 1792–94 the revolutionary soldier was fighting to defend his Patrie and to preserve the solid gains of the Revolution. He fought to prevent the reimposition of an unacceptable past. Today's guerrilla usually fights to seize his own country so that he may create a new and better system as yet only imagined. The French soldier could understand the evils of the past and the improvements of the present without extensive political education. He needed only to remember the past and to celebrate his present. The modern guerrilla, if he is to rise above the level of a bandit, must be educated and indoctrinated to see a future still over the horizon.

To say that personal experience and involvement were the strongest persuaders is not to deny all importance to propaganda. What can be said of the potential influence of this political education campaign? It was probably most effective at accomplishing the tasks set for it by the Committee of Public Safety and the Ministry of War. It insured that the troops understood to which authorities and institutions their ultimate loyalties belonged. The campaign guaranteed that soldiers heard an account of events acceptable to the government. And it increased troop suspicion of their own officers and willingness to reject beforehand any appeal by their commanders to act against the Convention or its committees. Official indoctrination almost certainly raised combat motivation among the troops, fostering patriotism by reaffirming a sense of purpose and by assuring the soldier that his efforts were appreciated by the French people.

The institutions of government and the interplay of factions were in continual flux from the creation of the Armée du Nord to well beyond the fall of Robespierre. Somehow the troops who fought to defend revolutionary France had to keep pace with the developments in Paris. Many of the troops who comprised the Nord had left for the front before the Convention began its meetings or the Committee of Public Safety rose to prominence. Political education was vital, since the troops could not possibly know at first hand the ins-and-outs of the ever-changing political collage in Paris and in the provinces. A Revolution that depended on a sense of participation to energize public spirit could hardly afford to leave its troops in the dark. More to the point, the government greatly feared that the troops might be misguided by generals who would use them to subvert the Revolution and its government. In order for soldiers to recognize where they ought to place their loyalty, they must be told of the work of the Convention, its committees, the Executive Council, and the Ministry of War. So that officers could not deceive and distort, explanations the government approved as correct and just must reach the troops. Speaking of their labors with the Nord in early June, two *commissaires* assured Bouchotte, "We have perfectly attained the goal that we set for ourselves. They now think in the army like they do in Paris; they reason the same."[101]

Some authors argue that the effort to increase the political awareness of the armies embroiled the troops in the struggle between revolutionary factions in Paris. Journals, and perhaps songs, became weapons in a battle for the allegiance or sympathies of the men in the ranks. But seen from the perspective of field soldiers, far removed from the political turmoils of the capital, the message of the journals and songs must have appeared fairly uniform. It condemned aristocracy, monarchy, federalism, the Vendée rebellion, and Girondists, while it praised liberty, equality, fraternity, patriotism, self-sacrifice, and loyalty to the Convention. These tenets were shared by all the major parties in France after 2 June 1793 and would have been equally acceptable to a range of political sympathies from moderate Jacobin to radical Hébertists. Only in town Jacobin clubs during the winter of 1793–94 is there evidence that some men of the Armée du Nord became caught up in centralist/Jacobin versus participatory/Hébertist controversy. Clear party prejudices seemed only to come into play when journals were used to justify the fall of a faction after the event, as the dominant majority sought to defend its actions.

Well within the range of what the Paris government could successfully transmit to the armies were her fears of the Revolution's internal enemies. Federalism and fanaticism were held up for scorn, and, most important, political education encouraged the soldiers to examine the civism and patriotism of their officers. Propaganda helped to free troops to challenge or denounce their officers and to prepare the rank and file to support the purge of suspect commanders. Uneasiness toward officers, particularly former nobles, played into the anxiety over an aristocratic conspiracy against the Revolution—a fear alive since 1789. This propaganda had as its ultimate goal to alert men against the potential treason of their generals. The questionable attacks made on some unlucky individuals were rooted in real threats posed by Lafayette and Dumouriez. The campaign of indoctrination probably made its point here, although no new Dumouriez arose to put it to the test. Not until several years later would the army intervene in internal politics, and by then things were very different.

Appeals made to patriotism, though the most difficult to gauge, cannot be dismissed as unnecessary or ineffective. Only history could forge the patriotic sword, but propaganda could sharpen it. Journals, and particularly songs, lavished more attention on patriotism than on any other theme. To a large degree, this patriotic rhetoric preached to the saved, but it still had value. Volunteer enlistments insured that patriotic sentiments would already be deeply rooted in the line regiments and in the battalions of volunteers. However, it is possible to argue that conscription diluted the native patriotism of the troops. Articles with a strong patriotic motif could support the sentiments of men in the field. The taking of a solemn oath or the singing of an inspiring song could reinforce a commitment. How much is impossible to know, but contemporaries clearly believed that propaganda could enhance feelings of patriotism. One proponent of songs had such confidence in their impact that he suggested the addition of four singers to each battalion. "The 'Marseillaise' enlightens, inspires, and cheers at the same time; it would be enough to subjugate the entire youth of Brabant." Representative on Mission Guiot even insisted that "one hundred thousand *écus* spent on revolutionary papers can save a hundred thousand patriots and five or six hundred million [*écus*]."[102]

There is another crucial impact of political education that must have influenced commitment and troop motivation. As already stated with regard to journals and songs, the campaign linked the troops to the government and the people. In subtle and direct ways political education continuously expressed the nation's respect for the soldier and his efforts. Without that recognition the soldier could have come to see himself as a victim and not as a hero. With it his trials became more a source of pride than of resentment. To the extent that troop motivation depends on the belief of the rank and file that its sacrifices and victories are appreciated, there is every reason to argue that the propaganda campaign contributed to the high combat effectiveness of the Armée du Nord.

Chapter 7

The *Ordinaire* and Motivation

THE QUESTION of troop motivation is central to any discussion of the revolutionary citizen-soldier. Forty years of research into combat effectiveness have established the paramount influence of the small group upon such motivation. Primary group cohesion is the most immediate, some have argued the dominant, element in the variety of forces that bind the individual to his duty. In this chapter a study of the primary group concludes with observations on motivation among the battalions of the First Republic.

As explained in Chapter 2, primary group cohesion receives virtually universal recognition as the sine qua non of combat performance. The character of that cohesion, however, still excites debate. Some insist that the structure of the group deserves the greater attention, while others argue that the standards established by the group determine the impact of the group on combat effectiveness. Considerably simplified, the controversy is over the degree to which the small group is the influence itself, and the degree to which it is a theater for the interplay of other influences.

Here, the structures and practices of the group will be weighed against its relationships and standards. The *ordinaire*, a mess group made up of individuals from the same combat squad or section, stands out as the obvious small group in the French army. As defined by regulations, the structures and practices of the *ordinaire* dated back at least to the mid-eighteenth century. It would be impossible to account for the contrast between the lackluster record of French troops during the late ancien régime and their triumphs under the Revolution solely in terms of the form of the *ordinaire*. On the other hand, there is good reason to argue that the Revolution, by altering the relationships and particularly the standards of performance within the *ordinaire*, brought great consequences.

The influences that contributed to troop motivation flowed through the *ordinaire*. To deny this would be to deny an overwhelming body of social science research. However, the physical presence of the *ordinaire* itself cannot adequately explain motivation. A comprehensive analysis must take into account matters discussed in the previous chapters of this work—the composition of the rank and file, the character of their officers, the nature of discipline, the climate of patriotic and political opinion, and the expression of public support for the army. These elements united with and through the influence of the *ordinaire*, forging a sense of commitment, even an enthusiasm, toward the goals of the war effort.

The *Ordinaire*: Structures and Practices

French regulations decreed that the soldier would live and fight surrounded by the primary group. As far as possible, the *ordinaire* was to be composed of men from the same squad or section, that is a half-company. The 24 June 1792 *Règlement concernant le service intérieur de l'infanterie* set the *ordinaire* at fourteen or sixteen men, a size to be maintained in any circumstances. At that time fusilier squads of volunteer battalions included fourteen soldiers, while similar squads from regular infantry battalions numbered sixteen. Therefore, when battalions were at full strength, the *ordinaire* and the squad were identical. Attrition could be expected to bring some reshuffling of men to keep the *ordinaires* at full strength, but even if squads were combined in the *ordinaire* they were still to come from the same section. In the infantry a corporal was to head both the *ordinaire* and the squad, and again, at full strength, there would be as many *ordinaires*, and squads, as there were corporals. Cavalry squads were somewhat larger than infantry squads and were headed by a *brigadier*; artillery squads included sixteen soldiers led by a corporal. Later reorganizations increased the sizes of infantry battalions and cavalry squadrons; however, the number of men in the *ordinaire* and squad remained constant.[1]

Soldiers were to procure, prepare, and eat their meals as an *ordinaire*. In garrisons, where troops received regular payments to purchase food, this function was administered through the *ordinaire*. In infantry *ordinaires* the duty of shopping fell to the corporal, who would also keep proper accounts. If the corporal did not have the capacity to administer the *ordinaire* properly, another man could be detailed to handle its funds and keep its books. In encampments, where the army supplied food directly to the soldiers, the men were to march off to distributions by squads or *ordinaires*. Their individual rations, each carried back in a standard cloth distribution bag, would then be put in a common pot.[2] In some circumstances a certain number of men per squad were to be detailed to get the food for the whole *ordinaire*. When encamped, water and wood for the entire *ordinaire* would be fetched by just a few men. Meals would be eaten at 10 A.M. and again at 4 or 5 P.M., according to regulations. Soup, or what could be called stew, was the staple of the *ordinaire* diet. The task of preparing it rotated among all the members of the *ordinaire*, except the corporal. A properly equipped *ordinaire* was to have a cooking pot, a *marmite*, large enough to cook for as many as sixteen men.[3]

The *ordinaire* could be quartered on the civilian population, camped together in tents, or lodged in barracks. When quartered, *en cantonnements*, the *ordinaire* was to be broken up to suit the accommodations available in the town or village. Ease of administration and supervision required that men from one *ordinaire* concentrate as closely as possible to their own corporal. In encampments an infantry *ordinaire* with the most modern equipment would sleep together in a large tent capable of sheltering sixteen men. Some smaller, old tents half the size of the new models were still in use in 1792; regulations allotted an *ordinaire* two of these tents.[4] The men slept on straw, which was to be distributed by *ordinaire*. Regulations required an orderly camp of a standard pattern in which each company, section, and *ordinaire* occupied a particular spot. There was even a regular place for washerwomen to pitch their tents, and these women were to be hired by the *ordinaire* to wash its linen. During the campaign season encamping was much preferred over quartering. During winter the severity of the weather rendered tents inadequate, and barracks of *cantonnements* were preferred.

In combat the infantry *ordinaire* became part of the section. For maneuver and combat each bataillon was broken up into companies, the number of which varied according to the kind of battalion, the period of time in question, and the particular circumstances. In 1792 a regular line infantry battalion could have as few as eight or as many as ten companies. Single companies at times played a combat role, particularly as skirmishers, but in most full-scale actions, the battalion itself was the basic combat unit, fighting and maneuvering as a whole. Each company was subdivided into two half-companies, called sections in line infantry, and sometimes called *pelotons* in volunteer battalions. The first section stood on the right of the company, the second on the left. In the normal three-rank line, the corporals stood on the extreme right of each rank in the first section and on the extreme left of each rank in the second section. Consequently, it would appear that each squad formed a rank in the section. Men of the *ordinaire* were thus to fight side by side in squad or section. Should a company disperse to fight as skirmishers, it is to be assumed that the squads and sections were still to act as units rather than disintegrating into individuals; however, it is very hard to know exactly how French skirmishers fought, since no formal instructions were written for them. Cavalry squadrons of roughly 145 men were divided into four subdivisions, each composed of two squads. Artillery squads became gun crews for one or two field guns, depending on caliber.[5]

It is legitimate to ask if the *ordinaire* as set down in the regulations existed in reality. Unprecedented national crisis, coupled with supply shortages and the influx of inexperienced troops, created a situation in which improvisation and innovation altered many established military practices. However, it is clear that commanders of the Armée du Nord labored to follow regulations. Officers received copies of them. The order of the day issued from headquarters at Valenciennes on 22 April 1793, for example, announced, "Each field grade officer will receive with this order a *Règlement du service de campagne*. They will want to conform to it scrupulously." A few weeks later, headquarters ordered all officers to obtain and study the field service manual for infantry.[6]

Since the *ordinaire* required certain equipment in order to live in the field according to regulations, a lack of these items could have profoundly altered the *ordinaire* and its practices. Shortages of nearly every manner of supply constantly plagued the Armée du Nord, and without proper equipment men were forced into *cantonnements*. Not only did quartering set limits on the life of the *ordinaire;* it also had dangerous strategic implications. Soldiers dispersed in villages were not as concentrated or mobile as men in camps. General Joseph Souham once wrote, "I am convinced of the principle that our forces consist only in the number of men which are in tents [*sous la toile*]."[7]

The Nord's environment of scarcity was probably least a problem in camping supplies. In 1792 this army seems to have suffered some limited, but not crippling, shortages. From October 1792 to January 1793 it received over 12,000 troop tents and 25,000 *marmites*. Precipitous retreat from the Austrian Netherlands caused inconveniences and shortages, so there were some bitter complaints in the summer of 1793.[8] But among the stacks of demands for needed shoes, clothing, and firearms, there were relatively few for camping equipment. It may not have posed the problems that other items did, since the materials and techniques required to make new camping equipment were more a natural part of the civil economy. The wagons loaded with tents often lagged days behind troops on the march, but in general the soldiers themselves wrote of tents and orderly encampments, and in March 1794 Souham could report, "Camping equipment is not in short supply." It is frequently said in general histories that the revolutionary armies abandoned the comforts thought essential by earlier forces, and tents are included in the list of equipment no longer thought necessary. The fact is that the Nord wanted and used tents and other standard camping supplies.[9]

This logic argues that the real *ordinaire* equaled or approached the *ordinaire* as set down in official regulations. More than ignorance or shortages, the constant fluctuations in unit strength must have been the major stumbling block to the maintenance of stable primary groups. Nonetheless, depleted battalions probably had time to integrate new levies into the *ordinaire* before they again faced the enemy in the field.

After considering the regulations, a study of the letters, diaries, and memoirs of common soldiers adds important human detail to an understanding of the *ordinaire*. Unfortunately, both these sources and the official records of the Armée du Nord provide a disappointingly sparse treatment of the *ordinaire;* perhaps they overlooked it because it was such a commonplace and unexciting reality. What can be found and interpreted in the light of twentieth-century findings concerning primary groups makes possible an estimate of the way in which the structures and practices of the *ordinaire* united the group.

That the men of the *ordinaire* depended on each other for almost every aspect of their welfare forged them into a community of interest even before they entered combat. Members of the *ordinaire* pitched their tent together; during winter quarters, or when tents were not available, they might construct a hut or barrack for the group.[10] Securing provisions, preparing food, and eating meals as a group also served to bind the *ordinaire* together. On campaign distributions went to the common store, and, when supplies were meager and men had to forage, such supplies must also have gone to maintain the *ordinaire*. Rotating the cooking chores meant that men served and were served by their fellows, creating subtle bonds of intimacy and obligation. One such soldier, Gabriel Noël, wrote that although he could have hired a substitute he felt it was important that he himself should do the "dirty and bothersome job of being cook." He did it "to set an example, to do this sort of labor with pleasure and good humor." He also boasted, "I have never eaten as good a soup as that which I made." Mealtime went as much as possible according to regulations, although campaign emergencies might force the men to drown their fires with their soup before it was finished. *Ordinaires* might develop their own customs, such as "greasing the *marmite*," as described by Gervais, when a new man was expected to buy *eau de vie* so that his new companions could have a drink on him. Eating *à la gamelle,* with mess tins around the *marmite,* could be a time of fellowship.[11]

Enduring the hard conditions of army life and fighting off boredom as a group must have drawn men together. Hours of drill in squad and section, manipulating heavy fusils through elaborate exercises, and long marches on ill-shod feet, while carrying heavy loads, exhausted men. Sleeping on the hard ground with straw as a mattress and a thin blanket or coat for warmth was never sumptuous, and rain made it dreadful. Despite precautions, tent floors became wet and muddy. Tents provided little protection from the cold. What solace and understanding life offered these troops came from the group, just as it has in wars since. Who else could they turn to? Noël described his fellows' reactions to dreary days in camp: "Instead of complaining in the tent when it rains, all of us sing together as loud as we can; this makes a noise to drive the clouds away."[12] The unifying effect of song was probably felt more in the *ordinaire* than at any other level.

During the public, obligatory reading of political journals or addresses, men probably stood together by company and *ordinaire*. As copies were passed around, they were probably read within the *ordinaire*, the literate men reading aloud to the illiterate. While any estimate of the time devoted to discussing political and patriotic topics remains sheer speculation, one thing seems fairly certain: Since the *ordinaire* consumed so much of the soldier's time and energy, what political discussion there was must have taken place primarily within its circle. In addition, the *ordinaire* must have laid special claim to the political songs that constituted such an important and lively patriotic medium.

Within this *ordinaire* corporals exerted considerable influence. Sergeants lived together in their own *ordinaires*, so the highest ranking NCOs constantly with the men were the corporals. Supposedly more experienced and able than the men below them, corporals trained new recruits. In line battalions, for example, in 1793, 65 percent of the privates had served less than four years, while 53 percent of the corporals claimed seven to twelve years' service. The disparity was certainly less in volunteer battalions. Though senior to his men, the corporal remained close to them, thus becoming the natural focus of the *ordinaire* and a role model for younger men. One corporal who served in 1789 boasted that "finding myself the corporal with the longest service and the head of the *ordinaire*, I had the assurance of being listened to with favor and interest."[13] Integrating senior men within the *ordinaire*, though done to aid command and administration, must also have helped impose military standards of conduct on new soldiers. The full implications of the corporals' pivotal role remain as yet unknown; more must be learned.

French soldiers seemed to have readily formed buddy relationships of two or three men within the *ordinaire*. With its fourteen or more soldiers the *ordinaire* was large for a primary group. Administrative convenience encouraged the large *ordinaire* in the eighteenth century. While the *ordinaire* as a whole is rarely mentioned in letters, diaries, and memoirs, two- or three-man friendships are more commonly described. Brothers, cousins, and friends enrolled together and served alongside one another. Louis Bricard signed up with his brother, and after the brother's death, deserted with two companions to avoid becoming part of Dumouriez's treason. Gervais enlisted with his friend, Tolin, and stayed with him through training. Delaporte writes of going to another bivouac, buying some ham there and sharing it with two comrades; the meat never made its way back to the *ordinaire*.[14] Some desertion records suggest the formation of buddy relationships and small groups within the companies, since men most commonly deserted in pairs or handfuls of comrades; however, this type of record is too rare to allow elaborate comment.[15]

The full richness of life within the *ordinaire* will probably remain hidden to the historian; records are so disappointingly mute concerning the mundane. Certainly the regulations did not box in all of the *ordinaire*'s practices and rituals, and they seem to have developed some of their own customs. Still, reading the available material leads me to conclude that the structures and practices of the *ordinaire* were extremely well fashioned to sustain French soldiers.

Although the *ordinaire*'s form lay at the base of its function, the historian who speaks only of its structure can say but little about the higher combat effectiveness of revolutionary troops as opposed to the less distinguished conduct of the battalions who served under Louis XV. In fact, the regulations that defined the shape of the *ordinaire* for revolutionary troops derived from those introduced at mid-century, and many of its details were simply copied from the 1778 field service regulation.[16] Yet similarity in structures and practices does not lead to a dead end in this inquiry, since primary group cohesion depends not only on these factors. Most important, the relationships between soldiers within the group and the standards set and enforced by them deserve attention.

The *Ordinaire:* Relationships and Standards

The study of relationships and standards challenges historians with extremely difficult problems of methods and sources. Even social scientists examining these questions in present-day armies confront serious problems, despite their questionnaires and interviews. Since the dead cannot be interrogated, the quality of evidence available to historians seldom matches the caliber of that generated by sociologists. Yet to abandon the subject because of the circumstantial nature of the evidence seems more cowardly than discrete. The crucial nature of the question demands an answer, even if it must be tentative.

In approaching the matter of relationships, it makes sense to begin with the basic element, the individual soldier. The men who marched behind the tri-color in the years 1792–94 differed sharply from those who stood in the ranks before the Revolution. No longer were they cast-offs of the economic and social systems. As discussed in Chapter 3, her new defenders represented the best young manhood that France could muster. It seems reasonable to suggest that in contrast to the troops who served before 1789, the new soldiers had every reason to value themselves more and set higher standards for their own conduct. Such was Jacques Fricasse, the gainfully employed son of a gardener, who believed himself courageous and able. He concluded that the war would go better for the French if he joined the troops at the front.[17] His naive confidence could not have been rare. Studies of twentieth-century soldiers demonstrate that those who think well of themselves, or expect to perform well, do better than those with low expectations. The new soldiers' positive self-image received further reinforcement from the praise heaped upon them by the French people and their government.

Compared with the armies of Louis XV, a far greater percentage of recruits must have been accustomed to success in their own lives. As they saw other similar men in service, often at their sides, they had every reason to respect their fellows as soldiers and as men and to expect much from them. If relations were indeed built upon mutual respect among men confident of themselves and of their comrades, it is to be expected that these young men would set and maintain high standards of behavior and performance. An army composed of such men would almost certainly have excelled on the battlefield under any commander, fighting for any *acceptable* cause. It could even be argued that the greater significance of French wartime enthusiasm was that it convinced the French people to send their best men to the army, not that it inspired those whom they sent.

This new soldier often fought alongside family and friends who volunteered or were conscripted from the home district. The Armée du Nord itself had a regional character, being drawn mainly from the departments of northeastern France.[18] Within the battalions of the Nord, there is good reason to believe that the regional character of many battalions helped to cement the *ordinaire* and raise performance standards. The royal army had not been a complete stranger to regionalism. Seigneurial recruitment often led a company to reflect a particular locality over others. Foreign regiments had regional identities or at least recruited men from German-speaking areas of France. The tendency for regiments to recruit most successfully along the frontiers gave their areas higher than average representation in the army. But these tendencies are faint in comparison with the regional character of battalions raised by the 1791 and 1792 volunteer levies and by conscription.

The regional focus of revolutionary battalions meant that local networks of family and friendship carried over into military life. Describing the volunteers of his own battalion, a canonneer with the Nord wrote, "Many brought their brothers; others brought their friends." He had volunteered with his brother, and he later reported running across two of his cousins serving together in another unit. Civilian relationships, translated into life in uniform, probably promised the kind of understanding and support a military primary group ought to provide. A Jacobin officer of the Nord argued, "We would like to serve altogether, for when a soldier is known and loved, defeats are less disastrous and successes more flattering." Many of these volunteers were reluctant to serve with strangers. One Volunteer of 1792 reported that when his undersized unit was broken up and incorporated into others at Soissons, "Little satisfied to serve with men whom they had never seen before, many comrades went back to Paris, and several returned to our Department."[19]

Regionalism could be expected to improve unit performance. Regional battalions probably jelled much more quickly than could battalions of strangers. And the social pressure of the battalion and the *ordinaire* must have been intensified by the fact that acts of bravery or cowardice would be reported home and remembered. The moral force of the civilian community was thus called upon to augment the moral force of the military primary group. As one petition from conscripts put it, "The interests of the Republic will only be served with more zeal by those citizens who fight alongside their friends and relatives."[20]

Within units from the same department, district origin seems to have been a significant factor influencing the formation of close relationships. A desertion report dealing with a Pas-de-Calais battalion drawn from two different areas in that department supplies an interesting insight into regionalism.[21] Over fourteen months there were twenty-eight cases in which two or more men deserted the same company on the same day; in all but four cases only men from the same district deserted on the same day.

The regional character of battalions, however, was not an omnipresent and permanent factor in the army of the Republic. Line army battalions were not regionally organized and from mid-1793 on, two practices, amalgamation and incorporation, eroded the regionalism of volunteer battalions. By combining and mixing battalions to create demi-brigades, the *amalgame* destroyed the identity of previous battalions. Although the original battalions were broken up during the *amalgame,* their companies maintained their integrity. However, squads might be adjusted to meet the requirement that each squad combine veterans with recruits. Of more danger to regionalism on the company level was the necessity to incorporate new draftees into established battalions. In one example with the Armée du Nord, a battalion of conscripts from Normandy reached Bouchain in early March 1794; there men were apportioned to three battalions from Paris, Deux-Sèvres, and the Somme.[22] Disbanding and incorporation were necessary; the gains of bringing understrength battalions back up to a full complement far outweighed the losses of polluting their regional purity. We do not know how incorporation affected the *ordinaire.* If volunteers and conscripts from the region generally congregated in *ordinaires,* then many of the benefits of regional units would still be enjoyed by a battalion that had incorporated "foreigners."

While regionalism deserves credit as an important factor in the armies that defended revolutionary France, esprit de corps played only a modest role in morale and motivation during the early years of the war. The term esprit de corps covers a range of attitudes: it can signify confidence and pride in a unit's proven ability; it can also mean an elitism or separatism that sees a unit as superior to and aloof from the rest of the army. While many battalions developed a healthy and natural self-confidence, elitism and separatism seem to have been minimal. In fact, egalitarian republicans expressed a distaste for elite units. They also associated esprit de corps with the potential for counterrevolutionary officers to lead their troops against the government, so revolutionaries discouraged it.[23] Nonetheless, as soldiers invested their efforts in learning difficult skills, enduring harsh conditions, and braving battlefield dangers they came to identify with their units and have pride in them. "No battalion is as good as ours," wrote a boastful recruit. "The more I see others, the more I can say this. . . . There are none which understand the service better than we do, who maintain better discipline or maintain so good an appearance." Proud battalions might even match their skills in contests with one another. The line army probably expressed this side of esprit de corps more than did the volunteers. Revolution did not entirely eliminate the old traditions of the regular army. At the battle of Jemappes line regiments shouted their old battle cries as they charged the Austrian redoubts. Regulars initially believed themselves better than volunteers, and they clashed on occasion. Particular units sometimes developed elite sentiments. Horse artillery, for example, was intensely proud. But by and large esprit de corps seems to have been a reasonable expression of the soldier's natural attachment to his battalion.[24]

As opposed to the particularism of esprit de corps, the troops were encouraged to see themselves as one great family, the relationships between soldiers thus being in accord with revolutionary fraternity. It was a theme throughout the early, heady years of Revolution, as the Christian trilogy gave way to the powerful secular trilogy of liberty, equality, and fraternity. If liberty set the people free, and equality raised them to the same level, fraternity decreed how they were to treat one another. Brotherhood would characterize the new society. It caught the fancy of common folk and political commentators alike and became "the cornerstone of the morality developed by the people." Oratory, newspapers, pamphlets, and the inevitable songs praised this popular ideal.

> Friends, a true Republican
> Ought to love and cherish his brothers.
> . . . .
> The *sans-culotte*, his pike in hand
> Fears not the mercenary hordes.
> He fights like a Republican,
> For the liberty of his brother.[25]

Of course, the notion of soldiers as a band of brothers has a long history. Since revolutionary France extended the concept of brotherhood to the entire society, is it any wonder that this ideal was encouraged and expected among the troops? Those who shaped military policy used the fraternal model as an ideal. "This army," wrote Edmund Dubois-Crancé when praising the Armée du Nord in November 1792, "seems to form but one family of brothers." A year later a circular from the minister of war argued that "our camps . . . ought to be composed only of brothers."[26] In the environment of the Revolution this choice of language was more than a mere figure of speech.

The soldier could not have avoided fraternity as an element of the revolutionary program for the army. Song and ceremony enshrined it in his consciousness. The following verses, meant only for soldiers' voices, are light in tone, but clear in object:

> No coldness, no haughtiness,
> Good nature makes for happiness;
> Yes, without fraternity,
> There is no gaiety.
> Let us eat together in the mess.

This song is particularly interesting, since it refers to life in the *ordinaire,* which is seen here as the setting for fraternity and good fellowship. The *fêtes de la fédération* of 1790 and later stressed fraternity. Smaller local celebrations and miscellaneous minor ceremonies within units also emphasized this sentiment. The ceremony of amalgamation involved oaths pledging fraternity. Sergeant Fricasse described one such ceremony. "[W]e drank the wine of alliance, we swore that fraternity would reign among us unto death; and since we served the same Patrie, we promised to live forever in peace as brothers."[27]

People being what they are, some soldiers acted in anything but brotherly fashion, but it would be excessively cynical to dismiss the talk of fraternity as pure cant. During the height of revolutionary action from 1792–94, when dreams and enthusiasms were still fresh, the fraternal ideal undoubtedly influenced the *ordinaire,* tightening bonds and defining the relationship between men as familial, based on affection, concern, support, and a strong degree of selflessness.

Another revolutionary ideal, the myth of the patriotic death, probably testifies to an important shift in the definition of responsibility and to the demand for self-sacrifice within the *ordinaire*. Fricasse told one of these common tales. "During the seige of Charleroi, an artilleryman . . . cried out as he died: 'Coburg, Coburg, with all your money you will not pay for one drop of my blood; I pour it out today for the Republic and for liberty.'"[28] Whether or not this account is literally true is almost inconsequential; it and numerous other such accounts were believed and repeated. They served as a myth, as an ideal toward which troops should aspire and by which they should measure their conduct.

The myth combined age-old themes with revolutionary motivation. Since death has always stalked the soldier in battle, courage has forever been a soldier's virtue. The fallen who bear a painful death with calm or defiance, rather than with anguish or tears, inspire admiration among those who may soon be struck down themselves. Brave words thus become a fundamental part of the soldier's vocabulary. Patriotic death included such elements, but there were differences. The choice of a patriotic death was not so much an act of bravery as an act of responsibility. It was not only the manner of dying that made the death praiseworthy; it was what the man died for. Above all, the patriotic death was not simply an act of courage; it was an armed martyrdom.

Soldiers expressed a sentimental, even melodramatic, but apparently sincere, resolve to die for the Patrie and the Republic if circumstances called for the supreme sacrifice. The great songs of the Revolution, enthusiastically adopted by Parisian crowds and troops alike, ring with this determination. Consider the "Chant du départ," second only to the "Marseillaise" as an anthem of the Revolution.

> The Republic calls us,
> We know how to vanquish, we know how to perish!
> The French ought to live for her,
> And for her the French ought to die!

As an example of a more humble song, take this piece copied in Joseph Tondeur's songbook and, consequently, a likely favorite with the troops.

> If by chance the despots
> Kill me with their cannon
> I ask the patriots
> To sing this song.
> And you, charming Julie,
> You will repeat this refrain:
> He has died for his Patrie
> Like a Republican soldier.[29]

Time and again during the years 1792–94 the government demanded that its soldiers swear to die a patriotic death rather than submit to the enemy. Even if these oaths were only acts of compliance, they at least made it clear that a soldier was expected to fight the enemy until death or victory. But, remember, it was an emotional time, when words possessed remarkable force, and oaths could be taken literally. Oaths seemed always to accompany revolutionary celebrations, like that held on 14 July 1792 when dragoon François Marquant swore "to uphold the rights of man to the last breath." During the fall of that year new oaths were taken, since the monarchy had just been toppled. In one of these ceremonies, at Avesnes, battalions paraded on the Grand Place and swore "to maintain liberty and equality or to die in defending them." During the summer of 1793, for the great Festival of Unity held all over France, troops of the Armée du Nord shouldered their weapons, formed up in front of their encampments, and swore "to live free or to die."[30] There were other great occasions, with other similar oaths.

Soldiers repeated their commitment in letters home, perhaps the last place where such statements would be expected, since a soldier's family and friends could hardly have been cheered by knowing of his willingness to die. François Joliclerc wrote to his mother: "When I see you grieving for my fate, this pains me more than all the troubles I face, and it brings tears to my eyes. On the contrary, you should rejoice; either you will see me return covered with glory, or you will have a son worthy to be called a French citizen, who will know how to die for the defense of the Patrie." François Mireur counseled his father that "in a free state it is good and sweet to die for the defense of the Patrie." In case after case "the defense of the Patrie" was viewed as worth the ultimate sacrifice. This grim but honorable resolve might be reinforced by the family of the soldier. One father wrote to his son: "The fever that you have had is only a slight indisposition for a republican who ought to know how to suffer and die for the defense of liberty and of his land. . . . When you march to combat, never forget that it is for your father, your mother, your brothers and your sisters, and know how to prefer even death to disgrace."[31]

Songs, oaths, and letters demonstrate that soldiers expressed such convictions openly and repeatedly, certainly within the *ordinaire*. The reader aware of the intellectual history of the late eighteenth century might see the myth of patriotic death as merely an expression of the melodramatic tastes of the times. The eighteenth century, was, after all, an age of sentiment as well as an age of reason. French soldiers employed emotional phrases that would have caused Willy and Joe to double up in laughter or blush through their grimy stubble. All true, but in an age of sentimentality, sentiment has a power that it loses in more cynical times.

If the rhetoric was only rhetoric, restricted to song and brave promises, then the charge that it was fashionable but hollow might stick. However, firsthand accounts justify the claim that some individuals did live up to the myth. Speaking of a grenadier from his own battalion, Sergeant Fricasse tells how this mortally wounded man said to those who stopped to aid him, "Leave me, my friends, let me die! I am content; I have served my Patrie." Pierre Girardon wrote to his brother in December 1793 that he had seen "many *sans-culottes* who had been shot in the arm or in the thigh, forget their wounds and cry out 'Vive la République' all along the road.

These are the republicans that I love."[32] It is not as important that some individuals did in fact die the patriotic death as it is that these acts affirmed the myth. The more that this reality came close to the *ordinaire,* the more conversation must have taken note of these sacrifices, thus validating ideal standards. As Girardon declared, "These are the republicans that I love."

As already stated, the standards of conduct set and maintained by the primary group will be a product of both group dynamics and the shared beliefs of the soldiers. On a minimal level, the primary group pressures the soldier to aid and support his comrades, since only in doing so will he receive aid and support himself. The group also demands that the individual act in a way consistent with group interest. What the myth of the patriotic death seems to indicate is that the ultimate perceived interest of the individual and of the group became not the mere survival of the group and its members, but the preservation of the Patrie and its Republic. If this is true, the motivation to perform well in battle, even at great personal risk, would have grown enormously. Could men who idealized deeds of sacrifice tolerate a patrol that consciously avoided contact with the enemy, or skirmishers who crouched in safe cover to avoid risk of wounds or death?

How self-consciously *ordinaires* defined their standards is impossible to know. There were official or semi-official attempts to set standards. Oaths made up part of this effort; other means were also used. In July 1792 a Monsieur Palis submitted a "Credo of the Good Soldier" to the *Argus de l'Armée du Nord.* Point seventeen read: "I believe, finally, that every good soldier, whatever his rank, should defend his Patrie to the last breath, while always crying out as did the brave Trénard: *live free or die!* Life is nothing without liberty." Perhaps an exaggerated expression, it was nevertheless considered appropriate by the writer and the editor to inspire the flesh-and-blood recruits and veterans of the Nord. Memoirs and letters speak of individual resolve but almost never give glimpses of group standards. A rare case involved Mireur and a friend. "We gave each other our word, my colleague and I, that we would run through the other with a sword if he tried to fall back. I live in this sound and manly resolution."[33] Certainly many cowered under fire; however, the myth of the patriotic death indicates that such conduct would be discouraged by the group and, if found out, would cost the guilty individual dearly.

Letters and memoirs supply virtually no information on the way primary groups treated offenders; this strongly suggests that the only means used was the informal denial of respect. That respect must have been priceless. It would have been a hard existence for one rejected by the *ordinaire,* since he had to eat with, sleep alongside, serve, and be served by these men day in and day out.

This glance at the *ordinaire* suggests that an existing primary group structure became the vehicle for potent and decisive combat behavior as war threatened the Revolution. The *ordinaire*, as a framework, existed before 1789, but there was little reason for its members to demand high standards of sacrifice and combat performance of one another. To gain obedience, officers relied heavily upon coercion, and little besides compliance was expected of the soldiers. As one military theorist wrote at mid-century, "Soldiers march at the enemy like Capuchins go to matins. It is neither interest in the war, nor love of glory or of country which animates our armies today. It is the drum which brings them up and back, like the church bells order the monks to go to bed or to rise."[34]

The Revolution cast aside force as the basis of obedience. Discipline and compliance were expected to be largely self-imposed. In such a transformed environment, the already intelligently structured *ordinaire* took on new importance. For the army to excel on the battlefield, the demand for sacrifice and the desire for victory had to emerge as group values. There is no reason to doubt that they did. A number of potent influences, working upon and augmented by primary group cohesion within the *ordinaire*, culminated in a compelling complex of impulses to fight bravely and efficiently.

The Complex of Motivation

A fuller understanding of morale and motivation emerges from the preceding chapters. No single influence explains the spirit and drive characteristic of the citizen-soldiers mustered by revolutionary France. Instead, each of the three phases of troop motivation resulted from interdependent factors.

Initial, Sustaining, and Combat Motivation

That men came to the army by different paths implies a variety of initial motivations. At first troops of the line army enlisted for long terms of service. In the main Volunteers of 1791 and 1792 rallied to the immediate defense of revolutionary France out of principle, patriotism, and a sense of adventure. Subsequent cohorts frequently had less noble or romantic motives. The Levy of 300,000 contained fewer volunteers, more hired substitutes, and a majority of draftees. Conscripts sent to the front by the *levée en masse* in late 1793 were raised by requisition rather than free will. Bearing this in mind, it could be anticipated that recruits marched to the front impelled by reasons ranging from enthusiastic support of a revolutionary ideal to dull obedience to the law.

The necessity to rely upon conscription in 1793 and the substantial desertion rates among conscripts on their way to the front argue that the patriotism of new recruits had waned when compared to the enthusiasm displayed in 1791 and 1792. A change in the character of initial motivation, even a decline in its intensity, however, does not necessarily entail a major drop in sustaining or combat motivation, the primary concerns of this study. In the camp and on the battlefield motivation derives from a set of factors different from those that first brought the soldier into the service.

Sustaining motivation demands emphasis and consideration in an army that had to survive and train under conditions of extreme hardship. Endemic shortages of arms, equipment, and clothing, aggravated by faltering logistics which provided inadequate or uncertain food supplies, meant that the republican soldier had to endure more than war's inevitable fatigues and dangers. Add to the suffering the proximity of home and the relatively light penalties for desertion, and it almost comes as a surprise that more men did not forsake the army for their villages. The lack of crippling rates of desertion in the combat units of the Nord, except for the special circumstances of December 1792 through April 1793, suggests a high level of sustaining motivation. So does the rapidity with which troops were trained and committed to battle.

Men in combat exist in a world vastly different from that of men in camps. In camp there is time for reflection and conversation, and boredom is more oppressive than fear. Under fire there is time only for action and reaction, and fear is pervasive. Although French troops suffered some early fiascos in combat, as a whole they performed well, especially considering their relative lack of training. Considering the tactical reliance upon the élan of troops massed in spirited bayonet assaults and the initiative of individuals dispersed as skirmishers, there is little reason to dispute that French combat motivation was strong.

Patriotism and Appreciation

Troop motivation traditionally has been ascribed to patriotism, but it is important to recognize that there is no simple equivalence between patriotic sentiment and high morale. Among the factors to be considered, patriotism was undoubtedly important for the armies of revolutionary France in general, and for the Nord in particular. Patriotic statements in soldiers' letters, diaries, and songs can be extensively documented. Unofficial and official reports attest to the high spirits and patriotic fervor of the Nord. Representatives on Mission continually reported that the troops "seem animated by that republican ardor which transforms men into heroes," that the spirit of the army is excellent," and that "the spirit of the soldier is excellent; he patiently suffers the hardships [*maux*] of war, he displays more ardor to fight and all cry 'Vive la République.'"[35] Few, if any, would deny that patriotic and revolutionary sentiments played a substantial role in the morale of the Nord.

The numerous and obvious assertions of intense nationalism in the army tempt historians to conclude that French troops were driven by something approaching fanaticism. That conclusion is too extreme, and it transforms the revolutionary soldier into a superhuman or subhuman being. Reality was more muddled. In a pensive movement one conscript serving with the Nord composed these revealing lines: "The law carried me to arms to defend my Patrie, which is dear to me; for her I left my family and fellow citizens. . . . I go, to repay my obligations toward the one and the other, to attack men that I have never seen, who have done me no harm, and who believe . . . their cause as good as ours. . . . In these attacks, often one forgets, on both sides, all humanity." Patriotism and compulsion put him into uniform. He expressed faith in his cause and revulsion at the hardships and inhumanity of war. This young man's anguish was not rare. Among the hundred soldiers' letters contained in one box at the war archives, Jean-Paul Bertaud counted only fifteen that expressed staunch patriotic or republican fervor; the rest, he found, spoke of "fear, fatigue, and despair."[36] Patriotism mattered, but it did not alone transform men into superb fighters. The level of patriotic sentiment among new recruits may even have fallen off in 1793 and 1794 from the heights reached in 1792. Of course, the political education campaign, which preached patriotism, did its work in this later period and may have helped to maintain the intensity felt by the men at the front.

Of crucial significance is that the French people continually expressed a sympathetic understanding of the sacrifices made by the troops and a profound gratitude for their efforts in the field. These sentiments, which buttressed the army's morale, were transmitted in a variety of ways and on many levels. Family and friends reinforced personal commitment through face-to-face contacts and letters. Local ceremonies during the enrollment and at the departure of troops reassured them of hometown support. Patriotic orators and journals praised the soldier as a model citizen, worthy of emulation. The government's campaign of political education left little doubt as to the importance of the Revolution and the value of the soldiers' struggle to defend it from foreign enemies.

Beyond the obvious republican and patriotic rhetoric, the central government instituted policies and programs that at first glance might not seem to have had much to do with troop motivation but that conveyed a sense of the people's concern for its soldiers. Paramount among such developments was the veterans' policy adopted by the Convention. Reform of veterans' legislation began in 1790, but the fundamental egalitarian change in previous policy came only with the law of 6 June 1793, which adjusted benefits more to wounds suffered than to rank or longevity of service. In confirming the state's obligations to its defenders, the Convention was well aware of the impact this would have on morale. In particular, those who advocated just compensation to wounded veterans believed that the example would make it easier to recruit new men into the army. Along with the reform of veterans' policy went a new law guaranteeing support to war widows. Circulation and public readings of the *Bulletin de la Convention Nationale* insured that all soldiers at the front knew of the promised benefits. The implications of these and related acts could not have escaped the common soldier; an article of 26 March 1794 in the *Journal des hommes libres* reminded the troops of the Convention's work. "Be assured ... brave soldiers of the Patrie, that the Patrie will not be ungrateful ... already the National Convention has fruitfully concerned itself with your wives, your children and all that is dear to you; it has equally concerned itself with you; you will find parcels of land to cultivate, positions, jobs, and especially public esteem, which is the true national reward."[37]

Through these various expressions of enthusiastic popular support for the army, civilian patriotism contributed to army morale. A military commentator must take care to distinguish sentiment within the general population from that among front line soldiers. It is commonplace when discussing twentieth-century armies to insist that patriotism inspired civilians more than troops in combat. But civilian patriotism cannot be dismissed as irrelevant to troop motivation if that fervor translates into a clearly expressed and effectively transmitted appreciation for the soldiers' efforts in the field. Among the rank and file of the Armée du Nord et des Ardennes during the tense period 1791–94, personal commitment was continually reinforced by public support.

Soldiers and Officers

The new soldiers and their officers differed from their predecessors who served before the Revolution and from the kind of individuals who still served in the armies arrayed against them. Revolutionary France committed an entire generation of young men who possessed the full range of skill and confidence characteristic of the French people. Much of the motivation to do well as soldiers could be expected to come from the high standards they would set for themselves.

The high spirits that the French army came to depend upon in the early years of the revolutionary wars probably was also related to the inexperience and idealism of the troops. The great majority of the soldiers entered the service after the Revolution began its work, and by mid-1794 most still had no more than one full campaign behind them. They were new to the army and new to war. The patriotic and revolutionary intensity of the times, combined with the freshness of the young men under arms, produced an army in which cynics were rare and enthusiasts common. If courage has its season, these French soldiers of June 1794 shone with the full brightness of a revolutionary spring.

The composition and character of the officer corps were similar to that of the rank and file. Unlike the aristocratic officers of the monarchy, republican commanders shared much in common with their men. Like the citizen-soldiers they led, French officers now came from a broad social spectrum. The very existence of so many lieutenants and captains who had once been common soldiers themselves acted as an incentive to their men, who clearly understood that promotion awaited those who did well. Subject to criticism and possible denunciation by his own men, the officer was encouraged to develop a relationship with his troops and a style of command consistent with the ideals of the Revolution and the men who rose to defend them.

Discipline, though hardly faultless, was pragmatic and ultimately sufficient for victory. Military justice did not foster resentment among the rank and file; it did not humiliate the common soldier, even if he was punished with severity. The revolutionary French did not fall back on coercion to maintain sustaining or combat motivation. Authorities expected French troops to greet orders to fight with willing obedience. Once in combat, troops displayed initiative, and the disciplinary system did not dampen this spirit. Coercion played a role in the struggle to maintain order and repress pillage, but it was not employed to drive men into battle. It was essentially consistent with the principle of normative compliance, so vital to an army of citizen-soldiers.

Groups and Individuals

Esprit de corps, historically a unifying and inspiring impulse in armies, was consciously discouraged in the forces of the Republic. As early as 1791 Robespierre cautioned against "a [particular] spirit which would be an esprit de corps." He feared it as a tool by which officers could turn their units against the state. This anxiety permeated the revolutionary leadership. The *amalgame* implied many things to many people, but one of its primary functions in the eyes of Bouchotte was "to inhibit that esprit de corps which grows daily through the secret maneuvers of the officers of the line."[38] This spirit not only threatened the government, but it also opposed the soldier's primary definition as citizen and defender of the nation. The man in the ranks was supposed to identify himself with the people, not with a military unit. The records suggest that soldiers felt an understandable pride in the proven competence of their battalions, but this unit self-confidence never grew into a unit identification so intense that it consumed the soldier's own individuality or larger loyalties.

The formal exaltation of the individual through awards for outstanding conduct seemed to have been of no more influence than was the formal exaltation of the unit through esprit de corps. There is evidence of fine weapons being given to soldiers of the Nord as a sign of recognition, as when Brette received a dagger for having captured a flag, or when a nameless sergeant was granted a sword for his conduct in a retreat. But there is little evidence that cash presentations were made to soldiers of the Nord who had distinguished themselves.[39] In any case, awards seem to have had little, if any, impact. Of far greater significance was the promotion of men who did well in the field. Advancement not only rewarded talent and bravery, but it also demonstrated the reality of equality and open careers in the army. The government certainly made effective use of its enlightened policy toward promotion.

Awards and promotions function to adjust self-interest to organizational goals. During the struggles of 1792–94, however, the individual French soldiers were already fully aware that their personal interests lay with the Revolution and with the defense of their homeland; thus, their self-interest merged with the goals of the army to defeat the enemy. Of course, in the heat of combat, self-interest translated into survival, not ambition. Thoughts of personal reward must have seemed remote to soldiers in fear of their lives; they were driven into greater dependence upon the good men around them. The primary group, of great importance to sustaining motivation, became paramount to combat motivation. The well-structured *ordinaire* reinforced revolutionary morale, setting its own demanding standards of conduct.

The high morale of revolutionary troops justified compliance with the orders of civil and military authorities. With rare exceptions, the values and goals of the *ordinaire* coincided with the values and goals of the government. The most notable cases in which the *ordinaire* seems to have endorsed what the government prohibited concerned pillage and desertion. If pillage was essential to the survival of the group, the *ordinaire* may have accepted it to such an extent that officials could never really stamp it out. In the very special circumstances of the winter of 1792–93, the small group probably tolerated and may even have promoted what it considered as legitimate desertion by volunteers. But in the main the small group effectively served as a conduit for patriotic and political ideals dear to the Revolution, and it supported rather than resisted the orders and demands of authority.

SECTION THREE
Doctrine, Training, and Tactics

Chapter 8

The Cult of the Bayonet: Enthusiasm and Tactics

Having taken into account the elements of composition, control, and opinion that determined the motivation of troops in the Armée du Nord, I now turn to the technical side of the ledger to explore the tactical system and its relation to combat effectiveness. As defined in Chapter 2, a tactical system includes doctrine, weapons, training, and experience as well as tactics. These factors will be examined in this section. Infantry receives the greater share of the discussion because the Armée du Nord et des Ardennes was fundamentally an army of foot soldiers.

The assumptions and assertions that epitomized revolutionary tactical doctrine can be summed up as the cult of the bayonet. It constituted the only tactical doctrine widely disseminated during 1792–94. It recognized the link between motivation and tactics; however, it promoted an extreme and simplistic notion of the army as an inspired body of *sans-culottes* under arms. Histories that uncritically accept the logic of the cult of the bayonet are forced into a view of French conduct on the battlefield that a closer study of their tactics cannot justify. Any reevaluation of the tactical system must deal with this extreme doctrine and, while not rejecting it totally, must separate its reasonable from its unreasonable tenets.

During the revolutionary era the cult of the bayonet captured the imagination of the French people and their civil and military leaders. Tactical doctrine, usually a concern only of professional officers and military theorists, was addressed in public forums. This doctrine focused on infantry alone; the proper use of cavalry and artillery remained technical issues, reserved for career military men. Popular wisdom held that the impetuous enthusiasm, or élan, displayed by the troops who fought for the Revolution particularly suited them to the tactical offensive. An equally strong contention insisted that edged weapons, expressively called the *arme blanche,* matched the temperament of the regenerated French. The result was a belief in the irresistible force of the mass bayonet charge when delivered by patriotic and spirited *sans-culottes*. Long before 1789, French military writers had expressed a similar confidence in the offensive élan of their troops, ascribing it to national character. Events of the Revolution, however, were believed to have inspired even stronger ardor, as patriotism and republicanism added their force to native French vigor.

The technology of the fusil determined that the bayonet must play a significant offensive role in any eighteenth-century army. A flintlock held only one charge, and during the lengthy reloading process its bearer remained defenseless. Any assault culminating in the bodily collision of opposing troops could only be an affair of the bayonet. Every army resorted to shock attacks on occasion, but the French placed much greater emphasis on the *arme blanche* than did their neighbors. Most revolutionary commanders favored a rapid approach and confrontation with cold steel when possible. Skirmishers and artillery were to supply whatever fire support the French required for the main body of attacking troops.

Belief in the omnipotent *arme blanche* reached such extremes that it blinded the French to reality. So adamant were the faithful that the government resurrected the archaic pike as a weapon for its new battalions. A shortage of fusils compelled the French to search for expedients, but advocates of the antiquated pike claimed that for Frenchmen it was a superior weapon. The cult of the bayonet won followers inside and outside the military by reassuring the French that their indomitable spirit could be directly translated into victorious tactics. The cult also played upon the political prejudices of the day. Transfixed by the emotional appeal of the *arme blanche*, the French failed to recognize the complexity of the flexible and adaptable tactical system that evolved at the front.

French Élan in the Ancien Régime

Faith in the invincibility of bayonet-armed French troops predated the Revolution. The tradition of the *furia francese* went back at least to Merovingian times and gained particularly wide acceptance in the eighteenth century. While the Enlightenment often dealt in universal truths, it also observed and reported the unique. Differences among men received considerable attention, and one focus of comparison was national character. Baron de Montesquieu's theory that climate helped form a people's makeup stands out as the best known contribution to the widespread view that each national group had its own traits. In terms of military prowess Frenchmen supposedly possessed unusual spirit and energy but were correspondingly difficult to discipline. These characteristics made the French formidable in the charge and particularly weak in controlled volley fire. No less a figure than François Voltaire wrote in his *Dictionnaire philoso-*

phique: "French artillery is very good, but the fire of French infantry is rarely superior and usually inferior to that of other nations. It can be said with as much truth that the French nation attacks with the greatest impetuosity and that it is very difficult to resist its shock."[1]

Great soldier-authors continually stressed the influence of national character on tactics. Marshal de Saxe, victor of Fontenoy, expressed himself on this subject in his widely read and valuable *Rêveries,* "It is the distinctive characteristic of the French nation to attack." The most important tactical writer of the century, and a lion of the salons, the comte de Guibert, held a similar opinion. "The French were without discipline, hardly suited to fire fights . . . , redoubtable in all attacks with cold steel and assaults on outposts. They had then, as today, that initial moment of vigor and impetuosity, that shock which one day nothing can stop, and which the next day, a slight obstacle throws back, that incredible combination of a courage sometimes above everything and a consternation sometimes carried on to a weakness."[2] Much of the column-line debate that filled the literature of the military enlightenment in France contrasted the virtues of fire power with those of bayonet shock. Those advocating columns for assault thought deep formations and the bayonet were particularly suited to the French character. In fact, François-Jean Mesnil-Durand proposed his mass column system in a work entitled *Projet d'un ordre français en tactique.* Yet many authors who favored linear combat formations still conceded that the French excelled in the *arme blanche.* And although the crushing success of the Prussians in the Seven Years' War won converts to their rigid system, few, if any, insisted that it was natural for the French.

Revolutionary Élan and the Bayonet

Revolution added further momentum to the traditional appeals to élan. Even before war struck in 1792 many believed that political and social changes only accentuated the old French traits of high spirit and low discipline. In a report to the Military Committee of the Constituent Assembly, Edmund Dubois-Crancé suggested that "the military spirit ought to acquire all the more energy, when it is guided by a more enlightened patriotism. . . . The French soldier is not an automaton."[3] His statements are particularly interesting because as a member of both the Constituent Assembly and the National Convention he heavily influenced the military policies of revolutionary France. Dubois-Crancé's view of the situation was by no means unique.

There was considerable logic in arguing that the Revolution amplified the strengths and weaknesses characteristic of French troops before 1789. If the infantryman of the ancien régime could not maneuver as well as his adversaries, everything indicated that after the breakdown of traditional authority he would be even less prepared for close order drill once war broke out again. Discipline, admittedly below European standards prior to social revolution, became even more lax with the new relationship between officers and men. But high esprit, a French attribute in the days of Maurice de Saxe, would rise to unprecedented heights with citizen involvement in the Revolution.

Wartime documents abound in references to the superior élan of the troops, and in the unprecedented conditions of French political life her politicians and soldiers offered new explanations for the gallant behavior they so vividly described. Some still praised French character in terms identical with those employed during the ancien régime. To most observers, however, the Revolution mixed additional elements into the old formula. Soldiers who marched under the tricolor were now patriots and republicans. As patriots they fought to defend their native soil, their Patrie. As republicans they fought to defend a set of institutions, a transformed society, which made their homeland even more their own. Patriotism and republicanism were related, yet distinct, and both differed from the attitudes and talents called national character.

Extreme accounts spoke of élan as if it were a totally revolutionary phenomenon, as if the mating of Jacobinism with the French nation gave rise to a new breed of men. As early as 30 October 1792 the Representatives at Maubeuge claimed that troops in that city "appeared animated by that republican ardor which transforms men into heroes." Reports defined the individual French soldier as inspired and free, while the Allies' armies contained only *esclaves* [slaves] of traditional despotisms. "What a difference there is, general, between free men and slaves!" exclaimed General Dominique Vandamme in a dispatch to Jean-Victor Moreau.[4]

Politicians and soldiers linked their belief in the superior élan of their troops with the conviction that the new citizen-soldiers excelled in the offensive. Combat reports and comuniqués issued from the Armée du Nord exemplify this confidence. The Nord won important battles by acting aggressively, especially during 1792 and 1793. Jemappes, Hondschoote, and Wattignies were all tactical offensives. Many men of influence drew naive conclusions from these victories. The Jacobin Representative Delbrel, who visited the Armée du Nord in the fall of 1793, flatly asserted, "Everytime we have attacked we have won, and . . . everytime we have been attacked we have almost always been defeated." Even as able and reasonable an observer as General Souham concluded that "we have few examples where the French have been beaten when they have attacked."[5]

This climate of opinion exalted the gleaming bayonet as a revolutionary symbol to rival the red liberty cap and the tricolor cockade. The bayonet evoked images of citizen-soldiers braving death at close quarters to defend the Patrie. Like a Crusader's cross, it seemed to insure victory by its very presence. As a weapon of war, it embodied the vaunted élan of the French and the offensive considered so essential. The *arme blanche* tangibly expressed psychological and tactical orthodoxy. So vividly did it symbolize Republican infantry tactics that when General Hugues-Alexandre-Joseph Meunier sought a motto to place at the beginning of his 1794 tactical study, he chose "Bayonet and Republic"; they were that closely joined.[6]

The rhetoric of the *arme blanche* pervaded the contemporary understanding of French tactics. Some lauded the bayonet as "the favorite weapon of republicans"; Houchard's chief of staff, General Etienne-Ambroise Berthélemy declared that it was "infallible with *sans-culottes*." Amidst this hail of praise it comes as no surprise that the Committee of Public Safety believed that "the success of our arms is due principally to the use of the bayonet."[7] Language employed to exalt this weapon became so intense and so political that one must question if it was almost an obligatory formula, which authors included to demonstrate their pure republican thought and to protect themselves from the suspicious zealots who were only too ready to guillotine reactionaries.

Insistence upon the value of the *arme blanche*, however, was not reserved for public reports alone; official directives also counseled the use of the bayonet. As general-in-chief of the Armée du Nord, Houchard advised his subordinates, "It is necessary to act a great deal with the *arme blanche*, like I do, it is the only way to succeed and to lose few men." Houchard personally ordered bayonet charges in several instances during the September fighting. At the victorious battle of Wattignies, Lazare Carnot, acting as a Representative on Mission with the Nord, was highly impressed by the bayonet combat he witnessed. Later when he drafted a plan of operations for the spring of 1794, he included a tactical directive to "on every occasion engage in combat with the bayonet."[8] Consistent and high-level advocacy of bayonet shock tactics demonstrates a self-conscious and very real reliance on them.

In fact, practically all French victories saw the enemy driven to defeat at the point of a bayonet, and every major battle fought by the Armée du Nord included significant shock action by republican infantry.[9] It occurred even at the defeats of Neerwinden and Famars. Only in the battle of Fleurus did musketry play the dominant role. On occasion, a shortage of ammunition left local commanders no option but to resort to the bayonet, but as a rule the decision to employ it represented a faith in the weapon and the tactics.[10]

The Pike

The adoption of pikes by Republican troops reveals the intensity of French devotion to the doctrine of the *arme blanche*. While flintlocks remained in short supply during 1792–94, many battalions unable to secure firearms carried pikes. The armies of Louis XIV had abandoned the pike as a standard infantry weapon before 1700. At first glance the revolutionary government's decision to resurrect this archaic weapon came as a last resort, imposed by the lack of proper arms. In fact, much more was involved in the efforts to manufacture and distribute pikes.[11] Paramount among the several reasons behind the decision were the same arguments stressing Republican offensive élan heard from advocates of the bayonet. Since the pike was itself a purer form of the *arme blanche* than was the bayonet, enthusiasts for the pike reached even greater extremes. To adherents of the *arme blanche*, the pike could even appear superior to the fusil.

By raising more troops than the government could properly equip, the French were faced with the need to search for expedients. Custine wrote from the Belgian frontier in June 1793, "We lack fusils . . . we must make up for this with pikes." Not only did shortages argue for the adoption of pikes, but also the easier and quicker task of training men to fight with them appealed to commanders swamped by the avalanche of recruits.[12] But neither the lack of previous firearms nor of time made the government's choice inevitable, since other options were possible.

Many already favored the use of the pike, for scarcity constituted just one more claim in favor of a more effective weapon. No less a figure than Carnot spoke exuberantly of the pike before the Legislative Assembly on more than one occasion: "If a troop of pikemen attacked one of fusiliers, necessarily the latter would be defeated, because the pike is longer than the bayonet, and this method of fighting is all the more suited to the French, since they have always been invincible with the *arme blanche,* and on the contrary, are very inferior to German and Prussian troops in the art of firing accurately and quickly." Only at the close of this particular presentation did he turn to expediency. "But if it is still denied, despite the testimony of all the generals that I have cited, that the pike is better than the fusil, it cannot be denied that it is better than nothing." Joseph Servan, minister of war after 10 August 1792, wrote in a circular on the organization of pikemen, "The pike is the most redoubtable weapon I know, when it is in the hands of a courageous body of troops whose valor is guided by an intrepid judgment." He considered it a tool of war "worthy of the regenerated French people."[13] Some of the praise may well have been making the best of a bad situation, but much was unquestionably sincere.

When it ordered the production of as many as half a million pikes on 1 August 1792, the Legislative Aseembly did so with the intention of arming all respectable and able-bodied male civilians in France. Thousands of these pikes were carried by newly formed battalions that joined the army in 1792–94. Battalions of pikemen appeared in the situation reports of the Armée du Nord. Baron Henri Jomini wrote of an entire division of pikemen in garrison at Guise.[14] As it turned out, pikemen saw little if any real action. By the time such battalions took their place at the front they had received fusils.

Advocates of the pike continued to plead their case through 1794. The obvious superiority of enemy cavalry lent added force to the plans that stressed the use of pikes in defense against onrushing horsemen. In at least one case the Ministry of War conducted experiments with new types of short pikes.[15] At any rate, when the supply of fusils eventually caught up with the expanded numbers of the army, no more was heard of pikes.

For the time it lasted, the discussion of this primitive weapon showed the depth of conviction behind the doctrine of the shock offensive and the cult of the bayonet. That so many French military and political leaders believed that an infantry armed with pikes could hold their own on contemporary battlefields reveals how much doctrine and expectation distorted the perception of reality.

Belief, Reality, and Rationale

During the revolutionary era the compelling rhetoric of élan, the offensive, and the bayonet won over soldiers and citizens alike. It was persuasive not only because it reflected certain realities of the battlefield, but also because it flattered and reassured the French people and touched their political prejudices.

A purely factual appraisal of the Nord's campaigns hardly proves that French soldiers were invincible in the assault. Perhaps those who so lustily boasted of republican prowess forgot the battles of Neerwinden and Famars, where Dumouriez and Dampierre attacked and failed. Moreover, the two great victories that turned the Austrian Netherlands into French departments were partly or wholly defensive engagements. At Tourcoing, Vandamme emerged triumphant in a struggle with the attacking Austrian forces under General Clairfayt, and at Fleurus Jourdan placed his combined army in a defensive position complete with entrenchments.

There is no question that the French often stormed enemy positions bayonet in hand. However, to conclude that they fought only with the *arme blanche* is to ignore a great deal of other evidence. A world of difference separates the observation that troops often finished combat by rushing at the enemy with cold steel from the conclusion that they relied exclusively on the bayonet or that bayonet charges alone decided the fate of battles. The study of French tactics presented in the following chapters describes a flexible tactical system of surprising variety, at least for infantry. Battalions of foot soldiers, ably supported by artillery, fought in close order lines and columns or dispersed as skirmishers, as circumstances required. A capacity to adapt to the field of battle gave the French greater eventual benefit than did their massed assaults.

Something more than empirical success in combat lay behind the rhetorical reliance on spirited offensives. Like all doctrines, this one was both descriptive and prescriptive of reality. Though to some extent a product of experience, it also altered the perception of events.

Emphasis upon élan reassured the French of the inevitability of victory. Civil and military officials expressed faith in the intense motivation of the troops to justify committing them to battle. After leading raw levies to defeat, General Jacob-Job Elie reported to the minister of war: "I marched persuaded of victory, hoping that the love of the Patrie, the character of the republican soldier, and the desire to defeat the tyrants would at least be the equal of experience and would prove disastrous to our enemies." The rhetoric of élan helped maintain morale, keeping expectations high in the face of shortages, hardships, and setbacks. It served as propaganda to boost the self-confidence of officers and men who often fought at a disadvantage in conventional terms of equipment and skill. Dumouriez issued this reassuring proclamation to his troubled battalions shortly before the disasters of March 1793: "If the enemy wants to cross the Meuse, close your ranks [*serrez vos batallions*], lower your bayonets, sing the hymn of the 'Marseillaise,' and you will win." More important, the documents leave the unmistakable impression that civil and military leaders themselves *needed* to believe in the superior spiritual qualities of republican soldiers. The question posed by Representatives Joseph-Charles Richard and Pierre Choudieu entailed its own hopeful answer: "But of what value are the tactics, even the courage of the most experienced veterans of the despots, against the devotion, the abandon of the sons of the French Republic? . . . The sacred image of the Patrie makes them endure everything and brave everything."[16]

In addition, it is interesting to speculate that political attitudes led the French, particularly the National Convention, to exaggerate the importance of patriotic élan and the *arme blanche*. A contemporary, General Maximilien Foy, pointed out the one-sided nature of official reporting. "The people . . . reading in the *Bulletin* of the Convention only stories of battalions in mass, lines broken through, and redoubts assaulted at the charge innocently believed that fusils and cannon had lost their value, and that all was taken with the bayonet." By minimizing art and maximizing élan the cult of the bayonet justified those who feared the officer corps and wished to discount the importance of its professional skills. Those who trusted only the *sans-culottes* wished to see their patriotic enthusiasm as sufficient to bring victory. As stated in a report by the Committee of Public Safety to the Convention, "The soldiers of the Republic . . . have more than one time gained victory in spite of their commanders."[17] Such men needed only a dedicated *sans-culotte* at their head.

There is a great deal of truth to the assertion that to be effective tactics must correspond to the value and temperament of the soldiers who employ them, but the cult of the bayonet erred in its extremes. The study of motivation presented in Section Two of this volume points as much to an increase in personal pride and in self- and group-enforced standards of military performance as it does to high levels of emotion. Overemphasis upon the mass bayonet assault obscures the fact that reliance upon the individual initiative of skirmishers or even upon the devotion of men standing resolutely in line was also consistent with the dedicated new armies of revolutionary France. It would be a mistake to judge as successful only those tactics that were channels for violent emotion, but the French themselves came close to being guilty of such an error, at least in their rhetoric. Fortunately for them, the evolution of a practical set of tactical alternatives in the field was not significantly crippled by the devotions of the new cult.

Chapter 9

Cavalry and Artillery in an Infantry Army

THE ARMÉE DU NORD was in essence an army of infantry ineffectively supported by cavalry and effectively seconded by artillery. Neither of the supporting branches explains the victories of the Nord, whereas the performance of the infantry does. For a number of reasons, cavalry did not develop either quantitatively or qualitatively to the point where it could assume its proper importance in the tactical system until after the spring and summer of 1794. Artillery enjoyed far greater, though uneven, success. The elite horse artillery units provided constant and invaluable assistance to infantry and cavalry alike. The foot artillery, on the other hand, rarely came into play, and the numerous volunteer artillery was dispersed and dissipated.

The Cavalry

French cavalry gained little credit through the first three years of the war.[1] The essential history of cavalry during 1791–94 is not a description of its tactics, but an account of the factors that kept it from fulfilling its proper role on campaign. The cavalry faced greater difficulties than those confronting the infantry. Creation of a mounted arm required assembling not only men but also horses. The quality of horseflesh could and did pose problems. All the experts agree that it took much longer to train a horse and rider for combat than it took to train a foot soldier. One authority estimated that it required three to four years before a cavalry recruit could take his place in the battle line. Beyond the technical complications lay political problems. Cavalry was regarded as the most aristocratic branch of the army, and in a revolutionary era its reputation made it suspect. Representative Joseph Le Bon fumed, "The cavalry is an assembly of émigré's sons, of show offs [*muscadins*], of young land holders [*fermiers*] and of all the enemies of holy equality."[2] Favoritism toward volunteer infantry and suspicion of line cavalry prolonged the latter's problems and delayed solutions.

The Quantitative Crisis in Manpower, Horses, and Equipment

Before the French could increase the strength of their cavalry to match the rapidly growing infantry, they had to overcome serious shortages of manpower, horses, and equipment.

Although the Republic boasted great resources of willing manpower, it was some time before adequate numbers of men joined the cavalry. The greatest and most rapid expansion of forces was in the volunteer infantry battalions, but, with only a handful of minor exceptions, the cavalry remained exclusively a line force. Even at the outset of the war, French horsemen were not present in sufficient quantities, and their numbers remained fairly static over the next year. Only in 1794 did they reach numbers in proper proportion to that of the burgeoning infantry.

On the eve of the Revolution the French line army numbered about 156,000 men, of which 33,000 were cavalry. The organizational and budgetary laws of 1789–91 maintained the official size of the mounted branch at roughly this same level. In fact, the cavalry suffered from two earlier decisions, the elimination of depots in 1788 and the suspension of domestic horse purchases in 1789. Organized in comparatively feeble regiments—of three squadrons for cavalry and dragoons, and four for hussars and *chasseurs à cheval*—the units were not able to expand quickly enough to meet the threat of war. When they rode to the front, regiments left one of their squadrons behind as a reconstituted depot to feed men and horses to the engaged units. In January 1792 the cavalry already fell short of its authorized strength by nearly 6,000 men. The losses of the 1792 campaign were replaced only with difficulty. Despite efforts to increase the numbers of mounted troops, in February 1793 the actual size of cavalry forces remained at roughly 30,000.[3]

Spurred on by the crisis at the front, the Convention took steps to rebuild its faltering cavalry. In its organizational decree of 21 February 1793 the Convention increased the number of squadrons in cavalry and dragoon regiments from three to four and the number of men per squadron from 150 to 170. Light cavalry, that is, hussars and *chasseurs à cheval,* went from four squadrons to six, again of 170 men each. Three days later a decree stated that squadrons were to be brought up to strength by accepting volunteers from existing infantry battalions. In April the Convention voted the levy of 30,000 men for the cavalry. Legislation of June created new regiments of mounted troops; some were built around volunteer cavalry units, such as the *Hussards noirs* with the Nord. Another law of 24 October 1793 restated the need to bring squadron strength up to 170 and authorized mounted regiments to accept volunteers from infantry battalions and from among men requisitioned by the *levée en masse*. In January 1794 Philippe-Charles-Aimé Goupilleau, speaking for the Military Committee, again pointed out, "The necessity to augment the number of our mounted troops has been felt for a long time in our armies; our old defeats in Belgium and on the banks of the Rhine are proof of it." At his urging the Convention decreed that all the remaining small volunteer cavalry units would be incorporated into regular regiments. Some of the various "free companies" and "legions" were combined to form additional new regiments.[4]

All the measures adopted finally showed results, but not before early 1794. According to Edouard Desbrière and Maurice Sautai, the French carried over 100,000 troopers on the rolls as summer began. This figure is impressive, but most of these men were new to the service and not yet skilled enough to be effective. For example, the 244 recruits received by the beleaguered 1st Cavalry on 7 February could hardly have become expert in the short span of four months. As it was, fully one-third of the troopers claimed by the June situation report served in depot.[5]

The government also had problems in providing the large numbers of horses required by the cavalry and in guaranteeing the quality of these animals. Even before the Revolution, the army could not boast of its horseflesh. Poor breeding practices had led to a deterioration in the quality of mounts. Unquestionably, the French secured their best cavalry horses from outside their own borders. In 1789, as an economy measure, the Assembly forbade the purchase of French-bred remounts. In January 1790 it closed down the state stud farms. These measures only made matters worse. By 1792 the cavalry lacked nearly 8,000 horses of its authorized strength.[6] The stress of war demanded a new system to supply great quantities of acceptable horses.

During 1792 and 1793 authorities tried several different systems of procuring horses. The outright purchase of horses at fixed rates was perhaps the simplest; however, it invited abuses. The fixed rates encouraged contractors to unload their worst animals on the army. Some even brought horses rejected by the army and then sold them back to the army. Newly created *dépôts de remonte* contained mounts of poor quality, and not enough of those. Representatives on Mission with the Adrennes complained in August 1793, "If this system [*régie*] of purchasing horses continues one more month, the Republic wil have spent immense sums, and it will have no more cavalry." A September inspection of the depots justified this fear. Only 39,700 horses were with the cavalry regiments or were in the depots at that time.[7] Alarmed by these findings, the Convention turned to requisitioning horses by quota.

Limited requisitions of remounts predated the final system of August-October 1793 by over a year. Horses once belonging to émigrés had been subject to expropriation by the army since August 1792. In March 1793 luxury horses became liable to seizure. When the Convention declared the *levée en masse,* it also placed all saddle horses under requisition, although only in October did it work out the details of the system. On 8 October it decreed that each canton of France must supply a minimum of six saddle horses for the cavalry. The Representatives on Mission named to carry out this requisition of mounts received authorization to raise the quota at their discretion. Ten days later the Convention added two draft horses to the quota of six saddle horses.[8] The horses were to be paid for with local revenues. According to the legislation, all horses were to be delivered to one of the twenty assembly points by 1 November.

The requisition went well and ultimately filled the cavalry's need for horses. Even if the 1 November deadline was not met, the zeal of the Representatives moved the process along rapidly. Situation reports of spring 1794 indicate that the army possessed nearly 100,000 saddle horses for the cavalry. The requisition alone accounts for the difference between this figure and the level of the previous fall.[9] Again, horses, like men, required instruction, and it would be some time before they could be expected to perform with front line regiments.

Shortages of equipment and arms continued to plague the French, even as they marshaled the men and horses required by expanded cavalry forces. The elaborate array of equipment needed for horse and rider far surpassed that necessary to make an infantryman useful. Without bridles and saddles, horses were just expensive inconveniences. Foot soldiers might stumble along in wooden shoes or straw sandals and sling their blankets over their shoulders; horsemen needed boots and the proper belts to secure their weapons and goods.

The first equipment shortage struck the cavalry as it began to expand in the late summer of 1792. A rapidly increasing infantry needed firearms, so on 31 August the minister of war was authorized to give the dragoons' fusils to the infantry. On 3 September the Assembly took the musketoons from cavalry regiments.[10] Light cavalry continued to carry their carbines, but even these fell into short supply.

Expansion of the mounted arm in 1793 and 1794 provoked all manner of shortages. The laws demanded equipment at the same time that they called up manpower and horses. The levy of 30,000 cavalry men in April 1793 stipulated that these men were supposed to be mounted and fully equipped. The October requisition of horses also demanded that the cantons supply not only the animals but their necessary furnishings. In addition, municipalities were supposed to send along one saber, two pistols, and a pair of boots with each horse.[11] Although this decree produced a great number of mounts in a short time, the equipment listed by the law came in slowly, if at all.

Turning from the general problems to their specific impact on the Armée du Nord, these crucial shortages of manpower, horses, and equipment crippled the cavalry forces along the northeast frontier, limiting this arm to a comparatively low percentage of the Nord's total forces. If only battle-ready cavalry is counted, the proportion of mounted troops falls to an even lower level. In general, eighteenth-century armies included 20 percent or more cavalry, at least in their field forces.[12] The line army preserved this proportion in the table of organization during the first years of the Revolution, since the mounted branch stood at 30,000 in an army of 150,000. As war approached and volunteer battalions bolstered the line at the front, the percentage of cavalry understandably decreased. Focusing on the Armée du Nord, a January 1792 report put the total forces at 54,448 and the cavalry at 8,592, or 16 percent. From this fairly respectable level, the proportion steadily declined.

The rare reports that can be assembled for the rest of 1792 suggest that mounted troops made up about 14 percent of the Nord's field forces, as opposed to garrisons. By March 1793 the proportion diminished to roughly 7 percent. Indeed, 1793 proved to be the nadir of French cavalry. The opening of the Nord's campaign that year reduced some units to skeletons. At Neerwinden the 1st Cavalry put only 250 men in the saddle, well less than half of its authorized strength. By the end of the battle only 100 effectives remained. Circumstances worsened to such a point during the spring that the Nord, already starved for cavalry, sent mounted regiments off the line to recuperate and reconstitute.[13] Even when paper figures for a regiment climbed to respectable heights, closer inspection reveals that a high percentage was in depot.[14]

By the summer of 1793 shortages of arms and equipment crippled even those units that had begun to rebuild. In early June the 9th Hussars at Amiens had only 136 sabers, forty-seven carbines, and thirty-seven pistols for 533 men. An inspection report from the Armée du Nord reveals the state of a number of other regiments at the end of June 1793. The 7th Dragoons, for example, lacked 439 helmets, 239 pairs of boots, 346 saddles, 302 bridles, and 352 bits. Since February the strength of dragoon regiments was authorized at 750 officers and men, but situation reports of the period state the real effectives of the 7th Dragoons at only 440.[15]

In late summer Representatives on Mission with the Nord complained to the Committee of Public Safety, "The infantry is in good enough a state and already rather well trained to fight. The cavalry is weak, we have no more than six to eight thousand men fit to fight and this includes those in garrison."[16] These Representatives estimated the full strength of the Nord at 140,000; therefore, they set the effective size of the cavalry contingent at 4–6 percent. But the fall battles concentrated available cavalry in the field armies, so that at Hondschoote, for example, General Jean Houchard's forces contained nearly 11 percent cavalry.

In 1794 the percentage of cavalry was enlarged, at least on paper. The 19 June 1794 situation reports for Nord troops list 26,540 cavalry (or 10 percent) out of a total of 262,416. Within the Nord there existed a serious imbalance during the spring, however, and the left wing stationed from Lille to Dunkirk boasted only 5 percent cavalry (3,200 out of 65,000 troops). A scarcity of horses held back the Nord until summer. In late March and early April Representative Vidalin reported that the Nord and Ardennes still lacked over 11,000 horses. Only in June was that deficit lowered to about 3,000, when these two sister armies claimed some 23,150 horses.[17]

The great influx of new mounted troops in 1794 only made the equipment problems still more appalling. Representative Vidalin reported to Bouchotte in April concerning the cavalry of the Armée des Ardennes. With 693 men, the 15th Cavalry Regiment approached its authorized strength of 750, but it armed these men with only 348 sabers and 341 pairs of pistols. The 20th *Chasseurs à cheval* numbered 1,022 men, essentially their authorized complement, but they mustered only 350 sabers in good condition, 289 pairs of pistols, and 407 musketoons. Even those weapons that the troopers possessed were often faulty. Representative Florent Guiot wrote from Lille to the Committee of Public Safety to complain that sabers sent from Paris "break at the first blow that our brave soldiers strike, and all that remains in their hand is a truncheon." General André de La Barre with another army wrote in April 1794, "The sabers have blades which are flexible like lead."[18] The larger numbers of cavalry in the spring of 1794 cannot be accepted as reflecting its true combat strength, when so few men carried the deadly tools of their trade.

The facts are clear; through most of the period 1791–92, the Nord functioned with only one-half to one-quarter of a standard contingent of cavalry. Although cavalry constituted a low percentage of the Nord, the Nord as a whole enjoyed such numerical superiority that had all its horsemen been battle-ready, they might have contested the field with the enemy. The quality of French cavalry, however, never equaled that of the Austrians and English. While the Austrian cavalry was superb and the English strong, the partially trained and equipped French horsemen suffered from serious qualitative weaknesses, which made them even less effective than their numbers would have implied.

The Problem of Quality

The cavalry of 1792–94 did not build upon a foundation of greatness laid in the recent past. During the last half century of the ancien régime,

French mounted regiments established a mediocre record. On the eve of the Revolution they were clearly no match for the cavalry of Prussia, Austria, and England. Each decade brought its tactical reforms. New cavalry regulations appeared in 1753, 1766, and 1788, but the systems they outlined remained inferior to those of potential enemies. Before 1789 French mounted troops did not equal their foes in sheer horsemanship, as insufficient attention had been given to training in equitation and jumping. French horses themselves were of poor quality; the best mounted regiments were those that had bought their animals across the border. Reforms instituted by Etienne, duc de Choiseul during the 1760s temporarily improved the cavalry, but his work was short-lived.

Revolution only brought further decline. More concerned with the free circulation of grain and with the preservation of civic order than with tactical expertise, authorities dispersed cavalry forces as detachments of thirty to fifty men and charged them with police duties. The number of troopers decreased, and their battlefield skills decayed from lack of practice. When the threat of approaching war forced the National Assembly to call out volunteers and build the line army to war strength, the cavalry had the furthest to go to attain adequate combat effectiveness. The colonel of the 11th Cavalry wrote in August 1791, "My regiment, dispersed for five years, has lost sight of all kinds of maneuver."[19]

As it struggled to reestablish itself and later to expand, the cavalry was hampered by the fact that it took much more time to create serviceable troopers than it did to fashion battle-worthy infantrymen. Throughout the years 1791–94 the longer period of training and seasoning meant that even when new recruits could be found, they could not be absorbed into the cavalry as quickly as could new men in the infantry. Simply replacing campaign losses could rob regiments of their effectiveness for months, and expansion placed even greater strains on the cavalry. The doubling of cavalry forces in the Nord between the fall of 1793 and the spring of 1794 implies a decline in quality at the same time that it denotes an increase in the numbers of mounted troops. This last problem becomes all the more obvious when the horse, as well as the rider, is considered. Horses needed extensive training to fit the needs of the cavalry. The tremendous increase in available horses in the short time from 39,700 in fall 1793 to nearly 100,000 in spring 1794 implies a cavalry mounted on green horses.

The relative lack of training provided to men and horses is undeniable, but another criticism of the quality of French cavalry is debatable, or at least more impressionistic. Too many officers were ill-suited by experience and age to command properly. The cavalry officers of 1792–94 were both new to command and advanced in age, an apparent paradox explained by the rapid promotion of long-service NCOs to fill command positions. It has been argued that both these characteristics sharply limited their effectiveness as officers; certainly Desbrière and Sautai share this opinion. The criticism rests on the assumptions that commanding the cavalry required considerable professional knowledge, plus a robust physique and dashing temperament. If nothing else, just the need to train and care for horses rendered the cavalry officer's job more complicated than that of the infantry officer. Yet it remained practically axiomatic that the exercise of command over cavalry was a young man's duty, because the extreme physical exertion of hard riding demanded a young and well-conditioned body, and because the psychology of cavalry placed a premium on impetuosity and vigor, virtues of youth.

Accordingly, the ideal cavalry captain or lieutenant was highly trained and experienced, yet still in his twenties or perhaps his early thirties. However, only 22 percent of the lieutenants and captains of April 1793 had served as officers before July 1789, meaning that 78 percent were comparatively new to such duties. In fact, since mass resignation and emigration really only began with the flight of the king in June 1791, the new replacement officers had less than a year of command experience before being called upon to lead their men in war. By April 1794 only 4 percent of the cavalry officers who had been on the army list in July 1789 still held commissioned rank. At the same time that company grade officers were new to their jobs, they were middle-aged. Samuel F. Scott's calculations place the median age for captains in early 1793 at forty-six to fifty and for lieutenants and sous-lieutenants combined at thirty-six to forty. Desbrière and Sautai, who employed a different sample, found that the average age of captains was 44.5, of lieutenants, thirty-nine, and of sous-lieutenants, thirty-three.[20]

Aspects of Cavalry Tactics

The formal tactical regulations that guided the mounted troops of the revolutionary army have also been criticized. During the years 1791–94 the cavalry employed the ordinance of May 1788 as modified in December 1789. These regulations failed to place sufficient emphasis on rapid movement and dash. There was too much maneuver at the trot and too little at a canter or gallop. The evolutions prescribed were too elaborate and complicated, and the ordinance lacked flexible and adaptable mass formations. When in line, a squadron stood two ranks deep along a front of forty-eight enlisted men; the remainder of the squadron gathered as a reserve troop, twenty paces to the rear. According to regulations, the charge began at a walk for 50 meters, increased to a trot for 150 meters, then a canter for 80 meters, and finished at a full gallop for the last 50 or 60 meters.[21] Charges were to be made in line against cavalry, but against infantry the ordinance permitted charges in column.

The reality of tactical usages in 1791–94 displayed limitations even greater than the formal deficiencies of the ordinance of 1788. In no major battle fought by the Nord was French cavalry a decisive factor. At Jemappes the squadrons acted boldly, but they were too dispersed to execute more than small charges of no great consequence. Neerwinden witnessed concentrated and effective attacks by the superb Austrian horsemen, but the French were incapable of responding in kind. The battlefields of Hondschoote and Wattignies were little suited to cavalry, and French mounted regiments saw slight action. General Joseph Souham gained the major victory of Tourcoing with such small cavalry forces that it comes as no surprise that they played only an insignificant role.[22] Fleurus did witness the use of General Paul Dubois's cavalry division in support of Jean-Etienne Championnet's infantry division, but, even though this was a step in the direction of future development, the cavalry was hardly decisive. Dubois's division at first met a rebuff, and only seized the offensive when Championnet himself attacked. Of course, during the early years of the war, some French cavalry regiments knew moments of greatness, but by and large the cavalry deserve little credit for French battlefield triumphs. Relentless pursuit after battle, so typical of Napoleonic cavalry, played no part in the victories of the Nord.

Beyond its role in shock assault, the cavalry did not perform its duties in skirmishing and reconnaissance with distinction. The withdrawal of fusils and musketoons from cavalry and dragoon regiments and the severe shortages of carbines in light cavalry regiments reduced the French to impotence when faced by the well-equipped and able enemy skirmishers. This fact helped tie French mounted troops to infantry support. On reconnaissance the lack of firearms and the need for support cut into the cavalry's ability to maintain contact with the enemy and report their movements. A reconnaissance detachment of 4 May 1794 demonstrates cavalry's dependence on support; it was composed of the 20th Cavalry, part of the 21st Cavalry, two horse artillery guns, and six companies of grenadiers. Even when stationed around encampments, as at the Camp de César, the cavalry occupied billets *behind* the infantry, that is, in less advanced positions. In more normal circumstances cavalry would be expected to occupy the most advanced outposts. The inability of republican cavalry in reconnaissance is also blamed for the practice followed in French encampments of waking the entire body of troops at 2 or 3 A.M. and having them stand to arms from well before dawn to mid-morning in order to avoid surprise by enemy troops who might approach undiscovered.

The records of the time and the historians who have studied them do not pass a favorable verdict on the value of mounted troops with the Nord. Harsh complaints by contemporaries witness the weakness of French cavalry along the Belgian frontier. In June 1793, Custine could write so black a judgment as, "The cavalry is almost destroyed and I am forced to send it to the rear to rebuild." Two months later General Charles de Kilmaine insisted to Bouchotte, "It is the Armée du Nord which has the greatest need for cavalry, and it is the Nord which has the least troopers." One of the most eloquent testimonials to the insufficiencies of French horsemen was the considerable correspondence accepting the superiority of enemy cavalry and suggesting schemes to provide infantry with the tools to fend off cavalry attacks that the French horse was unable to stop. Thus came the projects for pikes, stakes, and movable barriers.[23]

Arthur Chuquet, a historian of the revolutionary wars, dismissed the mounted arm, "From the month of April to the month of August 1793, generals and commissioners employed only one word, always the same, to point out its lamentable state: it is *nothing*." Henri Coutanceau, author of the classic account of the Nord's 1794 campaign, concluded, "The study of the cavalry shows that, whatever the efforts made by the Committee of Public Safety, it is impossible to improvise a cavalry worthy of the name."[24] These rough judgments (and still rougher ones have been committed to print) made it clear that the performance of republican cavalry did not account for victory. The mounted troops of France eventually claimed their hour of costly glory. Desbrière and Sautai mark Fleurus as the watershed; only after that battle did French cavalry come into its own. But during the period covered here, cavalry, generally defined as a supporting arm, was itself in need of infantry and artillery support to stand against the Austrians and English on the Belgian border.

The Artillery

Organization and Types of Artillery, 1789–94

During the revolutionary wars the French had not one but several artillery forces: foot artillery, horse artillery, and battalion artillery.[25] Each differed from the other. The force with the longest lineage was the foot artillery. Considered a part of the infantry under the ancien régime, it numbered seven regiments of twenty companies each in 1789. In October 1790 the Assembly declared the artillery to be a separate arm, on a level with infantry, cavalry, and engineers. The year 1792 saw the colonial artillery added to the total as an eighth regiment. A ninth regiment also seems to have been added, although the documentation is incomplete on this question. Although the regiments themselves grew in size from a paper figure of about 1,500 to one approaching 1,900 during the war, compared to the expansion of other arms the old foot artillery increased but little. Its limited growth was in accord with its limited role. Slow moving and cumbrous, it was marshaled in artillery parks and rarely came into play except in full-scale battles. Matti Lauerma concludes that during the years 1792–

94 foot artillery played only a modest role; certainly this was the case for the Nord.

While this traditional type of artillery remained relatively static, the artillery of the line army responded to the war crisis by multiplying the number of new horse artillery batteries. Such units possessed far greater mobility than foot batteries, because in horse artillery the crews did not march along on foot behind their cannon but were mounted on caissons and horses. Moreover, additional horses attached to the artillery teams allowed the cannon themselves to be maneuvered more rapidly. Since mounted batteries required more horses and equipment than did foot batteries, they were more expensive. However, the greater investment paid dividends in batteries that took a far more active part in full-scale battle and whose flexibility made them a decisive presence in small actions.

The French had intermittently experimented with horse artillery since the Seven Years' War, but its costs held back adoption. In December 1791 new experiments began, and on 11 January 1792 the Assembly authorized the creation of two companies of horse artillery. Each company normally constituted a battery of six guns. From this beginning, horse artillery grew rapidly. In April 1792 the number of companies was brought up to nine; in February 1793 the Convention raised the number of companies to twenty; in the summer of that year the number reached thirty. A memoir of the time exemplifies the logic behind such a rapid expansion: "A numerous horse artillery, well served, is the surest means of protecting the maneuvers [*évolutions*] of poorly trained troops by supporting its attacks *à l'arme blanche*, and by almost reducing to nothing, through taking up proper positions with speed, the advantage which better trained troops assure themselves because of their superiority in maneuver."[26] By legislation of 7 February 1794 the horse artillery became a separate branch of the service. Now termed *artillerie légère*, its nine regiments each included a staff, a depot, and six companies of eighty-four officers and men—a grand total of 513 officers and men, exclusive of the depot. The number of light artillery companies thus peaked at fifty-four. Tables of June 1794 report about 850 troops of light artillery serving with the Nord and Ardennes.[27] Throughout the campaigns of 1792–94, the horse artillery performed marvels.

Beyond the artillery parks and the horse batteries, the battalion guns of the infantry provided close material and psychological support. This artillery consisted of pairs of four-pounder cannons attached to infantry battalions. The use of battalion guns in the French army went back at least as far as 1757; however, they were abandoned after the Seven Years' War. An act of 29 September 1791 authorized National Guard battalions to add two light artillery pieces to their rosters. By a decree of 18 March 1792 these battalions could organize a company of volunteer artillerymen to serve their guns. The distribution of artillery to volunteers was further decreed in July, October, and December 1792. The organizational reforms of February 1793 recognized battalion artillery as integral to all battalions, including old line units. Demi-brigades were to include a company of sixty-four artillerymen serving six four-pounders. The crews of battalion guns generally came from the volunteers, but some units of regulars also performed this duty. These guns multiplied with the army in nearly direct proportion to the growth of infantry. By mid-1794 they represented a large share of the artillery of the Nord. At a time when the Armée du Nord numbered 222,000 soldiers on situation reports, it counted 226 battalion cannon, an overall ratio of one per thousand.[28]

To understand the favor volunteer battalion artillery enjoyed, factors other than sheer combat effectiveness must be weighed in the balance. Lauerma concluded, "It is . . . manifest that it owed the position it attained during the years 1791–1794 more to its special political character than to its military significance."[29] Free from the conservative taint of the regular army, it won praise as "the artillery of the Revolution." Increasing the number of battalion guns could multiply artillery in the field without strengthening the hand of the line army. Actually, theorists had questioned the real battlefield value of battalion guns for decades, and in general the French had rejected them in favor of concentration before the Revolution. However, the presence of artillery seemed to bolster the morale of the new battalions.

Volunteer artillery was not limited to the battalion guns, and some volunteer artillery companies served as horse artillery. The most substantial contribution of volunteer artillery came from Paris, which sent as many as seventy companies of artillery to the front.

Of Guns and Men

The cannon employed by France surpassed those of any other European army. Well before the Revolution, the French had adopted the Gribeauval system of artillery, both tubes and carriages. Before Jean-Baptiste Gribeauval the system designed by Jean-Florent de Vallière was the standard. It rested on the assumption that the cannon's ultimate targets were the walls of enemy fortresses, not the battalions. Designed for siege warfare, the tubes were thick-walled, to take more powerful charges, and long, to ensure greater range. These characteristics made them very heavy. The tube of a four-pounder in the Vallière system weighed over 500 kilograms. Gribeauval designed a true field artillery meant for the battlefield, not for siege warfare. The barrels of his cannon were neither as thick nor as long as previous models; a four-pounder weighed only 290 kilograms, roughly 40 percent lighter than the Vallière gun. Gribeauval turned his attention to gun carriages as well and even to the harnessing of the horses. The end result was a mobile system of field guns requiring fewer horses for each piece and allowing crews to manhandle the pieces more easily in the field. The standard calibers he based his system on were twelve-, eight-, and four-pounder cannon and a six-inch howitzer. Vallière denied artillerists the use of even the simplest aiming instruments; Gribeauval provided crews with graduated rear sights and an elevating screw at the breach, which allowed for much more accurate fire.

The change from the Vallière to the Gribeauval system came only after considerable controversy. Debate rose to such a pitch because the choice of guns rested upon important tactical assumptions, and these attracted most of the attention. Those who believed in the preeminence of siege warfare and trusted to counter-battery fire on the battlefield favored the Vallière system and became known as "Reds." Partisans of Gribeauval's field artillery thought more of battle and identified the enemy's troops as targets of choice for the artillery. They were called "Blues." The Blues had their way in 1765, when the army adopted the Gribeauval system. Seven years later the Reds turned the tables on the Blues, as the new system was rejected, but in 1774 Gribeauval's guns, with some modifications, won final acceptance.

Given the ubiquitous equipment shortages that plagued the revolutionary armies, it comes as somewhat of a surprise that the Armée du Nord did not suffer a crushing lack of field pieces. This is all the more surprising because perhaps the worst of all matériel hurdles stood in the way of the artillery. Barrels were difficult and expensive to forge; gun carriages and caissons represented major outlays of labor and money. The number of draft horses required and the necessary harnessing represented still another significant drain on French resources. The two four-pounders and their caissons attached to an infantry battalion required eighteen to twenty-two horses, and in the artillery parks the average rose to twenty-two horses per gun because of the heavier calibers and additional caissons kept by the parks. Horse artillery harnessed six horses to each gun and caisson, as opposed to the four in foot artillery; thus, more horses were required.[30] The demand was not met in full, to be sure, but numbers were brought up to acceptable levels by mid-1794.

The lack of artillery was felt most acutely in 1793. An artillery *état* of 18 July 1793 reported significant shortages of artillery in the Armée du Nord. Only half of the number of pieces thought necessary were available. The heavier calibers posed the worst problem, as 62 percent of the desired four-pounders were on line, but only 33 percent of the needed twelve-pounders stood in the batteries. The same report stated that of 14,545 horses needed, only 5,086 were with the Nord. The government strove to respond to the lack of cannon by forging barrels in new state factories. In one month of 1794 French foundries produced 597 cannons. In 1789 the French possessed

1,300 field pieces. By the end of 1795 they had about 2,550 bronze field pieces.[31]

As horse artillery continued to expand and the Republic's thirty companies of the summer of 1793 rose to fifty-six in the summer of 1794, the demand for horses skyrocketed. The requisition of cavalry horses ordered in October 1793 carried a proviso that each canton must also supply two artillery horses. In June 1794 the foot artillery of the parks in the Nord contained 2,958 men present under arms and 1,701 horses. The horse artillery had 523 men and 1,384 horses.[32]

By June 1794 the Nord claimed a reasonable number of guns in proportion to its field forces. The Nord alone, without the Ardennes, numbered 221,000 men at this point; however, only 128,000 were present under arms in its active field forces. For these men, the Nord mustered about 225 battalion guns. Since the Nord included about 175 infantry battalions in June, there were still not enough four-pounders to go around. The horse artillery can be estimated at perhaps forty cannon.[33] The artillery park must have contained more than eighty guns and perhaps as many as 150. Adding these estimates together, the total field artillery of the Nord amounted to something between 345 and 415 cannon. Consequently, the Nord could boast a reasonable proportion of artillery—2.7–3.2 guns per thousand for its troops in the field. The well-equipped Grand Armée had fewer than two guns per thousand in 1805, and the largest concentration of cannon Napoleon ever put into battle, according to David Chandler, was 3.3 per thousand.[34] The Nord never went begging for artillery, as it did for cavalry.

Measured against the standards of infantry and cavalry, artillery required personnel with elaborate technical knowledge. Both officers and those who manned the guns had to be highly trained in the special skills of the artillerist. During the ancien régime the artillery attracted an elite rank and file. Manhandling heavy cannon demanded men of above average size and strength. Their physical stature alone won elite status for cannoneers, who received the same pay as infantry grenadiers. On the other hand, judged by the social prejudices of the aristocracy, artillery officers were relatively low-born. Without the dash of a cavalry officer, or even an infantry leader, the battery commander seemed more a mechanic or a mathematician. Consequently, the artillery schools attracted young men of poorer, less prestigious noble families. It was formerly argued that a great many *roturiers* became officers of the artillery; however, David D. Bien's research indicates that this was not the case, especially after 1781.[35]

Many scholars have suggested that the elite status of rank and file and the relative low standing of artillery officers in ancien régime society insulated artillery from the worst effects of desertion and emigration brought on by the Revolution. Should the above logic prove correct, the artillery could be expected to have enjoyed an unusual stability, and, so the argument goes, it was an element of the old army called upon to rescue the new army from many a scrape. The facts challenge this argument. Artillery suffered severely from erosion of its personnel between 1789 and 1792. Scott's analysis of the rank and file of the line army in 1793 shows that, although cannoneers had longer service than the volunteers, they could not claim significantly more time in the ranks than their brothers in the line infantry and cavalry.[36] In 1789 enlisted men in all three branches claimed a median of four to six years' service, and in 1793 they looked back on a median of only one to three years' service. Line artillery had slightly fewer newcomers, since only 29 percent of its men, compared to 37 percent of cavalrymen, claimed less than one year's service. However, a survey of the evidence leads to the conclusion that the artillery was essentially no better in retaining its enlisted personnel than were the line infantry and cavalry.

Artillery officers may not have left the army at the same rate as infantry and cavalry commanders, but by April 1794, 81 percent of the officers who led it in July 1789 were no longer on the army list. The comparable figures for infantry and cavalry stood at 95 percent and 96 percent.[37] To overemphasize the stability of line artillery personnel distorts history. Most of its rank and file had only joined the service after the storming of the Bastille, and the overwhelming majority of its officers had not held commissions before the Revolution. Of course, the volunteer artillery was served by men and led by officers with little if any artillery experience.

A limited number of schools provided technical training for the new artillerymen of the revolutionary era. Enlisted personnel of foot artillery were trained in schools located in towns situated along the borders of France. Horse artillery depot companies established themselves in towns where the schools were located, so that the facilities of these institutions could be employed in the technical training of recruits. Instruction unique to horse artillery was undertaken by the depot company itself.[38]

Foot artillery lost much of its best manpower to the growing and glorious horse artillery, and recruits who filled the gaps created in foot artillery units often had little if any training. On the whole, the quality of expertise in the rank and file of the foot artillery declined over the years 1792–94. As one officer of this era wrote: "The foot artillery, enervated by the creation and growth of horse artillery, began to lose the military spirit, and the new cannoneers, limited to the manual labor of arsenals and artillery parks, remained peasants and became complainers."[39]

New officers of the line artillery received their training at Châlons, the only school established for such instruction. The first class took its exams in January 1792. Prospective officers received grounding in mathematics and theory, although practical training was thin.[40] Candidates attended classes for varying periods of time. The future General Maximilien Foy entered the school in March 1792 and left to join his company of foot artillery with the Nord in September. Pion des Loches, on the other hand, entered the school in April 1794 and took his final examination in June 1795. Classes were small; Pion des Loches belonged to a class of only forty-two. Châlons fell short of meeting the need for officers, and the army made do by commissioning NCOs without examinations. Thus there were many trained officers, but they served alongside many officers without the proper mathematical and technical preparation.

The worst manpower problems were posed not by men or officers, but by the drivers. An archaic method of supplying horses and drivers hampered the French, even after the Revolution ushered in considerable military reform. Teams and teamsters were hired by private contract. Four major contractors supplied tens of thousands of draft horses for the artillery through 1792 and 1793. Early in 1794 supply of these animals became the responsibility of a public monopoly, but the horses still did not belong to the army, and the system only degenerated under public control. It returned to private hands in 1795. Neither were the drivers soldiers, not even in the horse artillery. Many civilian teamsters performed their duties faithfully and bravely, but stories abound of drivers who cut the traces to gallop off to safety. Some officers had the elite artillerymen keep watch over the drivers, who were regarded as anything but elite.[41] This anachronistic system, dating back to medieval military practices, continued until 1800, when Napoleon organized the drivers as separate battalions within the artillery.

Artillery Tactics in Battle

To say that the artillery dominated battle along the Belgian frontier would rob the infantry of its hard-won glory. Still the Armée du Nord owed much to its gunners. A detailed description of their tactics along the northern frontier is beyond the scope of this chapter, and probably beyond what the sources provide. The picture of artillery on campaign with the Nord is yet one more puzzle lacking many of its pieces. To the extent that it is possible to outline tactical practice, a description must distinguish between the use of foot-and-horse batteries in the rare full-scale battles, the more common roles of horse artillery on campaign, and the function of the ubiquitous battalion guns in daily service.

Artillery tactics employed in the Armée du Nord evolved from ancien régime practices and theories as modified by the special circumstances of the Revolution. At mid-century the French typically marshaled their heavier field pieces from the artillery reserve in a few batteries at the flanks and center of the battle line or on some prominent ground that offered good fields of fire to these long-range, but essentially immobile, guns. At the same time each battalion possessed from one to three light cannon, and these pieces, dispersed in the field, garnished the entire front with their fire. In response to the debacle of the Seven Years' War, the French re-evaluated their artillery matériel and techniques. Beyond the controversy over the Gribeauval guns, the primary issues of contention were the concentration, mobility, and function of artillery on the battlefield. Reds and Blues eventually agreed on the need to concentrate guns in massed batteries, which called for the elimination of battalion guns and small batteries. The French were more deeply divided over the need for mobility. Gribeauval's victory gave the day to lighter guns, which could be more easily handled. Rapid battlefield mobility required horse batteries, but, although these were discussed, they were not instituted until 1792. Lastly, conservatives believed that the artillery's first targets were the enemy's guns. This had been a mid-century assumption. The well-known Joseph du Teil and other reformers persuasively insisted that the primary target was the enemy's troops. In place of counter-battery fire, he urged the use of artillery to prepare the way for assault by infantry and cavalry. The tactical theories of the late ancien régime would only become reality under Napoleon; they outlined the future.

The combined crises of Revolution and war forced French conceptions of artillery into a mode that, for a time, contrasted with theory before 1789. Rather than seeing artillery as an active and independent, even coequal, branch of the army, artillery now provided a means to remedy the weaknesses of an expanded, but untried and unsteady, body of troops. The need for support took precedence over the need for concentration. Battalion guns, abandoned after the Seven Years' War, reappeared to stiffen volunteer infantry; this practice was extended to all battalions in 1793. This meant that half or more of an army's artillery pieces would be dispersed along the line in battle.[42] The year 1792 did witness the birth of French horse artillery, desired by earlier theorists, but here the midwife was a desire to bolster an outnumbered and outclassed cavalry. As General Kilmaine wrote from the Nord in July 1793, "I beg you . . . to employ the most prompt means to furnish us with light artillery, it is the only way to make up for our scarcity of cavalry."[43] In the Nord light artillery commonly fought in half- or third-batteries, apparently to increase the number of units dispersed among cavalry formations. Not even the company was preserved as a concentration of guns. While a certain concentration might be expected among artillery from the parks, even these cannon usually stood in small batteries.

Much has been written concerning the tactical marriage of artillery fire and infantry attack columns during the wars of the Revolution. Frankly, the records of the Nord do not speak volumes on this subject; they rarely supply the details of cavalry or artillery tactics in the way that they cover infantry. However, there is no question that this technique developed early with the Nord. Paul Charles Thiébault's description of a small battle on 6 November 1792 at Le Blaton leaves little doubt concerning this development: "We were rapidly formed in battalion attack columns and put into motion at the charge [*au pas de charge*], under the protection of all our pieces. The enemy columns, cannonaded and then quickly attacked with the bayonet, were thrown back in disorder." Custine expressed his reliance on such tactics when he insisted "our cannon and our bayonets, these are our only arms." The higher mobility of horse artillery gave it the potential of accompanying attacking infantry and supporting its assault at close range. As stated above, the French valued mounted batteries as essential aids to infantry for "supporting its attack, *à l'arme blanche*."[44] The details of close support remain vague, but it did occur, as at Wattignies.

A battle-by-battle survey of Nord artillery in combat begins with Valmy, although the bulk of the Nord stood as passive reserves behind General François Kellermann's forces that day. Valmy was a victory of artillery, but its stunning success there should not be allowed to warp the perception of its role throughout the first three years of the war. Valmy was a compact battlefield with great open fields of fire offered to guns placed along the ridges overlooking the Prussian advance. Never again would the Nord see a battlefield so tailored to artillery.

At Jemappes the vastly superior French artillery took up position in several batteries along the front. Just as the infantry assault lacked focus, so did the utilization of cannon, which resembled mid-century practice much more than it foreshadowed Napoleonic tactics. In his classic study of French artillery, Lauerma criticizes the placement of French guns in this battle as too "linear," a criticism he repeats when discussing the defeat of Neerwinden. For all its superior numbers and vast consumption of ammunition, French artillery inflicted surprisingly few casualties at Jemappes. At Hondschoote marshy ground, restricted roadways, and thick hedges limited the scope of horsemen and cannon. Republican infantry battered its way to an indecisive victory largely on its own. However, a battery of ten field pieces was important in the final assault on Hondschoote itself.

Wattignies provided the artillery of the Nord a rare, perhaps unique, hour of glory. At the outset, the French dissipated their artillery in a linear dispersion across the entire front. Yet on 16 October a concentration of artillery fire on the French right prepared the way for the assault on the town of Wattignies. Some have gone so far as to credit the artillery with Jourdan's success that day. An English observer at the battle spoke of the "immense artillery" of the French.[45] The actual artillery involved in the crucial assault included three batteries of horse artillery and two of foot, a total of about thirty guns. As the horse batteries performed with great effect, accompanying the attacking infantry, the batteries of foot artillery engaged the Austrian guns in counter-battery fire.

The great battles the Nord fought in 1794 did not feature even the limited concentration of guns that appeared at Wattignies. Tourcoing resolved itself into a series of smaller battles in which concentration of the artillery park was out of the question. At Fleurus the great front of the battle, extending over eighteen miles, again led to a series of isolated combats. There was some massing of artillery fire in the separate engagements. François-Séverin Marceau, leading troops of the Armée des Ardennes, fell back in the face of the concentrated fire of over twenty-seven field pieces directed by the Austrian general, Johann Peter Freiherr von Beaulieu. In response, Marceau and François-Joseph Lefebrve finally assembled a battery of twelve guns on the French right. On other parts of the battlefield, horse artillery batteries performed magnificently with Championnet and with the cavalry division under Dubois.

By 1794 the French had learned from experience something of what the theorists advocated before 1789, particularly the value of mobile batteries as championed by du Teil. However, great batteries that united tremendous fire power focused on a crucial spot in the enemy's battle line would only come later. During the years 1792–94 the bulk of the Nord's cannon was still strung out along the front in combat.

Light Artillery on Campaign

Horse artillery exerted an influence on the course of battle and on the daily challenges of campaigning far in excess of foot or volunteer artillery. Mounted batteries were not reserved for great battles alone but committed to smaller combats, advance guards, and the like. The elite gunners who manned these cannon volunteered from foot artillery and cavalry. Their act of volunteering testified to their desire to face high risk and hard labor. Already proud men, they developed a particular pride in the unquestioned value and active omnipresence of their batteries. Séruzier characterized the high self-esteem of horse artillerymen, "They were renowned for their courage, and no less for their contentious spirit. They pushed esprit de corps far beyond the point of virtue and believed themselves infinitely superior to their comrades in foot artillery."[46] A glance at their performance on campaign, away from the major battlefield, adds to an appreciation of light artillery as a means of decisive intervention.

As stated above, horse artillery companies normally split in halves or thirds to multiply the number of units available for support. This would mean that each unit had only two or three guns, since as a rule each company was a battery of four eight-pounders and two six-inch howitzers. The records of the Nord show light artillery brigaded with cavalry, as would be expected. Marshaled in this fashion, mounted batteries both provided close support to cavalry and added their weight to quick moving reserves and reinforcements. In one exemplary instance, on 23 April 1794, the 5th

Paris and the battalions around it were broken by a charge of Austrian cavalry. The line dissolved in route; "however, the cavalry regiments came with some pieces of light artillery, and pushed back the enemy, inflicting great losses on them."[47]

Horse artillery also worked in conjunction with skirmishers, or *tirailleurs*. Again the clearest explanation for this coordination is the high mobility of mounted batteries. Even small caliber battalion guns could not keep up with the flow of the skirmish, particularly in broken ground. However, the extra draft horses and mounted gunners of light artillery made such mobility and flexibility possible for cannon of much more substantial caliber. For the foot artillery of the park to have performed such feats was out of the question. "I had three men and six horses wounded," reported General Jacques Desjardin concerning the attack on the village of Hautes. "The enemy's loss was much more considerable thanks to the light artillery and *tirailleurs*." On the march, standard practice in the Armée du Nord guaranteed that horse artillery would see constant small-scale action. Light artillery units were usually in the van of the army.[48]

Battalion Guns

The employment of battalion guns has received little attention from military historians, yet over half of the cannon of the Nord were distributed among the battalions. Acting as they did, only in conjunction with infantry, it is impossible to distinguish their effect from that of the battalions that they supported. It can be argued that even at their best battalion guns still frustrated the principle of concentration, thereby dissipating the potential destructiveness of massed artillery. The insignificance, or perceived insignificance, of volunteer artillery explains the neglect it has suffered. Among the few documents that allow some informed comment on the use of battalion guns, a valuable one deals with the Armée du Nord; it is the journal of Louis Bricard, a volunteer artilleryman in a battalion from Paris.

Bricard served as a cannoneer with the Parisian National Guard before he joined the 5th Paris, a volunteer battalion bound for the front. Enrolled on 3 September 1792, his company drew their equipment, two four-pounders and one caisson, two days later. On 15 September he fired his first shot against the enemy. Bricard mentions no specific training in the handling of pieces, but he must have learned the basics during his Guard service. Early in November his company of gunners was detached from the 5th Paris, then in garrison, and assigned to the 1st Haute-Vienne, a more experienced battalion ordered to go on campaign but which had no cannon of its own.

Bricard speaks of the two four-pounders of his company standing alone most times, but occasionally they joined with the guns of other battalions to form small ad hoc batteries of four or more guns. Sometimes guns were stationed in small redoubts or other prepared positions. In combat the battalion cannon commonly took the obvious position, with their battalions in the line of battle, but other options existed. When a battalion dispersed as *tirailleurs,* the guns might stand to the rear and fire in support of them. In one such instance Bricard reports that his piece fired into a woods in the direction where the enemy was thought to be. Frequently the guns stayed behind with little other intention than to provide covering fire in case of retreat.[49]

Volunteer battalion guns were not as immobile on the battlefield as is assumed by some analysts. Bricard's civilian drivers and their precious horses stayed up with the cannon; they did not retire to safety when bullets flew. Standard practice in the Nord, as reflected in Houchard's instructions, demanded that artillery teams stand in harness by their guns from before dawn to late afternoon. Bricard states that his cannon changed positions during battles, in one case limbering and galloping off to escape capture in the midst of a hot action.[50]

Reading Bricard leaves the impression of battalion guns more as defensive than offensive weapons. Even with the potential mobility of the pieces, he speaks little about using cannon to support infantry assaults in textbook fashion. This points to the matter contemporaries themselves singled out as paramount—the need for battalion artillery as a way of steadying inexperienced troops. It is interesting how often Bricard states that the cannon were situated not to press an attack but to cover a retreat.[51] In many tactical situations the rapidity of advance or the character of the battlefield would preclude guns advancing with their battalions, but I believe that there was more involved. Cannon were deployed as a backstop to reassure troops that they would not be overwhelmed, even if they were forced to concede ground. Such pieces provided a rallying point and a source of superior firepower. Battalion guns could shore up morale, promising an edge to republican infantry who faced capable enemy infantry and awesome enemy cavalry.

The conduct of cavalry and artillery in the field illustrates that patriotic enthusiasm alone could not guarantee victory. If all the rhetoric concerning élan, the offensive, and the *arme blanche* could be given exclusive credit, then revolutionary cavalry should have been splendid; however, it fell short because of crippling shortages, inadequate training, and suspect doctrine. Perhaps the excellent mounted batteries of the Nord expressed something approaching the cult of the bayonet as it applied to artillery. But the men who served these batteries were a select group, imbued with a strong esprit de corps. They also employed the finest pieces in Europe and were guided by an effective technical doctrine borrowed from forward-looking military theorists of the eighteenth century. Foot artillery and battalion guns played a much more questionable role. Acting contrary to the best professional opinion, they dispersed the potentially decisive power of their guns. High motivation may have been necessary for the success of revolutionary forces, but it was not sufficient. French battlefield performance also depended on at least three other factors: a force structure consistent with the resources of revolutionary France; an adequate degree of technical expertise, which could only be gained by training; and a tactical system that exploited the full range of techniques suited to the men and weapons of the era. Infantry achieved dominance because it met these criteria.

Chapter 10

Training an Evolving Infantry

THE PERFORMANCE of its infantry determined triumph or defeat for the Armée du Nord et des Ardennes. Popular wisdom holds that revolutionary infantry sank to the nadir of tactical finesse during the opening years of the war. Victory came, but only as a result of enthusiasm and horde tactics. A massive influx of green recruits coupled with a lack of effective training doomed the French to a clumsy and costly style of combat. According to this argument, in lieu of ability, numbers alone saved the Republic from defeat. In contradiction to the stereotype, French tactics actually displayed reasonable order, flexibility, and efficiency. But before one can plausibly assert that the Armée du Nord ever maneuvered effectively, one must dispel the image of an army in which training and drill were regarded either as impossible or as unnecessary luxuries.

The infantry drill masters of the Nord were vital to its success, just as their forerunners were to the armies of the ancien régime. Without question, they faced a Herculean task of military instruction, but it was far from impossible. Certainly, instructors of cavalry and artillery troops had a rougher go of it, since their novices took much longer to learn the skills of their trades. General Félix de Wimpffen, a savant who sat on the military committee of the National Assembly, gave this estimate of the time required to train men of the different branches: "Everybody knows . . . infantry recruits with six weeks service are in a condition to serve usefully, when they are incorporated with veterans. But it is not the same case with recruits in the cavalry and the artillery; the former require three or four years of drill, and the latter, up to seven or eight years."[1] Wimpffen almost certainly underestimated the time necessary to groom an infantry recruit. Eighteenth-century rule of thumb generally held that a man was still a recruit until he served through a couple of campaigns. However, the essential contrast between the training periods of infantry on the one hand and cavalry and artillery on the other remains the primary point.

Revolutionary armies did not normally have the luxury of surrounding recruits with veteran soldiers. The ability of battalions to maneuver effectively under fire depended upon their experience and the number of new men in their ranks. These factors pulled in opposite directions, training and experience heightening capacities, the influx of green recruits reducing them. Both deserve notice in any attempt to understand the growing technical competence of the Armée du Nord.

The Course of Instruction in the Nord

In their basic outlines instruction and exercise in the Nord strongly resembled their eighteenth-century predecessors, though not much spit and polish could be demanded of half-clothed volunteers. Two basic drill manuals guided the tactical exercises of French battalions—both prescribed a rather formal tactical system. The more important of the two, *Règlement concernant l'exercice et les manoeuvres de l'infanterie du 1er août 1791,* ordered a fairly stiff manual of arms, a normal marching pace of seventy-six steps per minute, and a quick step of 100 per minute. Battalions were to maneuver in a variety of set column formations, while in combat they were usually to deploy into lines of three ranks. The *Règlement* detailed several forms of volley fire plus a type of voluntary fire. A result of years of debate and experimentation, this bulky manual was at first intended only for regular infantry. The other drill regulation, a simplified version intended for use by volunteer battalions, was commonly called the *Instruction de M. Noailles,* after the chairman of the committee that composed it. In most ways the two manuals shared the same tactical system, except that the *Instruction* directed that troops form line in only two ranks.[2]

Certain orders issued by commanders of the Armée du Nord modified some aspects of drill, but the fundamentals remained the same. Custine, for example, went to great lengths to insure that his troops adopted a new cadence of ninety steps per minute on the march. Also, in the summer of 1793, the special school set up at Cambrai seems to have emphasized movements in mass battalion columns, but the form of these columns came out of the 1791 *Règlement.* In late 1793 commanders decided to discard the *Instruction* with its formation on two ranks, and the *Règlement* became the sole standard of instruction and drill.[3]

When reports and orders spoke of instruction, maneuver, and exercise, they generally referred only to the set-piece skills of the parade ground, since the looser tactics of the skirmisher did not regularly appear on the agenda of training camps. Even special light infantry units underwent the same course of close order drill learned by the heavy infantry. Light infantrymen, or *tirailleurs,* probably received more practice in markmanship than did line infantrymen.[4] But French military opinion held that the light infantryman could best learn the techniques of open order combat through actual experience, not formal instruction.

A normal course of instruction for a new recruit began with the *école de soldat,* i.e., the rudiments of marching and the manual of arms. Men usually drilled twice daily for one to three hours a session, circumstances permitting. A lack of muskets often forced a change in this routine, however. Without arms, only marching could be taught, and recruits would find themselves maneuvering with the entire battalion even though they were ignorant of the basic manual of arms. After the *école de soldat* came the *école de peloton,* or the elements of company drill. Once capable in these preliminaries, the recruit joined his battalion to perform the evolutions of the *école de bataillon.* In good circumstances it took about three months to prepare a novice to take his place with a battalion in the field.[5] Beyond the preliminaries, occasionally several battalions maneuvered together. Minor combat engagements formed part of the recruit's preparation for battle, since no matter how well drilled, until a soldier had seen real action he was considered unreliable. Events usually interrupted this course of training. Allied offensives or the pressures exerted by the Parisian government quite often forced partially trained recruits into action.

Four Periods in the Development of the Armée du Nord

Conditions that encouraged or inhibited training and the arrival of different recruit levies divide an account of training into four periods. Each will be considered in detail. At its inception in December 1791 the Armée du Nord included line regiments and recently mobilized volunteer battalions. New and inexperienced units of these Volunteers of 1791 had much to learn, but the regulars had so degenerated in 1789–90 that they too possessed little ability. When the campaign opened in April 1792, the troops met only with defeat. After a summer spent in training and in limited engagements designed to harden the soldiers, the Nord finally emerged in the fall as a seasoned force. Under Charles Dumouriez's command it fought well in September and triumphed at Jemappes, 6 November 1792.

Unfortunately, Dumouriez's proud army deteriorated during the following winter. Veteran battalions suffered heavily from desertion. At the same time, raw volunteer battalions raised during the summer and fall of 1792 now joined the Nord. Since most troops were on the move or scattered in small parties, little training took place; thus the winter months did not create skilled soldiers out of the new battalions. At the Battle of Neerwinden, 18 March 1793, an Austrian army dealt the unready Nord a severe setback. This period closed with a costly retreat.

A tremendous task now faced those generals who succeeded to command after Dumouriez went over to the enemy. Battalions reduced to skeleton force by a rigorous winter, bloody battle, and a disastrous retreat had to be brought up to strength by the massive incorporation of still one more levy of fresh troops. In April and May men who had been conscripted according to the law of 24 February 1793 began arriving. While the Volunteers of 1791 and 1792 retained their own battalions, the majority of this most recent levy found themselves doled out to established battalions in need of replacements. From April to August the Armée du Nord was virtually recreated. An intensive period of training directed by figures such as Custine and Hugues-Alexandre-Joseph Meunier paid off in the solid but indecisive victories of Hondschoote, 8 September, and Wattignies, 15–16 October.

As the Armée du Nord entered the winter of 1793–94, it did not repeat the mistakes of the year before. Again the Nord absorbed a great block of manpower—the thousands raised by the *levée en masse* of 23 August 1793. But this time battalions that incorporated the recruits were not as exhausted as they had been after Neerwinden. Training progressed throughout the winter and the following spring. When a new campaign began in April, the Allied armies inflicted some harsh blows on the Nord, but they could not reverse its momentum. Elements of the Armée du Nord displayed a high level of ability in the decisive victories of 18 May at Tourcoing and 26 June at Fleurus.

The Creation of Dumouriez's Army

Training to May 1792

In mid-1791 French line infantry still bore many scars inflicted through the ordeals of desertion and indiscipline, which plagued line regiments during the first two years of the Revolution. It also contained a high percentage of recruits. Consequently, on 15 June 1791 the Assembly, now fearful of war, ordered that regular battalions assemble in camps of instruction along the frontier. Only six days later, learning of the king's flight, the Assembly further directed that Volunteers of 1791 be activated, and in July it began ordering them to join the line troops marshaled on the borders. France at this time was divided into military administrative districts, called divisions, and Rochambeau held command over the 1st, 2nd, and 16th divisions in the northeast. There he labored to prepare his troops for war. Later, he wrote: "Our troops, as much those of the line as those of the National Volunteers, after a peace of thirty years, interrupted only by the partial wars of America and Corsica, had the greatest need to be disciplined, to be drilled, and to be hardened by gradual successes." By August 1791, 100,000 troops guarded the various borders of France, and roughly one-third of them belonged to Rochambeau's three divisions.[6]

As mentioned above, the regulars badly needed drilling. Since emigration removed the majority of experienced officers from the line battalions, Rochambeau's new officer cadre was made up largely of men promoted from the ranks of NCOs. That fall, before the volunteer battalions reached the frontiers, he held maneuvers with the regulars. These exercises apparently proved disappointing, although they were performed "with more precision than one could expect with such a considerable replacement of officers."[7] Much had to be done that winter, as the volunteer battalions joined the regulars.

In hopes of abandoning winter quarters early in 1792, the old Marshal labored diligently: "I am hurrying to put us in a state to form camps on our frontiers, there to work and instruct our troops in some formidable encampments [*positions*] which I have prepared, and to season them by victories if we are attached." Such was his program—no major offensive until the men were trained and acclimatized to combat. In a proposal of 15 April 1792 he argued that the Nord should be disposed in camps of instruction at Dunkirk, Maubeuge, and Valenciennes. Even with the declaration of war several days later, training, not offensive action, remained Rochambeau's goal. In fact, on 24 April he suggested to his Austrian rivals a truce applying to skirmishes and raids until both sides felt their troops to be prepared; the Austrians accepted.[8]

The kind of training Rochambeau detailed for his army during the months prior to the declaration of war can be inferred from the following order issued at this time. Section seven contains such rich material that it is quoted here in entirety:

> Commanders of infantry units will drill their troops, as much as the weather and the locality permits, in the different maneuvers of the line, particularly in the marches of columns, flank marches, forming the line, and in different manners of diminishing the fronts of sections, in the march in columns as well as in the maintenance of proper distances; but in every case, they will concern themselves with individual [*en detail*] drill and particularly with the loading and movements of the different ways of firing. Firing drills will be conducted individually [*en detail*] for the recruits or in groups for the privates, in which they will make certain that the soldier holds his fusil firmly and aims his shot. Line battalions will always assemble and drill, in maneuver and fire, in three ranks, and National Volunteers in two ranks.[9]

The evolutions listed above typified eighteenth-century combat. Yet it is important to notice that marches in line are not on the list; all movement is apparently performed in columns. Light infantry tactics are not even mentioned. Line and volunteer battalions must drill, but each according to their own regulations.

The respite the Marshal desired was not to be. Dumouriez, then minister of foreign affairs, ordered Rochambeau to invade the Austrian Netherlands with two columns led by General Théobald Dillon and Alexandre-Louis-Gontaut, duc de Biron. Rochambeau thought it unwise to invade Flanders with such an army, but Dumouriez remained adamant. In defense of his position Rochambeau later wrote that his troops were "without training, officers, or discipline."[10] Probably he exaggerated here, but his exasperation is understandable.

His battalions proved unready; their advance ended in disaster. Rochambeau had not had his chance to prepare his men by small engagements and small victories. Instead of fighting bravely, the advancing battalions broke and ran. General Dillon's column went forward from Lille toward Tournai but panicked on 29 April. The unfortunate Dillon was slain by his own troops. Those observers who wish to portray volunteer battalions as unreliable and line troops as steady and loyal should note that Dillon's entire column of 2,300 men included only one company of volunteers. Biron's column behaved better, though his troops also fled the field. After marching on Mons from Valenciennes, Biron resolved to withdraw, but on 30 April his men, over three-quarters from line units, bolted for Valenciennes.[11]

Within a few days, a disgusted Rochambeau resigned his command. Not given the time he requested and ordered to send into battle troops he knew to be unprepared, he felt justified in putting an end to a bad affair.

Training, May to September 1792

The defeats of late April 1792 did not really leave the army substantially weakened. Few men had fallen, and the troops had seen action, however inglorious. Some of the cockiness disappeared, but there was an improvement. Several months spent in one form or another of training now lay behind the regulars and the Volunteers of 1791. More maneuver and more experience would transform them into first-class battalions.

Back in their camps once again, French infantrymen continued the instruction begun under Rochambeau. Marshal Nicholas, baron de Luckner, who took command on 19 May, did not allow them much time before he began another invasion of the Austrian Netherlands. On 9 June he marched out of the Camp de Famars, near Valenciennes, with 20,000 men. Advancing by way of Lille, Luckner's column eventually seized Menin and Courtrai on 19 June. After some minor success, he decided to withdraw from these towns and returned to Lille on 30 June. In the words of Louis-Joseph Lahure, then a captain in the Belgian Legion marching with the French, "The expedition had thus been useless. However, it had this one advantage, to give a little confidence to the troops, showing them what they were capable of by a small success."[12]

The months of July and August gave the French further experience in marches and small combats. Duty in camps and the larger garrisons provided battalions the opportunity to drill together and adjust to war conditions. Best known among the Nord's several camps, the Camp de Maude contained as many as 8,200 soldiers during this period. Dumouriez, no longer minister of war, took command of Maude, where he devoted his considerable talents to readying the troops for serious campaigning. Drilling continued. In a law of 9 July the Assembly had just ordered that each volunteer battalion be sent a copy of the *Instructions de M. Noailles*. Beyond application of the manuals, Dumouriez also trained infantry in *petite guerre,* or small-scale combat, by the only means then believed appropriate, firsthand experience. He formed two bodies of "flankers" numbering 400–500 each. These he sent out constantly on patrols, raids, and ambushes. The flankers rotated every week so that eventually all the troops at Maude served in this kind of light infantry combat for some short time. Every skirmish helped turn regulars and volunteers into veterans. Dumouriez did not stand alone in his policy of conducting small operations to harden the men. From camps at Maubeuge, Famars, Valenciennes, and elsewhere, parties of line and volunteer infantry engaged Austrian detachments.[13]

During mid- and late July that weird exchange, the *chassé-croisé,* took place. Judging from the situation reports of line battalions, the Nord lost a bit more than it gained in this political-military maneuver. Taking into account the further switches that seemed to occur during Dumouriez's later march south, nineteen line battalions left the Nord, sixteen entered it, and thirty-seven were continually with the army:[14] Lafayette's battalions had experienced much the same rhythm of training and action as those of the Nord, so little change in quality and preparation must have attended the *chassé-croisé*.

By the time extensive operations began in September, regulars and Volunteers of 1791 had logged months of drill and a reasonable amount of battlefield experience. In the fall of 1792 they could be expected to perform, perhaps crudely but adequately, the tactical system contained in the drill manuals; they came up to expectations.

Performance in Combat, September and November 1792

When Dumouriez led the Armée des Ardennes south into the Argonne, it had become reasonably able. Units might still panic, as did Jean-Pierre-François, chevalier de Chasot's soldiers once the Austrians had turned the French position by seizing Croix-aux-Bois.[15] Still, by and large, his army marched rapidly and fought well. When General François Kellermann brought up the fresh Armée du centre, the Armée des Ardennes stood off as a spectator of the battle of Valmy. After a limited pursuit, Dumouriez's battalions returned north, but they now brought back something they had not had when they rushed south, a momentum of victory.

By late October, on paper the Nord loomed much larger than it had in early September. Swelled by battalions from the 1792 levies, the Armée du Nord mustered an invasion force of from 88,000 to 95,000 troops stretching from Lille in the north to Sedan in the south. But of this figure, only the 40,000 under Dumouriez's direct command at Valenciennes would play a decisive role. Of the sixty-four battalions with him, only thirteen were Volunteers of 1792.[16]

When the force assembled at Valenciennes advanced and confronted the Austrians at Jemappes, it possessed a numerical advantage of nearly three to one. But this should not detract from the fine tactical ability of Dumouriez's now veteran battalions. By all accounts they maneuvered like professionals. The day after the battle Dumouriez reported: "In all the movements that I made them perform under enemy fire, I saw them maneuver and march as if they were on a parade ground. In the preceding three days especially, I have myself admired their precision in executing the maneuvers and deployments that I ordered." Dampierre, in his story of the battle, supported Dumouriez. "I swear that it is impossible to execute better such a complicated movement under such a brisk and close fire of forty cannon." Further descriptions by César Berthier and General Théodore-François Leclaire leave little doubt that the line troops and Volunteers of 1791 were proficient and courageous infantrymen by November 1792.[17] The following winter, however, was to bring about the decay of these admirable battalions.

The Destruction of Dumouriez's Army

Dispersion and Desertion, November 1792 to March 1793

Winter treated any eighteenth-century army harshly; bad weather, inadequate rations, forced confinement, and increased sickness damaged all belligerents. Still, the months from November to March enervated the Armée du Nord to a greater degree than would normally be expected. Although casualties at Jemappes and related engagements were high, veteran battalions could not stop to replenish their ranks. The French pressed on, driving the retreating Austrians from the southern Low Countries. Then, depleted and tired, the Nord's battalions settled into winter quarters.

French logistical inefficiency ruled out concentration in a few large camps. Dispersed in order to supply themselves more easily, French soldiers devoted themselves to foraging rather than training. Generals protested against this situation, but their men had little other recourse. General Dominique Diettmann, commanding troops in the Armée des Ardennes, complained that the soldier gave little attention "to discipline and instruction when he is separated from his unit and from the eyes of his main commander."[18]

Not only did such conditions erode a unit's ability, but also they aided desertion, which in any case would have been a problem. The magnitude of the catastrophe emerges in appeals made by particular battalions. The colonel of the 104th Infantry Regiment requested that it be allowed to march back into France since it sustained heavy losses at Jemappes, suffered a high rate of mortality from the fatigues of the campaign, and lost a great many men through desertion. *Chef de bataillon* Claude Vézu of the 3rd Paris, a unit raised in 1791, reluctantly reported it "was reduced by sickness, desertion, and leaves to 300 men in a condition to fight." This same battalion, according to the situation report of 20 September 1792, once numbered 700 men.[19]

To bolster an army thus weakened, authorities ordered battalions stationed in the rear to take up positions with the main combat force. As early as 9 November 1792, Rolland, a *commissaire du pouvoir exécutif*, advised the minister of war, "It is all the more important to employ these battalions with field armies or in frontier fortresses, since so many volunteers are leaving their battalions and going home without leave." Such suggestions appear in dispatches from December to March.[20] They resulted in the introduction of many new 1792 battalions, which now advanced into Belgium during the winter months.

The Advent of the 1792 Battalions, September 1792 to March 1793

Newly raised battalions that came to fill the gap did not prove equal to the task. Volunteers of 1792 increased the size of the Nord, but at first they hardly added to its strength. Although they did not cause the deterioration, they did not make up for it.

Diversity, characteristic of the Nord in all aspects, especially typified the 1792 levy within its ranks. Battalions underwent widely differing experiences. A few units entered combat before Jemappes; the 1st Butte des Moulins numbered among them. Formed on 5 July 1792, it contained men from National Guard detachments in the Paris area. Paul Charles Thiébault served in this battalion and left a fine record of its early activities. His grenadier company was well trained and equipped.[21] By 24 October the 1st Butte des Moulins appeared on the Nord's order of battle, and on 6 November Thiébault and his comrades fought at Le Blaton. It stands to reason that battalions coming from urban areas with active National Guards probably were better prepared and armed. They certainly showed up sooner in the front lines.[22]

Different circumstances surrounded the 1st Haute-Marne, formed by August 1792. It remained in its native department until April 1793. This period of at least seven months allowed these volunteers to organize, equip, and train. Sergeant Jacques Fricasse, a soldier in this battalion, wrote of the spring of 1793 as a time of instruction. On 15 April he and his fellows marched out for Metz. Not until August 1793, no less than a year after its formation, did this battalion appear on the rolls of the Nord.[23]

Many battalions of the 1792 levies suffered serious problems. They arrived unarmed at the front. Thus, for want of flintlocks, they consumed rations without contributing to the operations of the army. September found General Anne-François La Bourdonnaye, for example, complaining, "I beg you to . . . write a circular to stop as soon as possible the march of the . . . unarmed companies who arrive here daily."[24] Even if equipped, most were at best poorly trained. Authorities concentrated thousands of unprepared recruits at Châlons and Soissons. Both camps, while covering Paris, gave battalions a chance to reorganize and drill. Unfortunately, the lack of discipline characteristic of these troops sometimes turned the camps into chaos, but at least the camps kept raw battalions from spreading that chaos along the front line.

Between September 1792 and March 1793 about 150 new battalions appeared on Armée du Nord situation reports. An increase of this magnitude called for an extensive training program, but this only began after Neerwinden. Still, surprisingly enough, this large influx did not in itself hurt the combat performance of the Nord as much as might be expected. By design and accident, Volunteers of 1792 played only a secondary role in events. Dumouriez massed thousands of these inexperienced troops to take part in the campaign of October and November, but their slow movement and their commanders' unwillingness to commit them to combat kept them pretty much out of harm's way. Many battalions sat out the winter and spring in safe garrisons.[25] When the Austrians advanced in early March, few units of 1792 actually confronted the enemy. Only in one of the Nord's component armies, the Armée de la Hollande, did 1792 battalions swamp older formations. Luckily for the Hollande and its commander, the only maneuver it performed was an unharassed retreat back to the borders of France. At Neerwinden Volunteers of 1792 did precipitate the retreat, but it must be realized that the veteran battalions had by then been severely weakened.

Defeat and Retreat

The month of March witnessed some attempts to put the Armée du Nord in fighting trim. Older units regained some of their manpower, as soldiers on leave and recovered invalids filtered back to their battalions. Apparently new recruits also entered established units. Weather permitting, some training occurred.[26] Unfortunately, the Austrian advance came so early that it allowed the French little time to prepare themselves.

On 18 March, 44,500 French troops under Dumouriez advanced toward the village of Neerwinden to challenge 39,000 Austrians under the prince of Coburg. Dumouriez had some hope of success. Only a minority of his battalions assembled at Neerwinden came from the 1792 levies, and many of those new units present fought during the fall and winter campaign, but they were rusty and below strength. Even though Coburg's army had just emerged from winter quarters itself, it was far better prepared and supplied. During the battle, the French center and right put up an unexpectedly good fight, but on the left, commanded by Francisco de Miranda, republican battalions fell back to Tirlement, thus necessitating a retreat by the entire force. Although Miranda claimed that most of his men fought bravely, there is otherwise general agreement that the Volunteers of 1792, which composed one-third of the left wing, panicked and deserted the rest of the battalions, throwing everything into disorder.[27] Three days after Neerwinden the Nord lost again at Louvain.

Then coming in the wake of two costly defeats, retreat nearly destroyed the Armée du Nord. To escape the worst, and to enable him to use his army for counterrevolutionary purposes, Dumouriez agreed to leave Belgium without disputing the Austrian advance, while the Austrians agreed not to harass the retreating French. But even unmolested, withdrawal brought heavy losses. Desertion proved the greatest problem. Individuals, companies, and, some say, whole battalions returned home. All seemed lost in Belgium, as it indeed was, so soldiers marched off to defend their hearths as they saw fit.[28] The long march out of Belgium reduced those who stayed with the Nord to the lowest levels of physical existence. Canonneer Louis Bricard, serving with the 5th Paris, wrote of this period in terms that can only inspire pity; he was "reduced to the worst misery, half naked, having no shirt to put on and filled with vermine. Most of the soldiers, and I was of this number, had lost their kit, and were reduced to begging."[29]

The Regeneration of the Armée du Nord

Precious Time Provided

The Armée du Nord that fought the battles of September and October 1793 only partially resembled its predecessor of a year before. Dumouriez's Armée du Nord consisted of battalions from the line regiments and the Volunteers of 1791 labouriously fashioned into a powerful instrument by November 1792. Though augmented with Volunteers of 1792, it fell before the Austrian advance and barely endured the aftermath. Essentially, the retreat prostrated the Nord. Working with the cadres of existing battalions, the Republic had to regenerate another Armée du Nord. Masses of new conscripts were ready to take their places alongside the veterans, but it would require precious time to integrate these conscripts into the Nord and to train them.

Allied strategy after the reconquest of Belgium could not have been better designed to provide the time needed to reconstruct the broken French battalions. Meeting in congress at Antwerp on 8 April 1793, an impressive assemblage of ambassadors and military commanders decided upon a course of siege warfare during the remaining months of 1793.[30] Six fortress cities constituted the Allied objective; these included Condé, Valenciennes, le Quesnoy, Maubeuge, Dunkirk, and Lille. In accord with military principles current in the eighteenth century, the Allies agreed that to strike deeply into France with hostile fortresses astride Allied lines of communication spelled disaster. Once the fortresses fell into their hands, the combined armies could safely and successfully march on Paris. Such a plan failed to take into consideration the weakness of the defeated Nord, which could have offered very little resistance to a bold advance during the spring or early summer. By undertaking a series of sieges, the Allies dissipated their efforts against strong walls instead of concentrating against weak battalions. It is true that twice Coburg attacked Nord field armies stationed around Valenciennes and Cambrai, but these efforts were of minor importance compared to the siege operations.

The Committee of Public Safety, however, believed that besieged fortresses must be relieved. Dampierre, who replaced Dumouriez, and Custine, who in turn succeeded Dampierre, both resisted the Committee's policies. Dampierre pleaded that "the Army of the Republic needs a respite. . . . Winter campaigns destroy armies; ours is in this case." He fell leading a premature attack undertaken at the insistence of the Representatives on Mission. The popular but suspect Custine resolved to forego all offensive action for the sake of training. Shortly after taking command, he explained to Minister of War Bouchotte: "It would be very dangerous to want to carry out an offensive in the position we find ourselves. I believe that we ought to temporize with wisdom, and wait in our camps until the Armée du Nord et des Ardennes are reorganized and trained."[31] Largely through Custine's efforts, the Nord that took the field in late August to relieve the siege of Dunkirk was capable, if not yet expert.

The Introduction of the February Conscripts

In April many Volunteers of 1792 plus the new men furnished by the 24 February 1793 Levy of 300,000 massed in camps and depots in the rear; these recruits now had to be integrated into established battalions. Volunteers brought into the Nord before March 1793 made their appearance as entire organized battalions of either 1791 or 1792 levies. Consequently, the number of battalions in the Nord skyrocketed during its first year of combat. By 1 March 1793 the Nord and the Ardennes included fully 283 battalions. After March 1793 comparatively few new units came to the Nord. In fact, although it grew in size from about 150,000 on 1 March 1793 to about 225,000 in December 1793, its total number of battalions rose by only thirty-five. When the Nord reached its maximum size of over 300,000 in April 1794, there were actually eighty-two fewer battalions than in December. Obviously, then, the growth of the Nord after March 1793 mainly entailed the size rather than the number of units.[32]

The March defeats and the subsequent introduction of large numbers of new recruits brought about rapid fluctuations in the size of battalions. Between 1 March and 1 May 1793 line regiments lost on the average about eighty men, or about 15 percent of their 1 March strength, and between 1 May and 30 June they jumped up by an average of 162 men. Average figures do not do justice to the reality of certain hard-hit line battalions, like the 1st, 8th, 14th, and 17th infantry regiments. The second battalion of the 1st Regiment fell from a 1 March figure of 607 to only 330 on 29 May. Volunteer battalions also suffered during the first six months of 1792. The 1st Aisne dropped from 417 on 1 December 1792, to 377 on 1 March 1793, to 223 on 1 May; the 1st Seine-et-Oise went from 567 to 406 over the same period.

Absorption of new recruits into established battalions consumed a great deal of administrative attention during April and May 1793. Already in late March Dumouriez and the minister of war, Pierre de Riel, marquis de Beurnonville, corresponded on the subject of integrating the new levies. With the change of command the concern still remained. One of Dampierre's first official letters to Bouchotte concerned his intention "to send all the volunteers of the new levy which can be made ready now to fill the veteran cadres."[33] The timetable for bringing in new recruits varied, depending on the type of unit. Sedan was the great repository of incoming recruits destined for the Nord and Ardennes. With representatives from various battalions coming to choose replacements, Sedan became a kind of military slave market. Citizen Rolland, *commissaire du conseil exécutif*, held much of the responsibility for incorporating the men at Sedan.[34] Fifty thousand recruits of the February levy were supposedly to flow through Sedan, although by 3 May only 8–10,000 had arrived.[35] Volunteer battalions of 1791 received the most benefit from the addition of these troops. Between 1 March and 30 June situation reports record nearly one hundred increases of battalion strength by at least 20 percent or by 100 men or more. These increases occurred in 63 percent of the 1791 volunteer battalions as opposed to only 23 percent of line battalions and 21 percent of 1792 battalions.

By feeding the great majority of new levies into understrength but experienced 1791 and line battalions, Citizen Rolland could accelerate the training of the 1793 recruits. Learning and fighting alongside veterans, green infantrymen would be sure to learn more rapidly than if kept in segregated units. Granted, for a time the efficiency of the veterans would decline, but the risk proved worthwhile.

Were not the influx of new soldiers enough of a challenge for the Nord, another confused manpower situation arose to complicate matters further. In response to that very conscription that now filled the ranks of the Nord, the Vendée rose in revolt against the Paris government. Realizing that civil war must be ended at all costs, the Convention massed an army to crush the insurrection. By an order issued to the Nord on 9–10 May 1793 all regular infantry battalions as well as volunteer units were each to supply a company of fifty-four veterans for service in the Vendée. The order expressly stated that chosen men must not be "newly arrived recruits."[36] This forced levy of veterans stripped the Nord of fifteen to twenty battalions. Apparently in exchange, an additional twenty-one raw volunteer battalions were sent from the Vendée army to the Armée du Nord. It was hardly a good bargain for the Nord.

Training the New Army

By mid-April 1793 the vital processes of instruction and drill had resumed. On the frontier between the Sambre and the sea, the main forces of the Armée du Nord concentrated in three large camps: la Madeleine, near Lille; Famars, near Valenciennes; and Maubeuge. On 16 April the Representatives on Mission at Lille reported of their visit to Madeleine, "Yesterday we visited the camp with General Lamarlière, and we found almost all the battalions working at their instruction." Orders issued at Valenciennes and Maubeuge indicate that many entire brigades maneuvered together in late April and May.[37] Troops were climbing up from the depths to which they had sunk by late March, but most of the upward trek still lay before them.

More than any other commander, Custine brought the Nord up the difficult path toward a new competency. He quickly and clearly recognized the weaknesses of the Armée du Nord and addressed himself to remedy them the moment he arrived at Cambrai, 27 May 1793. Although the incorporation and training of recruits had begun, many battalions were still far below strength. Those that could claim a full complement contained so many novices that they were often poorly suited to field duty. Just a day after arriving, Custine wrote the Committee of Public Safety: "This army exists only as the cadres of destroyed battalions. I have found line battalions with only sixty men, some with two hundred or one hundred fifty. A great number of volunteer battalions have their cadres filled only by recruits without arms."[38] Muskets were in short supply, as always, and many men lacked part or even all of their military kit.[39] One almost tires of the repeated complaints—too few veterans, too many recruits, and not enough equipment to go around. These seem constant factors in the French military equation of 1793.

To take stock of his new command, on 29 May Custine sent out orders that all battalions undergo a review. Such a review included surveys of each unit's ability, size, equipment, and finances. Reviews were dutifully held and the reports collected. Through a series of personal inspections Custine gained firsthand knowledge of conditions throughout the Nord. He drove home his intention to make the army a hardened fighting unit. He removed useless troops, evacuating sick and wounded men to Saint-Quentin and Peronne. He trimmed down field combat battalions to a smaller but more reliable force.[40] Custine also labored immediately to establish a respectable level of discipline in the Nord.

Under Custine the army occupied a series of camps and fortresses where sheltering walls gave the troops security and allowed them to devote their energies to training. The main body evacuated Famars and moved to the Camp de César near Paillencourt, just days before his arrival. According to figures of late June 1793, eleven camps and garrisons contained contingents numbering 3,000 or more: Dunkirk, Ghivelde, Bergues, Bailleul, Lille–La Madeleine, Condé, Valenciennes, Cambrai-César, Hecq, Maubeuge, and Carignan.[41]

The largest of the camps, the Camp de César, with about 40,000 soldiers, became a beehive of activity. Custine ordered the defenses of the camp shored up to better protect his inexperienced soldiers from attack. Battalions within these defenses drilled twice daily. *Commissaires* Varin and Celliez reported:

> What you will learn with no less interest is the incredible activity with which all the battalions drill daily. We can assure you that in the last two weeks the army, without growing in size, has doubled in force compared to what it had been before; one cannot see them without admiring them. The soldiers devote themselves to drill with indefatigable zeal, and the great number of battalions maneuver with a precision that one does not see in troops of the line. Wanting only to be as well trained as their comrades, the recruits drill almost ceaselessly and make incredible progress; we are assured that if they are not interrupted, in another week the infantry with the army will contain no more rookies [*second classe*].

Custine insisted that officers attend as well to the instruction of the individual recruits, and he delegated to brigade commanders the responsibility of overseeing instruction and insuring that their men made progress.[42]

Musketry as well as marching maneuvers received attention at the Camp de César. An order issued 12 July stated, "In every battalion, two cartridges will be given each day to men whose training demands firing drill." Firing only two cartridges a day could not turn a recruit into a marksman, but it could teach him how to load and fire efficiently. All this practice at the manual of arms and actual musketry must have proved quite a strain on the new recruits and on the veterans as well. A young man who joined up in 1794 wrote: "One will not be surprised at the extreme fatigue that this new drill caused us, if one considers our age and the fact that at this period the standard fusil with its bayonet weighed thirteen to fourteen pounds, sometimes more."[43] The vigorous commander and disciplinarian was whipping his army into shape.

Not only at the Camp de César, but in other camps and garrisons as well, men toiled at the task of becoming soldiers. Reporting his activities to the minister of war, General Charles-Edouard Kilmaine with the Armée des Ardennes simply stated, "At this time I am concerned with drilling the troops." Even in the besieged town of Valenciennes, men drilled.[44]

To insure uniformity, Custine formed a special training school at Cambrai. On 3 June he issued the first order summoning picked soldiers to this unusual camp: "One officer, one NCO, and one drummer from each battalion of all troops composing the Armée du Nord et des Ardennes, be they in camps or garrisons, will go immediately to Cambrai, there to be trained; that is, the drummers to a beat of ninety steps per minute, and the officers and NCOs to march only at this pace which from this moment on will be that of infantry on the march and during drill." Cadres trained at Cambrai could return to their mother units and themselves become instructors. At its inception the school's purpose seems extremely basic, but another directive, which appeared a month later, demonstrates that Custine's intentions had always been or had become more elaborate:

> Each battalion of the army in different garrisons and *cantonnements*, with the exception of the light infantry, will send to Cambrai one fusilier, well armed and well equipped, in order to receive instruction in the march and drill ordered by General Custine. He will be part of an instruction battalion which is established there, and he will live there in good order [*police*] and discipline under the orders of General Meunier and the officers detailed to train this battalion. Commanders are recommended to send a sensible and intelligent fusilier who can later be employed in his battalion to spread the training he will have received.[45]

According to this order, marching involved more than a step; it involved the use of the step in military evolutions as well.

Fortunately for the present-day enquirer, in 1794 General Meunier, who ran the school at Cambrai, submitted to the minister of war a report entitled "Changements en errata au *Règlement de 1791*, exécutés à Cambray à l'Ecole d'instruction au mois de juillet 1793." Meunier stated that instruction went on for six weeks, probably the last two weeks of June and all of July, but this is speculation. Even though the school functioned for only six weeks, "I cannot help but believe," he wrote, "that the ideas I propagated there were beneficially applied, later, in the plains of Beaumont [the Battle of Wattignies]." Mass maneuvers, i.e., those in column, must have been stressed more than in the 1791 *Règlement,* since Meunier felt it necessary to add "to the school of evolutions of the line a more extended treatise on maneuvers in masse," which he believed to be "of major utility in republican tactics."[46] It is clear from Meunier's "Changements" that the *école* dealt with line and column, musketry and bayonet. If Meunier's camp ceased at the end of July, the cadres Custine had summoned would only just have begun to teach their own battalions before combat overtook the Nord. Of course, this would not have meant that their battalions lacked instruction; after all, they were in training all along. Rather, the regularity desired by Custine would not have been completely attained. If nothing else, however, Custine's Cambrai school left a legacy of as many as 1,000 proficient drill instructors, who could contribute heavily to the on-going task of infantry training over the winter of 1793–94.

Preparing troops for large-scale battle required more than unmolested parade ground drill. Recruits needed some exposure to combat, preferably arranged in such a way as to guarantee success and thus increase their self-confidence. French commanders fully appreciated this fact throughout the history of the Nord. Gay de Vernon reports that, while the troops drilled behind their camps' defenses, they also "seasoned themselves by continual small engagements . . . prudently directed." Only such small combats without names could accustom the infantry, especially the light infantry, to battle. Even duty in the line of advance posts helped. The general correspndence of the Nord and Ardennes during late June and July contains one mention after another of skirmishes and small attacks.[47]

Summoned by the Committee of Public Safety, Custine left for Paris on 16 July; he never returned. His fall was not, however, the watershed that his arrival had been, and efforts he had accelerated kept up their momentum. General Kilmaine, interim commander of the Nord, had to abandon the main encampment at Paillencourt, when Coburg threatened to crush it in a giant pincers movement. On 7 and 8 August Kilmaine skillfully slipped the trap and withdrew to a new camp at Gavrelle, between Douai and Arras. There the endless drill continued. Bricard wrote of his experience at Gavrelle, "The battalions of our camp were drilled in maneuver, and several times, in major military evolutions by the generals." Training continued elsewhere without even the inconvenience of a change in camps.[48]

Houchard arrived at Vitry on 9 August to assume leadership of the Nord. He would be in command for only about ten days before his attention focused on the fall campaign. In his correspondence Houchard not only complained, he whined, about the Nord's condition. Mostly he decried the lack of organization. In the five months since Neerwinden the

Nord had six different commanders, each with his own staff. It endured a major retreat, a massive influx of new recruits, and three changes in headquarters. Not until Jourdan would a commander of the Nord last for more than six or seven weeks. No wonder the Armée du Nord was disorganized. Houchard's chief of staff, General Etienne-Ambroise Berthélemy, did effect an important change in organization by grouping the Nord in divisions. Stated more precisely, he completed the divisional organization, since parts of the Nord had previously been in divisions. Houchard and Berthélemy put great stock in the new organization: "This measure of organizing infantry in divisions is the only one, it can even be said that it is indispensable, to promise us success; without it we must fear disorder.... It only required four days to carry it out here."[49]

As mentioned before, training and maneuvers continued under Houchard, though without much attention from him. He did issue a lengthy instruction, which contained much on the conduct of outposts and something on marches and the choice of light infantry.[50] Since he only issued this order on 23 August, it seems unlikely that his orders affected training practices until after Hondschoote. The resumption of combat in late August should not be regarded as the conclusion of a period of instruction and drill, since troops not involved in an offensive or siege continued to train. In Maubeuge General Etienne Gudin issued this order, the day before Hondschoote, "The order previously given is renewed, to drill battalions in the morning from eight to nine and in the evenings from two to four."[51]

Performance in the Fall Battles

In late August 1793 the Armée du Nord, in training since April, mounted a major stroke. Though still limited in its capacities, the army proved equal to the task. Its performance contradicted the most quoted source on the Nord, the light infantry general, Philibert-Guillaume Duhesmes, who stated that it was incapable of most maneuvers. He insisted that battalions, "even those of the old regiments, barely knew the *école de bataillon*" and that "the French no longer knew any other tactics than those of skirmishers; of which they made on abuse." There is good reason to argue that Duhesmes misreported, misapprehended, or misinterpreted the situation. Certainly other participants in the revolutionary and Napoleonic wars disagreed with him. Kellermann wrote, "By mid-1793, order within the [French] armies began to be reestablished little by little; we still suffered reverses, but there was a little more regularity and better direction in the operation of war." He seems to come closer to the truth than Duhesmes. As early as 28 July 1793 Representatives on Mission Delbrel, Le Vaneur, and Charles-François Le Tourneur reported, "The infantry is in a fairly good state and already trained sufficiently ... to fight well."[52]

The two great battles of the fall campaign season did not call upon the full tactical resources of the Nord, but certain smaller combats, both successful and unsuccessful, revealed a distinct ability to use more elaborate tactical means. The landscape around Hondschoote forced the French to disperse and fight in loose order. Marshes, hedges, canals, and causeways made conventional lines and columns largely impractical. October brought the French another victory, this time over an Austrian army covering the siege of Maubeuge. Again the terrain allowed only a limited tactical choice. Here, however, evidence indicates that the French attacked in columns. In less important engagements battalions even maneuvered in line. In a 3 September attack on Abbaye d'Orval, for example, the topography allowed General Michel-François de Sistrières to tax his troops' full potential: "Since the terrain we had to cross was a vast plain . . . I marched in column to Chasse-Pierre . . . I put my forces into line. . . . I decided to march on Fl——, and I made this march, which was about three-quarters of a league, by dividing my troops into four columns whose heads marched at a set distance from one another, giving me the capacity to put my forces into line in three minutes."[53]

The Preparation for Victory

Incorporation and Reorganization

Although victorious during the fall of 1793, battalions suffered significant casualties. Winter witnessed a decline in battalion size after the summer peak. Some battalions lost as many as 200 or 300 men. Heavy losses meant that these battalions required considerable reorganization and training during the winter. Even as early as mid-September some battalions begged for a respite.[54] Between late August 1793 and April 1794, a flood of conscripts made good these losses and by April enlarged the average battalion size to over 1,000. The famed *levée en masse* furnished the bulk of this new manpower. Late summer and autumn of 1793 brought the first great surge of these *requisitionnaires,* as well as the remainder of the men raised by the legislation of February 1793. Representatives on Mission serving in northern departments declared a local *levée en masse* on 4 August, nearly three weeks before the Convention did the same. The men raised by the Representatives came in months ahead of those from the general levy. In fact, during the two days of 27 and 28 August, 19–20,000 arrived at the Nord depots.[55]

It is difficult to say exactly how many men entered the ranks of the Nord from late August 1793 to April 1794, but an estimate of at least 150,000 seems accurate. The Armée du Nord et des Ardennes totaled 177,647 men on 30 July 1793, but attrition due to fall battles and winter weather eliminated many of the men counted here; probably something less than 150,000 remained.[56] Yet situation reports for the first half of April 1794 state the army's total size was 310,000. If these figures are correct, then, by the spring of 1794 fully half the Nord consisted of recruits raised by the *levée en masse*. The spectacular increase in average battalion size bears this out, if some allowance is again made for attrition.

The Convention initially ordered whole battalions raised by the *levée en masse* to replace three-quarters of the troops then in garrison, thus releasing veterans for front line service. Although this was established practice, opposition rapidly crystallized. General Jourdan was among those who argued that the French ought to place "these young recruits among the ranks of seasoned soldiers, and soon they will learn to handle their weapons, to aspire to glory, and to despise danger." Finally, the Convention reversed its earlier decision to consign whole battalions of *requisitionnaires* to fortresses. On 22 November 1793 it decreed that soldiers raised by the *levée en masse* were all to be incorporated into battalions formed before 1 March 1793. This meant essentially that only battalions created by the line army, the Volunteers of 1791 and the Volunteers of 1792, would continue to exist. "I will receive with pleasure the decree which unites these new battalions with the veterans," Jourdan responded, "and I strongly hope that it can be executed promptly so that we will have the time to drill and instruct these youths."[57]

Incorporation generally progressed steadily throughout the winter months. Each army received an *agent supérieur* delegated by the minister of war to facilitate and direct the procedure. But there were a few snags in the process. At times there were not enough veteran battalions in a particular area to absorb all the *requisitionnaires* stationed nearby. As Representative Pierre Gillet reported, in mid-February nearly 10,000 of the *levée en masse* remained on garrison duty, since "they can neither be incorporated, for a lack of cadres, nor sent elsewhere because the towns they occupy would then be without defense." By law, incorporation should have been completed by 30 December 1793, but it went on through April 1794.[58]

In several notable cases absorption served political ends. The *armées révolutionnaires* were paramilitary instruments of the Terror, not actually part of the real army defending the frontiers. When the Paris government decided that they constituted more of an embarrassment than an asset, it ordered the dissolution of all the departmental contingents. By the law of 4 December 1793, only the Paris *armée* continued in being. Units of the Lille *armée revolutionnaire* found themselves forcibly incorporated into the battalions of the Nord.[59] Another variety of integration with political overtones involved battalions from the rebellious west of France. The

Committee of Public Safety apparently thought it best to remove these battalions from their home departments and to merge them into a distant army, like the Nord.[60]

Beyond incorporation, the Armée du Nord began the long delayed *amalgame* described in Chapter 3. Any attempt to start the *amalgame* in the Nord had to wait until the army ceased to be on campaign. Even then, incorporation generally preceded the *amalgame*. By the instructions of 8 and 10 January 1794 battalions had to be reviewed and united into demi-brigades under the supervision of proper authority, usually a Representative on Mission.[61] This took time, so that by the spring, although absorption was largely completed, the *amalgame* had only begun.

Training for the Spring Battles

After Wattignies, 15–16 October 1793, the Committee of Public Safety pressured Jourdan to continue offensive operations, but he balked. He undoubtedly realized that the winter of 1792–93 had greatly weakened the Nord. Dumouriez had undertaken a winter campaign and had cut up the Nord into small detachments, which neglected training and discipline. Jourdan now argued: "If we continue on campaign this winter, by spring we will only be able to field a tattered army, weakened by desertion and disease. On the contrary, if we can give the army some repose this winter, if during this time we expand and train it, we can assure ourselves of the most substantial advantages by the next spring."[62] Circumstances favored Jourdan's insistence, and he won out. The Nord gained a rest and used it well.

Problems the Nord chronically suffered did not disappear; shortages, indiscipline, and desertion seemed to be constant companions. Usually the *requisitionnaires* arriving at the Nord lacked muskets. Without arms, without uniforms, and sometimes without shoes, these conscripts must have presented a strange appearance. Equipped or not, the men had to be incorporated into veteran battalions, even if those were in daily contact with the enemy. In extreme cases unarmed recruits fought in minor combats during the spring in hopes of taking over the fusil of a fallen comrade.[63] By the time major field forces faced the enemy in battle during 1794, however, all battalions seemed to have been adequately armed. Indiscipline still afflicted the Nord, but authorities cracked down. The Representatives on Mission spearheaded a severe reemphasis of military discipline over the winter and spring. Desertion among the conscripts of the *levée en masse* rose to considerable proportions, but the Nord still grew. By the winter of 1793–94 the French were willing to use more effective coercion to keep good republicans in the ranks.

Even in the depths of winter troops drilled regularly. Repeated orders stressed the imperative need to instruct recruits and maneuver battalions.

In December Jourdan demanded that a subordinate "drill the battalions whenever weather permits; order commanders to use barns for the instruction of recruits." Again in January he issued a circular insisting on daily instruction and drill: "You will give orders to the effect that the troops will be drilled daily, you will hold the unit commanders responsible for the instruction of their battalions and regiments. You will order all brigadier generals to visit the troops under their command daily and to keep watch over their instruction." Orders given lower down on the chain of command indicate that Jourdan's directives were implemented.[64] His removal in mid-January 1794 did not alter the pressure on commanders to guarantee the training of their troops.

Wherever and whenever possible, men drilled. Fortunately, along the frontier north of Valenciennes the enemy remained relatively inactive. From Flanders a grateful Souham wrote on 13 February 1794 that the enemy "always leaves us alone. . . . I profit from this time to have the troops of the new levy trained."[65] Not every battalion had the luxury of long periods devoted exclusively to training. Sergeant Fricasse, serving along the embattled Sambre, had little rest from combat. "The rigor of the winter," he stated, "caused us many ills. At that time, there was no armistice; winter like summer, one was always on campaign." Another recruit, Ernouf, stationed in the same area as Fricasse, complained bitterly, "That winter was more murderous for us than battle had been."[66]

During the spring even units that had been unable to drill previously now massed in camps of instruction. During germinal (21 March-19 April 1794) "the troops [began] to leave their winter quarters to form small camps." General Desjardin, in command of the division in which Sergeant Fricasse served, now felt particular anxiety about the need to assemble his men in one camp.[67]

New orders issued in the spring demanded even greater attention to the serious work of preparing the Nord for a new campaign. This phenomenon should not be viewed as the beginning but rather as an intensification of a continuous process. General Jean Charles Pichegru now sent about an inspector to make certain that garrison troops were in training. Descriptions by the private soldiers confirm the effect of the numerous training orders and directives. Even battalions sent to the rear for rest and reorganization found themselves employed in training recruits. "We hardly give them any relief," wrote Sergeant Alexandre Brault, "three hours of drill in the morning and three in the afternoon keep anyone from getting bored."[68]

Although winter brought no major military moves on either side, a constant clash of outposts and small detachments provided ample chance for recruits to receive their baptism of fire. Such actions involved both experienced troops and the new recruits incorporated into the front line battalions. Commanders welcomed the chance to harden their soldiers and created opportunities for combat. General Dominique-Joseph Vandamme, for example, wrote that during germinal he conducted "two little attacks in order to harden and test in some manner the great number of recruits that each battalion had received."[69]

The Victorious Battles of Spring

Although the Nord suffered some reverses in April and May, on the whole by late spring it had been shaped into an effective military instrument. As always, comments and reports concerning the Armée du Nord contradict one another and confuse anyone obliged to sift through the material, yet some sense can be made of this apparent muddle. The keynote of the Nord throughout its existence was diversity, and that diversity was never greater than in early 1794. Raw conscripts poured into the army all through the winter and early spring and now stood with veterans of two years of continuous combat. If a battalion received its complement of *requisitionnaires* in November or December, it could have devoted as much as four or five months to their training before it marched into combat. Such lucky battalions probably performed well in April and May. Other battalions only took on their contingents in March or later. Gillet even reports the incorporation of recruits in May.[70] A lack of time for instruction in such units could doom them to defeat.

Also, as observed before, along the Sambre a heavy level of activity and dispersal of battalions did not allow the best circumstances for necessary drill. Whereas Souham and General Jean-Victor Moreau to the north reported long breathing spells devoted to training, Desjardin, in command of the division along the Sambre, complained that his men were too scattered for proper instruction. The situation in this area seemed to have been frustrated further by a late introduction of recruits.[71] Thus a certain diversity of accounts must be expected because of variations in the situation.

On balance the Nord proved itself ready. A general offensive launched in late April brought victory in the north, although the right flank of the army did receive a sharp setback. Souham, in command of the northern half of the army, wisely left behind many of the recruits deemed insufficiently trained. He felt confident of the trained soldiers he included in the field force. These troops won the impressive victory of Tourcoing on 18 May. Four days later the Allies fought them to a standstill, but even then the Nord displayed real ability. In the words of the French staff historians H. Coutanceau and H. Leplus, the setback at Pont-à-Chin during the Battle of Tournai on 22 May "still had a most important moral significance; it confirmed the valor of those republican troops who two years of skirmishes, struggles, and reverses, had finally rendered sufficiently solid that they could seriously pit themselves against a professional army in open battle [*en bataille rangée*]." Victory arrived by a more tortuous path for those divisions engaged in the fighting between Landrecies and Charleroi. Battalions tended to be less well trained than their brothers to the north, and a confused command structure hampered even the best of troops. At the same time that success eluded them, some battalions performed admirably. They even displayed an ability to resist enemy cavalry attacks over open ground, as during the engagements near Grand-reng on 13 and 21 May.[72] At Fleurus elements of the Nord and Ardennes, now under united and vigorous command, fought alongside units from the Moselle and triumphed.

The conduct of the Armée du Nord et des Ardennes bears out Gouvion St. Cyr's assertion that by the spring of 1794 the Republic's defenders "were passably seasoned and disciplined, and sufficiently trained."[73] They resembled the ragged figures of a Raffet lithograph, and their battle formations looked crude to their more traditional enemies; yet the troops of the Nord marched and fought in good order—and they won.

Motivation and Training

Although firm conclusions lie beyond the limits of the hard evidence, it seems appropriate and even necessary to speculate on the relationship between motivation and training. Sustaining motivation, as defined in Chapter 2, can affect the pace and quality of training. It is reasonable to expect that men who are proud of themselves and convinced of their mission will devote more attention and energy to learning the skills required of a soldier. Provided they understand the necessity of drill, such recruits would neither be hostile nor indifferent to it. All other things being equal, the new soldiers of revolutionary France probably reached a level of proficiency in less time than was required to train less spirited and dedicated troops.

Correspondence originating with the Nord frequently spoke of the enthusiasm of the troops as they trained, about the way trainees "put themselves into it with a will." In the summer of 1793 Representatives on Mission exclaimed, "One cannot see them without admiring them. The soldiers devote themselves to drill with an indefatigable zeal." These same Representatives wrote after observing training in Cambrai that the troops on their way to the twice-daily drills "marched along the streets to the sound of military music, and gaiety is seen on every one of their faces."[74]

But did their unquestionable zeal accelerate the training process? That is probably an unanswerable question, but some hints show that it did. "[T]he veteran soldiers are astonished when they see the precision with which our volunteers maneuver." Why the surprise if not to marvel at the speed with which the recruits had begun to master their new craft? Recruits spoke of their own "rapid progress."[75] Of course, a lack of arms or instructors could hamper training, so could the dispersal of units. Zeal alone was no guarantee of capacity. However, the documents, at least by the spring of 1794, repeatedly contain favorable comparisons between relatively new troops and veterans. "The young men of the first requisition fought like veterans." "[U]nder the fire of enemy cannon they marched and deployed with all the calm and assurance that could be displayed by veteran troops." "One can no longer tell any difference between veterans and the soldiers of the first requisition."[76] No doubt such glowing reports exaggerated to a degree, but the underlying theme is a pride that the newest levies could perform well in the field with no more than a few months' training. Certainly the evidence does not contradict the notion that spirited revolutionary French troops required less time than did their predecessors or their adversaries to prepare for service on campaign.

Chapter 11

Line and Column on the Battlefield

ARMIES ARE FASCINATING as social institutions and as political influences, but ultimately they are created for battle. When the Armée du Nord entered combat, it was the infantry that bore the brunt of the fighting. The tactics it employed have been a subject of historical confusion or controversy for nearly two centuries. This chapter analyzes the close order components of that tactical system through a quantitative methodology that promises to provide substantive evidence for a new set of conclusions.

Considering the momentous consequences of this period of warfare, it is all the more regrettable that confusion, not clarity, typifies our image of the past. Three sharply differing views of the revolutionary battlefield compete for acceptance. The first accepts the litany of the cult of the bayonet. Revolutionary enthusiasm inspired the republican soldier, and to capitalize on this sentiment commanders massed their troops in tightly packed but ragged columns. Men with little training or skill could be employed in this fashion. Protected by a screen of skirmishers, these columns—one could almost say "mobs"—then smashed into the enemy as best they could.

At the outset, this popular wisdom confronted opposition in the works of General Philibert-Guillaume Duhesmes, an important theoretician and high-ranking officer in the Nord. The analysis most forcefully presented by him claimed that in 1793 French troops lacked the ability to fight in any close order formation. They simply dispersed into disorganized bands of light infantry skirmishers, or *tirailleurs*. He virtually denied that training made up any part of the Nord's experience. Jean Colin offered the third and most scholarly description of republican tactics. In his study of the Armée de la Moselle, he claimed that the French did not use columns at all during 1793 and 1794, but neither did they rely on total dispersal. Colin asserted that the most traditional of all military formations, the line, served as the backbone of infantry tactics during those years. Each of the three positions mentioned not only emphasizes a single tactical element above all others but also is based on a particular image of the revolutionary soldier. The column is linked with élan, the band of skirmishers with both initiative and ineptitude, and the line with discipline. Although recent years have witnessed some attempts at moderation, in general these stridently conflicting opinions have ruled out a smooth synthesis.[1]

Any serious attempt to reconcile or supplant such authorities must begin with a different, not just another, attempt to establish the presence or the absence of specific tactical practices on the field of battle. Ideally, a tactical study should establish the elements of the system and their interrelationships by presenting a series of carefully described battles and drawing comparisons and contrasts between them. However, scarcity of information rules out such a narrative treatment, since only two of the major battles fought by the Armée du Nord or its elements allow meticulous tactical reconstruction. Some observers, Colin among them, have turned to a study of drill books and training instructions. But these sources can lead the inquirer to an uncertain destination; they mark the path of what might have been rather than what was. Some official materials become truly valuable only in *detailing* the form and deployment of a certain tactical formation once its employment is *already established*. Neither do the reveries of contemporaries supply the needed answers. As is the case for all armed conflicts, after the wars of the French Revolution ceased, generals wrote their views of what had occurred. They left a legacy of conflicting statements summing up tactical practice. Appeal to these statements without substantial factual backing can be dangerous. As fine an observer as a particular general may have been, he could only base his description on a limited range of experience, and even this may have been distorted by time or by the prejudices of the author.

The confusion can be eliminated, or at least minimized, by a quantitative approach based on a sample of tactical situations extracted from all types of available sources. This is the methodology adopted here. The body of documentation used includes the complete general correspondence of the Armée du Nord et des Ardennes from 1791 to 1 July 1794, order and correspondence registers for the same period, relevant manuscript memoirs and histories at the archives, and a large number of published letters and memoirs. The evidence collected here describes parts of 108 engagements from the battalion level up. It has been grouped into major categories, through which the tactical system has been broken down into elements that can be counted and compared. These examples are presented in table form as an appendix to this study. Whatever distortion this process creates, it promises great rewards.

The tactical system that emerges from this quantitative study is far more balanced and flexible than previous histories have suggested. An adaptable combination of line, column, and *tirailleurs* gave the infantry of the Nord the capacity to fit its tactics to the circumstances and terrain it faced. Let us turn first to the close order components of that tactical system.

The Nature of Close Order Formations

Several common traits typified the three close order formations—line, column, and square. They concentrated manpower in small areas to suit particular purposes. Although the resultant concentrations looked different, the infantry company standing in two or three ranks, shoulder to shoulder, served as the basic building block in each formation. Companies deployed into line, column, or square through a series of orderly, controlled maneuvers. These characteristics set close order apart from open order, where *tirailleurs* simply dispersed as individuals to perform their tasks on their own initiative. Because close order formations were fairly discrete, they are particularly well suited to study by quantitative techniques. Mere mention of such a formation in a battle report supplies the reader with a reasonably clear visual image of the battalion in combat, whereas to say a battalion fought as *tirailleurs* establishes only that it did not fight in close order.

Evidence presented in this chapter establishes that the Armée du Nord employed all three basic close order formations by the spring of 1794. Each of the three possessed different abilities. The linear order remained for the Nord what it had been for the armies of the monarchy, a basic and indispensable tactical element. Technology determined that the line would continue to possess crucial advantages. Troops deployed in line poured out a volume of musketry unequaled by infantry in any other order of battle. To exploit this firepower, Nord infantry characteristically stood in line when on the defensive. This formation also allowed a high degree of troop control while being less vulnerable to enemy artillery fire than was the column. Consequently, the line also appeared on the battlefield as a preliminary or waiting formation. For republican infantry, however, the line proved itself clumsy and brittle when advancing. The precision required for such a maneuver was generally beyond the grasp of the men. To achieve it took long experience or brutal discipline, neither of which was typical of this new army.

In just those very situations that least suited the line, the column operated best. Unlike the line, the attack column possessed high mobility but low firepower. It allowed rapidity of movement without loss of troop control or unit cohesiveness. In column assault the bayonet, not the fusil itself, was the primary weapon of French infantry. The vaunted French élan intensified the inherent power of such shock tactics.

While line and column appeared throughout the Nord's history, the square did not show up in the records until late 1793. Troops deployed into square as a defense against the encircling attack of cavalry. However, when facing an on-coming charge, it was often risky to alter formations; and a change from line to square was particularly complicated. Use of this kind of defense may be an indication that the Nord had arrived as a seasoned force by June 1794.

The Line

The Rationale behind Continuity

In physical appearance the line employed by revolutionary troops varied little from that utilized by defenders of the old order. Throughout the eighteenth century armies generally fought in line; the elegance and discipline exemplified by magnificent troops in long, straight ranks expressed the very spirit of enlightened despotism. When Jacobin orators extolled the prowess of the Republic's new armies, little wonder that they hardly mentioned linear combat. It possessed neither the massed élan of attack columns nor the personal dash of the individual *tirailleur*.

During 1792 French regulars formed line in three ranks while volunteer battalions stood in only two. As the war progressed, all French battalions adopted the three-deep line. The British later illustrated that a two-rank line was actually a superior formation for concentrated firepower, but the French, ever conscious of shock action, thought three preferable for resisting the *arme blanche*. A typical three-rank line was about two yards in depth.[2] The length of a battalion in linear order depended on that battalion's composition. Theoretically, an infantry battalion contained nine or ten companies, but on campaign an infantry battalion often had only eight. The number of soldiers per battalion differed from unit to unit and from time to time, but 700 would be a reasonable average figure. Standing shoulder to shoulder in three ranks, this number of men occupied some 160 yards. See Figure 3.

Several factors drove commanders to array troops in linear order, despite its brittle immobility. Smoothbore flintlock fusils took considerable time to load and proved quite inaccurate. In the best of circumstances a skilled infantryman could discharge his musket two or three times every minute, but in the midst of battle's confusion and fear the rate of fire probably fell to something like one round per minute. This round could reliably hit its mark only when that target was big and close.[3] On the defensive, the concentrated firepower of troops in line could decimate an attacking battalion or squadron in close order, since the attackers presented a widely exposed front. Though each individual fired slowly, the tightly packed ranks of the line could pour out a withering fire.

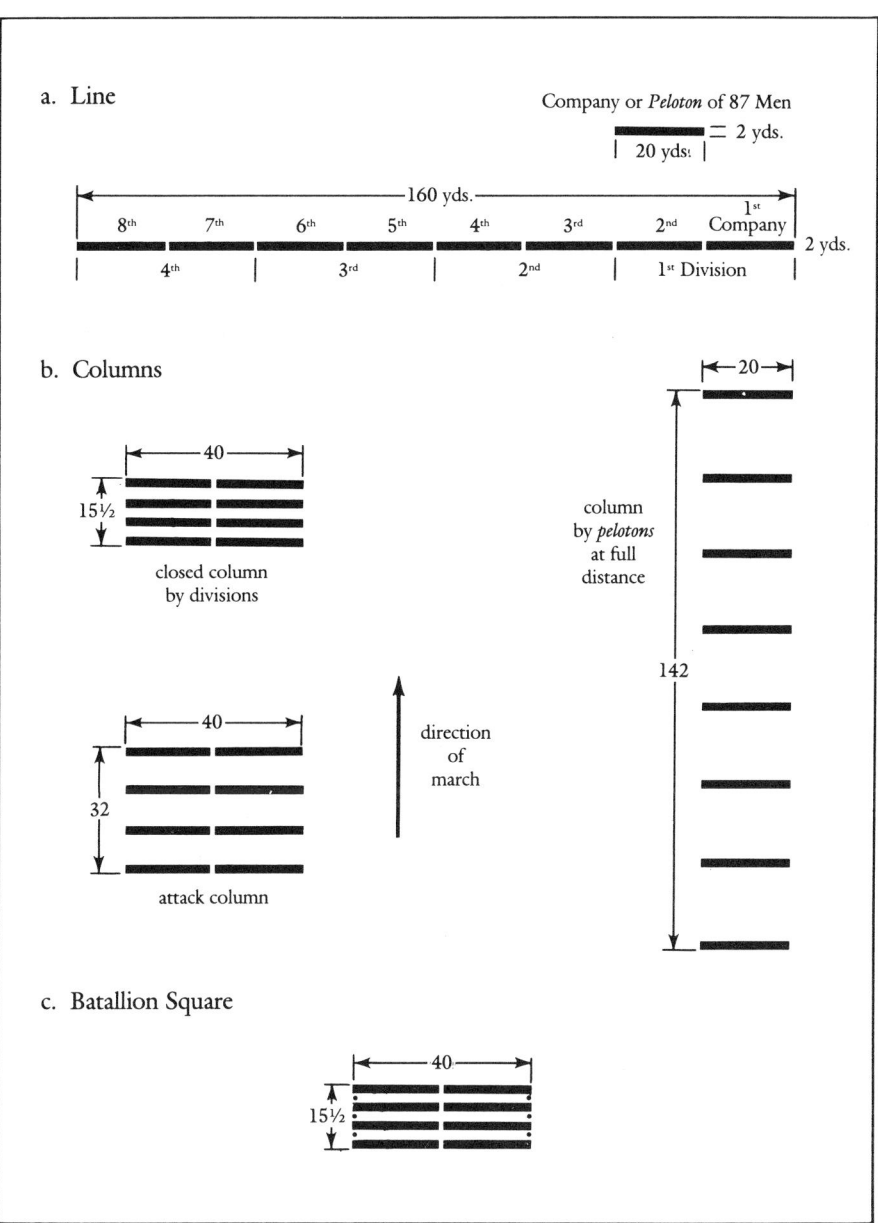

FIGURE 3.
Close Order Formations according to the Règlement of 1791

The *Règlement concernant l'exercice et manoeuvres de l'infanterie du 1ᵉʳ août 1791* laid down four types of musketry. Three methods consisted of commanded volleys, and for such salvos the first rank knelt as all three ranks discharged their pieces in turn. In the fourth method, the *feux de deux rangs,* only the initial round was fired by command; then troops fired at will. During the *feux de deux rangs* the first two ranks fired, while the third supposedly loaded for the first two. In fact, soldiers proved reluctant to pass around their treasured fusils, so the third rank generally stood idle. For most of the eighteenth century volley forms had been the rule, but now the French relied mainly upon the *feux de deux rangs*.[4]

Besides the need for concentrated firepower, the desire to keep troops in hand also moved commanders to favor the line. Infantrymen in line remained more under the control of their officers than did troops dispersed as *tirailleurs*. This high troop control made the line a good preliminary or holding formation, especially during a battle's early phase. Men standing in lines three ranks deep also presented a less attractive target to enemy artillery than did troops packed together in columns.

The Line in Formal Instructions

Jean Colin, in his classic *La tactique et la discipline dans les armées de la Révolution,* argued that with its very real advantages the line remained the dominant French combat formation after the outbreak of the Revolution. He based his comments largely upon the writings of General Alexis, comte de Schauenbourg, who directed a training camp in the Armée de la Moselle at roughly the same time that General H. A. J. Meunier labored with his *école* at Cambrai. The Moselle probably qualified as the most tactically conservative *armée,* and Schauenbourg was a proponent of the line. Using Schauenbourg's directives as an archetype, Colin concluded, "In the Armée de la Moselle, it was always in line that the battalions were formed." He contended that the *arme blanche,* so favored in Jacobin rhetoric, saw little real service: "In sum, one made almost exclusive use of fire combat, be it in line or in *tirailleurs*."[5]

Four years after Meunier composed his "Changements," he wrote a lengthy criticism of certain drill reforms suggested by Schauenbourg. Entirely in accord with the "Changements," Meunier's later work displays the contrast between the two officers and the armies they served. Meunier judged Schauenbourg's work too formal and too linear. This does not mean that Meunier avoided the linear order altogether. On the contrary, he himself suggested further refinements in the deployment of lines. But the line was not the only close order combat formation regularly used by the Armée du Nord. Certain instructions issued by generals in the Nord are in accord with Meunier's balanced evaluation of the line. General Jean-Baptiste Kléber, commanding troops of the Armée des Ardennes, prepared a tactical instruction in the spring of 1794, which recognized the line as an integral part of the tactical system. This general directed his commanders to employ the line as a support formation when engaged in villages. Kléber also ordered that "general officers will always hold their troops ready to put themselves in line."[6] He recommended, however, that attacks be made in column.

Documenting the Line in Battle: On the Defensive

At least some of the Nord's major officers valued the line, but only evidence of its use in battle can establish its real importance. Unfortunately, some real problems in documentation arise from the very wording of contemporary reports themselves. The usual eighteenth-century term for "in line," *en bataille*, muddles many records. Literally translated this means "in battle": but sometime before the late 1700s it came to mean "in line." However, at times the word implies only "in order of battle" without specifying the formation. This use is particularly common when referring to more than one battalion. The inquirer must consequently approach supposed cases of line usage with extreme care to avoid being misled by the words.[7] In many cases caution dictates than one seek corroborating circumstances before accepting a report as a description of linear combat.

Of the 108 engagements employed in this study, forty-four saw some use of the line, and in these forty-four there occurred fifty-five different recorded instances of the line in combat. Incidence of line usage followed roughly the same curve as reported engagements, neither increasing nor decreasing from April 1792 to July 1794. The sample collected here requires a further breakdown into types of usage, since the line filled several distinct roles.

Defense saw the largest number of cases, twenty-two. In defense, the concentration of firepower so basic to the line promised the greatest advantage. It proved especially valuable in situations demanding part of a force to defend the whole, as in retreats. One can establish no set rules concerning the size of unit likely to employ the line on defense or the type of situation that might call for the linear order. Examples in the defense category involved units from battalion to beyond brigade level. Usually French infantry stood in line to resist infantry, but Nord units sometimes chose to stand in line against charging cavalry as well. General Jean-Baptiste Cacault's engagement around Boussu, 26 April 1794, illustrates the use of a line as a last-minute emergency measure against cavalry. Cacault wrote that after galloping over to a threatened demi-brigade: "I commanded the last company of the third battalion stand firm, demi-brigade, companies half-turn to the right, forward in line, march. During this movement, I ordered a *feux de deux rangs* by successive companies."[8] This maneuver must have put the demi-brigade in an extended "L" with a short vertical bar.

In those situations that demanded that part of a force cover and protect the rest, a line's concentrated firepower was particularly appreciated. During retreats, covering troops often deployed into linear order. General Théodore-François Leclaire, for example, reported the professional behavior of the 56th Infantry Regiment at Wattignies on 15 October 1793: "By itself, it covered the retreat, from the position I had placed it in, with the most regular fires by half-battalion, by company, and by file during most of an hour." Volley fire, often thought to have been virtually absent in this period, poured into the pursuing Austrians. A French rear guard battalion here fought in the highest tradition of eighteenth-century disciplined warfare. In an action of 29 March 1794, on the Sambre, General Guillaume Soland successfully charged a series of redoubts at a crossroads, but he finally felt compelled to withdraw. As his soldiers turned about, "he ordered the 10th Paris to put itself in line beside the redoubt to protect it and to cover the retreat."[9] The 10th Paris did not equal the 56th Infantry Regiment, however; it panicked, fired on friend and foe alike, and fled to the rear.

Forced to retreat at Pont-à-Chin during the battle of Tournai, General Etienne-Jacques MacDonald's fine battalions seem to have executed a particularly complex maneuver, called a passage of lines.[10] According to the *Règlement du 1er août 1791,* one battalion in line passed through another in the following manner: each company of the first battalion withdrew by a flank march and moved through gaps in the second battalion created as each of the companies in this second battalion doubled its ranks; then the marching companies would loop about, coming into line again behind the second battalion.

The passage of defiles required that the first troops through a bottleneck stand in defense of their vulnerable comrades negotiating the obstacle. Such an operation occurred when General Leclaire's troops at Grand-Pré on 15 September 1792 covered General Jean-Pierre Chazont's retreat through the restricted forest road. Having marched his men safely through, Leclaire ordered "the column to halt and deploy in line facing the rear," to protect this confused withdrawal.[11] Judging from his "Changements," one would conclude that Meunier placed considerable emphasis on the correct passage of defiles, and for him the passage began and ended with troops standing in line.

As a Waiting and Preliminary Formation

Among the cases examined in this chapter appear seventeen examples of the linear order as a waiting or preliminary formation. Commanders who employed the line for this purpose were not responding to a direct enemy assault; instead they stood on guard as the battle developed. Here the line's high troop control and low vulnerability to artillery fire mattered more than its concentrated musketry. Occasionally, during a lull in combat, commanders reverted to a linear formation while their troops rested and awaited further orders.

September and November 1792 brought a series of victories for French arms, and these triumphs each began with almost the entire French force arrayed in the long ranks of linear order. At Jemappes nearly all battalions of the Nord stood in line before they formed into attack columns for the victorious assault. Neerwinden seems to have been the last full-scale battle, however, in which the line served as the preliminary formation for the army as a whole.[12] Terrain and circumstance rendered impossible the grouping of an entire French field force in line at the commencement of later engagements.

Units of divisional size and less continued to employ the line, often revealing a close continuity with the classic eighteenth-century two-line order of battle. General Jacob-Job Elie reported that at Beaumont, 16 October 1793, "I ordered the officers to do their duty and I put [my force] in line, in two lines." A startling example of both the old-style double-line formation and its weakness was supplied by General Réné-Bernard Chapuis's defeat at Troisvilles, 26 April 1794. As part of an attack on an enemy camp, he commanded 11,200 troops, the center column of the assault. Arnaudin, an émigré serving with the Austrians, wrote of this debacle: "He put the center column in line, in two lines, the left resting on the village of Aridencourt."[13] Chapuis believed his flanks secure; however, a large body of Austrian and English cavalry took his division in flank and rear and scattered it. The general ended the day a prisoner of the Allies.

The line might be utilized as a waiting formation not only at the beginning of a battle, but also in mid-battle. During his attack on Furnes, 22 October 1793 General Jean-Florimond Gougelot rushed for the bridges but failed to take them. Sending *tirailleurs* across the canal, he drew up his battalions to wait "in line to the right of the road along the town's ditch, covering his troops with the houses which are found near the canal. General Gougelot placed the other five battalions in a second line at cannon range."[14] Here the commander minimized the danger to his men by ranging them in two lines behind what cover the terrain afforded.

In Support of Light Infantry

A line could also back up infantry engaged in open order combat. Support troops in linear order offered fire assistance or shelter to retreating *tirailleurs*, while at the same time protecting successful light infantry from enemy turning movements. The fine troop control characteristic of the line allowed commanders to detach measured amounts of reinforcements if the assisted infantry required them. In six cases out of the sample of fifty-three battalions deployed in linear order to aid dispersed troops in these ways. General Duhesmes argued that *tirailleurs* thrown forward without a controlled reserve could not defend the gains they made. He wrote that the French only learned to appreciate this fully in the summer of 1794. Close order support of light infantry predates June 1794 in five of the six examples considered here. The night before Hondschoote, General Jean-Nicolas Houchard sent *tirailleurs* into the embattled town of Rexpoede and placed "the rest [of the infantry] in line behind the village so as not to be turned by the enemy." Sergeant Jacques Fricasse reported the use of a line in conjunction with an open order assault on the village of Grand-Reng: "They were put in line before the village, and a great quantity of *tirailleurs* were sent forward who took the village on the first assault."[15]

The Line in Movement

Brittle and slow, the line revealed its greatest shortcomings when it was on the march. To guard against disaster, the pace had to be held down to allow for maintenance of reasonable alignment. With the *Règlement du 1er août 1791,* the French relaxed their concern for rigid alignment, but certainly the line could not be permitted to snap. The sample collected for this study contains only three cases in which troops facing the enemy marched in line, and an additional seven examples of the line in attack. If the enemy was in the area, battalions moving carefully in line could be ready for immediate action. Leclaire's soldiers near Liege on 27 December 1792 "had marched more than two leagues in line as well as possible." Toward the end of May 1794, Duhesmes's own troops used the line for a most unlikely purpose—an advance at the charge [*pas de charge*].[16] This followed hostile action, and again there was probably a question of remaining battle-ready.

In the Attack

As an attack formation, the line saw service in two distinct manners and at two distinct times. Charles Dumouriez, a friend and follower of the noted theorist Jacques Guibert, agreed that the line was the proper combat formation and the column the best means of rapid maneuver. However, Dumouriez rated shock action higher than did Guibert. At Jemappes his troops stood in line during the cannonade; they then formed battalion attack columns for the advance and finally deployed into line at close quarters for the ultimate assault. August, marquis de Dampierre wrote of the charge: "We marched in . . . column up to one-quarter of cannon range. Then, since we were losing men, Generals Dumouriez and Beuronville ordered me to deploy the columns. . . . The movement was made like a peacetime maneuver. . . . As soon as the eight battalions had finished deploying, I commanded them to march forward and to beat the charge." Leclaire, also present at Jemappes, reported an attempted deployment into line, but one with less success: "I found a little plateau, and I wanted to deploy. I was able to carry out this maneuver only with three companies; we found ourselves in range of some battalions of Hungarian grenadiers who greeted us with a diabolical fire."[17] Much of Dumouriez's attacking force may have suffered difficulties similar to those witnessed by Leclaire. Even with a three to one numerical advantage, Dumouriez's attack stalled, and men began deserting their units. This crisis must have been due to the confusion that attended deployment into line at close quarters. Such problems apparently terminated the use of this form of attack.

Attacks conducted entirely in linear order, without the temporary deployment into column, continued to appear in the annals of the Nord after 1792, although it should be noted that all but one of the cases examined here come from 1794, when the Nord had reached a greater level of expertise. On 26 April 1794 General Cacault used a line attack to throw back his opponents at Boussu: "Our infantry advanced in line . . . we marched in this order with our weapons on our shoulders [*au bras*], braving the grape shot that their heavy artillery pieces were already vomitting; this audacity on the part of the French battalions caused their left to dissolve." On 29 April near Menin, MacDonald's brigade formed into line and obeyed Souham's order "to march in line on the heights."[18] Similarly, in the fighting near Grand-Reng, 13 May 1794, Duhesmes also seems to have used the line.

The Column

A Revolutionary Formation

To many commentators, the column symbolized a new style of warfare, yet advocacy of the column as a vehicle for attack dominated a tactical discussion that began in the 1720s. As early as mid-century, French drill books contained some kind of deep-assault formation. However, not until the war of 1792 did French infantry adopt the attack column as its characteristic offensive tactic.

Whereas the line extended manpower to facilitate musketry, the column compressed manpower to maximize speed and thus minimize losses. Since the attack column covered a narrower front, it encountered fewer obstacles and could more easily keep good order when it did. This allowed rapid movement without sacrificing troop control and unit cohesion. Though it could not compete in a firefight with the line, the increased speed of the column allowed it to close with an enemy before he got off many volleys. However, if the enemy was able to concentrate fire against a column the results could be disastrous. As a consequence, the column depended upon light infantry and artillery support to disturb the opponent and to divert his attention from the attacking columns until they were upon him. When properly supported, the spirited assault troops, often singing as they charged, could sweep the enemy off the field.

The Form and Function of Divisional and Attack Columns

Only three of the nine column formations listed in the *Règlement du 1er août 1791* merit description in this chapter—the column by companies at full distance, the closed column by divisions, and the attack column.[19] These three differed in purpose, dimensions, and deployment.

The column by companies at full distance was a route formation, intended for use by troops on the march. Its appearance presented the greatest contrast to that of the line. One company in a battalion of 700 men occupied a front of only about twenty yards. Intervals equal to the front of the company allowed troops in this column to deploy into line by simple wheeling maneuvers executed by each company. As a result of these large intervals, a battalion in this formation measured only twenty yards in breadth and about 140 yards in depth.

In contrast to the column by companies, that by divisions was employed primarily for maneuver on the battlefield. A division was a unit of two combined companies. The column by divisions occupied a greater front than depth. The closed column by divisions, usually called the *colonne serrée*, was composed of four divisions with an interval of two and a half yards, or three paces, between divisions. This formation covered a front of forty yards with a depth of fifteen and a half. As specified in the *Règlement*, the attack column possessed a greater depth than the *colonne serrée*, though it also had a front of two companies. An increased interval of one section, half the front of a company, separated the paired companies, making this column thirty-two yards deep. Not only did the attack column differ in size but also in the method by which it was deployed.

The question of deployment causes some confusion over tactical methods. A *colonne serrée* could be formed in several ways, but an attack column followed only one method. For the column by division, the division constituted the basic unit. A division was more than an ad hoc grouping of two companies; each battalion contained set divisions, e.g., the first and second companies always formed the first division. (In another context "division" meant a number of battalions joined in a permanent larger unit.) In the *colonne serrée* divisions maintained their integrity, and any of the four divisions could function as the base for a closed divisional column. In the attack column prescribed by the *Règlement*, the company, not the division, became the constituent element. The attack column took shape as the companies to either side made a flank march into position behind the two center companies. The divisional and the attack columns deployed into line by similar squared-off movements, each division or company making first a flank march and then a movement forward into line.

During the sunset of the ancien régime French military theorists experimented with certain ways to employ columns in the assault; thus many military historians have claimed with some reason that the inclusion of an attack column in the *Règlement du 1er août 1791* demonstrates continuity between tactical practices of the late ancien régime and those of the Revolution. In form and function, however, the revolutionary attack column evolved into someting different than expressly intended by the authors of the *Règlement*.

The wide intervals in the *Règlement*'s attack column argue that it was not intended for shock combat. As implied by the wording of the *Règlement*, the purpose of the attack column was only to facilitate a rapid approach march followed by deployment into line. The drill book also outlined a method of opening fire before the column completely deployed; this points to a close-up deployment under fire. Its large intervals would not lend themselves to the cohesion and mass needed in shock action. The *Règlement* required such large intervals so that a battalion might avoid possible confusion during deployment. If the preceding logic is correct, then the *Règlement du 1er août 1791* represented a victory for proponents of line combat, not a compromise between them and those who favored shock attack in columns. Certainly nowhere in its pages did it contain a detailed procedure for employing column assaults with the *arme blanche*.

Shock assault in column emerged as the decisive element in offensive tactics employed by the Armée du Nord. The formation chosen for such attacks seems not to have been the attack column as detailed in the *Règlement du 1er août 1791*, but rather a closed column with a front of two companies. General Meunier suggested that the *Règlement* needed some modification to bring it into line with the army's real needs. "It was necessary to organize movements by mass, which are, so to speak, only indicated in the *Règlement* of 1791. He thinks that in addition to their ease and rapidity, they can be infinitely useful for our combats *à la baionette*." The formation *en masse* he advocated was a closed column. Other officers in the Armée du Nord also worked out an offensive technique built around column assaults. While commanding troops from the Armée des Ardennes, General Kléber drafted a tactical instruction for the nine battalions he was to lead in a diversion against Mons in late May 1794. He ordered that "attacks will be made in column . . . the bayonet lowered." Another figure who served with the Nord, Barthélemy Schérer, occupies a particularly important place in the history of Napoleonic warfare. Instructions he drafted as commander of the Armée d'Italie during the winter of 1795–96 set out in detail the tactical system associated with Napoleon Bonaparte. There is good reason to argue that his system was chiefly based on his experience as a general in the Armée des Ardennes. His plan described a hypothetical attack by twelve battalions: "At the moment of the attack, the twelve battalions . . . would deploy in column by battalion, so that the twelve battalions would form twelve small columns along the same line, each column being composed of four divisions of the same size; each division at three paces distance from the proceeding one."[20]

If one distinctive element of the attack column, its wide intervals, underwent transformation; the other, its deployment by companies on the center, retained its supporters. Meunier argued in his critique of Schauenbourg: "In every case where the battalions ought to form a mass, it would seem most simple and advantageous to form each battalion in a closed column on its center, as the *Règlement* prescribes with the attack column; one would then need only half the time to form each battalion into *colonne serrée*. Independently of the precious advantage of speed that formation and deployment on the center of the battalion affords, it also could suit our bayonet attacks excellently."[21]

For simplicity's sake, during the rest of this chapter the terms attack column, divisional column, and *colonne serrée* will be used interchangeably in most cases.

Documenting the Column in Battle: In the Attack

After considering *Règlements,* criticisms, and instructions, battlefield evidence remains the final determinant of column usage. Forty-two examples and possible examples of divisional columns in battle constitute the sample for this study. As in discussing the line, a search for recorded examples runs into some linguistic confusion. "Column" in French as in English carries a double meaning. On the one hand, it means a particular tactical formation; on the other hand, it denotes a body of troops, as in the expression relief column. For this and other reasons, personal judgment comes into play in deciding between the meaningless and the meaningful.[22] The instances collected for this study fall into two categories, attack and non-attack. It is no surprise that "In the Attack" includes most of the cases, thirty-five. Here the column's mass and mobility lent it to shock assaults against enemy infantry or even cavalry.

This evidence confirms the importance of the attack column as a French offensive technique in the period before July 1794. The thirty-five cases of combat assaults are drawn from thirty-two engagements; all the major battles fought by the Armée du Nord and the Armée des Ardennes, except Neerwinden, number among these engagements. Consequently, Colin committed a serious error when he asserted that after Jemappes "attack columns and mass formations were abandoned for some time; at least we no longer find any trace of them in 1793 and 1794."[23]

The first evidence of a column attack by the Armée du Nord dates from Dumouriez's Argonne campaign, but it may well have occurred before. Dumouriez thought the column a sound formation for French troops. As minister of war before he took field command, he reportedly advised Marshal Luckner to put his volunteers in column, placing artillery and cavalry between the masses. As early as 14 September 1792, Leclaire reports that when attacking near Crois-aux-Bois, "I deployed five battalions in column . . . I directed the heads of the columns there, ordering the charge to be beaten and lowering our bayonets." At fifty paces enemy fire badly shook the attackers, who stopped and "executed a fire by files in column, fortunately firing in the air, and making a half turn to the right threw down their packs and fusils."[24]

At the battle of Jemappes, Dumouriez's army "exactly at noon . . . put itself into battalions in a flash, and advanced with the greatest rapidity and the best spirits toward the enemy entrenchments." The fighting of that November day has been considered as either typical of the revolutionary period as a whole, or as atypical. Jemappes saw column formations employed, and to that extent it was typical of French offensives. However, the type of column that was chosen was the formal attack column of the *Règlement* deployed back into line at close range. Dampierre was very specific: "We marched in central columns."[25] Jemappes remains the only battle in which the Armée du Nord can be shown to have advanced in attack columns and deployed into line for the assault. Thus, it constitutes an atypical battle. Perhaps if more details were known about the obscure battle of Neerwinden, there would be more examples of this tactical combination.

Shock warfare always suited the column. Even though Dumouriez encouraged deployment at close quarters, some of his officers preferred to send dense columns tearing into enemy ranks with no attempt at linear combat. In fact, the very day Dumouriez fought his particular kind of battle at Jemappes, Jacques O'Moran defeated the Austrians at Le Blaton in a very different manner. Paul Charles Thiébault reported: "We were rapidly formed into battalion attack columns and set into motion at the charge under the protection of all our cannon. The enemy columns, cannonaded and soon after attacked with the bayonet, were thrown back [*bouleversées*]."[26] Thiébault's praise of artillery support may provide another clue as to why the Armée du Nord abandoned last-minute linear deployment. It was thought that a successful assault required artillery support, but from the moment a column began to deploy it masked the enemy from support fire. Thus at the crucial juncture a deploying column robbed itself of an important asset.

Attack columns continued to appear throughout the tense year of 1793. Dampierre died leading what appears to have been an attack column during the battle of Famars, 8 May 1793. A clear example took place on 6 September, when Houchard ordered an assault against the town of Bambecke. He wrote, "General Barthélemy then proposed to the general in chief that we march at the enemy with the bayonet [*la baionnette en avant*]; the columns were formed and they advanced." Evidence indicates that French infantry attacked in column at both Hondschoote and Wattignies; however, owing particularly to the comments of General Duhesmes, considerable misunderstanding surrounds each battle. He implied that the French sought out the rugged terrain of both battlefields in order to avoid close order combat, which requires better country. But it should be remembered that Allied sieges compelled the Nord to fight at Hondschoote and Wattignies. Hondschoote, at one point, did become primarily a light infantry battle, but toward the end of the engagement column attacks precipitated a French victory. Comte Jean Baptiste Jourdan, then one of Houchard's divisional commanders, led a close order assault: "We will thus form the head of a column which will drive in the enemy skirmishers. Ours, pressed by our cavalry, and encouraged all the more by the presence of this battalion in good order, will doubtless rally to us. Our column, like a snowball, will grow as it advances." Leclaire apparently also charged in column at Hondschoote, and the crucial bayonet assault in the center seems to have come off in attack columns. Attack columns played such a crucial role at Wattignies that they left an indelible impression on Lazare Carnot, who was present with Jourdan at the battle.[27] From that point on Carnot always counseled the use of bayonet attacks in column.

Column attacks took place throughout the spring of 1794, and they were by no means restricted to *affaires de poste*, as some have asserted. At Boussu, on 26 April 1794, Cacault personally led an exemplary charge by two battalions. "After having rallied the units, I ordered a second charge. I put myself at the head of the 3rd Nord and the 9th Seine-et-Oise, and ordered the cavalry to charge along with these two battalions in attack column; this charge was tremendous, but we succeeded even better than would have been hoped. Never have as much audacity and good order been seen at the same time." Duhesmes himself described another explicit case, his 21 May attack on Grand-Reng. This latter account deserves special mention since it describes an order of battle assumed by a force of several battalions, each of which attacked in column. "Our infantry left the line and advanced with a great deal of firmness, in a checkerboard order."[28]

Attack columns proved their effectiveness against infantry, but they also had merit in assaults against cavalry. Essentially the *colonne serrée*, with certain minor changes, constituted one of the anti-cavalry formations prescribed in the *Règlement du 1ᵉʳ août 1791*. Thus it is not too surprising to see the attack column turned against cavalry. It is noteworthy that all the examples of this particular use of the *colonne serrée* occurred in the spring of

1794. Perhaps this is an indication that the Nord did not possess the required degree of training, experience, and confidence until then. Duhesmes more than once led his battalions against cavalry during the seesaw advances across the Sambre. He wrote of an encounter near Latombe on 26 May 1794, "Having crossed the woods, the battalions formed into masses to drive out a unit of skirmishers on horseback." The enemy cavalry appeared in great numbers and Duhesmes's force hesitated: "Recognizing their fear, General Duhesmes . . . dismounted, took the fusil of a dead soldier, put himself at the head of the first company and led them at the charge."[29] Considering the French infantry's almost paranoid fear of Austrian cavalry, these charges were significant feats.

The Non-Attack Uses of the Colonne Serrée

Battalions of the Armée du Nord stood in *colonne serrée* when performing several different functions, but the dramatic nature of battlefield reports submerges this formation's other roles in a flood of gallant attacks. Evidence, though very sparse, still exists to illustrate it as a support, waiting, and maneuver formation.

In support of light infantry attacks a reserve in close order could be essential to success. Duhesmes, who complained that without adequate reserves, *tirailleurs* met constant reversals, awarded General Jean-Victor Moreau the highest praise for his fine use of support formations *en masse*. Duhesmes himself apparently used a column in support at La Capelle, 21 April 1794.[30] However, more examples of the line in support come out of the sources, perhaps because the defensive firepower of the line mattered more in this situation than did the concentrated manpower present in the column.

High troop control and the capacity to maneuver quickly wherever troops were needed made the column a good assembly and waiting formation. At Hondschoote on the morning of 8 September, Jourdan's division stood in closed columns after abandoning the deeper route column as too vulnerable to artillery fire. The *colonnes serrées* later broke up when harassing artillery drove the soldiers to seek cover as best they could. Less vulnerable to artillery fire, the line may have been a better waiting formation within range of the enemy's cannon. At the siege of Maubeuge battalions drew up in column at each gate to respond to enemy thrusts.[31]

The closed column was intended for maneuver and certainly served in this role, although it remains difficult to get evidence establishing the fact. Battlefield reports mainly center on combat and even then often conceal as much as they reveal. What a unit did before and after it confronted the enemy concerned the reporters hardly at all. Only three examples of maneuver in *colonne serrée* were found, all of which took place in combat retreats. During the action of 16 June 1794 near Charleroi, Kléber covered

Jourdan's retreat: "I thus marched immediately to the bridge, passing on the flank of the enemy at a normal pace and in *colonne serrée;* disconcerted by this assured bearing, his cavalry dared try nothing against us."[32] Direct evidence is slim, but considering the facility of forming divisional columns, demonstrated by their use in attack, and their mobility, they must have been commonly employed in maneuver.

The ordre mixte

While there is no question that units of the Nord used both lines and columns on the battlefield, it is unclear whether the Nord witnessed the birth of the Napoleonic *ordre mixte*. This formation linked together three battalions, the central one in line flanked by two others in attack column. Such a combination may or may not have appeared as early as 1794; Kleber's Instructions possibly prescribed something like it. Yet despite uncertainty as to the exact patterns employed, it cannot be doubted that infantry of the Nord utilized varied and flexible combinations of line and column in battle.

Columns by Companies

Used both as a route column and as a column of maneuver on the battlefield, the column by companies served no assault role similar to the shorter and broader *colonne serrée*. Lacking this combat role, the route column appears rarely in engagement reports. The existence of several tactical instructions, however, makes it quite easy to establish the function and importance of the column by companies. During that self-conscious period after the disastrous defeat of Neerwinden, Nord commanders insisted that the column by companies must be the sole route formation. Custine on 31 May 1793 ordered, "In all marches infantry columns will march always by company and not otherwise." Houchard in his "Instruction" for the Nord, dated 23 August, wrote, "In all marches that the army makes from now on, the infantry will always march by company."[33]

Long before Custine's standing order, on 28 April 1793 those French troops that did not panic during the disastrous affair at Tournai marched off in column by company. Not only did this type of column appear on the road, but it also figured to some extent in battlefield maneuver. Cacault reported that during the combat around Boussu on 26 April 1794, enemy cavalry caught the 172nd Demi-Brigade off guard as it formed column by company at full distance. "Citizen Osté, commander of the 172nd, had already formed by a company left wheel; he thus found himself with distances by company [in column]." Duhesmes even states that his exemplary retreat in the presence of the enemy on 16 June 1794 "was made in the presence of General Kléber in the greatest order . . . , drums beating and arms shouldered, in column by companies."[34] But even in its combat role the route column remained very different from the attack column; all they really shared was an ability for rapid maneuver.

The Square

Function and Form

Other close order infantry formations served several purposes, but the square had only one rationale—defense against cavalry. The great strength of this formation lay in its ability to offer stern resistance on all four sides. Cavalry swirling around a well-ordered battalion would be unable to find a weak spot, while at the same time the horsemen themselves would become the targets of ceaseless musketry. Though a defensive Gibraltar, the square had no offensive capacity. Since embattled troops had to face out on all sides to receive the enemy assault, they could not move.[35] Immobile and dense, squares presented excellent targets for enemy artillery fire. A unit ideally put off forming square until the attackers masked it from hostile artillery, but deploying with enemy horsemen close at hand proved risky indeed.

The *Règlement du 1er août 1791* basically detailed two methods of forming square, depending on the size of the force involved. A large column of many battalions on the march could form a single, large hollow square. There is no evidence that this square was ever employed by the Nord. The other system was designed for as small a body of troops as one lone battalion. It required that units already be arrayed in closed divisional columns, such as one would commonly encounter on the battlefield. If more than one battalion was involved, the first two divisions faced forward, and the last two did an about-face. Intervening companies faced to either side. The three ranks all around the square then conduced a *feux de deux rangs*. Although the *Règlement* did not state who was to fill the gaps between divisions, it can be assumed that supernumerary officers and NCOs would stand in the openings. A solitary battalion could deploy into this type of square by facing only one division forward and one backward. Units standing in *colonne serrée* obviously had the easiest time in forming square. Meunier suggested a rather different one-battalion square in his "Changements," but his system appears to be only a suggestion.[36]

The Square in Battle

Given the Allies' quantitative and qualitative advantage in cavalry, one might expect the square to play a major defensive role in the Nord's tactical system. However, the difficulty of forming square in the presence of the enemy greatly lessened its desirability. Awkward French battalions apparently could not manage to do it properly until 1794. In an instruction for the tactical conduct of Allied troops, the Austrian General Mack advised that commanders always keep one-half to one-third of their cavalry in reserve for counterattacks. He then reminded his readers that their French opponents were at their weakest when deploying.[37]

Republican battalions often employed other formations against cavalry. A well-ordered line, facing an oncoming attack, could throw back charging squadrons, so if the enemy mounted a sudden charge, troops would probably be wiser to stay in line rather than begin a time-consuming deployment. Of course, if caught in the flank, as at Troisvilles, infantry in linear order crumbled before determined horsemen. As mentioned before, an attack column closely resembled a battalion square and had real strength against cavalry.

The *Règlement* not only stipulated that infantry form the square when opposing cavalry, but it also prescribed use of *feux de deux rangs* when battalions faced such an onslaught. Yet in battle reports bayonets received mention time and again as being particularly effective, and volley fire, which was also overlooked in the manual, came into play. In a 26 April 1794 case, Nord infantry in line staved off a sudden charge, as General Cacault ordered his men "to cross their bayonets in the first two ranks, and the third to fire."[38]

The sample for this study includes only six examples of the square in combat. The first two examples led to disaster; they occurred in late 1793 and early 1794. Successful instances did not take place until May and June 1794. Even when several battalions operated together, if threatened by cavalry, they seem to have deployed only into a series of battalion squares. At Grand-Reng, during the fighting of 21 May 1794, "General Kléber tried another sortie with some squadrons of cavalry and a column of three battalions commanded by General Poncet which he formed into square." This description of Duhesmes leaves some doubt as to how the battalions deployed, but General Desjardin, who also described this confrontation, states that they advanced "in battalion columns." In what was a clearer example, on 18 May 1794 General Jacques-Pierre Fromentin received orders that if the French advanced, he was to instruct the brigade commanded by General Depaux "to place itself in battalion columns in square, their left on Montplaisir," near the Bois de Bonne-Espérance.[39]

By May 1794 troops of the Armée du Nord clearly displayed an ability to form square and to stop enemy cavalry. The successful use of the square serves as a metaphor for the growing tactical maturity of the Nord. While it would be risky to hazard a confident judgment of all its battalions, by 1794 many, perhaps most, had come to display an order and flexibility that would surprise those historians convinced of a stereotype that condemns revolutionary troops to chaotic disorder.

Chapter 12

The Dimensions of Open Order Combat in the Armée du Nord

A CERTAIN MYTHOLOGY grew up around the use of open order tactics, although it was never as extravagant as the celebration of the bayonet and the column. Again the claim was heard that combat with skirmishers was somehow particularly French. "It is in this genre of combat, that the French genius shines with the greatest brilliance," wrote the light infantry specialist General Philibert-Guillaume Duhesmes.[1] The same patriotic devotion believed to inspire the serried ranks of the attack column could be trusted to impel the more individual effort of the *tirailleur*. On another plane, an emphasis on open order tactics was also believed to suit the unskilled recruit, since the French thought that open order tactics required more intelligent improvisation than formal training.

This myth will give way to reality only after several questions have been asked and answered. First, the nature of open order combat needs to be defined. Then it must be known if *tirailleurs* required special weaponry and, more important, whether all troops, recruits and veterans alike, fought as skirmishers or whether such duty required special abilities and thus fell to a picked elite. The inquiry can finally focus on the details of open order combat, both in independent action and in support of battalions marshaled in close order.

Open order tactics, in fact, involved a pattern of motivation and combat similar to the twentieth-century battlefield. As today, both personal commitment and group cohesion bound *tirailleurs* to their duties. Individualized combat required experience and skills that made the novice a poor skirmisher and gave specialists in open order fighting a real advantage. Unfortunately, much of the detail of the way they deployed and fought remains obscure and will not likely ever allow a precise reconstruction. The character of this style of combat did not lend itself to easy description, but what can be known of it establishes that it was ubiquitous along the Belgian frontier.

The Character of Light Infantry Combat and Forces

The Nature of Skirmishing

Open order tactics constituted a mode of combat altogether different from the more formalized tactics of line, column, and square. *Tirailleurs,* best translated as skirmishers, generally fought as dispersed parties of individual marksmen. Although they acted in coordination with one another, they moved independently as each *tirailleur* sought his own cover and concealment. This style of warfare differed in character, both technically and psychologically, from close order tactics.

The *tirailleur*'s open order tactics gave him unique advantages. He could unsettle and distract infantry in close order; deployed against enemy artillerymen, he could harass or even silence batteries. Disciplined volleys of musketry or salvos of artillery fire were merely wasted in opposing this elusive marksman. The *tirailleur* could better engage in street fighting, seize a wood, or provide the varied services of advance and flank guard than could his counterpart in close order. And when the French faced an enemy strong in light infantry, republican heavy battalions required the protection that only a *tirailleur* screen could provide.

This French light infantryman also suffered from a particular set of weaknesses. Without the cohesiveness and discipline of battalions in close order, dispersed *tirailleurs* on open ground could be easily ridden down by cavalry or swept from the field by advancing massed infantry. To hold its own effectively, light infantry often required the support of cavalry or heavy infantry. The *tirailleur* also wasted an inordinate amount of ammunition, a most precious item in those early, lean years of the Republic. Lastly, though the light infantryman often prepared the way for the decisive attack in a major engagement, he was usually incapable of delivering it. This duty was best left to massed heavy infantry.

The essence of skirmishing was its emphasis upon the individual. Proper performance rested upon his personal initiative. In terms of the theory of combat effectiveness, normative compliance alone became paramount, since close supervision and coercion of the *tirailleur* were usually out of the question. Consequently, this style of warfare particularly suited the revolutionary armies, which relied on normative compliance to a degree far in excess of previous forces. This fact was not lost on contemporaries, who were ready to trust patriotism as a source of dedicated initiative on the skirmish line. (Of course, the formula that made the French soldier reliable included more than raw patriotism.) The individuality of the *tirailleur* must also have resulted in what S. L. A. Marshall called the isolation of the battlefield—a fearful, helpless sense of being cut off and alone while facing the enemy. He argued that only confidence in a group of comrades and in their willingness to aid the individual soldier could overcome this potentially paralyzing anxiety. Such confidence came only with time and experience.

If it is fair to stress this mixture of independence and interdependence, then they can be seen to exist in a kind of tension, leading to conflicting expectations and decisions concerning the kind of men dispatched as *tirailleurs*. On the one hand, reliance on personal devotion as a source of combat motivation, linked with the low level of parade ground skills required by skirmishers, would have encouraged the use of new recruits who could fight as *tirailleurs, faute de mieux*. On the other hand, the need to build up the informal, but essential, bonds of confidence necessary to overcome battlefield isolation would argue that light infantry ought to be experienced and able, rather than raw and unskilled. Whether *tirailleurs* were specially armed experts, normal rank-and-file troops, or unskilled recruits is a question with more than technical implications.

Smoothbore and Rifle

The greatly increased use of *tirailleurs* during the war of 1792 cannot be ascribed to the adoption of a more effective rifled specialist's weapon by French light infantry. Until well into the nineteenth century, the French armed the overwhelming majority of their light infantry with the same smoothbore flintlock muzzleloaders that had been carried in the wars of the ancien régime. As early as the 1780s Prussian and English light forces came to favor rifled firearms for their greater accuracy and range. But rifles were much more expensive than smoothbores and more likely to foul. Furthermore, a long and complicated loading procedure doomed the muzzleloading rifle to a very slow rate of fire. To achieve the necessary tight fit between bullet and groove, the rifleman had to wrap his bullet in a greased patch and force it down the barrel with the aid of a ramrod driven home by blows from a mallet. All this caused the French to continue using smoothbores throughout the revolutionary and Napoleonic wars. The only significant difference in weaponry between heavy and light infantry is that some light infantry specialists preferred the shorter carbine to the full-sized infantry fusil.[2] Perhaps one or two of the free companies served with rifled muskets or carbines, and perhaps a few of the firearms commandeered for regular units had rifled barrels, but generally the *tirailleurs* of the Armée du Nord carried only the standard model 1777 smoothbore fusil.

Judged by modern standards, the accuracy of this fusil left much to be desired. Curious and enterprising officers performed tests with smoothbores and rifles during this period; consequently, the present-day inquirer can form a fairly precise picture of the capabilities of these arms. In one Prussian test marksmen armed with French and Prussian muskets fired at large targets, hitting their marks about 75 percent of the time at eighty yards, 50 percent at 160 yards, and a bit over 25 percent at 240 yards. The rifle scored a much greater percentage of hits, especially when fired at small targets; General Gerhard von Scharnhorst's test indicated that at 160 yards the marksman armed with a rifle scored slightly shy of two and a half times as frequently as one armed with the smoothbore musket. Interesting enough, however, the time consumed by riflemen in loading, aiming, and firing was two and one-half times greater at 160 yards. Summing up his inquiry, Scharnhorst concluded, "Rifle and musket fire have about the same effect in the same period of time; but the musket needs three to four times as much ammunition as the rifle."[3]

Assuming an adequate supply of cartridges, the *tirailleur* could be quite effective with a smoothbore. Of course, the Republicans regarded ammunition as a valuable commodity that they could ill afford to waste. Yet even in the best of circumstances the majority of shots fired by *tirailleurs* in battle flew wide of the mark. The hours of heated skirmishing that preceded the main French thrust in a battle consumed considerable amounts of ball and powder, often with disappointing results. It must be remembered that on occasion lack of ammunition forced the French to avoid or withdraw from combat. The Ministry of War at one point even accused the *tirailleurs* of imposing a premature end to encounters by purposely wasting ammunition. "If combats come to an end because of the lack of ammunition, it is because too much is wasted. Cannon fire at too great a range. *Tirailleurs* try to use all their cartridges as rapidly as possible, often firing in the air and returning to say they have no more ammunition."[4]

Since *tirailleurs* required considerable ammunition, resupply became a problem. There seem to have been three methods of getting ammunition to the skirmish line. First, the *tirailleur* himself could leave the line and go back for more cartridges, as implied in the above Ministry complaint. Second, certain light infantrymen could be given the duty of running up bags of ammunition from caissons in the rear. If there were not enough flintlocks to go around, the unarmed recruit could find himself in this supply capacity. Lastly, horsemen could carry up the bags of cartridges. Since they carried a heavier load than the foot soldier, and at a far more rapid pace, this last alternative was probably the most effective resupply technique.[5]

The charateristics of the eighteenth-century smoothbore musket exerted a dual influence on infantry tactics. Owing to the slow rate of fire and inaccuracy of their weapons, dispersed *tirailleurs* seldom found it within their means to decimate an enemy formation. Only if the opposing heavy infantry remained exposed and unresisting for a considerable length of time could light infantry inflict significant numbers of casualties. A linear formation alone could mass the infantry firepower required to destroy an enemy standing in close order. Accordingly, the musket made close order combat necessary. But the existence of tightly packed masses of men on the battlefield offered the light infantryman targets so large that his inaccurate musket became effective. Thus the *tirailleur* could easily harass and distract his enemies even if he could not destroy them.

Specialist and Non-Specialist Light Infantry

The extent to which combat as *tirailleurs* remained the province of a small elite corps of light infantry specialists and the extent to which it became generalized among all French infantry says something about the nature of the French soldier and the nature of combat as *tirailleurs*. Peter Paret argues that the wars of the French Revolution constituted a watershed in military history precisely because at this point all infantry became capable of fighting as light infantry. Specialist light infantry units predated the Revolution; in fact, they were on the rise during the decades before 1789. However, the republican army now called upon all men from heavy, or line, companies to disperse as skirmishers when circumstance required. As one émigré wrote concerning the Armée du Nord: "The Allies had sometimes concluded that the French armies were very much stronger than allied forces in free corps and light troops; this was not literally true. But since the infantry of the Republic were all armed in just about the same manner, they were all employed equally as *tirailleurs* and in the line, in so far as circumstances seemed to require." In the words of Duhesmes, "The French armies had only light infantry."[6]

Several factors permitted commanders to disperse their troops as *tirailleurs*. Since the French did not believe that *tirailleurs* needed distinct light infantry weapons, all infantry was thought to be properly equipped for light infantry action. In addition, the French rejected the notion that *tirailleurs* required special formal training to perform their duties adequately. Lastly, with good reason, republican officers trusted their men's dedication to their duty. The greatest single barrier to a wider use of light infantry earlier in the century had been the fear that once soldiers dispersed they would desert. Frederick the Great exemplified this apprehension. The French combat infantryman's commitment to the Revolution and to the war was never seriously questioned. These characteristics made it possible for all revolutionary battalions to fight as *tirailleurs,* but did they?

A direct examination of the sources dealing with the Armée du Nord produces a mixed answer. On the one hand, among the thirty-nine cases in which the origin of the *tirailleurs* was stipulated, specialist light infantry units were four times as likely to be mentioned than were *tirailleurs* from line units. This evidence suggests a marked tendency to employ distinct light infantry units if possible. On the other hand, there is ample evidence that line infantry dispersed as skirmishers when necessary. Furthermore, there is reason to believe that in many cases when *tirailleurs* are mentioned in reports without citing their units of origin, the *tirailleurs* very possibly came from line companies. In sum, deployment of entire line battalions as skirmishers was possible, but the use of specialists was preferred.

The number of specialist light infantry battalions and companies increased throughout the period and acquired an elite aura. Largest among the light infantry units were entire battalions, and later demi-brigades, given over to open order combat. After considerable discussion and experimentation during the eighteenth century, the French line army increased its light infantry contingent to twelve *chasseur à pied* battalions in 1788. These battalions more than proved their worth, and by May 1793 their number rose to twenty-five; by the summer of 1794 it reached fifty. The Armée du Nord and the Ardennes included at least ten of these battalions by late spring 1794.[7] A unique group of battalions derived from experiments with mixed forces of cavalry and infantry—the legions. Many volunteer battalions specialized in light infantry service. Some revealed their nature in their titles, such as the Chasseurs de la Meuse; others without such obvious labels also habitually acted as light infantry, such as the 5th Paris.

Without question light infantry battalions constituted something apart from the general run of line infantry. Commanders constantly differentiated between heavy and light troops and ascribed a certain elite quality to the latter. Correspondence dealing with the Chasseurs de la Meuse provides good examples of these opinions. An order of 11 December 1793 read in part: "Colonel Lenoble, commander of the Chasseurs de la Meuse, is authorized to take himself to Verdun so as to choose there among the battalions of conscripts the best trained, the most robust, and those most suited to service as *chasseurs*." A month later General Sistrières emphasized the need to bring this battalion up to strength: "I believe that it is indispensable that the process of bringing the battalions and regiments of this division up to strength and of organizing them begin before all else with the Chasseurs de la Meuse and the scouts whose service is the most active and necessary at the present."[8] Statements reflecting the elite character of light infantry battalions and betraying a particular urgency about their weakness hardly lend credence to assertions that all French infantry qualified as *tirailleurs*.

Elite companies that performed special duties constituted part of every regular or volunteer battalion. At the outset of the war heavy infantry battalions of the line army contained one grenadier company in addition to their eight fusilier companies, and volunteer battalions numbered one grenadier and seven fusilier companies. But in accord with standard practice during the eighteenth century, these elite companies were often separated from their original battalions and grouped together in ad hoc elite infantry battalions.⁹ The numerous gerrymandered free companies also concentrated on light infantry action.

Other specialist *tirailleurs* cannot be listed on a table of units because rather than being grouped together in particular companies they were scattered among the men of line infantry companies. Soldiers who displayed a talent or taste for open order combat might habitually fight *en tirailleurs* even though they were not part of a light infantry company or battalion.

Houchard attempted to regularize the practice of sending out men from fusilier companies to fight in open order. Instead of uniting these infantrymen into new companies, which could then possibly be detached from their battalions, he simply standardized the number and composition of the force to be sent out as light infantry. His "Instructions" of 23 August 1793 stated: "From now on there will be sixty-four men per battalion . . . selected as *tirailleurs,* these men to be chosen among the most valorous soldiers and the best shots: it will always be the same men who perform this genre of service; if the *tirailleurs* should lose a man from a company, the new man will always be chosen in the same company." Houchard absolutely insisted that only the chosen sixty-four would go out as *chasseurs* and under no circumstances could the number of *tirailleurs* be increased. To Houchard, a staunch believer in the *arme blanche,* an overabundance of *chasseurs* meant a waste of ammunition and a delay in the final resolution of a battle. Houchard was not the first (or the last) to oppose the indiscriminate and uncontrolled use of *tirailleurs*. Colonel Duplaisset even complained about the consequences of detailing a measured quantity of *tirailleurs:* "Hardly arrived on the field of battle, our brigadier general, Fuzier, ordered me to send forward ten volunteers per company to serve as *tirailleurs*. This number was furnished at once by the veteran soldiers of the battalion, so that there remained only men of the new requisition, cowardly men without energy."¹⁰

If other critics shared Houchard's objection to the manner in which *tirailleurs* left fusilier companies, apparently they also worked out alternative systems. As seen above, General Louis Fuzier sent out ten men in each company, and Pierre Delaporte also spoke of the same figure. Sergeant Jacques Fricasse reported some kind of rotation system in the Nord, although, unfortunately, the report lacks detail. Describing an engagement on 15 May 1794, Fricasse wrote, "The battle was begun by our *tirailleurs* taken from the companies by turns." In the preface to his "Changements," General H. A. J. Meunier proposed a new organization for infantry battalions with twelve companies of 100 men; he designated twenty soldiers in each company as light infantrymen.¹¹

This discussion of distinct light infantry units should not obscure the fact that some engagements witnessed entire battalions of line infantry dispersed in open order tactics. At the Battle of Hondschoote practically the entire army fought *en tirailleurs*. Paret's evaluation stands, though perhaps not exactly in the sense that he meant it. Yet the specialist predominated, and the argument that mass conscription necessarily brought a top-heavy reliance on light infantry tactics fundamentally distorts reality. As a general rule, *tirailleurs* were picked men. New conscripts were more likely to stand by in the ranks as veterans went out to skirmish than they were to fight on the skirmish line themselves. The proximity of comrades pressed together in close order promised to steady the recruit. Most men probably had to gain some experience and confidence, in themselves and in their comrades, before they could cope with the isolation of the *tirailleur*. Unaided patriotism might have promised an initial obedience, but more than revolutionary ardor was required to keep a man on station and active on the skirmish line.

Light Infantry in Battle with the Nord

Unfortunately, a detailed knowledge of light infantry tactics as practiced early in the wars of the French Revolution must largely elude the present-day scholar. This is a most embarrassing but necessary admission, since official directives were few, and contemporary descriptions are vague and unreliable. Compared to the tactics of line and column, those of the *tirailleurs* were relatively free in form. To say that a unit stood in line or attacked in column by division is to give a rather specific and detailed statement of their conduct. Yet to say a grenadier company dispersed *en tirailleurs* really supplies little information. This dispersal could have been executed in any number of ways; the men could have acted as a unit or as isolated individuals. They could have relied on marksmanship or simply laid down a barrage of relatively inaccurate fire. They could have acted without support or been backed by heavy infantry reserves. Light infantry combat was really an entire genre of tactics—to assert that men employed it leaves unanswered the question of technique.

Although the English and Prussians regularized light infantry tactics through instructions and drill books, the French generally held *tirailleur* tactics to be unsuited to official regulations. Commenting upon the *Règlement du 1er août 1791*, which said almost nothing about the use of *tirailleurs*, Jean Colin wrote: "It was found, not that it was necessary to stop the use of *tirailleurs*, but that it was absurd and a nuisance to draft regulations to fix the number and the mode of action of these *enfants perdus*." The light infantry expert General Le Couturier expressed the common opinion, "It is in effect so simple that intelligence can take the place of rules, and that some wise advice, given in writing or verbally, is worth more than artistically composed and described maneuvers." Rules were few, and a *tirailleur* was expected to improvise.[12]

It is certainly worth surveying the official regulations and instructions that bore on light infantry practices, but not much can be expected. The only time *tirailleurs* received tactical consideration in the *Règlement du 1er août 1791* was in the procedure for forming square on the march. It stated that when a marching column of several battalions was threatened by cavalry, if the commander so wished he could detach skirmishers to keep the cavalry at a distance. The 1792 *Règlement provisoire sur le service de l'infanterie en campagne* provided more information concerning open order tactics. This *Règlement* contained a paragraph on the use of *tirailleurs* in battle, directing them to seek out and harass enemy gun crews.[13]

Specifically from the Nord, there remain field instructions that devoted some attention to light infantry. In his August 1793 "Instruction" General Houchard stipulated a few details concerning the deployment of his sixty-four *tirailleurs* in each battalion. He also supplied some advice concerning outposts. General Jean-Baptiste Kléber's "Instruction" of 21 May 1794 constituted an attempt to coordinate a force of nine battalions in a diversion against Mons. March protection loomed largest in his "Instruction," yet light infantry received only two sentences that counseled commanders to employ light infantry as scouts and advance guards.[14]

With the exception of Duhesmes, the writings of major commanders of the Nord scarcely mention light infantry tactics. Descriptions of *tirailleurs* may have been omitted simply because knowledge of *tirailleurs* in battle was commonplace. Lafayette claimed that he originated the use of *tirailleurs* in support of massed infantry. He boasted that in 1791, long before war was declared, he "introduced . . . the principle, which is particularly favorable to French ardor, quickness, and intelligence, and which has since then been generally adopted; it is that of covering the active masses with a curtain of *tirailleurs,* ready to return to their units or pursue their advantages."[15] It is doubtful that he deserves credit for this crucial tactical innovation. It is true that one light infantry commander of the Armée du Nord, Duhesmes, wrote an extensive *Précis historique de l'infanterie légère;* however, as already pointed out, he is not a reliable witness regarding the early years of the wars of the French Revolution.[16] Duhesmes's categorical statements do not tally with the battlefield reports of the period; in fact, he contradicts his own dispatches and his own manuscript, "Mémoire militaire," a historical narrative of the era now in the Archives de la guerre at Vincennes. His *Précis* overemphasized the disheveled confusion of the Nord, and, while the rationale behind his exaggerations may be understandable, he still must be read with caution. Understandably but unfortunately, the lack of good accounts has forced many to turn to Duhesmes for their sole source of information on light infantry 1792–94.

Tirailleurs *in Independent Action*

When the few details contained in regulations and instructions are combined with examples gleaned from official correspondence, some of the outlines of open order combat appear. The cases of light infantry combat collected for this research can be separated into two major categories. The larger sample encompasses those instances in which the light infantry engagement constituted an independent or separate contest. Here the gamut runs from the isolated *tirailleur* struggles of outposts or advance guards, to those few examples of major battles that at one stage or another were fought entirely *en tirailleurs*. The smaller category includes those affairs in which light infantry simply supported heavy infantry. Under this rubric lie examples of skirmishers protecting the deployment or advance of battalions in close order and of *tirailleurs* covering the retreat of defeated Republican units.

This breakdown highlights some of the contrasts between the uses of light infantry before and after 1792. Roughly speaking, independent light infantry combats, with the exception of large engagements fought entirely *en tirailleurs*, often occurred on eighteenth-century battlefields. Certainly the scale and frequency of this form of warfare increased greatly, but it was common before the wars of the French Revolution. The extensive employment of light infantry in support of heavy infantry marked more of a departure from earlier practice. Thus the categorization attempts to bring out one significant contrast in open order tactics.

Another characteristic separates the two categories. When a significant body of troops employed open order tactics in independent action, the *tirailleurs* were more likely to fight in thick swarms. In the attack they constituted the primary effort, not a secondary support, so they had to concentrate in numbers great enough to overpower an enemy. The French classified such use of light infantry as *tirailleurs en grandes bandes*. In support of infantry in close order, *tirailleurs* deployed as a more dispersed cordon across the enemy front. Then their task was to harass, not to overcome, the enemy.

Forty-eight examples of independent light infantry engagements have been collected here, but in the case of light infantry action quantitative techniques say little about the details of tactics. Among examples of independent light infantry engagements, the frequency of known specialist light infantry involvement was high; about 52 percent were definitely specialist affairs, and in most of the uncertain cases the wording of the reports makes it seem likely that specialists were employed.

Employed in *petite guerre,* the *tirailleur* performed duties traditionally reserved to him. The term *petite guerre* covers several varieties of small-unit operations. Clashes of outposts, raids by minor detachments, and activities of advance and flank guards all constituted aspects of little war. This type of combat could hardly claim great novelty. A considerable literature throughout the eighteenth century discussed the conduct of small-unit operations, and every war involved a certain amount of activity on this level. No genre of military action would naturally be as underreported as this. In the general correspondence one can only glimpse the numberless minor encounters, or *affaires des postes*. "*Affaires des postes* are always the order of the day around here; our comrades are so accustomed to them that they second their officers perfectly. It is not necessary to order them to go; on the contrary, they have to be restrained."[17]

Houchard's "Instruction pour l'Armée du Nord" did say something about the use of *tirailleurs* on outpost duty, although he generally described outpost duties as if they fell almost wholly to light cavalry rather than to infantry. According to Houchard, major outposts "ought to be placed in such a manner that they cannot be seen by the enemy." The larger force would then send out small forward parties to protect the main outpost from being itself surprised. If a mixed force of infantry and cavalry manned the outposts, the forward posts were to be made up of cavalry during the day. At night the commander should draw in his horsemen, place them behind the infantry of the main outpost, and leave only a small party of horsemen forward "who will always be mounted with their sabers in their hands."[18] In his specific advice to the *tirailleurs* he counseled light infantry to remain within the protection of buildings or broken ground at all times. His warnings within the "Instruction" testify to his fear of uncontrolled and untrained light infantry.

Houchard's advice, based on his own experience prior to the wars of the French Revolution, probably reflected established French practice before 1792. The same can be said of his notes on infantry in advanced guards. The use of light infantry in advance and flank guards occurred almost universally. The only tactical instructions concerning *tirailleurs* in the *Règlement du 1er août 1791* dealt with this function. Commanders were instructed to send out "some men from the third ranks of the divisions, who will take themselves to both flanks, fifteen or twenty paces from the column, and will fire on enemy hussars and cavalry who approach to within fusil range; these *tirailleurs* will follow the march of the column about at the position of their divisions." Finally, when the enemy appeared ready to attack, the officer in charge should "order the *tirailleurs* to rejoin their respective divisions." The tactical instructions written by Houchard and Kléber also laid out some procedures for light infantry on the march. Houchard's "Instruction" contained slightly more detail. He insisted that advanced guards contain light cavalry and *tirailleurs* and that "in broken country, it will be light infantry who will open the march followed by light cavalry." He reversed the order of march in open country. Kléber simply reminded his field commanders to take great care in assuring proper march protection: "Every commander of a column will make certain that it is well covered in the march by hussars and *tirailleurs* who will be placed forward and on the flanks of the column. Before detaching these scouts and flankers, he will take care to assure himself that they have a perfect knowledge of the duties they must perform."[19]

According to reports about the actual composition of particular marching columns, in any troop movement involving several battalions, the advance party consisted exclusively, or in the main, of light infantry units. Often some unit or units of line troops were also included, and this may indicate the use of heavy infantry in close support of *tirailleurs*. If the *avant garde* contained a battalion or more, it might send out a small detachment to act as its own advance party, or point, made up of elite light infantry. As Desjardin reported, when Duhesmes's light infantry brigade acted as the *avant garde* of a larger force, it was "preceded by the *carabiniers* of his light infantry battalions."[20]

In addition to the combats of *petite guerre*, minor light infantry affairs also occurred as part of major engagements. With or without heavy infantry support, *tirailleurs* often fought to capture or defend a wood or village during the course of a battle. Since such terrain did not suit close order tactics, it constituted a field for independent light infantry action, rather similar to *affaires des postes*. Although armies of the ancien régime shied away from natural and manmade obstacles, they could not always be avoided. Small towns, forests, and canals dotted the map of Europe before, as well as after, 1789; consequently eighteenth-century armies committed troops against these objectives, just as did armies of the Republic.

French manuals and instructions current during the early years of the war skipped over this crucial employment of light infantry. Whereas the composition and placement of outposts could be sketched and the necessity of march protection stressed, the operations of dispersed *tirailleurs* in the seizure and defense of difficult terrain were best left to the soldiers' own initiative.

In roughly a quarter of the examples, battlefield reports mentioned cavalry or close order infantry support for light infantry engaged in independent action on the battlefield. Duhesmes stressed the need for close support by massed battalions, and in such matters it would be hard to doubt him. An interesting example of light and heavy infantry in coordination took place in October 1793. During a major sortie from the besieged French camp of Maubeuge, Desjardin deployed five battalions of heavy infantry and four of light. Some Austrian redoubts constituted the main objective of this attack, and the light infantry marched against them. Apparently to protect the main assault from turning movements, Desjardin flanked the light battalions with two heavy infantry battalions on each side. The fifth heavy battalion marched up behind the light infantry to support the latter's assault.[21]

It should be said in passing that although the very name *tirailleurs* implies that the light infantryman limited his activities on the battlefield to aimed musket fire, the *tirailleur* was no stranger to the use of the bayonet. Men dispersed in open order quite commonly carried the day by a final bayonet assault. At Roncq, Lannoy, and Tourcoing, for example, after a long musketry duel "had forced the enemy to prepare his retreat," the French *tirailleurs* "attacked these entrenchments, with bayonets fixed."[22] Moreover, skilled light infantry battalions acting on their own hardly restricted their tactics to dispersal *en tirailleurs*. On the contrary, they possessed the ability to maneuver in close order if the situation required. It will be recalled that during an engagement on 26 May 1794, Duhesmes massed his grenadier battalions in close order and charged enemy cavalry.[23] Such skilled performances were not all that unusual.

One subcategory of independent light infantry engagements does represent a decidedly novel aspect of open order tactics. Not until 1793 did large-scale combat during the eighteenth century see entire armies dispersed *en tirailleurs*. This style of total dispersal was not usually a matter of choice but was imposed by circumstance.

The sources yield reports on five engagements of major proportions fought entirely *en tirailleurs* at some stage of the combat. Of the five, Hondschoote alone involved an entire field army, and, as mentioned before, the French troops there fought in dispersed order only out of necessity. Two associated actions on the brigade level were apparently also fought *en tirailleurs*. General Théodore-François Leclaire sent his seven battalions to attack the town of Eckelsbecke on 24 August 1793. He reported that he left "a small reserve a bit to the rear with the caissons and limbers" and dispersed the remainder for the attack. Three days later, the main body of the French forces encountered the enemy at Roncq, Lannoy, and Tourcoing. The fighting around Tourcoing became quite severe; about ten battalions saw action. Owing to the thick woods and restricted roadways, Houchard launched the assault *en tirailleurs*. In his report he complained again of the casualties incurred in this kind of combat: "We have been cruelly mistreated, the woods and the hedges not permitting us to join with the enemy." These three instances show that the fall campaign to relieve Dunkirk was largely a light infantry affair. Two brigade-sized engagements in the spring of 1794 also ended with the French infantry scattered because of the difficulties of advancing over the rough country between the Scheldt and the Lys. As the enemy retired at Mouscron on 29 April

1794, the French infantry could not maintain its order in the pursuit. "Since the battalions were not able to follow in order," wrote General Jean-Louis Reynier in his journal, "the infantry was *en tirailleurs*."²⁴

Light Infantry in Support of Troops in Close Order

Of all the ways light infantry saw service in the wars of the French Revolution, the use of *tirailleurs* to support close order infantry during its approach, deployment, and attack stands out as the most innovative technique. Yet even it was not entirely without precedent, since light infantry frequently screened the main body at camps of instruction held previous to 1789. After the outbreak of war, peacetime experiments became combat reality, and the battlefield use of *tirailleurs* in support of heavy infantry increased in extent and frequency beyond eighteenth-century experience or expectations.

Only fragments of the technique using light infantry as support were outlined in regulations and instructions. The *Règlement provisoire*, for example, recommended that *tirailleurs* attempt to silence, or at least to harass, enemy batteries:

> While battle lines are being formed and batteries placed, the commanding officers order the light infantry to advance ahead of the line infantry, so as to discover the positions of the enemy's guns and to diminish their effect. The light troops are placed in small thickets behind hedges, ditches, or small rises, according to the nature of the ground. They are commanded to fire at the enemy batteries, and to try to kill the gunners. These men do not form in troops, so as not to draw artillery fire, but separate, profiting from features that may afford them cover, and remain attentive so that they can quickly reassemble at the first signal of their officers.²⁵

This directive for counterbattery activity actually came verbatim from the French *Règlement* of 1778, a fact that Paret uses to stress "the organic development rather than revolutionary emergence of the new tactics." In the Nord the most notable use of *tirailleurs* to silence enemy cannon occurred during the brief siege of Menin in April 1794. General Scharnhorst, a participant in this action, was impressed with the French skirmishers. Concerning his own men, General Dominique-Joseph Vandamme reported, "Throughout the duration of the siege, these *tirailleurs* succeeded so well that they kept the enemy from serving several cannon which their fire made too dangerous to approach."²⁶ Although Menin was not an example of open battle, it exemplified the effect *tirailleurs* could have on artillery crews, even when the artillerymen fought behind cover.

Another of the rare guidelines prescribed for *tirailleurs* was contained in Houchard's "Instructions." It outlined the way in which picked skirmishers were to assemble during actions: "When *tirailleurs* are requested, they will advance fifty paces in front of their battalions and form two platoons to receive their orders, and they will only leave their battalions on the orders of the general commanding their brigade; it is necessary that *tirailleurs* show the greatest obedience to the orders of their officers."[27] The above sentence once again reveals Houchard's determination that *tirailleurs* had to be controlled by responsible officers. By advancing only when ordered, and receiving clear instruction before the firefight, the *tirailleurs* under his command ought to become a more orderly and military body of infantry, less likely to waste time and ammunition.

More important than official directives, experience shaped light infantry practice. Time and again in battle, circumstances dictated that French *chasseurs* counter the effective Austrian light infantry. In a graphic example of concern over enemy light infantry, the commander of the French brigade at Zucotte received orders that in case of attack he was to place his main body in line and station "many *tirailleurs* in the houses and behind the hedges a little forward and to stop the enemy *tirailleurs*."[28]

Light infantry deployed against the enemy's main line of battle lay open to considerable danger. That the men were screening heavy infantry means that they probably occupied terrain suitable for close order maneuver; thus, charging Allied cavalry or advancing hostile line infantry possessed the ability to drive the *tirailleurs* off the field. Skirmishers had always to keep a wary eye on enemy movements and to be ready to withdraw rapidly. For example, at Courtrai on 11 May 1794, Vandamme's light infantry retreated to the main line when Austrian cavalry thundered down upon his steady battalions of heavy infantry. When the horsemen withdrew, the *tirailleurs* moved out ahead again.[29]

Since *chasseurs* screening their own heavy infantry faced serious opposition, which they could not adequately resist, the skirmish line often also required some kind of close support. Companies, or perhaps battalions, of infantry in close order might back them up. At Mouscron General Etienne-Jacques MacDonald detached part of his brigade to protect his battered *tirailleurs*. Similarly, during an encounter around Courtrai, Vandamme employed grenadier battalions to support the skirmishers who covered the deployment of his line infantry.[30] Coordination between heavy battalions and *tirailleurs* developed only with time and practice. All but one of the examples of light infantry support collected here come out of the nine months from September 1793 to June 1794.

It is a great paradox that the battle records of the Armée du Nord supply such meager detail concerning the use of *tirailleurs* in support of close order infantry. Only thirteen cases have been collected in this research, and most of the major battles are not represented in this sample. However, the constant general mention of *tirailleurs* makes it absurd to argue that infrequent specific citations in the sources mean that such tactics were rare. The explanation of this paradox goes back to the fact that reports and narratives of actions focused on the main decisive action, and by nature *tirailleurs* in support only prepared the way for the primary forces. In most of the examples collected here, it remains unclear which close order formation was employed, and the rest of the cases are split between column and line.

The use of attack columns in conjunction with *tirailleurs* became a hallmark of revolutionary tactics by 1796, but had this combination evolved in the Nord by June 1794? Most certainly yes; however, the frustrating lack of detailed description obscures its technique and frequency. The emphasis upon the mass attack *à la baionette* at Wattignies and the ubiquitous use of *tirailleurs* by late 1793 make it almost inconceivable that these elements were not put together there, but the exact tactical nature of Wattignies is still veiled. We do know that in 1794 Meunier stressed the bayonet assault *en masse* with the fire of skirmishers "as curtain and prelude." And consider a field report such as that written by General Jean-Louis Dessaubaz on 5 May 1794, "I deployed my left column [*demi-column*] in order of battle and *en tirailleurs*. . . . My column having rallied, I advanced part of it by division in mass and stopped the enemy."[31]

An excerpt from the journal of Delaporte richly illuminates the relationship between *tirailleurs* and close order infantry under fire. An unsurpassed soldier's view of combat, it makes a fitting, and very human, conclusion to this discussion of infantry tactics. The account by this young conscript tells of his part in the victory of Tourcoing.[32] Delaporte served in Vandamme's brigade and fought near Roncq. The battle began for him as his battalion marched along a forest road toward the sound of gunfire. Presumably it proceeded in column by companies, but upon reaching a wheat field swept by enemy fire "we marched at the charge pace, or rather we ran, to put ourselves into line." English cavalry threatened the advance. "We had hardly covered fifty paces when it was ordered that the *tirailleurs* move out and that [the battalion] close ranks." Delaporte remained in the second rank behind a fellow named Le Blond. Enemy cannon looming in front of them fired two shots, one was grape or canister, and a piece of it "struck the unfortunate Le Blond who covered me in the first rank. I saw him . . . cross his hands, fall to his knees, and then roll on his belly, with a total expresion of pain. I deeply wanted to help him, but seized by fear . . . I drew back just like my company, which broke to find cover from this battery."

All was now confusion; his and another battalion, the 9th Paris, were mixed together. Finally the men formed up again, but six ranks deep. The doubled ranks probably offered a stouter resistance to the threatening cavalry. Once order was restored, the battalion's fusillade drove back the English horsemen, who had closed to pistol range. Now "we formed a rather large body of *tirailleurs* of which I was one." This renewed effort to send out skirmishers must have involved more than just the picked *tirailleurs*, since Delaporte writes of it as being an unusually large band. With the battalion standing in close order to the rear, the *tirailleurs* pressed ahead. Delaporte linked up with a comrade named Filippeaux. Having a companion must have helped the inexperienced Delaporte deal with his fear. The two kept advancing, meeting stiff fire but urged on by surrounding cries of "En avant!" With their uneasiness growing, they were met by a French hussar who galloped up to them and ordered all *tirailleurs* to retreat. To their surprise they saw that only a dozen skirmishers had kept up with them. He and Filippeaux "retreated precipitously while loading our fusils, which we shot each time we were behind cover." They fired in the direction of the enemy but were unable to see what they shot at, because thick willows obstructed their view. They assumed that they were backed up all the time by their battalion, but it had already again withdrawn. Finally they rejoined its ranks. "The rest of the affair engaged only the *tirailleurs*, reinforced by volunteers taken from each company of the different battalions," i.e., it became exclusively an open order combat, apparently with specialists aided by men from the line companies. That night the exhausted men bivouacked in fields behind the village of Roncq.

Conclusion

Motivation and Tactics: The Experience of the Armée du Nord in Context

V ICTORY CROWNED the Armée du Nord in May and June 1794. These laurels came as reward neither for outstanding generalship nor for overwhelming numbers, although the French did enjoy a numerical superiority. At the foundation of triumph lay the great national effort by the French people and their government. On the battlefield, the combat effectiveness of the rank and file—their tactics and their spirit—explain success. By their exertions in the first years of the war, the troops of the Armée du Nord, aided by their brothers in the other armies of the Republic, preserved the Revolution and forged the weapons that eventually led to the conquest and reshaping of Europe.

The Emerging Tactical System

By the summer of 1794 the Armée du Nord employed an effective, although not yet perfected, tactical system. This system had yet to crystallize into its Napoleonic form; it was still evolving. Its essential component was an infantry that combined varied and flexible tactics in a rough but potent manner. Infantry progressed further than the other branches, and the elements of its tactics associated with the genius of General Napoleon Bonaparte were all present; the battalions of the Nord lacked only the uniform and self-confident skill to give them their later polish. New artillery techniques also surfaced by 1794, although the procedures and principles of concentration and mobile support were only partially developed. In major and minor combats artillery, particularly the new mounted batteries, ably seconded the all-important battalions. Cavalry, while not entirely without merit, suffered so severely from shortages and inadequacies that it contributed little to the victories won by the Nord.

The tactical system emerging in the Armée du Nord was not expressed as a conscious, reasoned doctrine. Only the cult of the bayonet approached the level of a military doctrine, and it encapsuled but part of the reality of battle. During the first two years of combat, experience produced a successful ad hoc combination of tactical elements matched to the technology of the times and the character of the new republican soldier. Accidents of personality and terrain that made the Nord unique also exerted considerable influence on the final product. The great German military figure, Gerhard von Scharnhorst, who participated in the events he analyzed, summed up the character of the resultant tactics: "The French armies, compelled by the situation in which they found themselves and aided by their national genius, had developed a practical system of tactics that permitted them to fight over open or broken ground, in open or close order, but this *without their being aware of their system.*"[1]

In Petite Guerre *and on the March*

Probably as no modern conflict before, the wars of the French Revolution entailed an emphasis on small-scale actions involving forces well below the brigade level. A continual series of minor clashes fought by outposts, foraging detachments, and raiding parties took place along the front lines of the Armée du Nord from Dunkirk to Carignan. Usually these encounters resulted from the tensions arising between two hostile armies confronting each other. On the French side there was an added incentive to use small actions as training exercises for recruits. Insufficient good light cavalry caused the French to place the main responsibility for *petite guerre* on the shoulders of the infantry. Normally battalions or companies of special light troops performed these duties. Yet, if necessary, heavy infantry also fought *petite guerre*.

In these small but deadly encounters the personal skills of the soldier could not alone insure success. Coordination and control were essential to the proper conduct of *petite guerre*. Major officers in command of the Nord labored continually to improve French performance in this genre of warfare. Charles Dumouriez, Jean Houchard, Jean Kléber, and Jean Jourdan, to name several, demonstrated concern over what they felt to be inept conduct of small actions and issued instructions to impose their own standards. It is ironic that this, the form of conflict involving the least ability in close order drill, should have caused republican commanders so much anxiety. By the spring of 1794 the French had learned the intelligent use of reserves, which seems to have constituted one of the essential aspects of *petite guerre*.

Napoleon said that the art of war was in the legs; for the Nord, the ability to cover distances rapidly proved vital. On the march the Armée du Nord resembled an army of the ancien régime in its formation, though not in its bearing. Battalions on the road marched in columns by company. Should the need arise, units in this formation could easily disperse *en tirailleurs* or deploy into line or attack column. A large body of troops marching together would be arranged in a predetermined order of battle. If a marching column were carefully organized and controlled, it would be capable of quickly presenting a strong front to the enemy. During a retreat the individual battalion columns were often *renversée* (reversed), meaning that the company usually in the lead would now march in the last place. This allowed the retreating battalion to deploy toward its pursuers in the same fashion as it would have in the advance.

To avoid being surprised by a full-scale enemy attack before battalions could properly deploy, a column on the march protected itself with light infantry, cavalry, and horse artillery. The *avant garde* possessed enough strength to seize villages along the route of march and to delay enemy attacks. Flank guards composed of small bodies of light infantry and cavalry on either side of the main body warned it of danger. In retreat a strong rear guard composed primarily of infantry, usually light infantry, and artillery would cover the escape.

Occasionally a division or some other large body of troops maneuvered over open country in a series of brigade or demi-brigade columns marching abreast of each other. From such a formation, a large unit could quickly form into order of battle.

In Battle

Battles alone decided the issue between the Armée du Nord and its opponents. Neither lengthy sieges nor grand maneuvers, the mainstays of eighteenth-century limited warfare, produced victory on this front. In full-scale combat the Nord had a checkered career before mid-May 1794. Even the victories of Hondschoote and Wattignies were called into question by Allied successes during April 1794. When skill and courage mattered most, however, the Nord rose to the occasion in May and June. No one claims that the crucial infantry of the Nord matched the degree of excellence reached by the Grande Armée, but it maneuvered and fought well enough.

At every battle fought by the Armée du Nord in 1794, light infantry played a conspicuous role. After the approach march, *tirailleurs* set up a screen to cover the heavy battalions as they deployed. During the battle, villages, woods, or other terrain suited to their form of combat might become special zones dominated by *tirailleurs* alone. At times light infantrymen provided security for a flank of the main army by holding the village or wood anchoring that flank. As skirmishers, *tirailleurs* distracted enemy infantry and harassed enemy artillery crews.

French artillery, and especially horse artillery, aided light infantry in its task of crippling the enemy. French cannoneers of the mounted batteries handled their pieces expertly and aggressively. Infantry depended heavily on artillery support, and without it the victories of late 1793 might have turned into defeats. There seems to be some truth to the assertion that the less experienced the infantry, the more it required numerous artillery; even battalion guns were at least a psychological prop. Battles commonly opened with extensive artillery barrages that continued through the main assault. Cavalry rarely fulfilled the offensive role normally associated with it; however, its mobility suited it to service as a quick-responding reserve. Stiffened by horse artillery, republican troopers countered enemy thrusts as best they could.

Behind the support provided by *tirailleurs* and artillery, the main body of the army generally deployed into an initial order of battle organized in some depth. Many units stood well back from the first row of battalions to act as support and reserves. Classic eighteenth-century practice dictated that an army arrayed for battle form two long lines with an interval between them of about 200 yards. On occasion troops from the Armée du Nord did adopt this practice. The use of three-rank lines proved most successful in engagements on the northern flank of the Nord. Battalions along the Sambre were seemingly more prone to form attack columns from the start. In at least one major instance, the combat near Landrecies on 21 May 1794, these columns attacked in a checkerboard formation, with the rear battalions staggered to cover the intervals between the attack columns in the front.

A bayonet assault inevitably climaxed the major offensive battles won by the Armée du Nord. It is not always certain whether the bayonet administered the *coup de grace* to a fallen enemy, or whether it delivered the decisive stroke against a foe who could be driven from the field in no other way. In most cases it was the latter and not the former. Mass infantry shock attacks not only suited the spirit of the new republican soldier, but they also may have been dictated by the lack of good cavalry, which, if it had been more plentiful, might have dealt the crucial blow to a shaken opponent.

The tactical system evolving in the Armée du Nord claimed a high degree of adaptability and flexibility. Commanders placed their soldiers, primarily their infantry, in ways which exploited the terrain and met the tactical challenge. Battalions stood in a full close order repertoire of line, column, and square or dispersed in open order, either as large bands of *tirailleurs* or as thin skirmish lines. Artillery, especially horse artillery, could adjust to the changing situations of combat. With such tactical alternatives available, no tactical element was forced to perform duties for which it was unsuited. This gave the French an immense advantage over enemies limited to the narrow alternatives of formal eighteenth-century warfare.

Motivation and Tactics

Historians of the Revolution traditionally ascribe the offensive tactics of the *armées* to the élan of their troops. This almost obligatory judgment touches upon, but hardly explores, the highly complex relationship between combat and motivation. So many factors need to be examined in any one case, and ways of measuring them are so elusive, that it is generally impossible to understand sustaining and combat motivation completely. As historians strive to fill obvious gaps in their knowledge, they are tempted to go beyond what the evidence really provides. Sometimes findings from related social sciences can supply a framework of understanding to bridge those gaps, but the chasms remain. All too often, wishful thinking and convenience lead historians to disguise the missing facts with a tangle of fancies. The cult of the bayonet ranks as one such fancy. It provides a plausible substitute for a potentially baffling reality. After all, contemporaries proclaimed the creed with great conviction—revolutionary soldiers were driven by patriotic enthusiasm, so without need of skill they hurled themselves at the enemy in spirited bayonet assaults. However, the variety of the tactical systems employed and the emphasis given to training and expertise call into question the facile generalizations about élan and the bayonet.

There is no intent here to deny all credit to the argument that the assault in *colonne serrée* expressed the patriotic enthusiasm of the troops. Accounts of spirited charges fill the documents; they cannot be dismissed as fairy tales. In fact, the cult of the bayonet dealt in self-fulfilling prophecy. To the extent that the French were convinced by their own rhetoric of their superiority in this form of combat, they would choose to employ it. However, both tactics and motivation were more complex than the traditional formula allows.

The French rightfully boasted of the high spirits of their front line troops. Although their strong motivation may never be completely understood, its main outlines can be sketched. At the foundation lay the very sort of men who now found themselves in uniform. They represented the entire range of French society, not just its losers. These valued and honored recruits were led by an officer corps that was close to the rank and file in social origin and sympathies. Discipline and control eventually kept adequate order without dampening the spirit, and even the idealism, of the common soldier. The campaign of political education fostered patriotism, republicanism, and a sense of cause. But beyond these, it repeatedly expressed the nation's gratitude to its soldiery, which had endured and risked much. These influences flowed through the *ordinaire,* a thoroughly encompassing primary group of the kind that military sociology has established as essential to cohesion and performance.

The particular complex of French motivation 1791–94 evidences an undeniable enthusiasm, but it also encouraged a high level of normative compliance and a rise in self- and group-imposed standards of performance and sacrifice. Without strong normative compliance, large-scale reliance on open order combat would have been out of the question. The rapid training of French recruits in conditions of deprivation so typical of the Armée du Nord demanded healthy sustaining motivation, as did the ability to march and fight, underfed and in rags. It can equally be argued that elevated standards found expression in linear combat as much as they did in the more renowned column.

The fact is that in an army in which the troops care about what they are doing and in which personal pride and group pressures compel men to execute their duties with energy and initiative, soldiers can apply their talents to a range of tactical possibilities. The final tactical system is not just a product of a specific motivation, though to be effective it must be consistent with that motivation. Technology, precedent, doctrine, terrain, and circumstance all influence the evolving system. In the case of the Armée du Nord the technology of smoothbore, muzzle-loading weapons set limits. The theory and experimentation of the military enlightenment, represented by the Gribeauval system, the *Règlement* of 1791, and the tactical convictions of the generals, helped shape the Nord's responses as it faced the challenges of campaign and battle. Revolutionary crisis dictated that a rapidly expanding rank and file, poorly supplied and possessing varied levels of technical proficiency, must fight a skilled opponent over terrain that included a range from flat, unobstructed plains to heavily wooded hills. Guided by the past and preconception, the French adjusted to circumstance in a revolutionary environment and thus evolved a tactical system of tremendous potential.

The Experience of the Nord, 1791–94: A Caveat to the Reader

Fundamental to both the argument and the methodology of this volume is the assertion that generalizations based on superficial knowledge or narrow samples have led only to misconception and confusion regarding the armies of the First Republic. To be consistent with this point of view, I caution against stretching the conclusions reached here beyond their proper limits. A study of the Armée du Nord does not establish the combat style of all the other *armées* during the early years of conflict; experiences varied. In addition, the tactical system, particularly as it employed artillery and cavalry, continued to develop past the time boundary established for this study. Lastly, the essential and complicated question of troop motivation also underwent a subtle and important change after the fall of Robespierre. Consequently, the patterns of commitment described here must be taken as a beginning and not a conclusion for the revolutionary period through 1799.

At the height of the Terror the Committee of Public Safety directed eleven armies; the Nord and the Ardennes were only two of these. The rest confronted different enemies, fought over different terrain, and were led by different commanders. This variety of circumstances produced a variety of tactical systems, similar and yet distinct. The comte de Schauenbourg's training reports, discussed by Jean Colin, reveal the Armée de la Moselle as tactically conservative and wedded to the line. The mountainous terrain that troops encountered in the Pyrenees and the Alps must have influenced tactical development along distinct lines. Certainly the Armée de l'Ouest, sent to suppress the Vendée rebellion, was a special case. Since the Ouest faced only occasional major actions but encountered frequent small-scale ambushes and raids by guerrilla forces, its war was very different. Because the Nord and Ardennes together constituted by far the largest of the Republic's *armées,* the style of combat evolved there could be expected to have exerted an especially strong influence, and several of its generals went on to command *armées* in the years after 1794. But even if its influence was great, there is no reason to believe that its tactical system was universal. Other styles and levels of warfare deserve study as well.

This volume leaves off with the victory at Fleurus and the coup of thermidor, but the tactical system had not entirely matured at that point, so this study's findings ought to be qualified past 1794. All the major elements of the infantry tactics associated with Napoleon had emerged along the Belgian border by 1794. That in itself is quite a statement. It classes this style of infantry combat as one more creation of the Terror. However, artillery tactics had a long way to go in 1794, and French cavalry had barely begun to have an impact. Effective concentration of field guns was still in the future, although horse artillery batteries were already used to good purpose. Cavalry would not decide the fate of battles nor assume its proper reconnaissance and screening duties until it reached a quantitative and qualitative level beyond what it achieved with the Nord by mid-1794.

The analysis of motivation presented in these pages also requires care when taken beyond the confines of this work. Since much of the discussion was far less focused on the Nord alone than was the treatment given tactics, the caveat concerning applying findings to other *armées* in the same period need not be so strident. To be sure, a certain degree of variation complicated some of the details. The campaign of political education in the Armée du Rhin, for example, seems to have involved the local Jacobin clubs more than was the case for the Nord. In the Ouest the same campaign may have followed very different lines, since the forces opposing this army were composed of counterrevolutionary Frenchmen, not foreign invaders. Still, I am inclined to generalize my findings on motivation to the entire Republican army. However, a serious interpretive danger threatens those who would borrow an analysis of motivation based on the years through 1794 and apply it uncritically to the years following the Terror. Emotional commitment to the defense of the Revolution peaked before Robespierre fell from power. Up to that point, a sense of common purpose and shared suffering bound society and army together. After that point, they began to diverge. The army became alienated, doubting the good will and concern of the government and the people. As the troops became more remote from society, they developed a stronger esprit de corps among themselves. If many factors remained that had contributed to motivation from 1791 to 1794, it is equally true that the forces that impelled the army shifted notably after 1794. The loyal army of citizen-soldiers who resisted the appeal of Lafayette and Dumouriez became an army of coup d'état by 1797. In a profound sense the commitments and enthusiasms of 1791–94 were special, and ultimately fragile, creations not to be duplicated in subsequent years, so later motivation must be subject to new analysis.

I would hope that these warnings do not detract from the central purpose of this volume. Limitations notwithstanding, the case of Armée du Nord from 1791 to 1794 provides the best example for an inquiry concerning the tactics and motivation of the troops who preserved the Revolution in its hours of greatest crisis. The triumph of the Nord goes a long way to explain the defeat of the Allies in the first, and critical, phase of the war. While holding the Belgian frontier against the most adamant of the Republic's enemies, the troops of the Nord created a tactical system that made victory possible. The way in which the Nord accomplished these tasks illustrates the impact of revolutionary fervor upon the armed forces of a new France. To say this is to say a great deal. Ultimately, an examination of the Armée du Nord leads to a better understanding of the power behind the bayonets of the Republic.

Appendix

Tables Concerning Tactical Practice

TABLE A.1
Examples of the Line in Combat

Date	Place	Source
On Defense		*13 Examples*
15-9-92	near Chalons	Bricard, 5.
2-11-92	Boussu*	AG, B^{1}30, 26 Apr. 1793, General Chapuis.
10-2-93	Maestricht	Bricard, 27.
11-2-93	Maestricht	Bricard, 28.
18-3-93	Neerwinden	Girardon, 32.
22-3-93	near Pessemberg	AG, B^{1}11, 22 Apr. 1793, Lt. col. of the 1st Manche.
12-9-93	Avesnes-le-Sec	AG, B^{1}18, 14 Sept. 1793, General Declaye.
29-9-93	near Maubeuge	Fricasse, 13.
16-10-93	Wattignies*	Orders of 16 Oct. 1793 in Dupuis, *1793*, 2: 173–4.
21-3-94	unspecified camp*	AG, MR 273, General Lacroix.
26-4-94	Boussu	AG, B^{1}30, 26 Apr. 1794, General Cacault.
13-5-94	Grand-Reng*	AG, MR 271, General Desjardin.
24-5-94	Erquelinnes*	Fricasse.
On Defense: In Retreat		*7 Examples*
7-8-93	Fontaine-Natre-Dame	Bricard, 71.
8-8-93	near the Camp de César	Bricard, 73.
15-9-93	Menin	AG, B^{1}19, 16 Sept. 1793, Representatives Lavasseur and Bentaboule.
29-9-93	near Maubeuge	Fricasse, 68.
15-10-93	Wattignies	Leclaire, 88–89.

TABLE A.1 (continued)

Date	Place	Source
29-3-94	on the Sambre near Maubeuge	AG, B¹28, 29 Mar. 1794, General Soland.
22-5-94	Pont-à-Chin	AG, MR 273, General Lacroix.

On Defense: Passage of Defiles:		*2 Examples*
15-9-92	Grand-Pré	AG, MR 270, Colonel Leclaire.
31-5-94	Fontaine-l'Evêque	AG, B¹30, 26 Apr. 1794, General Cacault.

As a Waiting and Preliminary Formation		*17 Examples*
15-9-92	Grand-Pré	AG, MR 270, Colonel Leclaire.
2-11-92	Boussu	AG, B¹30, 26 Apr. 1794, General Chapuis.
6-11-92	Jemappes	AG, B¹6, 7 Nov. 1792, General Dumouriez.
4-3-93	Tongres	AG, B¹17, 19 Aug. 1793, report from the 2nd Division Armée des Ardennes; Bricard, 31–32.
17-3-92	near Neerwinden	AG, Bricard, 39.
18-3-93	Neerwinden	AG, Bricard, 39–43.
3-10-93	Abbaye d'Orval	AG, B¹18, 3 Sept. 1793, General Tardy
16-10-93	Wattignies	Orders for 16 Oct. 1793 in Dupuis, *1793*, 2: 173–74.
16-10-93	Beaumont	AG, B¹20, 19 Nov. 1793, General Elie.
22-10-93	Furnes	AG, B¹23, 6 Dec. 1793, Adj.-Gen. Durulte.
?-4-94	Landrecies	AG, B¹23, n.d. Apr. 1794, General Rolland.
24-4-94	near Cambrai	Bricard, 95.
26-4-94	Troisvilles	AG, B¹30, 26 Apr. 1794, General Chapuis; AG, MR 277–8, Colonel Arnaudin.
26-4-94	Boussu (1st case)	AG, B¹ 30, 26 Apr. 1794, General Cacault.
26-4-94	Boussu (2nd case)	AG, B¹30, 26 Apr. 1794, General Cacault.
1-5-94	Strée	AG, MR 271, General Desjardin.
11-5-94	Courtrai	AG, B¹18, 5 Sept. 1793, General Vandamme, "Récit abrégé."

In Support of Light Infantry		*6 Examples*
19-8-93	Lincelles	AG, B¹17, 19 Aug. 1793, General Jourdan.
7-9-93	Rexpoede	AG, B¹18, 29 Sept. 1793, General Houchard.
30-4-94	Mouscron	AG, B¹30, 26 Apr. 1794, General Reynier, "Journal."

TABLE A.1 (continued)

Date	Place	Source
12-5-94	near Grand-Reng*	AG, B¹*298, 17 May 1794, General Muller.
13-5-94	Grand-Reng	Fricasse, 25.
27-6-94	Audenarde*	Bricard, 113.
On the March		*3 Examples*
27-12-92	near Liege	AG, MR 270, Col. Leclaire manuscript Mémoire.
12-5-94	near Grand-Reng	AG, B¹*298, 17 May 1794, General Muller.
20-5-94	Grand-Reng	AG, MR 291, General Duhesmes.
In the Attack		*7 Examples*
6-11-92	Jemappes	AG, MR 270, Col. Leclaire; General Dampierre's account in La Jonquière, 165–68.
16-3-93	Louvain*	Bricard, 35–36.
26-4-94	Boussu	AG, B¹30, 26 Apr. 1794, General Cacault.
29-4-94	Menin	AG, MR 273, General Lacroix.
13-5-94	Grand-Reng	AG, MR 291, General Duhesmes.
18-5-94	near Roncq	Delaporte, 345–46.
26-6-94	Fleurus*	AG, B¹*137, 26 June 1794, General Kléber.

*Indicates a somewhat confusing or doubtful case.

TABLE A.2
Examples of the Column in Combat

Date	Place	Source
In the Attack: With Deployment into Line		*1 Example*
6-11-92	Jemappes	AG, B¹6, 7 Nov. 1792, General Dumouriez; MR 270, Colonel Leclaire; General Dampierre's report in La Jonquière, 165–68.
In the Attack: "Column" Specifically Stated		*14 Examples*
14-9-92	Croix-aux-Bois	AG, MR 270, Colonel Leclaire; B¹*104, 29 Dec. 1792, letter.
5-11-92	Quaregnon	Lombard, 153.
6-11-92	Le Blaton	Thiébault, 1: 343.
29-3-93	Helles	AG, B¹10, 29 Mar. 1793, General Champmorin.

TABLE A.2 (continued)

Date	Place	Source
8-5-93	Famars*	Letter by Private Savary in Foucart and Finot, 1: 429; Lahure, 45.
7-8-93	Bambecke	AG, B¹18, 11 Sept. 1793, General Houchard.
8-8-93	Hondschoote*	Leclaire, 94–95; paintings cited by Dupuis, *1793*, 1: 479.
24-9-93	Maubeuge*	Thiébault, 454–55.
15-10-93	Wattignies	Dupuis, *1793*, 2: 164–65, 167.
5-5-94	Florenne	AG, B¹*298, 5 May 1794, General Dessaubay.
17-5-94	Mouscron	AG, B¹32, 19 May 1794, General Thierry.
18-5-94	Bois-de Bonne-Espérance	AG, MR 271, General Desjardin.
21-5-94	Grand-Reng	AG, MR 271, General Desjardin; MR 291, General Duhesmes.
31-5-94	Fontaine-l'Evêque	AG, B¹30, 26 Apr. 1794, General Cacault.

In the Attack: The Charge "In Order" and "In Mass"		*9 Examples*
12-9-93	Avesnes-le-Sec	AG, B¹18, 12 Sept. 1793, General Declaye.
12-9-93	Werwik	AG, B¹18, 13 Sept. 1793, General Beru.
29-3-94	on the Sambre to the east of Maubeuge	AG, B¹28, 28 Mar. 1794, General Soland.
10-4-93	Hesrud	AG, MR 271, General Desjardin.
21-4-94	Nouvion	Extract of General Favereau's "Journal" in Coutanceau, pt. 2, 1: 625.
26-4-94	Marque	AG, B¹31, 12 May 1794, General Reynier, "Journal."
26-4-94	Menin	AG, MR 273, General Lacroix; B¹31, 12 May 1794, General Reynier, "Journal."
16-6-94	near Charleroi	General Duplaisset letter in Dupuis, *1794*, 557.
26-6-94	Fleurus	AG, B¹34, 26 June 1794, General Ernouf.

In the Attack: The Charge "à la baionnette" and "battant la charge"		*7 Examples*
7-11-92	Halluin	Representative Delmas Letter in La Jonquière, 184–85.
27-8-93	Roncq	AG, B¹17, 27 Aug. 1793, Representatives.
23-10-93	Tilleul	AG, B¹21, 28 Oct. 1793, General Ferrand.
21-4-94	Nouvion	AG, B¹*134, 23 Apr. 1794, General Duhesmes.
12-5-94	near Grand-Reng	AG, Fricasse, 23.

Appendix

TABLE A.2 (continued)

Date	Place	Source
18-5-94	Tourcoing	AG, MR 273, General Lacroix.
30-6-94	near Maubeuge	AG, B¹*135, 30 May 1794, General Favereau.

In the Attack: Against Cavalry		*4 Examples*
26-4-94	Boussu	AG, B¹30, 26 Apr. 1794, General Cacault.
13-5-94	Grand-Reng*	AG, MR 291, General Duhesmes.
26-5-94	Latombe	AG, MR 291, General Duhesmes.
16-6-94	near Charleroi	AG, B¹34, 26 June 1794, General Ernouf.

In Support of Light Infantry		*1 Example*
21-4-94	Nouvion	AG, MR 272, General Favereau.

As a Waiting and Preliminary Formation		*3 Examples*
8-9-93	Hondschoote	Dupuis, *1793*, 1: 468–69.
23-9-93	Maubeuge	Thiébault, 454.
15-10-93	Wattignies	Dupuis, *1793*, 2: 189.

As a Maneuver Formation: In Retreat		*3 Examples*
28-2-93	near Aldenoue*	AG, B¹10, 4 Mar. 1793, commander of the 3rd Paris.
8-5-93	Famars*	Letter by Private Savary in Foucart and Finot, 1: 429.
16-6-94	near Charleroi*	AG, B¹*298, 17 June 1794, General Kléber; MR 291, General Duhesmes.

Columns by Pelotons		*5 Examples*
29-4-92	Tournai	AG, B¹2, 3 May 1792, General d'Aumont; De Sérignan, 144.
8-9-93	Hondschoote	Dupuis, *1793*, 1: 468–69.
26-4-94	Boussu	AG, B¹30, 26 Apr. 1794, General Cacault.
31-5-94	Fontaine l'Evêque	AG, B¹30, 26 Apr. 1794, General Cacault.
16-6-94	near Charleroi*	AG, MR 291, General Duhesmes.

*Signifies a case that is only probable.

Table A.3
Examples of the Square in Combat

Date	Place	Source
The Square		*6 Examples*
12-9-93	Avesnes-le-Sec*	Dupuis, *1793*, 2: 30; B¹18, 12 Sept. 1793, report.
24-4-94	unknown	*Oesterreichische militarische Zeitschrift* in Coutanceau and La Jonquière, pt. 2, 1: 379.
10-5-94	Besieux	AG, MR 279, General Bonnaud, *Journal*; B¹31, 12 May 1794, General Reynier, "Journal."
18-5-94	Bois de Bonne-Espérance	AG, MR 271, General Desjardin.
21-5-94	Grand-Reng	AG, MR 271, General Desjardin; MR 291, General Duhesmes.
16-6-94	near Charleroi†	AG, MR 608², General Jourdan.

*This case is at best possible.
†Since this clear case of the square in combat occurred after Jourdan had brought up troops from the Moselle, it is uncertain whether this example involved soldiers from that army or the Armée du Nord et des Ardennes.

Table A.4
Specialist and Non-Specialist Light Infantry Actions

Categories of examples: (1) unspecified; (2) non-specialists; (3) total dispersal of line battalions *en tirailleurs*; (4) specialists from an indefinite unit; (5) specialist company; (6) specialist battalion.

Date	Place	Source	1	2	3	4	5	6
Infantry Actions		*73 Examples*						
28-4-92	Mons	AG, MR 264, General Foissac-Latour.	x					
28-4-92	Tournai	AG, B¹2, 28 Apr. 1792, account by a grenadier of the 24th Infantry Regiment.					x	
17-9-92	Clermont	Money, 85–86.						x
2-11-92	Boussu	AG, B¹30, 26 Apr. 1794, General Chapuis.	x					
6-11-92	Jemappes	General Dumouriez, in La Jonquière, 146.					x	
6-11-92	La Blaton	Thiébault, 343.					x	
4-3-93	near Liege	Mastrick's account in Foucart and Finot, 1: 345.	x					

TABLE A.4 (continued)

Categories of examples: (1) unspecified; (2) non-specialists; (3) total dispersal of line battalions *en tirailleurs*; (4) specialists from an indefinite unit; (5) specialist company; (6) specialist battalion.

Date	Place	Source	1	2	3	4	5	6
18-3-93	Neerwinden	AG, B¹10, 29 Mar. 1793, General Champmorin.		x				
21-3-93	Louvain	Bricard, 43–44.	x					
22-3-93	Louvain	Bricard, 44.	x					
26-4-93	Bois de Bonne Espérance	Bricard, 62–63.						x
26-5-93	Rousbrugge	AG, B¹12, 6 May 1793, report.						x
23-5-93	?	AG, B¹12, 23 May 1793, commander of 1st Battalion "républicain."	x					
1-8-93	Givet	AG, B¹16, 1 Aug. 1793, General Poutier.	x					
19-8-93	Lincelles	AG, B¹17, 19 Aug. 1793, General Jourdan.	x					
24-8-93	Esquelsbeque	Leclaire, 82–83.			x			
27-8-93	Tourcoing	AG, B¹17, 29 Aug. 1793, General Houchard.			x			
7-9-93	Rexpoede	AG, B¹19, 29 Sept. 1792, General Houchard.	x					
8-9-93	Hondschoote	AG, B¹19, 23 Sept. 1793, Representative Delbrel; Gay de Vernon, 267–72.			x			
11-9-93	Fontaine	Thiébault, 449–50.					x	
24-9-93	Maubeuge	Thiébault, 454–55.						x
29-9-93	Maubeuge	Fricasse, 13.	x					
7-10-93	Maubeuge	AG, MR 271, General Desjardin.						x
13-10-93	Tilleul	*Guerres de la Révolution et du premier empire*, 1: 302.						x
16-10-93	Wattignies	Orders for 16 Oct. 1793, in Dupuis, *1793*, 2: 173–74.	x					
16-10-93	Beaumont	AG, B¹20, 19 Nov. 1793, General Elie.					x	
20-10-93	Cysoing	AG, B¹*124, 20 Oct. 1793, General Souham.	x					
22-10-93	Furnes	AG, B¹23, 6 Dec. 1793, Adj.-Gen. Durulte.	x					
23-10-93	Tilleul	AG, MR 271, General Desjardin.						x
28-2-94	?	AG, B¹*124, 28 Feb. 1794, General Souham.					x	

TABLE A.4 (continued)

Categories of examples: (1) unspecified; (2) non-specialists; (3) total dispersal of line battalions *en tirailleurs*; (4) specialists from an indefinite unit; (5) specialist company; (6) specialist battalion.

Date	Place	Source	1	2	3	4	5	6
6-3-94	near Philippeville	AG, B¹28, 6 Mar. 1794, General Hardy.	x					
3-4-94	?	AG, B¹*109, 3 Apr. 1794, General MacDonald	x					
21-4-94	La Capelle	AG, MR 272, General Favereau.	x					
21-4-94	Nouvion	AG, MR 271, General Desjardin.					x	
24-4-94	Nouvion	AG, MR 291, General Duhesmes.	x					
24-4-94	Silenrieux	AG, B¹*308, 24 Apr. 1794, General Charbonnier						x
24-4-94	near Rousbrugge	Coutanceau, pt. 2, 2: 70–71.						x
26-4-94	Boussu	AG, B¹30, 26 Apr. 1794, General Cacault.						x
26-4-94	Dickebusch	Coutanceau, pt. 2, 2: 78–79.						x
26-4-94	near Mouscron	General Souham's orders to General MacDonald dated 25 Apr. 1794 in Coutanceau, pt. 2, 2: 82.	x					
26-4-94	Prisches	AG, MR 271, General Desjardin.	x					
26-4-94	Troisvilles	AG, B¹30, 26 Apr. 1794, General Chapuis.						x
27-4-94	Werwik	AG, B¹18, 5 Sept. 1793, General Vandamme, "Récit abrégé."						x
27-4-94	near Leugnies	AG, MR 271, General Desjardin.						x
29-4-94	Hautes	29 Apr. 1794, General Desjardin to General Favereau, in Coutanceau, pt. 2, 1: 755.	x					
29-4-94	Mouscron (1)	AG, B¹31, 12 May 1794, General Reynier, "Journal."				x		
29-4-94	Mouscron (2)	AG, B¹31, 12 May 1794, General Reynier, "Journal."	x					
1-5-94	Strée	AG, MR 271, General Desjardin.	x					
5-5-94	Florenne	AG, B¹*298, 5 May 1794, General Desaubay.	x					

Appendix

TABLE A.4 (continued)

Categories of examples: (1) unspecified; (2) non-specialists; (3) total dispersal of line battalions *en tirailleurs*; (4) specialists from an indefinite unit; (5) specialist company; (6) specialist battalion.

Date	Place	Source	1	2	3	4	5	6
10-5-94	near Courtrai	Coutanceau, pt. 2, 2: 227.					x	
10-5-94	Strée	AG, MR 271, General Desjardin.					x	
11-5-94	Courtrai (1)	AG, B¹31, 12 May 1794, General Reynier, "Journal."				x		
11-5-94	Courtrai (2)	AG, B¹31, 12 May 1794, General Reynier, "Journal."	x					
11-5-94	Courtrai (3)	AG, B¹18, 5 Sept. 1793, General Vandamme, "Récit abrégé"; B¹31, 12 May 1794, General Reynier, "Journal."						x
12-5-94	near Courtrai	General Souham's orders to General Daendels dated 11-5-94 in Coutanceau, pt. 2, 2: 232.						x
12-5-94	near Grand-Reng	AG, B¹*298, 17 May 1794, General Muller.	x					
12-5-94	near Grand-Reng	AG, MR 291, General Duhesmes.				x		
13-5-94	Grand-Reng	AG, MR 271, General Desjardin.	x					
13-5-94	on the Sambre	Fricasse, 25.	x					
15-5-94	on the Sambre	Fricasse, 26.		x				
18-5-94	Roubaix Battle of Tourcoing)	Coutanceau, pt. 2, 2: 242.	x					
18-5-94	Bousbecque (Battle of Tourcoing)	AG, B¹18, 5 Sept. 1794, General Vandamme, "Récit abrégé."						x
19-5-94	on the Sambre	Instructions of General Charbonnier in Dupuis, *1794*, 479.	x					
20-5-94	Bois de Bourgogne	Dupuis, *1794*, 483.						x
20-5-94	Grand-Reng	AG, MR 291, General Duhesmes; orders of General Charbonnier in Dupuis, *1794*, 479.	x					
23-5-94	on the Sambre	General Kléber's "Instructions" in MR 291, General Duhesmes.	x					

296   Appendix

TABLE A.4 (continued)

Categories of examples: (1) unspecified; (2) non-specialists; (3) total dispersal of line battalions *en tirailleurs*; (4) specialists from an indefinite unit; (5) specialist company; (6) specialist battalion.

Date	Place	Source	1	2	3	4	5	6
24-5-94	Grand-Reng	Ernouf, 35–37.	x					
27-5-94	near Charleroi	AG, MR 291, General Duhesmes.						x
31-5-94	near Fontaine	AG, B¹30, 26 Apr. 1794, General Cacault.						x
n.d. 6-94	Vlamertingue	General Dumesny report in Foucart and Finot, 2: 114.	x					
8-6-94	near Ypres	Jouan, 103.					x	
16-6-94	near Charleroi	Dupuis, *1794*, 557.				x		
27-6-94	near Audenarde	Bricard, 113.	x					

Total sample	73
Cases uncertain (1)	34, 47 percent of the total sample
Total non-specialist cases (2, 3)	8, 11 percent of the total sample
Total specialist cases (4, 5, 6)	31, 31 percent of the total sample

TABLE A.5

Independent Light Infantry Actions

Code: (1) Terrain: B-broken or wooded, V-villages, R-redoubts and entrenchments; (2) Role: PAG-*petite guerre*, avant and flank guards; PAP-*petite guerre, affaires des postes,* IC-independent combat role, TD-total dispersal; (3) Light infantry were supported, "X" if so; (4) Specialist light infantry, "yes" or "no"; and *=questionable case.

Date	Place	Source	1	2	3	4
Independent Light Infantry Actions		*48 Examples*				
28-4-92	Tournai	AG, B¹2, 28 Apr. 1792, account by a grenadier of the 24th Infantry Regiment	?	PAG		yes
17-9-92	Clermont	Money, 85–86	B	IC		yes
6-11-92	Jemappes*	General Dumouriez in La Jonquière, 146.	V	IC	X	yes

Appendix

TABLE A.5 (continued)

Code: (1) Terrain: B-broken or wooded, V-villages, R-redoubts and entrenchments; (2) Role: PAG-*petite guerre*, avant and flank guards; PAP-*petite guerre, affaires des postes,* IC-independent combat role, TD-total dispersal; (3) Light infantry were supported, "X" if so; (4) Specialist light infantry, "yes" or "no"; and *=questionable case.

Date	Place	Source	1	2	3	4
6-11-92	Le Blaton	Thiébault, 343.	B	IC		yes
4-3-93	near Liege	Mastrick's account in Foucart and Finot, vol. 1: 345.	?	IC		?
21-3-93	Louvain	Bricard, 43–44.	B	PAP		?
22-3-93	Louvain	Bricard, 44.	B	IC		?
26-4-93	Bois de Bonne Espérance	Bricard, 62–63.	B	IC		yes
26-5-93	Rousbrugge	AG, B¹12, 6 May 1793, report.	?	PAP		yes
24-8-93	Esquelsbeque	Leclaire, 82–83.	V	TD		no
27-8-93	Tourcoing	AG, B¹17, 29 Aug. 1793, General Houchard.	R&B	TD		no
7-9-93	Rexpoede*	AG, B¹19, 29 Sept. 1793, General Houchard.	V	IC		?
8-9-93	Hondschoote	AG, B¹19, 23, Sept. 1793, Representative Delbrel; Gay de Vernon, 267–72.	B	TD		no
7-10-93	Maubeuge	AG, MR 271, General Desjardin.	R	IC	X	yes
13-10-93	Tilleul	*Guerres de la Révolution*, 302.	B	IC		yes
16-10-93	Wattingnies	Orders for 16 Oct. 1793, in Dupuis, *1793*, 2: 173–74.	B	IC		?
16-10-93	Beaumont	AG, B¹20, 19 Nov. 1793, General Elie.	B	PAG		yes
20-10-93	Cysoing	AG, B¹*124, 20 Oct. 1793, General Souham.	B	IC	X	?
22-10-93	Furnes	AG, B¹23, 6 Dec. 1793, Adj.-Gen. Durulte.	V	PAG		?
23-10-93	Tilleul*	AG, MR 271, General Desjardin.	B	IC		yes
21-4-94	Nouvion*	AG, MR 271, General Desjardin; AG, MR 291, General Duhesmes.	B&V	PAG	X	yes
24-4-94	near Rousbrugge*	Coutanceau, pt. 2, 2: 70–71.	V	IC		yes

TABLE A.5 (continued)

Code: (1) Terrain: B-broken or wooded, V-villages, R-redoubts and entrenchments; (2) Role: PAG-*petite guerre*, avant and flank guards; PAP-*petite guerre, affaires des postes*, IC-independent combat role, TD-total dispersal; (3) Light infantry were supported, "X" if so; (4) Specialist light infantry, "yes" or "no"; and *=questionable case.

Date	Place	Source	1	2	3	4
24-4-94	Silenrieux	AG, B¹*308, 24 Apr. 1794, General Charbonnier.	B	IC		yes
26-4-94	Troisvilles*	AG, B¹30, 26 Apr. 1794, General Chapuis.	B	IC	X	yes
26-4-94	Boussu	AG, B¹30, 26 Apr. 1794, General Cacault.	B	IC		yes
26-4-94	Dichebusch	Coutanceau, pt. 2, 2: 78–79.		PAG		yes
26-4-94	near Mouscron	General Souham's orders to General MacDonald dated 25 Apr. 1794, in Coutanceau, pt. 2, 2: 82.		PAG		?
27-4-94	Werwik	AG, B¹18, 5 Sept. 1793, General Vandamme, "Récit abrégé."	V	IC		yes
27-4-94	near Leugnies	AG, MR 271, General Desjardin.	V	IC		yes
29-4-94	Mouscron (1)	AG, B¹31, 12 May 1794, General Reynier, "Journal."	B	TD		no
29-4-94	Hautes*	29 Apr. 1794, General Desjardin to General Favereau in Coutanceau pt. 2, 1: 755.	V	PAG		?
1-5-94	Strée	AG, MR 271, General Desjardin.	V	IC		?
5-5-94	Florenne*	AG, B¹*298, 5 May 1794, General Desaubay.	B	IC	X	?
10-5-94	near Courtrai	Coutanceau pt. 2, 2: 227.		PAP		yes
10-5-94	Strée	AG, MR 271, General Desjardin.		PAG		yes
11-5-94	Courtrai (1)	AG, B¹31, 12 May 1794, General Reynier, "Journal."	B	TD		no
12-5-94	near Courtrai	General Souham's orders to General Daendels dated 11-5-94, in Coutanceau, pt. 2, 2: 232.		PAG		yes

Appendix

TABLE A.5 (continued)

Code: (1) Terrain: B-broken or wooded, V-villages, R-redoubts and entrenchments; (2) Role: PAG-*petite guerre*, avant and flank guards; PAP-*petite guerre, affaires des postes,* IC-independent combat role, TD-total dispersal; (3) Light infantry were supported, "X" if so; (4) Specialist light infantry, "yes" or "no"; and *=questionable case.

Date	Place	Source	1	2	3	4
12-5-94	near Grand-Reng (1)	AG, B¹*298, 17 May 1794, General Muller to General Desjardin.	V	IC	X	?
12-5-94	near Grand-Reng (2)	AG, MR 291, General Duhesmes.	B	IC		yes
13-5-94	Grand-Reng	AG, MR 271, General Desjardin.	V	IC	X	?
18-5-94	Bousbecque (Battle of Tourcoing)	AG, B¹18, 5 Sept. 1793, General Vandamme, "Récit abrégé."		PAP		yes
18-5-94	Roubaix (Battle of Tourcoing)	Coutanceau, pt. 2, 2: 242.	V	IC		?
19-5-94	on the Sambre	Instructions of General Charbonnier in Dupuis, *1794*, 479.		PAG		?
20-5-94	Bois de Bourgogne*	Dupuis, *1794*, 483.	B	IC		yes
20-5-94	Grand-Reng	AG, MR 291, General Duhesmes; orders of Gen. Charbonnier in Dupuis, *1794*, 479.	B	IC		?
23-5-94	on the Sambre	General Kléber's "Instructions," in MR 291, General Dehesmes.		PAG		?
31-5-94	near Fontaine	AG, B¹30, 26 Apr. 1794, General Cacault.	B	PAG		yes
n.d. 6-94	Vlamertingue	General Dumesny report in Foucart and Finot, 2: 114.	V	PAG		?

Table A.6
Light Infantry in Support of Close Order Formations

Code: (1) Close order formation employed by the main body; (2) Light infantry specialists. *Indicates a somewhat doubtful example; † action only on the company level.

Date	Place	Source	1	2
Close Order Formations		*13 Examples*		
2-11-92	Boussu*	AG, B¹30, 26 Apr. 1794, General Chapuis.	Line	?
11-9-93	Fontaine†	Thiébault, 449–50.	?	yes
29-9-93	near Maubeuge	Fricasse, 13.	Line	?
6-3-94	near Philippeville*	AG, B¹28, 6 Mar. 1794, General Hardy.	?	?
26-4-94	Prisches*	AG, MR 271, General Desjardin.	?	?
29-4-94	Mouscron	AG, B¹31, 12 May 1794, General Reynier, "Journal."	?	?
5-5-94	Florenne	AG, B¹*298, 5 May 1794, General Desaubay.	Col.	?
11-5-94	Courtrai (1)	AG, B¹18, 5 Sept. 1793, General Vandamme, "Récit abrégé"; B¹31, 12 May 1794, General Reynier, "Journal."	?	yes
11-5-94	Courtrai (2)	AG, B¹31, 12 May 1794, General Reynier, "Journal."	Line	?
15-5-94	on the Sambre*	Fricasse, 26.	?	no
18-5-94	near Roncq	Delaporte, 345–48.	Line	Both
24-5-94	Grand-Reng	Ernouf, 35–37.	?	?
16-6-94	near Charleroi	Dupuis, *1794*, 557.	Col.	no

Notes

Notes to "The Elements of Victory"

1. This treatment of compliance theory relies on that presented by Stephen D. Wesbrook, "The Potential for Military Disintegration," in Sarkesian, *Combat Effectiveness*, 244–78.
2. Colby, *Masters*, 83.
3. Baynes, *Morale*, 94; Marshall, *Men against Fire*, 158.
4. See Mandelbaum, *Soldier Groups*; Shibutani, *Derelicts of Company K*; Stouffer, *American Soldier*, 10–15, 33–38.
5. See Stouffer, *American Soldier*, 131–35; Moskos, *American Enlisted Man*, 154–56.
6. Stouffer, *American Soldier*, 150–53, 169; Baynes, *Morale*, 99–100; Marshall, *Men against Fire*, 160–61; Shils and Janowitz, "Cohesion and Disintegration"; Moskos, *American Enlisted Man*, 148–50; Dollard, *Fear in Battle*; Henderson, *Why the Vietcong Fought*, 96. Helmer, *Bringing the War Home*, views at least some American troops in Vietnam as being more political.
7. Stouffer, *American Soldier*, 321. In another impressive survey 85 percent answered that their family and friends were doing what they should to help win the war, that is, they were committed to the war effort. Committed people could be expected to appreciate the war effort more (322).
8. Currey, *Self-Destruction*, 27.
9. Moskos, *American Enlisted Man*, 148–51; Guenter Lewy, "The American Experience in Vietnam," in Sarkesian, *Combat Effectiveness*, 101.
10. An unexcelled work on fear in battle and the wearing effect of time is Moran, *Anatomy of Courage*.
11. Ibid., ch. 15; Sarkesian, *Combat Effectiveness*, 102; Stouffer, *American Soldier*, 87–88; Ellis, *Sharp End*, 290–92.
12. Helmer, *Bringing the War Home*, 153–208.
13. These three works were Marshall, *Men against Fire* (1947), Shils and Janowitz, "Cohesion and Disintegration" (first published 1948), and Stouffer, *American Soldier* (1949).
14. Stouffer, *American Soldier*, 169.
15. Ibid., 130–31.

16. Marshall, *Men against Fire*, 145–53; Shils and Janowitz, "Cohesion and Disintegration," 178.

17. Marshall, *Men against Fire*, 161. For similar statements that good people make good soldiers, see Anthony Wallace, "Psychological Preparation for War," in Fried, *War*, 181–82, and Moran, *Anatomy of Courage*, 159–60.

18. Marshall, *Men against Fire*, 76; Stouffer, *American Soldier*, 34–35; Moran, *Anatomy of Courage*, 52–53. See Stouffer, 108, for the argument that hatred may *not* have been a combat motivation, however.

19. Moskos, *American Enlisted Man*, 141–43, 156; Roger W. Little, "Buddy Relationships and Combat Performance," in Janowitz, *New Military*, 195–223.

20. Moskos, *American Enlisted Man*, 135; Helmer, *Bringing the War Home*, 153–208.

21. See George, *Chinese Communist Army*.

22. Moskos, *American Enlisted Man*, 135.

23. Helmer, *Bringing the War Home*, 40–41, 47, 199; Sarkesian, *Combat Effectiveness*, 96–98, 257–59; Prebble, *Mutiny*.

24. Sarkesian, *Combat Effectiveness*, 257.

25. For a definition and diagram of combat effectiveness that places great emphasis on leadership, see Alexander L. George, "Primary Groups, Organization, and Military Performance," in Little, *Handbook of Military Institutions*, 245–318.

Notes to "The New Soldier"

1. The crucial social profiles of the line army are Corvisier, *L'armée française* and Scott, "Line Army, 1787–1793." Scott's *Response of the Royal Army* is excellent but contains less detail concerning troop composition than does his dissertation. Unless otherwise noted, all information presented here on the statistical characteristics of line army troops has been taken from Corvisier, *L'armée française*, 1:406, 511; 2: 624–27, 640, and from Scott, "Line Army, 1787–1793," 136, 144, 150, 185, 219–20, 223, 231–37.

2. Lynn, "Growth of the French Army," and Scott, "Regeneration of the Line Army," 310.

3. Scott, "Line Army, 1787–1793," 223.

4. Bertaud, *La Révolution armée*, 37. This classification of rural and urban is accepted by Corvisier, Scott, and Bertaud. It goes back to works of the eighteenth century.

5. My figures generally differ slightly from Scott's because I subtract unknown or indeterminant cases from the total before calculating percentages. This method makes Scott's figures more consistent with Corvisier's.

6. Scott, "Regeneration of the Line Army," 318, reached this figure by studying the *contrôles*. Alexander Lameth, in his presentation to the National Assembly on 22 July 1791, estimated the army's strength at the beginning of the year to have been 133,000. A more alarming figure of 120,000 was given by Lameth on 28 Jan. 1791 before the Assembly. Unless otherwise noted, in this and subsequent chapters, the details of actions taken in and by the National Assembly, the Legislative Assembly, and the National Convention have been taken from the *Archives parlementaires*, vols. 1–92 (Paris: 1867–1980). Such details will not be footnoted when the

date of an action or address is sufficient to guide the reader to the proper volume and page of the *Archives parlementaires*. When cited, the *Archives parlementaires* will be simply referred to as *AP*.

7. Scott, "Regeneration of the Line Army," 319.
8. Scott, *Response of the Royal Army*, 166.
9. *AP*, 22:531–42; 25:225–30, 364–73, 381–94.
10. *Règlement pour l'infanterie—nationale—parisienne*. The Guard excluded non-domiciled workers and domestics.
11. For this statistical profile of the Volunteers of 1791, see Bertaud, *La Révolution armée*, 67–68, 82–83. Some of the percentages he presents in *La Révolution armée* differ sharply from those contained in his *Valmy*. This is cause for some confusion.
12. Mathiez, *La victoire*, 68, speaks of battalions from the Marne and from Marseille composed largely of the poor. For other cases of large numbers of workers involved in 1791 battalions, see Bertaud, *Valmy*, 292–94.
13. Mathiez, *La victoire*, 74; *AP*, 44:550–56, 649.
14. Rousset, *Les volontaires*, 307–35, lists all volunteer battalions raised, 1791–93.
15. Bertaud, *La Révolution armée*, 80–81; Chuquet, *Lettres de 1793*, 137.
16. Bricard, *Journal*, 8.
17. Bertaud's profile of the Volunteers of 1792 is contained in *La Révolution armée*, 82–83. See as well his *Valmy*, 300–302.
18. Thiébault, *Mémoires*, 1:328.
19. Dubois-Crancé estimated the infantry at 113,000 line and 289,000 volunteers in early December 1792; with 35,000 cavalry and 10,000 artillery the total force would have been 447,000. *AP*, 58:358–59. The estimate presented in the consideration of February levies set the volunteers at only 113,500, while Scott puts line strength at 178,000, for a February total of 291,500. *AP*, 59:174; Scott, *Response of the Royal Army*, 178. For a statement of desired strength, see *AP*, 58:359.
20. Archives de la guerre (AG) $X^w 74$, folder 7.
21. Bertaud, *La Révolution armée*, 102; Carnot letter of 13 July 1793 in Mathiez, *La victoire*, 112; Picard, *Au service*, 149–50.
22. What statistical profile of the Levy of 300,000 Bertaud offers can be found in *La Révolution armée*, 103.
23. See *Père Duchesne*, #234; *Révolutions de Paris*, #199, #200.
24. Bertaud, *La Révolution armée*, 104; AG, $B^1 16$, 1 Aug. 1793, printed order. See as well AG, $B^1 16$, 4 Aug. 1793 orders; AG, $X^w 78$, order on details of levy.
25. Bertaud's count and statistical profile of the *levée en masse* can be found in *La Révolution armée*, 137–39.
26. Unless otherwise noted, in this and later chapters statements concerning the units present in the Nord, their size and brigading, as well as estimates of the strength of the entire Nord, are based on orders of battle, situation reports, and troop tableaux found in AG, $B^{1*}249$–54. These figures are, of course, paper figures.
27. Bertaud, *La Révolution armée*, 96–99. Article 8 of the decree postponed *enbrigadement* until further notice.
28. Cochon in Bertaud, *La Révolution armée*, 171. See Dubois-Crancé's direct reply to Cochon's criticism on 9 Jan. 1794 in the Convention; and Dubois-Crancé, *Rapport sur l'embrigadement*, 13–14.

29. Bertaud, *La Révolution armée*, 174; list of demi-brigades of the first and second *amalgames* in Rousset, *Les volontaires*, 336–99.

30. Godechot, *Les institutions de la France*, 362; Bertaud, *La Révolution armée*, 271.

31. Bertaud's examination of the composition of the army in 1794 can be found in *La Révolution armée*, 174–75.

32. See breakdown of years in service for artillerymen in Scott, "Line Army, 1787–1793," 138.

33. Le Roy, *Souvenirs*.

34. Excerpt from the contemporary *Des causes de la desertion* by de Vietinghoff in Desbrière and Sautai, *La cavalerie de 1740–1789*, 110.

35. Duruy, *La'armée royale*, 42.

36. Delarue, "L'éducation politique," 207.

37. Guibert, *Essai générale*, vi. See as well Vauvenargues and Voltaire in Léonard, *L'armée et ses problèmes*, 152, 225. Iung, *Dubois-Crancé*, 2:23. See statement from a memoir of the 1780s in Desbrière and Sautai, *La cavalerie de 1740 à 1789*, 115. Even someone of modest means "regarded a son who enlisted as a soldier as a disgrace to the family."

38. Concerning barracks life see Corvisier, *L'armée française*, 2:828–31, 848; Desbrière and Sautai, *La cavalerie de 1740 à 1789*, 115.

39. Rogers, *Spirit of Revolution*, 210.

40. Woloch, *French Veteran*, 66; statement of 12 Dec. 1789 in Iung, *Dubois-Crancé*, 2:16; memoir of 18 Sept. 1789 in Bertaud, *La Révolution armée*, 46.

41. Iung, *Dubois-Crancé*, 2:19; Michon, "L'armée et la politique intérieure," 13–14; Dumouriez, *Mémoire sur l'armée*

42. "Chanson guerrier," in *Le chansonnier patriote*, 78; untitled song in *Soirée de camp*, 11 (30 July 1794), 4; AG, X^{w}2; Bertaud, *La Révolution armée*, 207.

43. Rogers, *Spirit of Revolution*, 207–8; *Argus*, 79 (10 July 1792); Bertaud, *La Révolution armée*, 128.

44. Mathiez, *La victoire*, 149; Herlaut, *Bouchotte*, 2:128.

Notes to "The New Officer Corps"

1. Concerning officers of fortune, see Wrong, "French Infantry Officer," 139, 177–89. Wrong estimates the share of infantry officers of fortune at 10 percent. Bodinier, "Les officiers," 61, presents figures demonstrating that in July 1789 officers of fortune constituted 10.6 percent of infantry officers and 12.9 percent of all officers.

2. Bien, "La réaction aristocratique." The best of earlier works, Tuetey, *Les officiers*, estimated that at least one-third of infantry officers had been of non-noble birth during the Seven Years' War.

3. Scott, *Response of the Royal Army*, 23.

4. Bien, "La réaction aristocratique," is essentially a fundamental redefinition of the importance of the Ségur decree. It makes all other analyses obsolete.

5. Scott, *Response of the Royal Army*, 191; Scott, "Professionalization of the French Officer Corps," 25–26.

6. Bodinier, "Les officiers," 67, 68. Greer, *Incidence of the Emigration*, 112, sets the

number of officer-émigrés at 7,513. Only 8 percent of officers of fortune resigned or abandoned their commissions.

7. The November law supposedly applied until 1 Feb. 1792, but it was extended by legislation of 10 Apr. 1792. The 10 Apr. 1792 legislation is misreported in Scott, "Line Army, 1787–1793," 107; Belhomme, "Histoire de l'infanterie"; and Hanoteau, *Histoire militaire*. They claim the order reserved all positions of sous-lieutenants to NCOs. It does not; rather, it reasserts articles 3–7 of the November order.

8. Details on length of service and social composition of the officer corps come from Scott, "Line Army, 1787–1793," 256, 260–62, 271, 274. My figures differ slightly from Scott's, since I subtract the indeterminate cases from the total sample before computing percentages. For ease of comparison, although the ranks of colonel and lieutenant-colonel were replaced by newer titles of *chef-de-brigade* and *chef-de-bataillon*, I employ only the traditional ranks here.

9. The social analysis of officers from the Volunteers of 1791 is taken from Bertaud, *La Révolution armée*, 68–70, and Bertaud, *Valmy*, 297–99.

10. Details concerning officers of the Volunteers of 1792 are taken from Bertaud, *La Révolution armée*, 83–84, and Bertaud, *Valmy*, 303–5.

11. *AP*, 59:172.

12. Thus between two sous-lieutenants both aspiring to a vacant lieutenancy, if one was a Volunteer of 1791 with three years total service, all as a sous-lieutenant, and the other a veteran line soldier with ten years total service, but only one as a sous-lieutenant, the veteran would receive the promotion. See Bertaud's discussion in "Le recrutement et l'avancement des officiers," 519–20.

13. Sous-Lieutenant Galdon in ibid., 520.

14. Ibid., 523; Bertaud, *La Révolution armée*, 178; Six, *Les généraux*, 107. NCOs objected to the February law, and in at least one case frustrated NCOs went to the enemy. *Receuil des actes du Comité de salut public (RACSP)*, 13:565–67.

15. Bertaud's profile of the officer corps in 1794 is in *La Révolution armée*, 182–84, 189, 191.

16. Six, *Les généraux*, 115.

17. Bertaud, *La Révolution armée*, 277–78, 280–81.

18. See comments on illiterate officers made 13 Sept. 1793 before the Convention.

19. Bertaud, *La Révolution armée*, 192.

20. Woloch, *French Veteran*, 142.

21. Dupuis, *La campagne de 1793*, 1:310.

22. Representative Duhem on 24 Sept. 1793.

23. Duchet, *Deux volontaires*, 93.

24. AG, B¹11, 9 Apr. 1793, poster signed Cochon, Lequinio, and Bellegarde.

25. *RACSP*, 3:465; Six, *Les généraux*, 204.

26. Herlaut, *Bouchotte*, 2:225–27, 232; Legrand, *La justice militaire*, 17–18; Bricard, *Journal*, 65–66; Girardon, *Lettres*, 37.

27. AG, B¹13, 6 June 1793; Herlaut, *Bouchotte*, 2:254.

28. Six, *Les généraux*, 203–5; *AP*, 69:632; Herlaut, "Le républicanisation des états-majors," 389. Bouchotte had been pushing for such authority as early as 6 May.

29. The most convenient source for the professional details of generals' lives is Six, *Dictionnaire biographique*.

30. Six, *Les généraux*, 26–27, 236. Six counts more than one sanction for one

man at times; if, for example, a man was suspended, then arrested, and finally sentenced to death, the total came to three sanctions.

31. Order of battle for main forces of the Nord on 24 Oct. 1792 in La Jonquière, *Jemappes*, 49–51; Six, *Dictionnaire biographique*.

32. Thiébault, *Mémoires*, 1:444.

33. *Père Duchesne*, #260, #259.

34. Herlaut, *Bouchotte*, 2:203, 186.

35. Bertaud, *La Révolution armée*, 153.

36. Herlaut, "Le républicanisation des états-majors," 399.

37. See Duhem's comments in *AP*, 75:84; 5 Sept. 1792 report by Carnot in Charavay, *Correspondence de Carnot*, 1:151; Reinhard, *Carnot*, 2:45–46.

38. Bertaud, *La Révolution armée*, 177.

39. Archives nationales (AN), AF^{II}234, dossier 2015. See as well correspondence in AG, B^{1*}146.

40. September 1793 instruction in Bonnal des Ganges, *Les représentants du peuple*, 1:131.

41. Maréchal, *La constitution*, 115.

42. *AP*, 64:216.

43. Bricard, *Journal*, 76. See as well pp. 65, 69.

44. Bertaud argues that the campaign against Custine and the demand to drive all nobles away from the army were *sans-culotte* issues more than they were Jacobin policies. Although they were often divided against themselves, on the whole the Jacobins spoke for a more middle-class constituency and favored a more centralized government than did the Hébertists, who relied upon the heavily working-class *sans-culottes* and who desired more direct democracy on the local level. With good reason, the Jacobin lynchpin was the Committee of Public Safety, while the *sans-culotte* loci of power were the sections, or wards, and the Commune of Paris.

45. Bonnal des Ganges, *Les représentants du peuple*, 1:131.

46. AG, B^{1}15; Chuquet, *Lettres de 1793*, 172, 174–84, 244–47, 257–65.

47. AG, B^{12*}2; AG, B^{1}23, 2 Dec. 1793; *AP*, 87:260; Gross, "Saint-Just," 1032–33. See AG, B^{1*}146 for lists of suspensions and arrests in the Nord during fall 1793.

48. Calandini's letters AG, B^{1}13, 15 June 1793, and Chuquet, *Lettres de 1793*, 231; Representative Dubarran report on 23 Mar. 1794, *AP*, 87:260–61; Bouchotte in Herlaut, *Bouchotte*, 2:293; *RACSP*, 15:283; Bertaud, *La Révolution armée*, 177.

49. See AG, B^{12*}29 for club denunciations; order in AN, AF^{II}233, dossier 2009; Moreel, *La société populaire*, 145.

50. Circular of 14 frimaire an II, *RACSP*, 9:181–84.

51. Lombard, *Un volontaire de 1792*, 217; AN, AF^{II}234, dossier 2013, 22 Dec. 1793.

52. AN, D 2 1.

53. Scott, "Line Army, 1787–1793," 256; Desbrière and Sautai, *La crise*, 246; Dupuis, *La campagne de 1793*, 1:311.

54. Thiébault, *Mémoires*, 1:327–28.

55. Biron in Soboul, *Les soldats*, 169; AN, AF^{II}242, dossier 2072, 26 Aug. 1793; *Argus*, #217 (20 Dec. 1792).

56. 12 Aug. 1793 letter in Dupuis, *La campagne de 1793*, 1:312; AG, B^{1}18, 14 Sept. 1793; Jourdan in Charavay, *Correspondance de Carnot*, 3:314.

57. The stories surrounding Charbonnier are both amusing and disturbing. One

day when he was eating, an aide rushed in to report, "General, the enemy is attacking your lines." "Yes then, they will be well received!" replied Charbonnier. "But, General, aren't you going to join your troops?" "My troops!" cried Charbonnier, "Oh, don't worry, they are all tough little dogs who know their business better than I do." Thiébault, *Mémoires*, 1:446.

58. *AP*, 83:179–82, 193–203; *RACSP*, 15:283; Bertaud, *La Révolution armée*, 183.

59. Le Roy, *Souvenirs*, 46.

60. Bertaud, "Voies nouvelles," 191.

61. For absenteeism, see Grille, *Lettres*, 1:23; Duchet, *Deux volontaires*, 51–52; for women, see Herlaut, *Bouchotte*, 2:230–31; Six, *Les généraux*, 24–25.

62. Rousset, *Les volontaires*, 176.

63. *Père Duchesne*, #321; 23 Nov. 1793 circular is in Herlaut, *Bouchotte*, 1:254; *AP*, 78:92–93; see also Herlaut, *Bouchotte*, 2:135.

64. Roch Godart clubbed two of his men who addressed him in this fashion. Godart, *Mémoires*, 26.

65. Herlaut, *Bouchotte*, 2:133; AG, X^{w}73, folder 4, 27 Nov. 1793.

66. 1 Jan. 1794 circular in Herlaut, *Bouchotte*, 1:245–46.

67. See execution of Lieutenant-Colonel Evard in Bricard, *Journal*, 103.

68. AG, MR 291.

Notes to "Discipline in an Army of Citizen-Soldiers"

1. Dubois-Crancé, *Observations*, 2.

2. *AP*, 31:637; Herlaut, *Bouchotte*, 1:242–43.

3. *Argus*, #79 (10 July 1792). Martin, "Journaux d'armées," 594, argues that "the new conception of discipline is thus inseparable from a constant effort of explication. . . . The army journals were a means of instruction to found this new order in the army." The *Argus* was full of appeals for discipline in May 1792.

4. Bertaud, *La Révolution armée*, 84; letter of 15 May 1792 in Rousset, *Les volontaires*, 54–55.

5. Herlaut, *Bouchotte*, 2:133; AG, B^{1}106, 13 Nov. 1793.

6. Coutanceau, *La campagne de 1794*, part 1, 1:xliii.

7. Michon, *La justice militaire*, 9.

8. Ibid., 27.

9. *AP*, 49:558.

10. Michon, *La justice militaire*, 61, states that tribunals were established in the Nord in August and September. But two letters by Representative Laurent with the Nord complain that the tribunals still had yet to be set up properly in December. AG, B^{1}23, 21 Dec. 1793; AG, B^{12*}15, 27 Dec. 1793. See *AP*, 72:617, for an August 1793 *compte rendu* of why tribunals were slow in forming.

11. Michon, *La justice militaire*, 38.

12. Desdevises du Dézert, *Lettres du sergent Brault*, 12; Herlaut, *Bouchotte*, 1:255.

13. Marquant, *Carnet d'étapes*, 31. A similar regulation was issued as late as the siege of Lancrecies in April 1794. Coutanceau, *La campagne de 1794*, part 2, 1:663.

14. See Houchard's instruction of 23 Aug. 1793 in Dupuis, *La campagne de 1793*, 1:320, and Kléber's march order of May 1794 in Dupuis, *Les operations militaires*, 170–71.

15. Bricard, *Journal*, 65–66.
16. Charavay, *Correspondence de Carnot*, vol. 2; see correspondence of Representative Laurent, AG, B¹23, 21 Dec. 1793, and AG, B¹²*15, 27 Dec. 1793.
17. In Coutanceau, *La campagne de 1794*, part 1, 1:74; Gross, "Saint-Just," 1030–31.
18. AG, B¹*22, 10 May 1794, order from Guise; AG, B¹*146, 29 Apr. 1794; Mathiez, *La victoire*, 194; Michon, *La justice militaire*, 63; Bricard, *Journal*, 102, 105–6.
19. Houchard's instructions in Dupuis, *La campagne de 1793*, 1:320. General Lamarche struggled to get his men out of the cabarets during battle. AG, B¹13, 5 June 1793.
20. Charavay, *Correspondence de Carnot*, 2:116–17; *RACSP*, 3:309–10; Bertaud, *La Révolution armée*, 198.
21. AG, B¹30, 23 Apr. 1794; Coutanceau, *La campagne de 1794*, part 2, 1:645.
22. Godart, *Mémoires*, 8–12; Desbrière and Sautai, *La crise*, 138; AN, D 2, 10 Jan. 1792.
23. Thiébault, *Mémoires*, 1:332–33; AG, B¹11, 1 Apr. 1793; Gay de Vernon, *Mémoire*, 184–86; Duchet, *Deux volontaires*, 53.
24. AG, Xʷ2, 27 Mar. 1793; AG, Xʷ97, 4 Mar. 1794; Charavay, *Correspondence de Carnot*, 2:173; AG, Xʷ96, printed order from Dunkirk; AG, B¹²*28, 19 Nov. 1793.
25. Lynn, "Revolution on the Battlefield," 118–19.
26. AG, B¹10, 24 Mar. 1793.
27. Legrand, *La justice militaire*, 15.
28. *Argus*, 1280–91; AG, B¹7, 7 Dec. 1792; letter from representatives in Wallon, *Les représentants en mission*, 2:41.
29. Herlaut, *Bouchotte*, 1:17; Le Roy, *Souvenirs*, 86; Dumouriez in Wallon, *Les représentants en mission*, 1:40; Desbrière and Sautai, *La crise*, 167.
30. AG, Xʷ73, 2 Nov. 1793.
31. AG, Xʷ78.
32. Michon, *La justice militaire*, 58n; Bricard, *Journal*, 102–3; Gross, "Saint-Just," 1034.
33. Pion des Loches, *Mes campagnes*, 12–13.
34. Marquant, *Carnet d'étapes*, 79–80; AG, B¹12, filed as 1 May 1793 but dated 19 Mar. 1793; letter from Patin-Wilder to his uncle, written 23 Dec. 1792 in Chuquet, *Lettres de 1792*.
35. Letter of 1 June 1793 in Charavay, *Correspondence de Carnot*, 2:302.
36. The most important account of Furnes is Carnot's letter of 1 June 1793, ibid., 2:299–302. Reinhard, *Carnot*, 2:50.
37. See order of 29 Apr. 1794, AG, B¹*146; Bricard, *Journal*, 113.
38. AG, B¹10, 18 Mar. 1793; Charavay, *Correspondence de Carnot*, 2:260.
39. Legrand, *La justice militaire*, 80–95.
40. Ibid., 79.
41. Bricard, *Journal*, 102–3.
42. AG, B¹121; AG, B¹137 bis.; *RACSP*, 13:76–77; AG, B¹²*15, 14 Dec. 1793.
43. By an act of the Convention of 1 June 1794, general officers sentenced to death were to be executed at the head of their troops.
44. Bricard, *Journal*, 126–27. Vivien provides an equally graphic account of an execution in the fall of 1794 in his *Souvenirs*, 45–49.

45. Desdevises du Dézert, *Letters du sergent Brault*, 12.

Notes to "The Political Education of the Armée du Nord"

1. Two unpublished *mémoires de maitrise* deal with political education in other armies of the first Republic. Sibon-Cattaui, "L'éducation politique à l'armée des Pyrénées-Orientales en l'an II," and Delarue, "L'éducation politique." My research on political education in the Nord was greatly aided by the work of Delarue.

2. Scott, *Response of the Royal Army*, 81–97.

3. Concerning plans for 14 July celebrations in the territory occupied by the Nord, see Legrand, "Les fêtes civiques," 378–80, for Abbeville; AG, X^{w}83, 6 July 1792, for Arras; Marquant, *Carnet d'étapes*, 48–49, for La Capelle; and *Argus*, #83 (13 July 1793), for Valenciennes.

4. See Mathiez, *La victoire*, 58–59, for 1791 volunteers, and 74–75, for 1792 enrollment in Paris; for blessings, see pieces concerning Somme battalions in 1791 in AG, X^{w}96; and AN, D^{1}16, 5 Sept. 1792.

5. Scott, *Response of the Royal Army*, 98–99. De Cardinal, *La province*, 342–44, argues that the 8 May decree simply recognized the status quo; to guage soldier membership, see figures for Lille club in Leleu, *La société populaire de Lille*; address by the president of the Bergues club to men of the 78th Regiment in April 1791 in Moreel, *La société populaire*, 59–60.

6. Moreel, *La société populaire*, 62–63; De Sérignan, *La première invasion*, 6; and *Argus*, #8 (10 Apr. 1792).

7. *Argus*, #52 (2 June 1792).

8. AG, B^{1}2, 29 June 1792; Bertaud, *La Révolution armée*, 76.

9. *AP*, 52:513–14. The letter that precipitated the Convention's decision was sent by Representatives Georges Doulcet, E.D.E.J. Duquesnoy, and Jean-Marie d'Aoust from Lille on 14 Oct. AG, B^{1}8, 1 Jan. 1793; and orders of the day filed in AG, B^{1}8–12 and in B^{1*}121.

10. Martin, "Les origines de la presse militaire"; Maeght, "La presse," 323; Morel, "Historie de Valenciennes," 129, argues that the name derived from *Le Cousin Jacques*, a Parisian paper.

11. See Martin, "Les origines de la presse militaire," 249–55, and Morel, "Histoire de Valenciennes," 109.

12. Martin, "Journaux d'armées," 594; and *Argus*, #79 (10 July 1792), #124 (31 Aug. 1792), #167 (20 Oct. 1792), and #108 and #109 (13, 14 Aug. 1792).

13. *Argus*, prospectus, 18 June 1792. Compare *Argus*, #83 (10 Nov. 1792) with Dumouriez's report in La Jonquière, *Jemappes*, 148.

14. *Argus*, #165 (18 Oct. 1792), #117 (23 Aug. 1793), #119 (25 Aug. 1792), #161 (14 Oct. 1792), and #177 (1 Nov. 1792).

15. Representatives Doulcet, Duquesnoy, and d'Aoust to the Convention, 14 Oct. 1792, in *RACSP*, 1:142. This letter argued for the regular distribution of the *Bulletin*.

16. Herlaut, *Bouchotte*, 2:82.

17. AN, AF^{II}232, 12 May 1793.

18. Herlaut, *Bouchotte*, 2:82–83. The funds came from a grant of six million livres made by the Convention to the Executive Council on 16 Apr.; see *AP*, 62:192–93. AG, B^{13}306, 24 May 1793; AG, B^{13}306, 24 May 1794. The timing of the second

order opens up the possibility that the subscription to the *Père Duchesne* was an afterthought imposed by the political complexion of the Ministry of War.

19. Bouchotte in Bonnal des Ganges, *Les représentants de peuple*, 1:131–32.

20. The mémoire was written in the 1820s or early 1830s as a response to the writings of Adolphe Thiers. Much of it was published by Bouchez and Roux in their *Historie parlementaire*, 31; 234–38.

21. Unless otherwise stated, the figures listed in this section for the size and cost of subscriptions have been taken from two financial accounts presented by Bouchotte to the Committee of Public Safety in ventôse and germinal year II. These accounts have been reproduced in Herlaut, *Bouchette*, 2:96–100, and in Mathiez, "La presse subventionnée," 112–13.

22. Herlaut speaks of 8,000 copies of the *Père Duchesne* going out before the rise to 12,000 in September. Herlaut, *Bouchotte*, 2:86. See AG, $B^{13}306$, 24 May 1794 order; AG, $B^{13}306$, 17 Sept. 1793 order; and AG, $B^{12}*15$, 14 Mar. 1794 order.

23. The original order was 2,000 copies, but Bouchotte's 1794 accounts list it as 3,000 copies. The best guess is that Bouchotte put it down as 3,000 copies for three months when he meant 2,000 copies for four months. Delarue, "L'éducation politique," 154; AG, $B^{12}*15$, 4 Oct. 1794, order.

24. The accounts published in Herlaut, *Bouchotte*, 2:100, state the figure as 1,200 copies, but the cost listed for the germinal subscription makes it clear that 1,200 is far, far too low a number. Delarue, "L'éducation politique," 157–60, interprets the actual figure as 12,000. But a comparison of subscription cost with the reliable *ventôse* figures yields a total subscription of 10,200. The 1,200 must be a clerical error. There is at least one other in Herlaut's transcriptions of the accounts.

25. *RACSP*, 6:396. The order here is for only 1,000 copies.

26. Ibid., 10:493; Delarue, "L'éducation politique," 155–56.

27. Herlaut, *Bouchotte*, 2:86, states that the *Publiciste* was sent to the armies.

28. *RACSP*, 12:67; 13:571; 14:774–75; 15:26, 131, 166, 699–700.

29. Ibid., 5:549, 506; 6:374. To understand this publication venture one must read Aulard, "La presse officieuse," 227–40.

30. *RACSP*, 15:699–700; 16:185.

31. Martin, "Journaux d'armées," 604.

32. Pache's 1 Jan. 1793 order that the *Bulletin* would be sent and distributed to the troops stipulated that orders of the day must list which issues were to be distributed that day, and, if no *Bulletins* were received, that fact must also be stated in the orders. AG, $B^{1}8$, 1 Jan. 1793. This practice was continued through the first week of October but abandoned thereafter. The archives' collection of orders of the day for the period prior to mid-April 1793 is hit or miss at best. What orders are available can be found in AG, $B^{1}8$–11. Two fine sources pick up from April on; these are registers of orders, AG, $B^{1}*121$, Register of orders for the *Armée du Nord*, 18 Apr. 1793–5 Jan. 1794, and AG, $B^{1}*132$, Register of orders given by General Pichegru, 9 Feb. 1794–7 Oct. 1794. These can be supplemented by orders in AG, $B^{1}13$ for the month of June 1793. Some similar orders for troops headquartered at Maubeuge can also be found in the B^{1} general correspondence series.

33. AN, $AF^{II}232$, 5 May 1793.

34. AG, $B^{1}13$, 27 June 1793, *commissaires* Celliez and Varin at Cambrai to Bouchotte; see AG, $B^{1}13$, 18 June 1793, Celliez and Varin to Bouchotte; AG, $B^{1}14$, 10

July 1793, Varin to Bouchotte; AG, B¹15, 21 July 1793, Celliez to Vincent; AG, X⁵3, 28 Aug. 1793, Varin to Bouchotte; and AG, B¹15, 19 July 1793, Celliez to Hébert.

35. Letters of 24 and 27 June 1793 in Herlaut, *Bouchotte*, 2:257; Custine order in ibid., 2:250; AG, B¹15, 19 July 1793, Celliez to Hébert; AG, B¹14, 7 July 1789, Celliez to Bouchotte; and AG, B¹14, 2 July 1793, Custine to the Committee of Public Safety.

36. AG, B¹15, 19 July 1793, Celliez to Hébert.

37. AG, X⁵3, 19 Oct. 1793.

38. November Sijas order in Herlaut, *Bouchotte*, 2:86–88; Sijas July order in AG, B¹14, 5 July 1793, poster published by *commissaire* Defrenne at Maubeuge; Vincent letter of 12 Nov. 1793 in Herlaut, *Bouchotte*, 2:87; AN, F¹⁸10A, "Rapport au Comité du salut public sur l'état du service des Postes en pluviôse an II"; Martin, "Les origines de la presse militaire," 313; Mathiez, *La victoire*, 135; *RACSP*, 6:512.

39. AG, B¹27, 22 Feb. 1794, Guiot to Bouchotte; AG, B¹²*15, 26 Feb. 1794, Guiot to Bouchotte; *RACSP*, 2:457; Bouchotte's response, 1 Mar. 1794, AG, X⁵3.

40. AG, B¹8, 1 Jan. 1793, Pache order; complaint of a soldier in Bertaud, *La Révolution armée*, 147.

41. AG, B¹12, 7 May 1793, order of the day from Valenciennes; Martin, "Les origines de la presse militaire," 590; AG, B¹*200, 16 June 1793, order by Hulin.

42. AG, B¹13, 12 June 1793.

43. *Journal des hommes libres*, second prospectus, filed with November 1793 issues at the Bibliothéque Nationale, Paris.

44. The first issue of *Soirée* praised the style of *Père Duchesne*, while attacking its politics. See Bertaud, *La Révolution armée*, 216–17.

45. Hébert, who had no love at all for priests, relentlessly hammered at the church only in the issues of October and November 1793. Delarue, "L'éducation politique," 216, claims that after a spurt in October, "anti-clericalism hardly played any part in the education given to soldiers." *Père Duchesne*, #301, 7.

46. Bricard, *Journal*, 126.

47. *Père Duchesne*, #296, 1–2; *Soirée de camp*, #2 (22 July 1794); and *Père Duchesne*, #342, 2–3.

48. Laveaux in Delarue, "L'éducation politique," 198; *Père Duchesne*, #302, 4.

49. *Journal des hommes libres*, #99 (29 Mar. 1794).

50. *Père Duchesne*, #346, 7.

51. Delarue, "L'éducation politique," Appendix II.

52. AG, *Ordonnances militaires*, 20 Feb. 1793; Delarue, "L'éducation politique," Appendix II; AG, B¹13, 30 June 1793, Celliez to Bouchotte; Bouchette in Delarue, "L'éducation politique," 141; Bouchotte in Herlaut, *Bouchotte*, 2:121; *RACSP*, 6:576; AG, B¹*121, 29 Aug. 1793.

53. AG, B¹23, 16 and 17 Dec. 1793, Celliez and Berton to Bouchette; AG, B¹15, 19 July 1793, Celliez to Hébert.

54. Constant Pierre's count runs as follows: 1789—116; 1790—261; 1791—308; 1792—325; 1793—690; 1794—701; 1795—137; 1796—126; 1797—147; 1798—77; 1799—90; and 1800—25. Pierre, *Les hymnes et chansons*, 34. Rogers, *Spirit of Revolution*, 14–15, argues that Pierre dates many songs too early, so he underestimates the surge of songs under the Convention. Pierre, *Les hymnes et chansons*, 2–3, 7–30, 50; Rogers, *Spirit of Revolution*, 7–8, 10–11; *RACSP*, 8:570.

55. Tiersot, *Les fêtes et les chants*, 100–102.

56. Gervais, *A la conquête*, 19; *Chansons patriotiques*, chant VII (Paris, 1792), advertisement.

57. *Soirée du camp*, #1 (the decade was the revolutionary week); Pion des Loches, *Mes campagnes*, 8–9; see as well Chuquet, *Lettres de 1792*, 301; Noël in Mathiez, *La victoire*, 95; and Chuquet, *Les guerres de la Révolution, Jemappes*, 92–102.

58. Chaumette before the General Council of the Paris Commune in *Journal de Paris*, #270 (27 Sept. 1793).

59. AG, B^{12}29, 67 and 159; Herlaut, *Bouchette*, 2:98; Rousseau in Pierre, *Les hymnes et chansons*, 71. If the cost of songbooks sold to the Ministry was the same as those later offered to the Committee of Public Safety, 80,000 livres could have brought in the neighborhood of 500,000 booklets!

60. *RACSP*, 11:157; 14:25–26, 398, 688; Pierre, *Les hymnes et chansons*, 132–33.

61. Pierre, *Les hymnes et chansons*, 132–33.

62. *Journal de Paris*, #263 (20 Sept. 1793) and #270 (27 Sept. 1793); Potevin et al., *Le sans-culotte*.

63. AN, AF^{II}129, dossier 991, 25 Jan. 1794.

64. See Pierre, *Les hymnes et chansons*, 70–72, on Rousseau.

65. Ibid., 70. Copies of the *Ame* were neither numbered nor dated and are best differentiated by the title of the first song they contained. Six consisted of sixteen pages, and one had only four. Rogers, *Spirit of Revolution*, 301.

66. The best description of their work is in Pierre, *Les hymnes et chansons*, 119–42, his chapter, "Le Magazin de Musique à l'usage des fêtes nationales, ses collections d'hymns et chansons." *Procès verbaux de Comité d'instruction publique* (*PVCIP*), 2:800–803; 3:294–304; *AP*, 78: 597–98; *RACSP*, 11:157; 13:3, 69, 571.

67. Pierre, *Les hymnes et chansons*, 128–29; *RACSP*, 14:25–26; 15:668.

68. *RACSP*, 7:537; 12:751–52; 13:288–89.

69. Pierre, *Les hymnes et chansons*, 140–41.

70. *AP*, 83:367; *RACSP*, 11:157; 15:26; *Rougyff*, 17 Nov. 1793, in Bertaud, *La Révolution armée*, 148; and November 1793 Rousseau letter in Pierre, *Les hymnes et chansons*, 32.

71. Loy, "Le livre de route," 404; Rousseau, *L'âme du peuple et du soldat*, beginning with "Le portrait du héros-guerrier aux prises avec le sort," 7; Delarue, "L'éducation politique," 190.

72. Rousseau, "Cri de mort contre les rois"; Potevin et al., *Le sans-culotte*; "La philosophie des républicains français," *Soirée de camp*, #30 (18 Aug. 1794), 41; and "A nos frères et amis des fauxbourgs Saint-Antoine et Saint-Marcel, dit les sans-culottes," in Rousseau, *L'âme du peuple et du soldat*, beginning with "Hymne pour la fête d'un citoyen soldat," 12.

73. "Chansons patriotiques chantée à Lille," 5; "Les principes du vrai républicain," in Rousseau, *L'âme du peuple et du soldat*, beginning with "Idée du l'ancien gouvernement," 14; and "Hymne patriotique" in Potevin et al., *Le sans-culotte*, 8.

74. The song Hébert so praised is printed in the *Journal de Paris*, #263 (20 Sept. 1793).

75. "Chant de guerre," in Rousseau, *L'âme du peuple et du soldat*; Rousseau, *Chants du patriotisme*, #29; *Chansonnier de la Montagne*, 27; "Quelles vains reproches" in Piis, *Chansons patriotiques*, 24; and Bertaud, *La Révolution armée*, 151.

76. Loy, "Le livre de route," 402–4. The romances were remarkably sentimental. Off-color lyrics were not unknown, but the songs were not usually bawdy.

77. "Les exploits des sans-culottes," in *Soirée de camp*, 28 (11 Aug. 1794); Rousseau, "Sur le succès de nos armées," in Bertaud, *La Révolution armée*, 149; "Hymne en l'honneur de Michel Le Pelleteir," in Rousseau, *L'âme du peuple et du soldat*, beginning with "Le portrait du héros-guerrier aux prises avec sort," 13.

78. Bertaud, *La Révolution armée*, 129.

79. AG, B^{1}14, 8 July 1793, letter from headquarters at Cambrai.

80. Bricard, *Journal*, 67; AG, B^{1}14, 10 July 1793, Celliez to Bouchotte.

81. Herlaut, *Bouchotte*, 2:124; AG, B^{1*}121, 10–11 Aug. 1793, order of the day; Bricard, *Journal*, 73; AG, B^{1}16, 11 Aug. 1793, address by the curé of Ivay-Carignan; Legrand, "Les fêtes civiques," 382.

82. Legrand, "Les fêtes civiques," 382–89; Bricard, *Journal*, 80.

83. Bertaud, *La Révolution armée*, 145.

84. AN, AF^{II}233, dossier 2009, order of 18 Sept. 1793; B^{1}23, 30 Dec. 1793, Celliez to Bouchotte; Moreel, *La sociéte populaire*, 145, 190.

85. AG, B^{1}22, 17 Nov. 1793; AG, B^{12*}20, 4 Dec. 1793.

86. Gossuin's attack on Bouchotte in the Convention 12 August 1793 in Herlaut, *Bouchotte*, 2:48.

87. Brinton, *Jacobins*, 201.

88. AG, B^{1}27, 19 Feb. 1794.

89. Charavay, *Correspondance de Carnot*, 3:17; AG, B^{1}13, 30 June, 19 July 1793, Celliez letters; AG, B^{1}27, 13 Feb. 1793, Lespomaredy to the Committee of Public Safety.

90. AG, B^{1}13, 15 June 1793, Calanding to Jacobins of Paris; Statement at Paris Jacobins, 27 Oct. 1793, in Wallon, *Les représentants en mission*, 5:57.

91. AG, B^{1}27, 13 Feb. 1793, Lespomaredy to the Committee of Public Safety; Desdevises du Dézert, *Lettres du sergent Brault*, 11.

92. Cobb, *Les armées révolutionnaires*, 241.

93. Ibid., 752; AN, AF^{II}234, dossier 2019, Guiot to Committee of Public Safety.

94. 6 Nov. 1793 letter in Chuquet, *Lettres de 1793*, 284–86; AG, B^{1}23, 30 Dec. 1793, Celliez to Bouchotte; AG, B^{1*}133, 28 Feb. 1794.

95. Duchet, *Deux volontaires*, 34; Herlaut, *Bouchotte*, 2:99; AG, B^{12*}29, piece 127, 12 Dec. 1793; Wallon, *Les représentants en mission*, 5:54, 127. In Lorient actors received draft exempt status from the Representatives on Mission in November 1793, since "the theatre which has always [*à toujours du*] been the school of morals is now the only patriotic school, since national education is not yet in existence [*constituée*]." Bertaud, *La Révolution armée*, 119.

96. AG, B^{1*}121; Bertaud, *La Révolution armée*, 23.

97. Concerning cockades, see AG, B^{1*}199, 28 May 1793. The Convention voted the decree against white uniforms on 6 May, and it first appeared in the Armée du Nord orders of 8 May. Continued reminders were issued by Bouchotte as late as August. See AG, B^{12*}15, order of 11 Aug. 1793. On buttons see AG, B^{1*}121, 21–22 Aug. 1793, order of the day, and Bertaud, *La Révolution armée*, 73–74. For flags see *Journal militaire*, 2 Dec. 1792, and AG, B^{12*}15, 13 Oct. 1793.

98. Duchet, *Deux volontaires*, 96; Dubois-Crancé, *Rapport sur l' embrigadement*, 13–14; Dubois-Crancé in Jaurès, *L'armée nouvelle*, 169–70.

99. Citizen Falize, *chef de battalion* of a battalion formed in the district around Amiens, in Bertaud, *La Révolution armée*, 219; AN, AF^{II}232, 9 Apr. 1793, poster explaining Dumouriez's treason to the Armée du Nord.

100. *Soirée de camp*, #10 (29 July 1793); E. Picard, *Au service*, 117.

101. AG, B^{1}13, 12 June 1793, Celliez and Varin to Bouchotte.

102. Rousel in *Chronique de Paris*, Oct. 1793, in Pierre, *Les hymnes et chansons*, 31–32; *RACSP*, 11:457, letter of 28 Feb. 1794.

Notes to "The Ordinaire and Motivation"

1. The infantry *ordinaire* is defined in the following regulations: *Règlement provisoire sur le service de l'infanterie en campagne* of 5 Apr. 1792; *Instruction provisoire sur le campement de l'infanterie* of 1 Mar. 1792; and *Règlement concernant le service intérieur, la police, et la discipline de l'infanterie* of 24 June 1792. For the unit size of line infantry, see *Règlement sur la formation des bataillons d'infanterie destinés à entrer en campagne* of 15 Mar. 1792. For volunteer bataillons see the law of 4 Aug. 1791 in *AP*, 29:172–73. For cavalry see *Ordonnance . . . sur la formation . . . de la cavalerie* of 17 Mar. 1788. For artillery organization, see Lauerma, *L'artillerie de campagne*, 116. Squads of artillerymen attached to infantry demi-brigades contained fourteen men only. *Journal militaire* (1793), 776. Legislation of 12 Aug. and 22 Nov. 1793, which increased battalion size to 777 and then to 1,067, maintained the size of fusilier *ordinaires* at thirteen or fourteen men. *AP*, 72:83–84; 79:649.

2. For a list of soldier's basic equipment, see *Journal militaire* (1791), 627.

3. In the morning meat and dried or fresh vegetables would be cooked in a large wrought-iron pot called a *marmite*. After boiling, the meat was removed and set aside for the afternoon meal. Broth and vegetables were then divided. Half the soup was poured out into the lid of the *marmite*, bread added, and finally portioned out. This recipe for soup and the description of cooking it came from a 1788 or 1789 description of a field test of the new sixteen-man *marmite*. AG, MR 1772. The official ration for a French soldier in the year II was: 1 pound of meat, 1¾ pounds of bread, 1 ounce of rice, and 2 ounces of dried vegetables. Bertaud, *La Révolution armée*, 245. For changes in their allotment, see *Journal militaire*, (an II), 866. The *marmite* before 1788 was large enough for eight men; later *marmites* were large enough for sixteen. Both types were used during the early years of the war. *Instruction provisoire sur le campement de l'infanterie* of 1 Mar. 1792.

4. *Instruction provisoire sur le campement de l'infanterie* of 1 Mar. 1792.

5. The *Règlement sur la formation des bataillons d'infanterie destinés à entrer en campagne* of 15 Mar. 1792; *Règlement concernant l'exercice et manoeuvres de l'infanterie* of 1 Aug. 1791; *Ordonnance . . . sur la formation . . . de la cavalerie* of 17 Mar. 1788. For a useful chart concerning the characteristics and crews of French cannon, see Chandler, *Campaigns of Napoleon*, 358–59.

6. AG, B^{1*}121, order of 22–23 Apr. 1793; AG, B^{1*}121, order of 13–14 May 1793. For the intention to honor regulations scrupulously in other armies, see, for example, Colin, *La tactique et la discipline*, 22–23, 169.

7. AG, B^{1}28, 27 Mar. 1793, Souham to Pichegru.

8. See Dumouriez's request for camp equipment in La Jonquière, *Jemappes*, 96–97; *Journal militaire* (1793), 33; Charavay, *Correspondance de Carnot*, 2:173.

9. AG, B¹28, 27 Mar. 1794, Souham to Pichegru. An order issued 22 Apr. 1793 also implies that for the main body of the Armée du Nord there were sufficient camping supplies in the magazines. AG, B¹121. For comments on tents and encampments, see Duchet, *Deux volontaires*, 39, 41, 59; Bricard, *Journal*, 4; Gervais, *A la conquête*, 39; Grille, *Lettres, mémoires, et documents*, 3:160; Mathiez, *La victoire*, 95; Lombard, *Un volontaire de 1792*, 154; Terrade, "Journal d'un volontaire," 270.

10. See, for example, Bricard, *Journal*, 106, 113; Delaporte, "Campagne de l'an II," 342; Desdevises du Dézert, *Lettres du sergent Brault*, 13; AG, B¹22, 26 Nov. 1793, Ferrand to Bouchotte. Men without tents might also sleep in the open air.

11. Gervais, *A la conquête*, 28–30; Noël in Mathiez, *La victoire*, 84–85; see the song "La gamelle" in *Soirée de camp*, #8 (27 July 1794), 4.

12. See Duchet, *Deux volontaires*, 41; Bonneville, *Journal d'un volontaire*, 23; Noël in Mathiez, *La victoire*, 95.

13. *Règlement concernant le service intérieur* of 24 June 1792, 10–11; *Règlement pour la formation, organisation, solde, police et administration de l'infanterie—national—parisienne*, 33–34; Scott, "Line Army, 1787–1793," 138; Fricasse, *Journal de marche*, 7; Gervais, *A la conquête*, 35–37; Le Roy, *Souvenirs*, 51.

14. Bricard, *Journal*, 2, 52; Gervais, *A la conquête*, 15–38; Delaporte, "Campagne de l'an II," 352.

15. One particularly useful report concerns the 2nd Pas-de-Calais, a battalion of 1791 volunteers serving with the Armée du Nord. AG, Xʷ78. This unusual piece lists the names of 205 deserters, the company to which they belonged, and the days they deserted for the period October 1791 through December 1792. Before the victories of the fall of 1792, a soldier would have had to break military law and the moral code of his fellows to desert. Deserters consequently left as individuals in most cases (seventy-two) before 25 Nov. 1792. Interestingly, there were ten cases in which pairs of men from the same company left on the same day, presumably together. This suggests that buddy relationships were important. It is equally significant that there was no desertion by groups larger than two. Since the men of the 2nd Pas-de-Calais were Volunteers of 1791, they had enlisted to serve only one campaign. After the victory of Jemappes on 6 Nov. 1793, they would have felt free to leave the army as they wished, even if they had not received formal permission to return home. With little moral pressure against desertion, it soared. In the month between Nov. 24 and Dec. 28 the battalion lost 113 men. All but seven left in groups of from two to sixteen men from the same company. The pattern strongly suggests the formation of small groups within the company structure, which persevered even when the army itself no longer commanded the men's obedience. These small groups, if the deserters were indeed this, seem to have been formed only within, not across, company lines. Scott reports that deserters often left in pairs during the ancien régime. Scott, *Response of the Royal Army*, 37.

16. AG, MR 1897, "Service des armées en campagne: Comparison des règlements antérieurs à 1809, jusqu'à et y compris 1809."

17. Fricasse, *Journal de marche*, 5.

18. Bertaud, *La Révolution armée*, 176.

19. Bricard, *Journal*, 2, 64; 14 Dec. 1793 petition from the Bataillon des Amis in Bertaud, *La Révolution armée*, 167; Chuquet, *Lettres de 1793*, 137.

20. 28 Dec. 1793 petition by conscripts serving in the 3ᵉ bis Haute Garonne in Bertaud, *La Révolution armée*, 167.

21. AG, Xʷ78.

22. *AP*, 72:85; Bricard, *Journal*, 89–91.

23. Noël in Mathiez, *La victoire*, 84; Thiébault, *Mémoires*, 1:23–25; and for fear of esprit de corps, see 5 Jan. 1794 Projet de décret in Desbrière and Sautai, *La crise*, 205.

24. Noël in Mathiez, *La victoire*, 96; Thiébault, *Mémoires*, 1:251–52; La Jonquière, *Jemappes*, 164; Bertaud, *La Révolution armée*, 158–60; Lauerma, *L'artillerie de campagne*, 120, 127.

25. Censer, *Prelude to Power*, 42; "Le sans-culotte républicain," in Potevin et al., *Le sans-culotte républicain*, 1.

26. AG, B¹6, 13 Nov. 1792, printed report by Dubois-Crancé; and 13 Nov. 1792 circular written by Jourdeuil in Herlaut, *Bouchotte*, 1:254.

27. "La gamelle" in *Soirée de camp*, #8 (27 July 1794), 4; Pion des Loches, *Mes campagnes*, 17–18; Fricasse, *Journal de marche*, 43.

28. Fricasse, *Journal de marche*, 36–37.

29. Gauthier, *Les chansons de notre histoire*, 122; Loy, "Le livre de route," 405.

30. Marquant, "Carnet d'étapes, 48–49; AN, D1 16, 5 Sept. 1792, letter from Representatives Delmas, Dubois-Dubais, and Bellegarde; AG, B¹*121, Ordre du jour, 10–11 Aug. 1793, Etat-major de l'Armée du Nord. For oaths in local ceremonies see, for example, Duchet, *Deux volontaires*, 13–15, and Moreel, *La société populaire*, 65. See George, *Chinese Army*, ch. 7, for the importance of oaths and pledges in the Chinese army.

31. Joliclerc, *Ses lettres*, 103; Lombard, *Un volontaire de 1792*, 152; and a letter from a father in the Department of the Meuse to his son, from AG, Xʷ66 in Bertaud, *La Révolution armée*, 222.

32. Fricasse, *Journal de marche*, 29; Girardon, *Lettres*, 40. For other firsthand accounts see Bricard, *Journal*, 40; Picard, *Au service*, 137.

33. *Augus* #17 (10 July 1792); Lombard, *Un volontaire de 1792*, 152.

34. Vauvenargues in Léonard, *L'armée et ses problèmes*, 152.

35. Representatives on Mission at Maubeuge, 30 Oct. 1792, in La Jonquière, *Jemappes*, 84–85; minister of foreign affairs to Bouchotte, 29 Apr. 1793, in Rousset, *Les volontaires*, 189; Representatives Bentabole and Levasseur at the Camp de la Madeleine, 9 Aug. 1793, AG, B¹16.

36. Delaporte, "Campagne de l'an II," 389; Bertaud, *La Révolution armée*, 222.

37. Woloch, *French Veteran*, 90; Woloch, "War-Widows Pensions"; *Journal des hommes libres*, #96, in Delarue, "L'éducation politique," 221–22.

38. In Delarue, "L'éducation politique," 28, and in Rousset, *Les volontaires*, 198–99.

39. Brette, "Récits d'un volontaire," 524; and *Argus*, 456. On cash, see the case of St.-Just with the Rhin in Soboul, "Sur la mission de Saint-Just," 321, 337; see Bertaud, *La Révolution armée*, 204. There is some reason to argue that some soldiers saw money as demeaning to their sacrifices. Scott, *Response of the Royal Army*, 163.

Notes to "The Cult of the Bayonet"

1. Voltaire in Léonard, *L'armée et ses problèmes*, 235.
2. De Saxe in Carrias, *La pensée militaire française*, 170; Guibert, *Essai général*, 7.
3. Dubois-Crancé, *Observations*. Dumouriez used identical logic and also denied that French troops could be "reduced to the state of automatons." Dumouriez, *Mémoire sur l'armée*, 3.
4. La Jonquière, *Jemappes*, letter of 12 Apr. 1794 in Coutanceau, *La campagne de 1794*, part 2, 2:48–49.
5. AG, B¹19, 23 Sept. 1793, Representative Delbrel; General Souham in Coutanceau, *La campagne de 1794*, part 2, 2:5–6.
6. AG, MR 2041, Meunier, "Changements en errata au *Règlement de 1791*."
7. General Hardy in AG, B¹28, 6 Mar. 1793; Berthélemy in Dupuis, *La campagne de 1793*, 1:493; Committee of Public Safety decrees of 5 and 4 Mar. 1794, respectively, in Coutanceau, *La campagne de 1794*, part 1, 1:404.
8. Leclaire, *Mémoires et correspondance*, 91–92; Reinhard, *Carnot*, 2:80; Carnot in Coutanceau, *La campagne de 1794*, part 2, 1:5. Bouchotte reflected this directive when he wrote to Jourdan, who had just been reinstated and given command of the Armée de la Moselle. The letter ordered that French troops "without cease act offensively; it is necessary to haggle with our enemies no longer, but to march intrepidly at them and charge them with the bayonet as at Wattignies." Bouchotte's letter in AG, MR 608¹, Jourdan, "Mémoires militaires."
9. A document must be mentioned here, although it was not composed by an officer of the Nord. Dated 22 Nov. 1793, this report by an officer in the Armée du Rhin points up the use of the bayonet in another portion of the French frontier. Unpublished elsewhere, it deserves notice. Concluding his lengthy criticism of a suggested reform in battalion organization and drill, the commander of the 41st Demi-Brigade wrote: "The war of today proves the uselessness of a bunch of maneuvers which are brilliant on parade and seductive in their mathematical precision; these vaunted tactics give way everywhere to the bayonet and the charge; therefore, it is to the perfecting of the bayonet and the order and manner of making use of it that military men ought to direct their attention." AG, MR 2041, "Observations du commandant du batallion de la 41ᵉ Demi-Brigade." The above comments take on all the more meaning because of a postscript by General Mengaud, apparently the commander of the division of the *Bas Rhin:* "The undersigned general has found the observations made by the commanders of the 41st demi-brigade *Bas Rhin* . . . , very valid."
10. AG, B¹19, 29, Sept. 1793, General Houchard; AG, B¹298, May 1794, General Favereau; AG, MR 291, General Duhesmes; General Berthélemy in Dupuis, *La campagne de 1793*, 1:435.
11. For a discussion of the rationale behind the resurrection of the pike, see Lynn, "French Opinion and the Military Resurrection of the Pike."
12. AG, B¹13, 25 June 1793; AG, B¹18, 14 Sept. 1793, letter by General Beauregard.
13. *AP*, 47:121–24; Servan, *Plan d'organisation*, 1.
14. *AP*, 47:265–66; for example, the 10ᵉ *bataillon des piquiers* at Lille in AG, B¹*250, 1 Mar. 1793, Tableau; Jomini, *Histoire critique*, 4:123.
15. AG, B¹*243, correspondence of General Gougelot.

16. AG, B¹20, 19 Oct. 1793, General Elie; AG, B¹12, 4 Mar. 1793, General Dumouriez; and 14 May 1794, letter from Representatives Richard and Choudieu in Coutanceau, *La campagne de 1794,* part 2, 2:annexes.

17. Foy, *Histoire des guerres de la Péninsule,* 1:101; *AP,* 83:173.

Notes to "Cavalry and Artillery in an Infantry Army"

1. The four-volume history by Edouard Desbrière and Maurice Sautai stands as the classic account of cavalry during this era. *La cavalerie de 1740 à 1789. La cavalerie pendant la Révolution du 14 juillet 1789 au 26 juin 1794: La crise. La cavalrie pendant la Révolution du 19 juin 1794 au 27 octobre 1795: La fin de la Convention. La cavalerie sous le Directoire.* Fortunately for this study Desbrière and Sautai emphasized the Armée du Nord in their *La crise.* In this chapter, unless otherwise cited, the tactical and organizational details concerning cavalry have been taken from *La crise.*

2. Report presented to the National Assembly on 15 Dec. 1789 by General Félix de Wimpffen. *AP,* 10:587; letter of 15 Feb. 1794, *RACSP,* 10:168.

3. Scott, *Response of the Royal Army,* 5–6, and documents in Desbrière and Sautai, *La crise,* 6, 56–57, 151n.

4. *AP,* 59:166–67, 172; 77:475–77; 83:173.

5. *Etat* of 1 messidor an II, 19 June 1794, in Desbrière and Sautai, *La crise,* 293–96.

6. *AP,* 11:393; 2nd *état* of 1 Jan. 1792 in Desbrière and Sautai, *La crise,* 56–67.

7. Cales and Massieu, 21 Aug. 1793, *RACSP,* 6:51; Gauthier's estimate in Desbrière and Sautai, *La crise,* 184.

8. *AP,* 76:240–42; 76:713.

9. Godechot speaks of more than 10,000 cantons in France. *Les institutions de la France,* 475. At six horses per canton this would yield over 60,000 horses, which when added to the 39,000 horses of September, adds up to the nearly 100,000 estimated by Desbrière and Sautai, *La crise,* 297.

10. *AP,* 49:198.

11. *AP,* 62:187; 76:240.

12. Rothenberg argues that European armies prior to the Revolution contained 20–40 percent cavalry. Rothenberg, *Art of War,* 71. As specific examples that bracket the period consider the following cases. In 1758 the French army of the Lower Rhine boasted 112 battalions of infantry and 121 squadrons of cavalry with battalions of about 720 and squadrons of perhaps 170; the resultant proportion of cavalry was 20 percent. Kennett, *French Armies,* tables I, II. The Grand Armée of 1805 listed 226 battalions, 233 squadrons, and 161 companies of artillery and engineers. Manceron, *Austerlitz,* 79–80. With contemporary battalion and squadron strengths as shown by Chandler, *Campaigns of Napoleon,* 340, 352, cavalry strength amounted to about 23 percent including dismounted squadrons. In his 15 Dec. 1789 report to the National Assembly Wimpffen estimated than an army of 26,000 meant to fight in Germany should contain 5,000 cavalry, that is, 19 percent of the total number. *AP,* 10:587. The expansion of armies brought a general decline in the percentage of cavalry, and hard-pressed forces might have much less than 20 percent cavalry. Wellington had only 6 percent at Fuentes de Onoro. Rothenberg, *Art of War,* 71.

13. Situation reports in Desbrière and Sautai, *La crise,* 103–5, 151–53, 350, 361; La Jonquière, *Jemappes,* 49–51, 146; AG, B^{1*}250, situation reports.

14. Consider the 6th *Chasseurs à cheval* in mid-March. With an authorized strength of 1,020 men, it had 606 men and 634 horses on 15 Mar. 1793. Of these, 391 men were with the Nord and 305 were in depot. Desbrière and Sautai, *La crise,* 153.

15. Inspection reports in ibid., 194, 197–99; AG, B^{1*}251, situation reports.

16. AG, B^{1}15, 28 July 1793.

17. Situation reports in Desbrière and Sautai, *La crise,* 300, 409–13; AG, B^{1*}253, situation reports.

18. Desbrière and Sautai, *La crise,* 287–88; 20 Feb. 1794, *RACSP,* 11:300.

19. Desbrière and Sautai, *La crise,* 19.

20. Ibid., 271; Bodinier, "Les officiers," 67–68; Scott, "Professionalization of the French Officer Corps," 37.

21. For an analysis of the 1788 tactical ordinance, see Desbrière and Sautai, *La cavalerie de 1740 à 1789,* 99–103.

22. Moreau's division had only 176 cavalry out of 14,611 men, and Michaud's division had only 328 cavalry in a total force of 12,558. Situation report in Desbrière and Sautai, *La crise,* 412–13.

23. AG, B^{1}13, 1 June 1793; and AG, B^{1}16, 10 Aug. 1793. For anti-cavalry schemes advocating the pike, see AG, B^{1}15, 24 July 1793, Vézu; AG, B^{1}19, 23 Sept. 1793, Representative Delbrel; and the Gougelet correspondence in AG, B^{1*}243, 26 Dec. 1794, 2 Feb. 1794.

24. Chuquet, *Valenciennes,* 10; Coutanceau, *La campagne de 1794,* part 1, 2:vi.

25. The standard work on artillery is the excellent Lauerma, *L'artillerie de campagne.* When not otherwise cited, details on artillery matériel, organization, and performance have been taken from it.

26. Ibid., 99.

27. AG, B^{1*}253.

28. *AP,* 59:165; an order of the day from Valenciennes, dated 23–24 May 1793, stipulated that "each squad of line artillerymen attached to battalions of the army" should submit an updated *état.* AG, B^{1}12; tableau of 8 June 1794 in AG, B^{1*}253. The total number of effectives was 221,994, but this does not include the Armée des Ardennes. Of the gross figure, only 174,000 were listed as present under arms, giving an average of 1.3 battalion gun per 1,000 men.

29. Lauerma, *L'artillerie de campagne,* 131.

30. See 22 July 1793 report by Dormier in Coutanceau, *La campagne de 1794,* part 1, 2:264–65; 20 May 1794, General Elbé to General Leprun in Coutanceau, *La campagne de 1794,* part 1, 2:271.

31. Dupuis, *La campagne de 1793,* 1:48; Richard, *Le Comité du salut publique,* 228–76 (Lauerma, *L'artillerie de campagne,* 115, misapplies his figures); Rothenberg, *Art of War,* 123. A high percentage of the cannon forged were seige, garrison, and naval pieces; in 1789 the army had a total of 7,300 field pieces. Lauerma, *L'artillerie de campagne,* 115.

32. *AP,* 76:713; AG, B^{1*}253. These figures exclude the Ardennes.

33. The situation report of 8 June 1794 shows four entire companies, three half-companies, and parts of two others. AG, B^{1*}253.

34. Manceron, *Austerlitz,* 79–80, quotes a report showing 396 guns for 212,000

men. Chandler, *Campaigns of Napoleon*, 360, claims the highest concentration of cannon was the 600 cannon at Leipzig.

35. Bien, "La réaction aristocratique," 27–28.

36. Scott, "Line Army, 1787–1793," 138.

37. Bodinier, "Les officiers," 68.

38. *AP*, 84:430–31. Judging from situation reports of the Nord and Ardennes, the most likely centers for artillery schools and horse artillery depots were Douai and Lille.

39. Foy in Lauerma, *L'artillerie de campagne*, 119. See Pion des Loches, *Mes campagnes*, 24–25, on the poor quality of men in the 5th Regiment of foot artillery.

40. See the description of the school by Pion des Loches, *Mes campagnes*, 20–49.

41. See letters in Dupuis, *La campagne de 1793*, 1:214, 387, and in Coutanceau, *La campagne de 1794*, part 1, 2:158–62.

42. Using Nord figures of June 1794 already discussed, in a total of 345 to 415 pieces, 225, that is, 65 to 54 percent, were dispersed.

43. AG, B¹15, 28 July 1793, Kilmaine to Bouchotte.

44. Thiébault, *Mémoires*, 1:343; Custine in Lauerma, *L'artillerie de campagne*, 160; memoir on horse artillery in ibid., 99.

45. See Phipps, *Armies of the First Republic*, 1:261; Verney, ed., *Journals and Correspondence of Calvert*, 156.

46. Séruzier in Lauerma, *L'artillerie de campagne*, 127.

47. An 8 June 1794 tableau shows twelve stations for parts of eight companies. Only two companies were shown intact. AG, B¹*253. Bricard, *Journal*, 97.

48. 29 Apr. 1794 letter from Desjardin to Favereau in Coutanceau, *La campagne de 1794*, part 1, 1:755. See Houchard, "Instruction," in Dupuis, *La campagne de 1793*, 1:317.

49. Bricard, *Journal*, 20, 35, 45–46, 65, 107, 129–30, 134, 136.

50. Ibid., 35–36, 44–45, 97; Houchard, "Instruction," in Dupuis, *La campagne de 1793*, 1:323. Sir Harry Calvert wrote concerning practice before Houchard in 1793: "May 10, the Prussians and Austrians carried five of the enemies batteries; no guns were taken, owing to the enemy's practice of each night retiring their guns in the rear of their batteries and keeping them always limbered, ready to make their escape." Calvert, *Journals and Correspondence*, 73.

51. Bricard, *Journal*, 41–42, 46, 63, 134, 136.

Notes to "Training an Evolving Infantry"

1. 15 Dec. 1789 address in *AP*, 10:587.

2. Colin, *L'infanterie au XVIIIe siècle*, for an account of the systems contained in both the *Règlement* and the *Instruction*.

3. See B¹*111, 2 July 1793, order; AG, MR 2041, Meunier, "Changements an errata au *Règlement de 1791*"; B¹17, 24 Aug. 1794, order.

4. Line infantry fired only two shots daily, not enough to develop real proficiency. But Representative on Mission Gillet stated that "carabiniers," elite light infantry, should be chosen from the best marksmen in a light infantry battalion. Certainly, then, the *tirailleurs* must have practiced more than line units.

5. Gervais, who supplies one of the best accounts of training during 1794, required three months of actual drill before he went on campaign. In that time he had finished the *école de soldat* and the *école de peloton* and had at least begun the *école de bataillon*. Gervais, *A la conquête*, 35–39. A letter in the *Argus* of 26 July 1792 stated that a recruit needed "three months of musket drill at least . . . before he could render effective service."

6. AG, MR 254, Marshal Rochambeau; AG, B^1*245, 1 Jan. 1792, report.

7. Rochambeau in De Sérignan, *La première invasion*, 49.

8. Rochambeau, *Mémoires militaires*, 1:395–96; AG, B^{1}1, 15 Apr. 1793, instruction; De Sérignan, *La première invasion*, 121–22.

9. AG, B^{1}1, n.d. (This order must predate 15 Apr. 1792).

10. Rochambeau in De Sérignan, *La première invasion*, 83.

11. Ibid., 139–40, 156–57.

12. Lahure, *Souvenirs*, 18.

13. AG, B^1*249, 10 Aug. 1792, order of battle; "Décret relatif à l'instruction," in Deprez, *Les volontaires nationaux*, 207; for examples of such combat, see AG, B^{1}3, 3 Aug. 1792, Dumouriez to Balan; AG, B^{1}2, 25 July 1792, General A. Dillon; B^{1}2, 27 July 1792, *Bulletin;* AG, B^{1}2, 29 July 1792, General A. Dillon.

14. Situation reports from December 1791 to December 1792 contained in AG, B^1*249.

15. AG, B^{1}4, 18 Sept. 1792, General Dumouriez.

16. AG, B^1*249, 24 Oct. 1792, order of battle.

17. Dumouriez, Dampierre, and Berthier in La Jonquière, *Jemappes*, 147–48, 165, 169; AG, MR 270, Leclaire, "Mémoire."

18. AG, B^{1}8, 14 Jan. 1793.

19. AG, B^{1}8, 31 Jan. 1793, Colonel d'Hahu; AG, B^{1}10, 4 Mar. 1793, Chief of Battalion Vézu; AG, B^1*249, 20 Sept. 1792, order of battle.

20. AG, B^{1}6, 9 Nov. 1793, Commissioner Rolland; AG, B^{1}9, 7 Feb. 1793, *commissaire du conseil exécutif.*

21. Thiébault, *Mémoires*, 1:328.

22. In the order of battle dated 24 Oct. 1792 for Dumouriez's immediate command at Valenciennes, only thirteen 1792 battalions appear. Of these at least seven are from the Paris area. B^1*249, 24 Oct. 1792.

23. For this battalion see Fricasse, *Journal de marche;* situation reports contained in AG, B^1*250 and B^1*251.

24. AG, B^{1}4, 7 Sept. 1792.

25. See situation reports in AG, B^1*249 and B^1*250.

26. A decree of 5 May 1792 ordered that old battalions be augmented by 124 recruits; later this figure was raised to 226. Belhomme, *Histoire de l'infanterie*, 3:491; see Terrade, "Journal d'un volontaire."

27. Compare Miranda, *Correspondance*, with Dumouriez, *Mémoires*, 2:107.

28. At least this is how Dumouriez explained it in *Mémoires*, 2:119.

29. Bricard, *Journal*, 48.

30. Sorel, *L'Europe et la Révolution francaise*, 3:336.

31. Dampierre in Lachouque, *Aux armes citoyens*, 206; AG, B^{1}13, 7 June 1793, General Custine.

32. Figures on the size of the Nord and on the number and size of its battalions

are based on the situation reports contained in AG, B¹*250–53. For a detailed set of figures and charts concerning these details, see Lynn, "Revolution on the Battlefield," 115–19.

33. AG, B¹*240, 29 Mar. 1793, the minister of war to Dumouriez; AG, B¹11, 9 Apr. 1793, General Dampierre.

34. Commissioner Rolland ordered that each brigadier general report the strengths of his battalions. See, for example, B¹*121, 11–12 May 1793, order. Once it was decided that a battalion was to receive a definite number of recruits, men from that battalion were summoned to Sedan in order to fetch its contingent. One such order issued at Maubeuge read: "It will be commanded . . . one captain, two sergeants, four corporals, and two drummers taken in each one of the 18th and 68th Regiments to go to Sedan, there to find recruits from the contingent." AG, B¹12, 29 May 1792, order. Waiting at Sedan, the recruits who had marched in as groups ranging from a few men to entire battalions now formed into provisional companies of 100 men. AG, B¹11, 21 Apr. 1793, Representatives. It is simply unclear whether the battalion representatives simply chose a quota of men or whether Commissioner Rolland assigned them particular individuals.

35. AG, B¹12, 3 May 1793, Representative Deville.

36. AG, B¹*121, 9–10 May 1793, order. Each company of the battalion was to furnish six men.

37. 16 Apr. 1794, letter by Representatives on Mission in Foucart and Finot, *La défense nationale,* 1:425; AG, B¹*121, 24 Apr. 1793, order; AG, B¹12, 23 May 1793, order.

38. AG, B¹12, 28 May 1793, General Custine.

39. Gay de Vernon stated that of 36,000 infantry at the Camp de César, 6,000 had no muskets. In addition, "many were without shoes or coats, and a great number have lost some pieces of their armament." Gay de Vernon, *Mémoire,* 184, 189.

40. AG, B¹*121, 29–30 May 1793, order; AG, B¹*104, 20 May 1793, circular; AG, B¹*105, 79, 80–82, 89–90; Lachouque, *Aux armes citoyens,* 214; Phipps, *Armies of the First Republic* 1:186. A law of 18 Apr. 1793 had demanded these examinations, but circumstances had delayed implementation; between 5 and 11 June Custine received review reports from fifty-two battalions outside the Camp de César.

41. Gay de Vernon, *Mémoire,* 196.

42. For the efforts to strengthen the camp, see AG 270, Leclaire, "Mémoire"; AG, B¹11, n.d. Apr. 1793, letter by Varin and Celliez (misfiled, letter in fact dates from June 1793); AG, B¹*111, 19 June 1793, order; AG, B¹*111, 22 June 1793, order.

43. AG, B¹14, 12 July 1793, order; Bricard, *Journal,* 78, speaks of firing practice twice a day at César; Gervais, *A la conquête,* 37.

44. AG, B¹13, 18 June 1793, General Kilmaine; AG, B¹15, 31 July 1793, General Ferrand.

45. AG, B¹*121, 3 June 1793, order; AG, B¹*111, 2 July 1793, order.

46. AG, MR 2041, Meunier, "Changements."

47. Gay de Vernon, *Mémoire,* 197. Contrary to Gay de Vernon's account, however, which argues that Custine and his generals set up one skirmish after another, most of the combats that find their way into the reports were small defensive engagements brought about by Allied probes. See AG, B¹14, 2 July 1793, report; AG, B¹14, 7 July 1793, report.

48. Bricard, *Journal*, 76; see training orders issued at Maubeuge in AG, $B^1$17, Aug. 1793, order and by General Wisch down on the Semoy in AG, $B^1$17, 21 Aug. 1793 order.
49. AG, $B^1$17, 22 Aug. 1793, General Barthélemy.
50. AG, $B^1$17, 23 Aug. 1793, General Houchard, "Instruction."
51. AG, $B^1$18, 5 Sept. 1793, order.
52. Duhesmes, *Précis historique*, 154–55, 157; Kellermann, *Instruction*, 39; AG, $B^1$15, 28 July 1793, Representatives Delbrel, Le Vaneur, and Le Tourneur.
53. AG, $B^1$18, 3 Sept. 1793.
54. For example, see AG, $B^1$19, 20 Sept. 1793, administration of the Département du Nord; AG, B^{1*}223, 18 Sept. 1793, letter by Colonet Boguet.
55. AG, $B^1$17, 28 Aug. 1793, Representative Perrin; AG, $B^1$17, 28 Aug. 1793, Rochette; AG, $B^1$17, 27 Aug. 1793, Chaumont.
56. For the 30 July 1793 total, see Dupuis, *La campagne de 1793*, 1:7–24, 26–29.
57. *AP*, 75:252; 79:649; AG, MR 608^1, Jourdan, "Mémoires militaires"; AG, B^{1*}223, 4 Oct. 1793 and 8 Nov. 1793; AG, $B^1$19, 25 Sept. 1793; AG, $B^1$22, 8 Nov. 1793; AG, B^{1*}223, 4 Dec. 1793, General Jourdan.
58. Coutanceau, *La campagne de 1794*, part 1, 1:xviii, 347; AG, B^{1*}133, 14 Feb. 1793, Representative Gillet. See Cobb, *Les armées révolutionnaires*.
59. Bricard reported that at Cambrai on 15 Dec. 1793 "the garrison was assembled on the place d'armes, and a strong detachment of the *armée révolutionnaire* was then disarmed; the soldiers were incorporated into every unit, and the commander was arrested." Bricard, *Journal*, 83.
60. See Coutanceau, *La campagne de 1794*, part 1, 1:354–55.
61. *AP*, 83:125–26, 179–82, 199–203.
62. AG, B^{1*}223, 6 Nov. 1793, General Jourdan.
63. See AG, B^{1*}240, 17 Jan. 1794, letter by General Colaud; Gervais, *A la conquête*, 32; AG, $B^1$26, 25 Jan. 1974, General Ferrand; General Bertin to General Mareau in Coutanceau, *La campagne du 1794*, part 2, 2:annexes, 51.
64. AG, B^{1*}223, 20 Dec. 1793, General Jourdan; AG, B^{1*}223, 3 Jan. 1794, General Jourdan; AG, B^{1*}108, 19 Jan. 1794, order; AG, B^{1*}108, 27 Jan. 1794, order; AG, $B^1$26, 27 Jan. 1794, General Ferrand.
65. See AG, $B^1$18, 5 Sept. 1793, General Vandamme, "Récit abrégé"; AG, B^{1*}124, 13 Feb. 1794, General Souham.
66. Fricasse, *Journal de marche*, 21; Ernouf, *Souvenirs militaires*, 7.
67. AG, MR 280, General Reynier, "Operations"; AG, MR 271, General Desjardin.
68. Coutanceau, *La campagne de 1794*, part 1, 1:102; Gervais, *A la conquête*, 35; Ernouf, *Souvenirs militaires*, 12; Brault in Lachouque, *Aux armes citoyens*, 387.
69. AG, MR 273, General Lacroix; see as well Ernouf, *Souvenirs militaires*, 12; AG, $B^1$18, 5 Sept. 1793, General Vandamme, "Récit abrégé."
70. Gillet in Dupuis, *Les opérations militaires*, 509.
71. See Coutanceau, *La campagne de 1794*, part 1, 1:387.
72. AG, B^{1*}124, 25 Apr. 1794, General Souham; Coutanceau, *La campagne de 1794*, part 2, 2:360–61; AG, $B^1$33, 14 June 1794; AG, MR 291, General Duhesmes, "Mémoire militaire."
73. Gouvion St. Cyr, *Mémoires*, 1:4.
74. AG, $B^1$11, 25 Apr. 1794, General Lamarlière to Bouchotte; AG, $B^1$11, n.d.

(probably June), Representatives Varin and Celliez; AG, B¹13, 5 June 1793, Representatives Varin and Celliez to Bouchotte.

75. AG, B¹13, 5 June 1793, Representatives Varin and Celliez to Bouchotte; letter dated 11 Mar. 1794 in Ernouf, *Souvenirs militaires*, 12.

76. AG, B¹*133, Representative Gillet to the National Convention; AG, B¹28, 29 Mar. 1793, General Pichegru to Bouchotte; AG, B¹30, 29 Apr. 1793, General Souham.

Notes to "Line and Column on the Battlefield"

1. Over the last decade three works in particular have presented balanced views of French infantry tactics. Bertaud, *La Révolution armée*, and Ross, *From Flintlock to Rifle*, both derived their treatments of revolutionary infantry tactics from my dissertation. Rothenberg, *Art of War*, reached a moderate conclusion apparently just by splitting the difference between extremes.

2. Only a foot separated the ranks one from another. This distance was to be measured from the chest of the man in the rear to the back of the man in front of him. If the men wore packs, then the interval would be measured from chest to pack, and the line would be correspondingly thicker. *Règlement du 1ᵉʳ août 1791*.

3. See test results taken from Scharnhorst in Paret, *Yorck*, 273.

4. *Règlement du 1ᵉʳ août 1791*, 42–44, 68–70, 247–50; Colin, *La tactique et la discipline*, xvii–xxvii; Colin, *L'infanterie au XVIIIᵉ siècle*, 274.

5. Colin, *La tactique et la discipline*, lxv, lxvii.

6. Meunier, *Rapport*; Kléber's instructions in AG, MR 291, Duhesmes, "Mémoire militaire." Duhesmes stated that Kléber's instructions were the first written during the wars of the Revolution; interestingly enough, Schérer was present at the drafting of these instructions.

7. Further confusion results from the apparently loose definition of a line in the minds of some contemporary witnesses. Technically the linear formation was a rather tidy affair composed of reasonably well aligned ranks. But at times the term *en bataille* seems to have meant something far less regular. Consider, for example, Duhesmes's description of a 1793 infantry attack: "Is it necessary to go at the enemy to attack an outpost? A part of the force is detached *en tirailleurs;* the rest marches in line, moving off at a run without keeping ranks, leaving the flag in the rear, where it is often encountered after the combat, isolated without even ten men to guard it." Duhesmes, *Précis historique*, 155–56.

8. AG, B¹30, 26 Apr. 1794, General Cacault.

9. Leclaire, *Mémoires et correspondance*, 88; AG, B¹14, 29 Mar. 1793, General Soland.

10. AG, MR 273, Lacroix, "Précis des opérations."

11. AG, MR 270, Leclaire, "Mémoire."

12. Documentation for Neerwinden is far sketchier than that for Jemappes; in fact, we scarcely know how they fought there. But Bricard supplies information that implies that the French were in line. In his journal for 18 Mar. 1793 he recorded, "Never have we seen such a multitude of men ranged in line [*en bataille*], as this day. Our army, divided in two columns, deployed in three lines." And later, describing the bravery of a certain Morel of the 5th Paris, he wrote, "This brave

fellow had his two thighs carried away by a cannon ball. . . . The same ball cut off a leg of each of the two volunteers who were in closed file behind him." Bricard, *Journal*, 39, 40–41. These two comments certainly indicate a linear order in three ranks. This is sparse information, but some of the best available.

13. AG, B¹20, 19 Nov. 1793, General Elie; Arnaudin in Coutanceau, *La campagne de 1794*, part 2, 1:20.

14. AG, B¹23, 6 Dec. 1793, General Durulte.

15. Duhesmes, *Précis historique*, 157; AG, B¹19, 29 Sept. 1793, General Houchard; Fricasse, *Journal de marche*, 25.

16. AG, MR 270, Leclaire, "Mémoire"; AG, MR 291, Duhesmes, "Mémoire militaire."

17. Dampierre in La Jonquière, *Jemappes*, 165; AG, MR 270, Leclaire, "Mémoire."

18. AG, B¹30, 26 Apr. 1794, General Cacault; AG, MR 273, Lacroix, "Précis des opérations."

19. The columns detailed by the *Règlement* are listed below.

A.	Column by division— at full distance, at distance of a *peloton*, at distance of a section, closed	B.	Column by *pelotons*— at full distance, at distance of a section, closed
C.	Column by sections— at full distance	D.	Attack column

"At full distance" means that the intervals between the subdivision of a column were equal to the front of that subdivision. Thus, a column at full distance could deploy into line by a series of quarter-wheels by its constituent elements.

20. Meunier, *Rapport*, 17 (here Meunier wrote in the third person); Kléber in AG, MR 291, Duhesmes, "Mémoire militaire"; Schérer in Fabry, *Compagne d'Italie*, 3:63.

21. Meunier, *Rapport*, 37–38.

22. The vagaries of battlefield reports require a fairly awkward categorization in pursuit of accuracy. In Table A.2 of the appendix, the three largest subcategories of "In the Attack" do not reflect different uses of the column, but rather different degrees of specificity in the evidence. Under "In the Attack: 'Column' Specifically Stated" appear all those examples gleaned from reports that actually called the assault formation a *colonne serrée*, *colonne d'attaque*, or *colonne*. Cases in which the explicit information states that a force attacked in good order and in mass fall under "In the Attack: The Charge 'In Order' and 'In Mass.'" It would be most unlikely that this choice of words could describe anything other than attack columns, although one must be cautious in working with this evidence. Most difficult to handle, the third subcategory includes cases that appear to be column assaults, although a source only records that a bayonet assault occurred, perhaps as the commander ordered the charge to be beaten on the drums. In Table 4 this last group of examples receives the title, "In the Attack: The Charge '*à la baionette*' and '*battant la charge*.'" To count as definite column usage every possible case would risk distorting the evidence, but to leave out all but the most obvious cases would result in underestimating the role of the attack column.

23. Colin, *La tactique et la discipline*, lxiv.

24. Carrias, *La pensée militaire française*, 205; AG, MR 270, Leclaire, "Mémoire."
25. AG, B¹7, 7 Nov. 1792, Dumouriez; Dampierre in La Jonquière, *Jemappes*, 165.
26. Thiébault, *Mémoires*, 1:454–55.
27. Letter from Savary dated 11 May 1793 in Foucart and Finot, *La défense nationale*, 1:429; AG, B¹18, 11 Sept. 1793, General Houchard; Jourdan in Dupuis, *La campagne de 1793*, 1:472–73, 478–79; Leclaire, *Mémoires et correspondance*, 94–95; Reinhard, *Carnot*, 2:66–72, 80.
28. AG, B¹30, 26 Apr. 1794, General Cacault; AG, MR 291, Duhesmes, "Mémoire militaire."
29. AG, MR 291, Duhesmes, "Mémoire militaire."
30. Duhesmes, *Précis historique*, 160–61; AG, MR 272, Favereau, "Journal des opérations."
31. Dupuis, *La campagne de 1793*, 1:469; Thiébault, *Mémoires*, 1:454.
32. AG, B¹*298, 7 June 1794, General Kléber.
33. AG, B¹12, 31 May 1793, order; AG, B¹17, 23 Aug. 1793, General Houchard, "Instruction."
34. De Sérignan, *La première invasion*, 144; AG, B¹30, 26 Apr. 1794, General Cacault; AG, MR 291, Duhesmes, "Mémoire militaire."
35. In other European armies the outer rank knelt, braced the butts of their muskets against the solid earth, and slanted their bayonets outward to impale any unlucky horse that ventured too near. The *Règlement du I*ᵉʳ *août 1791* prescribed the *feux de deux rangs*, during which the first rank stood, but at least General Cacault's report leads one to believe that in the Nord the first rank also knelt when facing cavalry.
36. *Règlement du I*ᵉʳ *août 1791*, 339–45; AG, MR 2041, Meunier, "Changements."
37. General Mack's instruction for the 1794 campaign in Coutanceau, *La campagne de 1794*, part 2, 1:169.
38. AG, B¹30, Apr. 1794, General Cacault.
39. AG, MR 291, Duhesmes, "Memoire militaire"; AG, MR 271, Desjardin, "Journal des opérations."

Notes to "The Dimensions of Open Order Combat"

1. Duhesmes, *Précis historique*, 152.
2. Both Meunier and Duhesmes favored the smoothbore carbine as the best light infantry weapon. AG, MR 2041, Meunier "Changements"; Duhesmes in Paret, *Yorck*, 272.
3. Paret in *Yorck*, 271–73, presents test results reported in Scharnhorst, *Uber die Wirkung des Feurergewehr* (Berlin, 1813). See as well Chandler, *Campaigns of Napoleon*, 342; Rogers, *Weapons of the British Soldier*, 94.
4. AG, B¹*22, 26 Aug. 1793, Minister of War.
5. For an example of infantry running up ammunition, see the letter by General Bertin, in Coutanceau, *La campagne de 1794*, part 2, 2:51. These runners were recruits who had no muskets. A picture and story in Championnet, *Le livre du soldat français*, 86, tells of a French cavalryman named Mandeville who carried sacks of cartridges to *tirailleurs*.

6. AG, MR 277, Arnaudin "Mémoire historique"; Duhesmes, *Précis historique,* 154–55.

7. Situation reports in AG, B¹*250 and B¹*253.

8. AG, B¹*130, 11 Dec. 1793, order; AG, B¹*125, 13 Jan. 1794, General Sistrières.

9. For reactions to this practice, see AG, B¹2, 16 July 1792, General La Bourdonnaye; Gouvion St. Cyr, *Mémoires,* 29.

10. AG, B¹17, 23 Aug. 1793, General Houchard, "Instruction"; Duplaisset in Dupuis, *Les opérations militaires,* 557. See as well AG, B¹18, 5 Sept. 1793, Vandamme, "Récit abrégé."

11. Delaporte, "Campagne de l'an II," 360; Fricasse, *Journal de marche,* 26; AG, MR 2041, Meunier, "Changements."

12. Colin, *La tactique et la discipline,* lxviii; Le Couturier in ibid., c; Paret, *Yorck,* 70.

13. *Règlement provisoire* in Paret, *Yorck,* 68–69.

14. General Kléber's "Instruction" in AG, MR 291, Duhesmes, "Mémoire militaire."

15. Lafayette, *Mémoires,* 3:296.

16. For an extensive criticism of Duhesmes as a source, see Lynn, "Revolution on the Battlefield," 255–66.

17. AG, B¹28, 1 Mar. 1794, Representative Varin.

18. AG, B¹17, 23 Aug. 1793, General Houchard, "Instruction."

19. *Règlement du 1er août 1791,* 340; AG, B¹17, 23 Aug. 1793, General Houchard, "Instruction"; General Kléber's "Instruction" in AG, MR 291, Duhesmes, "Mémoire militaire."

20. AG, MR 271, Desjardin, "Mémoire des campagnes."

21. Ibid.

22. AG, B¹17, 27 Aug. 1793, Representatives.

23. AG, MR 291, Duhesmes, "Mémoire militaire."

24. Leclaire, *Mémoires et correspondance,* 82–83; AG, B¹17, 29 Aug. 1793, General Houchard; AG, B¹30, 26 Apr. 1794, General Reynier, "Journal."

25. *Règlement provisoire* in Paret, *Yorck,* 68–69.

26. Paret, *Yorck,* 69, 258; AG, B¹18, 5 Sept. 1793, General Vandamme, "Récit abrégé."

27. AG, B¹17, 23 Aug. 1793, General Houchard, "Instruction."

28. AG, B¹26, n.d. 1794, Poste of Zucotte, instructions.

29. AG, B¹18, 5 Sept. 1793, General Vandamme, "Récit abrégé."

30. AG, B¹31, 12 May 1794, General Reynier, "Journal"; and AG, B¹18, 5 Sept. 1793, General Vandamme, "Récit abrégé."

31. AG, MR 2041, Meunier, "Changements"; and AG, B¹*298, 5 May 1794, General Dessaubay.

32. Delaporte, "Campagne de l'an II," 345–48.

Note to "Conclusion"

1. From Scharnhorst's 1811 essay on infantry tactics in Paret, *Yorck,* 258.

Bibliography

I. Archival Sources

Archives de la guerre, Vincennes

Materials in the *Archives de la guerre* (AG) formed the basis of this study. Series B contains the general correspondence of the *Armée du Nord et des Ardennes*, while B^{1*} contains the registers of correspondence for the Nord and Ardennes. B^{1*} 244–54 comprises the situation reports of the Nord and Ardennes through August 1794.

B^{12*} consists of correspondence registers for the Ministry of War; more such registers are catalogued under X^s. B^{13} contains registers of orders from the Ministry of War.

The series MR, Mémoires et Reconnaissances, is a gold mine of reports, technical essays, and historical memoirs. Its rich funds have been catalogued by Louis Tuetey in *Catalogue des manuscrits des bibliothèques de France . . . Archives de Guerre*. 3 vols. Paris, 1912.

Series X^w provides the historian with a wealth of documents copied from departmental archives and collected at the *Archives de la guerre*. These pieces deal with volunteers and conscripts. They were collected by a military commission directed by General Dumont. Cartons dealing with different departments are of uneven quality and differing focuses.

Archives nationales, Paris

In preparing this volume, I was able to supplement the materials in the *Archives de la guerre* with cartons from series D and AF^{II} from the *Archives nationales* (AN). Series D contains correspondence of Representatives on Mission. The vital, and huge, series AF^{II} consists of the papers of the Committee of Public Safety, including their correspondence with Representatives on Mission.

II. Journals and Songbooks

Argus du Départment et de l'armée du Nord. Complete run available only at the municipal library of Valenciennes, Département du Nord.
Bulletin de la Convention nationale.

Chansonnier de la montagne ou recueil de chansons, vaudevilles, pots-pourris et hymnes patriotiques. Paris, an II.
Chansonnier national. n.p., n.d.
Chansonnier patriote ou receuil de chansons, vaudevilles et pots-pourris patriotiques. Paris, an I.
Chansons patriotiques chantée à Lille. Lille, an II.
Chansons patriotiques imprimés par ordre de l'Assemblée genéralé de la Section du Contrat-sociale. Paris, n.d.
Couplets chantés au banquet civique des employées au Département des affaires étrangères, et à la plantation de l'arbre de la liberté. Paris, an II.
Ferrand, veuve. *Le triomphe de la liberté et de l'égalité: Almanach républicain*. Paris, 1792.
Gerard. *Almanach de la Mère Gerard*. Paris, 1792.
Journal des hommes libres. (Le Républicain.)
Journal de la Montagne.
Journal de Paris.
Journal militaire.
Ladré. *Le chansonnier patriote, ou recueil de chansons nationales et autres, choisies, composées et chantées par Ladré père accompagné de son fils*. Paris, 1791.
La soirée de camp.
Maréchal, Sylvain. *La constitution française en chansons*. Paris, 1792.
Père Duchesne. Facsimile reproduction. 10 vols. Paris, 1969.
Piis. *Chansons patriotiques*. Paris, an II.
Potevin et al. *Le sans-culotte républicain*. Paris, an II.
Révolutions de Paris.
Rousseau, Thomas. *L'âme du peuple et du soldat*. 7 cahiers. Paris, n.d.
———. *Les chants de patriotisme avec des notes, dediés à la jeunesse citoyenne*. Paris, 1792.

III. Printed Materials

Archives parlementaires (AP), première serie, 1787–99. Originally edited by J. Mandival and E. Laurent. The volumes began to appear in 1867; the most recent volume appeared in 1980.
Ardant du Picq, Charles. *Battle Studies*. Harrisburg, 1947.
Audouin, Xavier. *Histoire de l'administration de la guerre*. 4 vols. Paris, 1811.
Aulard, Alphonse. *Le patriotisme française de la Renaissance à la Révolution*. Paris, 1921.
———. "Le presse officieuse sous la Terreur." In *Etudes et leçons sur la Révolution française*, edited by Alphonse Aulard. Paris, 1921.
Babeau, Albert. *La vie militaire sous l'ancien régime*. 2 vols. Paris, 1890.
Balland, J. B. *Mémoire sur l'organisation et l'administration des corps militaires*. Vannes, an X.
Barbé, J. J. "Le théâtre à Metz pendant la Rèvolution," *Annales historiques de la Révolution française*, 4 (1927): 359–88.
Baynes, John. *Morale; A Study of Men and Courage*. New York, 1967.
Belhomme. *Histoire de l'infanterie en France*. Tome III. Paris, 1899.

Bell, D. Bruce, and Beverly W. Bell, "Desertion and Antiwar Protest: Findings from the Ford Clemency Program," *Armed Forces and Society* 3 (1977): 433–43.
Belliard, Augustin-Daniel. *Mémoires*. 3 vols. Paris, 1842.
Bertaud, Jean-Paul. "Apercus sur l'insoumission et la désertion à l'époque révolutionnaire: Etudes et sources." In *Bulletin d'histoire économique et sociale de la Révolution française: Année 1969*. Paris, 1970.
———. "Le recrutement et l'avancement des officiers de la Révolution," *Annales historiques de la Révolution française*, 44 (1972): 513–36.
———. *La Révolution armée: Les soldats-citoyens et la Révolution française*. Paris, 1979.
———. *Valmy, la démocratie en armes*. Paris, 1970.
———. "Voies nouvelles pour l'histoire militaire de la Révolution," *Annales historiques de la Révolution française*, 47 (1975): 66–94.
Bien, David D. "La réaction aristocratique avant 1789: l'exemple de l'armée," *Annales: économies, sociétés, civilizations* 29 (1974): 23–48, 505–34.
Biron, Armand-Louis de Gontaut, duc le Lauzun, puis duc de. *Mémoires de M. le duc de Lauzun*. Paris, 1822.
Bled, O. *Les sociétés populaires à St. Omer pendant la Révolution*. St. Omer, 1907.
Bodinier, Capt. "Les officiers de l'armée royale et la Révolution." In *Le métier militaire en France aux époques des grandes transformations sociales*, edited by André Corvisier. Vincennes, 1980.
Boisantais, Bernard. *La bataille de Valmy n'a pas eu lieu*. Paris, 1967.
Bonnal, M., ed. *Les armées de la République*, 3d ed. Paris, 1894.
Bonnal de Ganges, Edmond. *Les représentants du peuple en mission près les armées, 1791–1797*. 4 vols. Paris, 1898–99.
Bonneville de Marsangy, Louis, ed. *Journal d'un volontaire de 1791*. Paris, 1888.
Bouchez, B., and P. Roux, ed. *Histoire parlementaire de la Révolution française*. 40 vols. Paris, 1834–38.
Brette. "Récits d'un volontaire de 1792." *Carnet de la Sabretache* (1911): 522–28.
Bricard, Louis. *Journal du cannonier Bricard, 1792–1802*. Paris, 1891.
Brinton, Clarence Crane. *The Jacobins*. New York, 1961.
Buck, James H., and Lawrence J. Korb, eds. *Military Leadership*. Beverly Hills, 1981.
Carnot, Lazare. *Décret de l'Assemblée nationale du premier août 1792, l'an IVe de la Liberté, sur une fabrication de piques, précédé du rapport fait le même jour, au nom de la Commission militaire*. Paris, 1792.
———. *Exploits des Français*. Bale, 1796.
———. *Rapport et projet de décret sur la distribution de piques*. Paris, 1792.
Carrias, Eugene. *La pensée militaire française*. Paris, 1960.
Censer, Jack Richard. *Prelude to Power: The Parisian Radical Press, 1789–1791*. Baltimore, 1976.
Championnet. *Le livre du soldat français*. Paris, n.d.
Chandler, David G. *The Campaigns of Napoleon*. New York, 1966.
Chassin, Charles L. *L'armée et la Révolution*. Paris, 1867.
Chuquet, Arthur. *Dumouriez*. Paris, 1914.
———. *Le général Dagobert*. Paris, 1914.
———. *Les guerres de la Révolution*. 11 vols. Paris, 1886–96.
———, ed. *Lettres de 1792*. Paris, 1911.

———, ed. *Lettres de 1793*. Paris, 1911.
———. *Quatre généraux de la Révolution: Houche & Desaix, Kléber & Marceau*. Paris, 1911.
Clapham, J. H. *The Causes of the War of 1792*. Cambridge, 1899.
Cobb, Richard C. *Les armées révolutionnaires, instrument de la Terreur dans les départements*. 2 vols. Paris, 1961–63.
Coignet, Jean Roch. *Les cahiers du capitaine Coignet, 1799-1815*, edited by Lorédan Larchey. Paris, 1899.
Colby, Elbridge. *Masters of Mobile Warfare*. Princeton, 1943.
Colin, Jean. *L'infanterie au XVIIIe siècle: La tactique*. Paris, 1907.
———. *La tactique et la discipline dans les armées de la Révolution: Correspondance du général Schauenbourg du 4 avril au 2 août 1793*. Paris, 1902.
———. *The Transformations of War*, translated by Pope-Hennessey. London, 1912.
Correspondance générale de Carnot, edited by Etienne Charavay. 4 vols. Paris, 1892–1907.
Corvisier, André. *L'armée française de la fin du XVIIe siècle au ministère de Choiseul: Le soldat*. 2 vols. Paris, 1964.
———. *Armies and Societies in Europe, 1494-1789*, translated by Abigail T. Siddall. Bloomington, Ind., 1979.
———. "Les généraux de Louis XIV et leur origine sociale," *XVIIe siècle* (1956): 23–53.
———. "Hiérarchie militaire et hiérarchie sociale à la vielle de la Révolution," *Revue internationale d'histoire militaire*, 30 (1970): 77–91.
Coutanceau, H., H. Lepus, and Clément La Jonquière. *La campagne de 1794 à l'armee du Nord*, part 1, 2 vols., and part 2, 2 vols. Paris, 1903–8.
Currey, Cecil B. [Cincinnatus]. *Self-Destruction*. New York, 1981.
Davout, Louis. *Le maréchal Davout, correspondance inédite 1790–1815*. Paris, 1887.
De Cardinal, L. *La province pendant la Révolution: Histoire des clubs Jacobins, 1789-1795*. Paris, 1929.
Defay, Pierre. *Les sociétés populaires et l'armée, 1791-1794*. Paris, 1913.
Delaporte, Pierre. "Campagne de l'an II: Journal du conscrit Pierre Delaporte." *Nouvelle revue retrospective*. 11(1899): 337–60, 385–417.
Delarue, M. "L'éducation politique à l'armée du Rhin, 1793–1794." Mémoire de maitrise, Université de Paris–Nanterre, 1967–68.
Déprez, Eugène. *Les volontaires nationaux, 1791-1793*. Paris, 1908.
Desbrière, Edouard, and Maurice Sautai. *La cavalerie de 1740-1789*. Paris, 1906.
———. *La cavalerie pendant la Révolution du 14 juillet 1789 au 26 juin 1794: La crise*. Paris, 1907.
Desdevises du Dézert, ed. *Les lettres du sergent Brault*. Clermont-Ferrand, 1897.
De Sérignan. *La première invasion de la Belgique*. Paris, 1903.
Dollard, John. *Fear in Battle*. New Haven, Conn., 1943.
Dubois-Crancé. *Compte rendu à la Convention nationale de la mission des Representants du Peuple à l'Armée des Alpes 3 mai-12 oct. 1793*. Lyon, 1793.
———. *Décret de la Convention nationale 21 fevrier 1793*. Paris, 1793.
———. *Dialogue entre le père Duchêne et Carra, sur l'état actuel de la République française*. Paris, 1793.
———. *Discours de M. Dubois de Crancé à son bataillon, juin 1791*. Paris, 1791.

———. *Discours sur notre situation politique*. Paris, 1794.
———. *Observations sur la constitution militaire*. Paris, n.d.
———. *Rapport sur l'embrigadement des armées*. Paris, 1793.
———. *Rapport sur les moyens de défense général pour l'année 1793*. Paris, n.d.
———. *Second rapport du Comité militaire sur l'etablissement des milices nationales et le recrutement de l'armée*. Paris, 1789.
———. *Sentiments d'un républicain*. Rennes, n.d.
———. *Suite de Rapport sur l'embrigadement des armées*. Paris, 1793.
Du Casse, A. *Le général Vandamme et sa correspondance*. vol. 1. Paris, 1870.
Duchet, L., ed. *Deux volontaires de 1791, Les frères Favier de Montluçon: Journal et lettres*. Montluçon, 1909.
Duhesmes, P. G. *Précis historique de l'infanterie légère*. Lyon, 1806.
Dumas, Mathieu. *Souvenirs de Mathieu Dumas de 1770–1836*. 3 vols. Paris, 1836.
Dumouriez, Charles-François. *Mémoire sur l'armée de ligne lu à la société des amis de la constitution à Nantes, 21 juin 1791*. Nantes, 1791.
———. *Mémoires du Dumouriez*. 2 vols. Hamburg and Leipzig, 1794.
Dupuis, Victor. *La campagne de 1793 à l'armée du Nord et des Ardennes*. 2 vols. Paris, 1906–9.
———. *Les operations militaires sur la Sambre en 1794: La bataille de Fleurus*. Paris, 1907.
Duruy, Albert, *L'armée royale en 1789*. Paris, 1888.
Elbée Comte d'. *La veritable manière de composer les troupes réglées en France, d'après l'esprit et le caractère de la nation*. Paris, 1789.
Ellis, John. *The Sharp End*. New York, 1980.
Ernouf. *Souvenirs militaires d'un jeune abbé, soldat de la République, 1793–1801*. Paris, 1881.
Fabry, G. *Campagne d'Italie 1796–1797*. Vol. 3. Paris, 1901.
Flocon. *Milice et volontaires du Puy-de-Dôme*. Paris, 1911.
Foucart, Paul, and Jules Finot, eds. *La défense nationale dans le nord 1792 à 1802*. 2 vols. Lille, 1890–93.
Foy. *Histoire de la guerre de la Péninsule*. Vol. 1. Paris, 1827.
Frémont, Paul. *Les payeurs d'armées 1293–1870*. Paris, 1906.
Friant. *Vie militaire du lieutenant-général Comte Friant*. Paris, 1857.
Fricasse, Jacques. *Journal de marche du sergent Fricasse de la 127e demi-brigade*. Paris, 1882.
Fried, Martin, ed. *War: The Anthropology of Armed Conflict*. Garden City, N.J., 1968.
Fuller, J. F. C. *Sir John Moore's System of Training*. London, 1924.
Gasmann, Emile, trans. *La bataille d'Hondschoote*. Hazerbrouck, 1857.
Gauthier, André. *Les chansons de notre histoire*. Paris, 1967.
Gay de Vernon, Louis. *Mémoire sur les operations militaires pendant les années 1792 et 1793*. Paris, 1844.
George, Alexander L. *The Chinese Communist Army in Action: The Korean War and its Aftermath*. New York, 1967.
———. "Primary Groups, Organization, and Military Performance." In *Handbook of Military Institutions*, edited by R. W. Little. Beverly Hills, 1971.
Gerome. *Essai historique sur la tactique de l'infanterie*, 2nd ed. Paris, 1903.

Gervais. *A la conquête de l'Europe: Souvenirs d'un soldat de la Révolution et de l'Empire*. Paris, 1939.
Gibbs, Norman H. "Armed Forces and the Art of War," in *The New Cambridge Modern History*, vol. 9, edited by C. W. Crawley. Cambridge, 1965.
Girard, Georges. *Le service militaire en France à la fin du règne de Louis XIV: Racolage et milice, 1701–1715*. Paris, 1924.
Girardon, Pierre. *Lettres de Pierre Girardon*, edited by Louis Morin. Barsur-Aube, 1898.
Glasser, Ronald J. *365 Days*. New York, 1972.
Glover, Richard. *Peninsular Preparation*. Cambridge, 1963.
Godart, Roch. *Mémoires du général Roch Godart, 1792–1815*, edited by J. B. Antoine. Paris, 1895.
Godechot, Jacques. *Les institutions de la France sous la Révolution et l'Empire*, 2nd ed. Paris, 1968.
———, ed. *Fragments des mémoires de Charles-Alexis Alexandre sur sa mission aux armées du Nord et de Sambre-et-Meuse*. Paris, 1941.
Gosset, Pol. "Le comité de surveillance de Mars, Reims, 1793–1794," *Nouvelle revue de Champagne et de Brie*, 6 (1928): 129–43.
Gouvion Saint-Cyr. *Mémoires sur les campagnes des Armées du Rhin et de Rhin-et-Moselle de 1792 jusqu'à la paix de Campo-Formio*. 2 vols. Paris, 1829.
Greer, Donald. *The Incidence of the Emigration during the French Revolution*. Cambridge, Mass., 1951.
Grille, François, ed. *Lettres, mémoires, et documents publiés avec des notes sur la formation, le personnel, l'esprit du 1er bataillon des volontaires de Maine-et-Loire*. 4 vols. Paris, 1848–50.
Grindel, E., and Richard, eds. *Cahiers de vieux soldats*. Paris, 1903.
Gross, J. P. "Saint-Just, représentant en mission." Thèse, Université de Paris—I, 1973.
Guerres de la révolution et du premier empire. Vol. 1. Paris, 1876.
Guibert, Jacques-Antoine-Hypolite de. *Essai général de tactique*. 2 vols. London, 1773.
Hanoteau, Gabriel, ed. *Histoire de la nation française*. Tome VII, *Histoire militaire et navale*. 2 vols. Paris, 1925.
Hardy, Jean. *Mémoires militaires 1792–1802*. Paris, 1883.
Hartmann, L. *Les officiers de l'armée royale et la Révolution*. Paris, 1910.
Hauterive, M.A.d', ed. *Lettres d'un chef de brigade du 33e de ligne, 65e et 68e demi-brigades, 56e de ligne*. Paris, 1891.
Helmer, John. *Bringing the War Home*. New York, 1974.
Henderson, William Darryl. *Why the Vietcong Fought: A Study of Motivation and Control in a Modern Army in Combat*. Westport, Conn., 1979.
Herlaut, Auguste Philippe. *Le colonel Bouchotte, ministre de la guerre en l'an II*. Paris, 1946.
———. "Le republicainization des états-majors." *Annales historiques de la Révolution française*, 14 (1937): 385–409, 537–51.
Hilliers, Baraguay d'. *Mémoires du général Custine rédigés par un de ses Aides de camp*. 2 vols. Hamburg and Frankfort, 1794.

Houchard, fils. *Notice historique et justificative sur la vie militaire de général Houchard par son fils*. Strasbourg, 1809.
Hyslop, Beatrice Fey. *French Nationalism in 1789 according to the General Cahiers*. New York, 1934.
Instruction provisoire sur la campement de l'infanterie du 1ᵉʳ mars 1792.
Iung, Theodore. *L'armée et la Révolution, Dubois-Crancé, mousquetaire, constituant, conventionnel, général de division, ministre de la guerre, 1747–1814*. 2 vols. Paris, 1884.
Jacob, Louis. "Un essay de fédération de sociétés montagnardes à Arras en octobre 1793," *Annales historiques de la Révolution française*, 4 (1927): 476–80.
Jannin, J. C. "Lettres de J. C. Jannin, sergent-major vaguemestre au 1ᵉʳ bataillon de la Haute-Saone." *Carnet de la Sabretache* (1899): 400–414.
Janowitz, Morris. *Sociology and the Military Establishment*. New York, 1959.
Jarry. *Projet de formation de l'armée française*. Versailles, 1789.
Jaurès, Jean. *L'armée nouvelle*. Paris, 1915.
Joliclerc, François. *Joliclerc, Volontaire aux armées de la Révolution: Ses lettres, 1793–1796*. Paris, 1905.
Jomini, A. H. *Histoire critique et militaire des campagnes de la Révolution*. 15 vols. Paris, 1820–24.
Jouan, Louis. *La campagne de 1794–1795 dans les Pays-Bas*. Vol. 1. Paris, 1915.
Keegan, John. *The Face of Battle*. New York, 1976.
Kellermann, François-Etienne-Christophe. *Exposé de la conduite de Kellermann depuis l'année 1790, jusqu'à l'éqoque de son arrestation au 18 octobre 1793*. N.p., n.d.
———. *Instruction pour les troupes de la république*. Nice, an III.
———. *Règlement militaire pour l'Armée des Alpes*. N.p., 1791.
Kennett, Lee. *The French Armies in the Seven Years War*. Durham, 1967.
Lachouque, Henry. *Aux armes citoyens! Les soldats de la Révolution*. Paris, 1969.
Lafayette. *Mémoires*. Vol. 3. Paris, 1837.
Lahure, Louis-Joseph. *Souvenirs de la vie militaire du lieutenant-général Lahure*. Paris, 1895.
La Jonquière, Clément de. *La Bataille de Jemappes*. Paris, 1902.
Lallemand. *Tactique française*. Paris, 1793.
Lancelin, H. *Histoire de Valenciennes depuis ses origines*. Valenciennes, 1933.
Lang, Kurt. *Military Institutions and the Sociology of War*. Beverly Hills, 1972.
Latreille, Albert. *L'oeuvre militaire de la Révolution: L'armée et la nation à la fin de l'ancien régime: Les derniers ministres de la guerre de la monarchie*. Paris, 1914.
Lauerma, Matti. *L'artillerie de campagne française pendant les guerres de la Révolution*. Helsinki, 1956.
Lavasseur, R. *Mémoires*. Paris, 1829.
Leclaire, Théodore-François-Joseph. *Mémoires et correspondance du général Leclaire, 1793*. Paris, 1904.
Lecluselle, A. *Histoire de Cambrai de 1789 à nos jours suivie de tablettes cambresiennes*. 2 vols. Cambrai, 1872–74.
Legrand, Antoine. *La justice militaire et la discipline à l'armée du Rhin et a l'armée du Rhin-et-Moselle 1792–1796*, edited by L. Hennequin. Paris, 1909.
Legrand, Robert. "Les fêtes civiques à Abbéville," *Bulletin de la société d'émulation historique et litteraire d'Abbéville*, 24 (1978): 373–426.

———. "Les structures sociales de la société populaire d'Abbéville," *Bulletin de la société d'émulation historique d'Abbéville* (1965): 562–80.
Leleu, Edmond. *La société populaire de Lille, 1789–1795.* Lille, 1919.
Lemaire, L. "Les Jacobins à Dunkerque, histoire d'un club, 1790–1795," *Bulletin de l'Union Faulconnier*, 16 (1913): 317–464.
Léonard, Emile G., *L'armée et ses problèmes au XVIIIe siècle.* Paris, 1958.
———. "La question sociale dans l'armée française au XVIIIe siècle," *Annales: économies, sociétés, civilizations*, 3 (1948): 135–49.
Le Roy, Claude F. M. *Souvenirs de C.F.M. Le Roy, major d'infanterie vétéran des armées de la République et de l'Empire, 1767–1851.* Paris, 1908.
Leuillot, Paul, ed. *Les Jacobins de Colmar: Procès-verbaux des séances de la société populaire, 1791–1795.* Strasburg, 1923.
Levi. *Les Français à Furnes (1792–1794).* Dunkirk, 1911.
Lhomel, Georges de. *Journal de la Révolution à Montreuil-sur-Mer.* Abbéville, 1905.
Little, Roger W. "Buddy Relationships and Combat Performance." In *The New Military*, edited by Morris Janowitz. Beverly Hills, 1964.
Lombard, Jean. *Un volontaire de 1792.* Paris, 1892.
Loy, ed. "Le livre de route du caporal Joseph-Claude Tondeur de la 94e demi-brigade, 1793–1801." *Carnet de la Sabretache* (1928): 394–417.
Lynn, John A. "Esquisse sur la tactique de l'infanterie des armées de la République," *Annales historiques de la Révolution française*, 44 (1972): 539–58.
———. "French Opinion and the Military Resurrection of the Pike," *Military Affairs*, 41 (Feb. 1977): 1–7.
———. "The Growth of the French Army during the Seventeenth Century," *Armed Forces and Society*, 6 (1980): 568–85.
———. "The Revolution on the Battlefield: Training and Tactics of the *Armée du Nord*, 1792–1794." Ph.d. diss., University of California, Los Angeles, 1973.
MacDonald, Alexandre. *Souvenirs.* Paris, 1892.
Maeght, Xavier. "Deux journaux du Département du Nord en 1792," *Annales historiques de la Révolution française* (1974): 216–34.
———. "La presse dans le Département du Nord sous la Révolution française." Thèse, doctorat de 3e cycle, Université de Lille–III, 1971.
Manceron, Claude. *Austerlitz.* Paris, 1960.
Mandelbaum, David G. *Soldier Groups and Negro Soldiers.* Berkeley, 1952.
Mangerel, Maxime, ed. *Le capitaine Gerbaud, 1773–1799.* Paris, 1910.
Marquant, François. *Carnet d'étapes du dragon Marquant*, edited by G. Vallée and G. Pariset. Paris, 1898.
Marshall, Samuel L. A. *Men against Fire.* Gloucester, Mass., 1978.
Martin, Marc. "L'information de guerre dans la presse parisienne de 1792 à 1800: L'exemple du *Moniteur universel.*" In *Voies nouvelles pour l'histoire de la Révolution française*, edited by Albert Soboul.
———. "Journaux d'armées au temps de la Convention," *Annales historiques de la Révolution française*, 44 (1972): 567–605.
———. "Les origines de la presse militaire en France à la fin de l'ancien régime et sous la Révolution, 1770–1799." Thèse, doctorat de 3e cycle, Université de Paris–II, 1972.

Mathiez, Albert. "La presse subventionnée en l'an II," *Annales révolutionnaires* (1918): 112–13.
———. *La victoire en l'an*. Paris, 1916.
Mention, Léon. *L'armée de l'ancien régime de Louis XIV à la Révolution*. Paris, n.d.
Mercer, Charles. *Legion of Strangers*. New York, 1964.
Merchier, A. *La bataille de Tourcoing*. Roubaix, 1894.
Merilys, Jean. "La propaganda révolutionnaire dans l'armée en 1789." *La revue hebdomadaire* (22 May 1937).
Meunier, H. A. J. *Evolutions par brigades*. Paris, 1814.
———. *Rapport fait au ministre de la guerre par son ordre sur l'instruction du général Schauenburg, concernant les exercises et manoeuvres de l'infanterie*. Paris, an VII.
Michon, Georges. "L'armée et la politique intérieure sous la Convention," *Annales historiques de la Révolution française*, 4 (1927): 529–46.
———. *La justice militaire sous la Révolution*. Paris, 1922.
Miranda, Francisco de. *Correspondance du général Miranda avec le général Dumouriez, les ministres de guerre, Pache et Beurnonville, depuis janvier 1793*. Paris, 1793.
Money, J. *The History of the Campaign of 1792*. London, 1794.
Moran, Lord. *The Anatomy of Courage*. Boston, 1967.
Moreel, Leaon. *La société populaire de Bergues, 1789–1795*. Lille, 1926.
Morel, Jean. "Histoire de Valenciennes sous la Révolution d'après une étude de l'imprimé." Mémoire de maitrise, Université de Lille–III, 1971.
Moskos, Charles C., Jr. *The American Enlisted Man*. New York, 1970.
"Nouveautés touchant l'artillerie." *Carnet de la Sabretache* (1899): 89–100.
Ordonnance . . . sur la formation . . . de cavalerie du 17ᵉ mars 1788.
Palmer, R. R. "Frederick the Great, Guibert, Bulow: From Dynastic to National War." In *Makers of Modern Strategy*, edited by E. M. Earle. Princeton, 1941.
Paret, Peter. "Colonial Experience and European Military Reform at the End of the Eighteenth Century," *Bulletin of the Institute of Historical Research*. 37 (May 1964): 47–59.
———. *Yorck and the Era of Prussian Reform*. Princeton, 1966.
Pastoors, A. *Histoire de la ville de Cambrai pendant la Révolution 1789–1802*. 2 vols. Cambrai, 1908.
Petitfrière, Claude, ed. *Le général Dupuy et sa correspondance, 1792–1798*. Paris, n.d.
Phipps, Ramsay. *The Armies of the First Republic*. 5 vols. London, 1926–39.
Picard, Ernest, ed. *Au service de la nation: Lettres de volontaires, 1792–1798*. Paris, 1914.
Picard, Louis. *La cavalerie dans les guerres de la Révolution et de l'Empire*. 2 vols. Saumur, 1895–96.
Pierart, Z. J. *La grande épopée de l'an II*, 2nd ed. Paris, 1864.
Pierre, Constant. *Les hymnes et chansons de la Révolution*. Paris, 1904.
Pioger, A. "Lettres de Pierre Cohin volontaire à l'armée du Nord et de membres de sa famille, 1777–1794." *Annales historiques de la Révolution francaise* (1955): 124–42.
Pion des Loches, Antoine. *Mes campagnes*, edited by Maurice Chipon and Léonce Pingaud. Paris, 1889.
Poisson, C. *L'armée et la garde nationale*. 4 vols. Paris, 1858–62.
Prebble, John. *Mutiny*. London, 1975.

Procès verbaux de Comité d'instruction publique, edited by J. Guillaume. 6 vols. Paris, 1891–1907.
Quimby, Robert S. *The Background of Napoleonic Warfare.* New York, 1957.
Reboul, F. *La vie au dix-huitième siècle: L'armée.* Paris, 1931.
Recueil des actes du Comité de salut public. Edited by Alphonse Aulard and completed by P. Mautouchet and G. Lefebvre. 28 vols., 2 vols. of index. Paris, 1889–1951.
Règlement concernant l'exercise et manoeuvres de l'infanterie du 1ᵉʳ août 1791.
Règlement concernant le service intérieur, la police et la discipline de l'infanterie du 24ᵉ juin 1792.
"Règlement pour l'armée de Dumouriez." *Carnet de la Sabretache* (1899): 57–63.
Règlement pour la formation, organization, solde, police, et administration de l'infanterie—nationale—parisienne, 1789.
Règlement provisoire, concernant le service intérieur, la police et la discipline des troupes de l'infanterie du 1ᵉʳ juillet 1788.
Règlement provisoire sur le service de l'infanterie en campagne du 12ᵉ août 1788.
Règlement provisoire sur le service de l'infanterie en campagne du 5 avril 1792.
Règlement sur la formation des bataillons d'infanterie destinés à entrer en campagne du 15ᵉ mars 1792.
Reinhard, Marcel. *Le grand Carnot.* 2 vols. Paris, 1950–52.
Ringer, Alexander L. "Cherubini's *Médée* and the Spirit of French Revolutionary Opera." In *Essays in Musicology in Honor of Dragon Plamenac,* edited by Gustave Reese and Robert J. Snow. Pittsburgh, 1969.
———. "The Political Uses of Opera in Revolutionary France." In *Sonderdruck aus Bericht uber den internationalen musikwissenschaflichen Kongress.* Bonn, 1970.
Rochambeau, Jean-Baptiste de Vimeur, comte de. *Mémoires militaires, historiques et politiques de Rochambeau.* vol. 1. Paris, 1809.
Rogers, Cornwall. *The Spirit of Revolution in 1789.* Princeton, 1949.
Rogers, H. C. B. *Weapons of the British Soldier.* London, 1960.
Rojas, Aristides, ed. *Miranda dans la Révolution française.* Caracas, 1889.
Ropp, Theodore. *War in the Modern World.* Durham, 1959.
Ross, Steven T. "The Development of the Combat Division in Eighteenth-Century French Armies," *French Historical Studies,* 4 (1965): 84–94.
———. *From Flintlock to Rifle: Infantry Tactics, 1740–1866.* London, 1979.
———. *Quest for Victory: French Military Strategy, 1792–1799.* New York, 1973.
Rothenberg, Gunther. *The Art of War in the Age of Napoleon.* Bloomington, Ind., 1970.
Rousset, Camille. *Histoire de Louvois.* 4 vols. Paris, 1879.
———. *Les volontaires, 1791–1794.* Paris, 1892.
Saint-Albin, A. R. C. de. *Championnet général des armées de la République française,* 2nd ed. Paris, 1861.
Samion, L. *Kellermann, l'homme du 20 septembre.* Paris, 1893.
Sarkesian, Sam C., ed. *Combat Effectiveness: Cohesion, Stress, and the Volunteer Military.* Beverly Hills, 1980.
Saxe, Marshal Maurice de. *My Reveries on the Art of War,* trans. T. R. Phillips. In *Roots of Strategy,* edited by Thomas R. Phillips. Harrisburg, 1940.

Scott, Samuel F. "The French Revolution and the Line Army, 1787–1793." Ph.d. diss., University of Wisconsin, 1968.

———. "The French Revolution and the Professionalization of the French Officer Corps, 1789–1793." In *On Military Ideology*, edited by Morris Janowitz and Jacques van Doorn. Rotterdam, 1971.

———. "Les officiers de l'infanterie de ligne à la veille de l'Amalgame," *Annales historiques de la Révolution française*, 40 (1968): 455–71.

———. "The Regeneration of the Line Army during the French Revolution," *Journal of Modern History*, 42 (1970): 307–30.

———. *The Response of the Royal Army to the French Revolution: The Role and Development of the Line Army 1787–93*. Oxford, 1978.

———. "Les soldats de l'armée de ligne en 1793," *Annales historiques de la Révolution française*, 44 (1972): 493–512.

Servan, Joseph. *Plan d'organisation pour des bataillons de piquiers*. Paris, 1792.

———. *Recherches sur la force de l'armée française, depuis Henri IV jusqu'à la fin de 1806 en Tableau historique de la guerre de la révolution de France*. Vol. 1. Paris, 1808.

———. *Soldat citoyen*. Neufchatel. 1780.

———. *Tableau historique de la guerre de la révolution française*. Vol. 2. Paris, 1808.

Shanahan, William O. *Prussian Military Reforms, 1786–1813*. New York, 1945.

Shibutani, Tamotsu. *The Derelicts of Company K: A Sociological Study of Demoralization*. Berkeley, 1978.

Shils, Edward. "A Profile of the Military Deserter," *Armed Forces and Society*, 3 (1977): 427–32.

———, and Morris Janowitz. "Cohesion and Disintegration in the Wehrmacht in World War II." In *Military Conflict*, edited by Morris Janowitz. Beverly Hills, 1975.

Sibon-Cattaui, M. "L'éducation politique à l'armée des Pryenées-Orientales en l'an II." Mémoire de maitrise, 1970–71.

Simon, Claude. *Correspondance de Claude Simon, lieutenant des grenadiers, du régiment de Walsh aux armées du Nord, des Ardennes, et de Sambre-et-Meuse, 1792–1793*, edited by Emmanuel Delorme. Grenoble, 1899.

Sirich, John B. *The Revolutionary Committees in the Departments of France, 1793–1794*. Cambridge, Mass., 1943.

Six, Georges. *Dictionnaire biographique des généraux et amiraux français de la Révolution et de l'Empire, 1792–1814*. 2 vols. Paris, 1934.

———. *Les généraux de la Révolution et de l'Empire*. Paris, 1947.

Soboul, Albert. *Les soldats de l'an II*. Paris, 1959.

———. "Sur la mission de Saint-Just à l'armée du Rhin." *Annales historiques de la Révolution française*, 26 (1954): 193–231, 298–337.

Soult, Nicolas. *Mémoires du maréchal-général Soult, duc de Dalmatie*. Part I, vol. I. Paris, 1854.

Stengel. *Le général Stengel au citoyen Marat*. N.p., 1793.

Stouffer, Samuel A., et al. *The American Soldier: Combat and Its Aftermath*. Princeton, 1949.

Susane, Louis. *Histoire de l'artillerie française*. Paris, 1874.

———. *Histoire de la cavalerie française*. 3 vols. Paris, 1874.

———. *Histoire de l'infanterie française*. 5 vols. Paris, 1876–77.
Terrade, Albert, ed. "Journal d'un volontaire au 10ᵉ bataillon composé de jeunes gens de la ville de Versailles, parti le 21 septembre 1792." *Le carnet historique* (1898): 267–79, 508–16, 666–77.
Thiébault, Paul Charles. *Mémoires du général bon. Thiébault*. 5 vols. Paris, 1894.
Thiry, Louis. *Après Fleurus, la bataille de Sprimont: 18 septembre 1794*. Brussels, 1936.
Tiersot, Julien. *Les fêtes et les chants de la Révolution française*. Paris, 1908.
Tiger, Lionel. *Men in Groups*. New York, 1969.
Tuetey, Louis. *Les officiers sous l'ancien régime*. Paris, 1908.
Verney, Sir Harry, ed. *The Journals and Correspondence of General Sir Harry Calvert. Adjutant-General of the Forces under H.R.H. the Duke of York*. London, 1853.
Vivien, Jean-Stanislas. *Souvenirs de ma vie militaire 1792–1822*. Paris, 1907.
Wallon, Henri. *Les représentants du peuple en mission et la justice révolutionnaire dans les départements en l'an II, 1793–1794*. 4 vols. Paris, 1889–90.
Westbrook, Steven D. "Sociopolitical Alienation and Military Efficiency," *Armed Forces and Society*, 8 (1980): 170–89.
Woloch, Isser. *The French Veteran from the Revolution to the Restoration*. Chapel Hill, 1979.
———. "War-Widows Pensions: Social Policy in Revolutionary and Napoleonic France," *Societas* (Autumn 1976): 235–54.
Wrong, Charles John, "The French Infantry Officer at the Close of the *ancien régime*." Ph.d. diss., Brown University, 1968.

Index

Abbaye d'Orval, 234
Abbéville, 152
Active citizens, 50
"Adieux d'un républicain à sa maitresse," 148
Affaires des postes, 271–72
Agent supérieur, 235
Amalgame: described, 57–60; to limit officers' influence, 83; in Nord, 93–94; as political education, 158–59; effect on regionalism, 171; ceremony of, 173; effect on esprit de corps, 181; mentioned, 48, 90
Âme du peuple et du soldat: described, 145; patriotic themes in, 148
Antifédéraliste: subscription, cost, numbers, 126–30 passim; frequency of distribution, 132–33
Appreciation: and morale, 28; in French army, 140, 150, 162
Ardant du Picq, 30
Argus du Département et de l'armée du Nord: on soldier as a victim in ancien régime, 66; on abuses of electing officers, 89; code of conduct for soldiers, 99, 176; political clubs and soldiers, 121; description of Argus, 122–24
Arme blanche: suited to French temperament, 185; French excel with, 187, 190; rhetoric of *arme blanche,* 189, 214; French exaggeration of, 192; and artillery support, 204, 211; and the line, 244; and *Règlement of 1791,* 253; mentioned, 186, 190, 191
Armée des Ardennes: description and history, 7–20
Armée de la Belgique: description, 7, 10

Armée du centre: created, 4; at Valmy, 9, 222
Armée de la Hollande: created, 7, 10; 1792 Volunteers in, 225
Armée de la Moselle: joins Nord on the Sambre, xii, 18; at Fleurus, 239; tactics in, 241, 284; mentioned, 15
Armée de l'Ouest: tactical character of, 284; mentioned, 146
Armée du Rhin: created, 4; retreat in 1793, 11; treatment of deserters in, 111; military justice in, 115–16; mentioned, 134
Armée de Sambre-et-Meuse, 18
Armée française du fin du XVIIe siècle au ministère de Choiseul: le soldat, 44
Armée révolutionnaire: of Paris and of Lille, 155–56; units absorbed into Nord, 235–36
Armées révolutionnaires, 326n59
Arnaudin: on French defeat at Troisvilles, 249
Arnould, 152
Artillery: esprit de corps in horse artillery, 172; in the Nord, 194; organization and types of, 203–5; description and creation of horse artillery, 204; in support of unsteady infantry, 204; men and equipment for, 205–9; greater need for horses in horse artillery, 206, 207; "blues" and "reds," 206, 210; training of horse artillery, 208; artillery schools, 208–9; drivers, 209; tactics, 209–12; in support of cavalry, 210; battalion guns, 210, 213–14; special role of horse artillery, 212–13; on the march, 280, 281
Audouin, 126
Avesnes: political *fête* at, 121

341

Index

Awards: to soldiers for good service, 181–82

Bailleul: camp at, 230
Baisieux: engagement at, 17
Balland, Antoine, 15
Bambecke, engagement at: use of columns, 256
Barère, Bertrand: proposal for *levée en masse*, 56; desire for a *sans-culotte* general, 80
Barracks: eighteenth-century construction, 63
"Bataille de Fleurus," 144
Batave: purchase and distribution, 127–33 passim
Bayonet: in song, 150; in attacks, 178, 281; cult of, 185–93, 241, 279, 282; Bouchotte directive ordering use of, 319n8; use in the Rhin, 319n9
Beauchant, 142
Beauharnais, Alexandre: advocates soldiers attend clubs, 99
Beaulieu, Johan Peter, 212
Beaumont, engagement at: use of line, 249
Belloque, François: imprisoned for sale of equipment, 116
Bentabole, Pierre: backed plays in Lille, 157–58
Bergues: political club at, 121; camp at, 230
Beril, Pierre de: condemned to death, 116
Bertaud, Jean-Paul: *contrôles*, 49; Volunteers of 1791, 50; Volunteers of 1792, 52; Levy of 300,000, 53–54; conscription, 55; *levée en masse*, 57; composition of army in 1794, 60–61; officers, 76, 89, 90; revolutionary *fêtes*, 151; political clubs in the army, 153; on motivation of French troops, 179
Berthel, Nicolas: promoted, 89; retired, 90
Berthélemy, Etienne-Ambroise: chief of staff of Nord, 13; on patriotism and officers, 90; praise of bayonet, 189; organized divisions in Nord, 233; favored column attacks, 256
Berthier, César: skill of troops in 1792, 223
Bertin, Nicholas: at Mouscron, 16; punished officers, 95
Béru, Antoine: at Linselles, 13
Beurnonville: on subordination, 94; integration of new levies, 228; at Jemappes, 250
Bien, David, 207

Billaud-Varenne, J.-Nicolas: against aristocratic officers, 82
Biron, Armand-Louis: advance on Mons, 4, 6, 221; traitor, 85; against election of officers, 89
Bodinier: on emigration of officers, 72
Bonaparte, Napoleon: on morale, 26; rapid rise of, 76; elements of his tactics present by 1794, 258, 278; on mobility, 279; mentioned, 284
Bonnaud, Jacques-Philippe: replaces Chapuis, 16; at Baisieux, 17; at Tourcoing, 17
Bouchotte, Jean-Baptiste: goodness of soldier, 66; controversy with Custine, 80; purge of aristocratic officers, 82, 83, 86; evaluation of, 84, 94; power to appoint officers, 90; equality between officers and men, 94; officers to live with their men, 94–95; need for discipline, 101; purchase and distribution of journals, 124, 126, 129, 135, 138; on reading of journals, 136; distribution of copies of the Constitution, 141; revolutionary songs, 143, 144; Fête de l'unité, 152; political clubs, 154, 155; distribution of revolutionary plays, 157; fraternity, 173; esprit de corps, 181; on sending up replacements, 228; recommends bayonet attacks, 319n8; mentioned, 125, 145, 147, 161, 203, 227
Bounties: recruitment, 52
Boussu, engagement at: importance, 16; use of line in, 247, 251; use of column at, 256, 258
Brault, Alexandre: disdain for Levy of 300,000, 53; military law read to, 105; *armée revolutionnaire* at Dunkirk, 156; treatment of French people by the enemy, 160; trained constantly, 237
Brette: received dagger as reward, 182
Bricard, Louis: volunteered for service, 52; accustomed to treason of officers, 84; Custine's impact on discipline, 106; described executions, 115–17; reaction to fall of Robespierre, 139; and *fêtes*, 152; signed up with brother, 168; deserted with friend, 168; battalion artillery, 213–14; retreat out of Belgium, 226; *armée revolutionnaire*, 325n59; Neerwinden, 326–27n12
Brissot, Jean-Pierre: Girondist journalist, 123; vilified in political journals, 138
Brouard, Etienne: on Maubeuge political club, 156

Brunet, Gaspard-Jean: named traitor, 85
Brunswick, duke of, 7
Brunswick Manifesto, 7
Bulletin of the National Convention: praise of Hérault plan, 55; advocacy of *tu* forms, 94; as explanation of the law, 105, 180; description of, 122; distribution to army, 122, 128, 131, 132–33, 135; display of, 136; message of, 136; distribution after Thermidor, 146; praise of bayonet, 192; mentioned, 130, 140

"Ca ira!," 142, 148
Cacault, Jean-Baptiste: at Boussu, 16; use of line by, 247, 251; use of columns by, 256, 258; use of square by, 260
Calandini, 86
Cambon, Joseph: reported on Hérault system to Convention, 54
Cambrai: training camp at, 12, 231; military court, 113; *fêtes* at, 151; political club, 155, 156; Custine's headquarters, 229
Camille, 129
Carignan: *fêtes* at, 152; camp, 230
"Carmagnole," 148, 152
Carnot, Lazare: at Wattignies, 14, 256; on substitutes, 53; modified exclusion of noble officers, 82, 90, 91; inspection of officers, 91; rights of soldiers, 99; disciplinary problems of the Nord, 107, 109, 110, 114–15; purchase and distribution of journals, 125, 131; *Soirée de camp*, 129, 137; favors bayonet attacks, 189, 256; praises pike, 190
Carra, Jean-Louis, 123
Cateau-Cambrésis, engagement at: 15
Cavalry: peasant preference for, 45; in the Nord, 194–203; problems in securing men, horses, and equipment, 195–99; low quality of, 199–201; tactics, 201–3, 278–84 passim; training, 216; cavalry as a percentage of Nord, 320–21n12
Celliez: struggle with Custine regarding journals, 85, 134; on reading of journals, 136; suggests distributing copies of Constitution, 141; on Cambrai *fête*, 152; on drill at César, 230
Certificates of civism, 83, 87, 153–54
César, camp de: established and abandoned, 12; civic *fête* at, 152; training at, 230, 231
Châles, Pierre: Lille political club, 155

Châlons: artillery school at, 208–9; camp at, 225
Championnet, Jean-Etienne: at Fleurus, 202, 212
Chandler, David, 207
"Changements en errata au Règlement de 1791," 231
Chansons et romances civiques, 146
"Chant du départ," 144, 146, 147, 174
"Chant des victoires," 144
Chapuis, René-Bernard: defeated at Troisvilles, 16; use of line at Troisvilles, 249
Charbonnier, Louis: replaced Sistrières, 90
Charleroi: seige of, 18
Chasot, Jean-Pierre: at Croix-aux-Bois, 222
Chassé-croisé, 6, 222
Chasseurs à pied: creation before Revolution, 266. *See also* Skirmishers
Chaumette, Jean-François: praised song, 143
Chaumont, Jean-François: sentenced for insubordination, 116
Chazont, Jean-Pierre: at Grand-Pré, 248
Chénier, Marie-Joseph: association with National Institute of Music, 146
Choiseul, Etienne, duc de: reform of cavalry, 200
Choudieu, Pierre: authorized generals to set up military courts, 108; on spirit of French troops, 192
Chuquet, Arthur: on revolutionary cavalry, 203
Citizen soldier: ideal, 43–44; praise of, 63–66
Clairfayt, Charles de Croix: at Wattignies, 14; at Mouscron, 16; at Courtrai, 17; at Tourcoing, 17, 191
Cobb, Richard: on *armées révolutionnaire,* 156
Coburg, prince of: commanding Austrian forces against France, 10–14 passim, 17, 18; at Neerwinden, 226; objectives for 1793, 227; mentioned, 79, 173
Colin, Jean: on the line, 241–42, 246; denied column use, 254; on lack of regulations for skirmishers, 268; on Schauenburg, 284
Column: use at Cambrai, 232; use at Wattignies, 234; ties with *élan,* 242, 243; characteristics, 243; Kléber recommends, 249; use at Jemappes, 250; discussion of, 251–58; table listing instances of use of, 289–91; columns in *Règlement de 1791,* 327n19;

mentioned, 191, 280, 281, 282
Colonne serrée: described, 252. *See also* Column
Combat effectiveness: general theory of, 21–40; and interest, 21; morale, 26–30; primary group cohesion, 30–35, 163; troop motivation, 35–36; the military system, 36–38; tactical combat strength, 38–40; mentioned, 20, 21, 185
Combat motivation: theory, 35–36; in French army, 178
Commissaires des guerres: and military courts, 103
Commissaires du conseil exécutif: surveillance over officers, 83, 86; powers of, 84–85; distributing journals, 126, 135; controversy with Custine over journals, 134; reading of journals, 136; on importance of political education, 161
Committee of General Defense, 125
Committee of Public Safety: great power of, 11, 125; ordered Custine to Paris, 12; relations with Houchard, 13; and Hérault plan for conscription, 54; *levée en masse*, 56; purge of officers, 67, 81–83; survey of officer competency, 86; on traitors, 87; appointments of officers, 90; military justice system, 104, 105; and Representatives on Mission, 106; disciplinary measures, 109; purchase and distribution of journals, 124, 126, 127, 129, 135, 136, 138, 139; purchase and distribution of songbooks, 143, 144, 147; National Institute of Music, 145–46; Lille political club, 156; faith in bayonet, 185; faith in troops, 192; demanded sieges be relieved, 227; Custine reported condition of army to, 229; demanded Jourdan take up offensive, 236; abolished *armées révolutionnaires*, 236; mentioned, 114, 119, 147, 159, 160, 161, 199, 203, 284
Committee on Public Instruction: financed songbooks, 143, 144; backed National Institute of Music, 144
Committees of Surveillance: founded, 11; purge of officers, 86–87; mentioned, 157
Commune of Paris: Hérault plan of conscription, 55; exclusion of nobles from office, 82; songs and songbooks, 142, 143, 144
Compliance theory, 23–25
Condé: seige of, 12, 227; garrison of, 230

Conseil d'administration: composition and role in officer selection, 74–75, 91
Conseil de discipline: description and duties, 102–5 passim; mentioned, 113
Conseil exécutif provisoire. See Executive Council
Conseil de guerre, 141
Constitution of 1793: praised in journals, 139; distributed to troops, 141; *fêtes,* 151–52, 153
Contrôles, 44, 49
Convention. *See* National Convention
Cordelier Club: condemnation of officers at, 77, 82
Corvisier, André: and *contrôles,* 44; peasant in army, 45; recruitment, 62
Court-martial: in ancien régime, 101; revolutionary, 102–13
Courts, military. *See* Military justice
Courtrai, combat at: 16, 17, 275
Coutanceau, Henri: on cavalry, 203; on French proficiency at Pont-à-Chin, 238–39
"Cri de mort contre les rois," 148
Croix-aux-Bois, combat at: 8–9; mentioned, 222
Cromwell, Oliver: Dumouriez compared to, 79
Custine, Adam Philippe, baron de: took command of Nord, 12; guillotined, 14; caused government to distrust officers, 78, 79–80; controversy with Celliez over journals, 85, 134; attacked by journals, 85, 139; as disciplinarian, 98, 100, 106; need for pikes, 202–3; condemned cavalry, 202–3; on infantry and artillery, 211; for faster march pace, 217; training, 219, 227, 229–32; summoned to Paris, 232; on columns, 258; mentioned, 11, 82, 84, 107, 155
Cysoing, combat at: 14

Daendels, Hermann-Wilhelm, comte: at Mouscron, 16; at Courtrai, 17
Dampierre, Auguste, marquis de: command of Nord, 11; death, 11, 255; line, column, and skill at Jemappes, 223, 250–51, 255; on need for training, 227; on need to incorporate new levy, 228; mentioned, 85, 191
Danton, Georges Jacques: Vendeé levy, 54; on limited competence of officers, 88; attacked in journals, 138; banning singers from Convention, 142

Davaine, Jean-Baptiste, 14
Declaration of the Rights of Man, 104
Defeated Arsitocrat, 157
Delacroix, Jean-Baptiste: complains of women in camps, 109
Delaporte, Pierre: life in *ordinaire,* 168; on skirmishers, 267, 276; description of battle, 276–77
Delbrel, Pierre: complained of officer seniority, 89; praised the offensive, 188; on training of troops, 233
Demi-brigades: creation of, 58
Democracy, 157
Depaux: use of square at, 260
Desbrières, Edouard: on cavalry, 196, 201, 203
Desertion: 1789–91, 3; winter of 1792–93, 10; and primary group cohesion, 34, 317n15; among *levée en masse,* 56–57; as a problem in Nord, 110–13; winter of 1793–94, 236; mentioned, 98, 100, 104, 108
Desjardin: training along the Sambre 1793–94, 237, 238; use of columns at Grand Reng, 260; on avant gardes, 272; on infantry to support skirmishers, 272–73
Desmoulins, Camille: soldiers as brothers of civilians, 64
Dessaubay: report on skirmishers and columns, 276
Dictionnaire philosophique, 186–87
Diettmann, Dominique: complains of dispersed units, 224
Dillon, Théobald: advance on Lille, 4; shot by troops, 4, 98, 109, 221
Discipline: decline 1789–91, 3; in combat effectiveness theory, 36–37; and election of officers, 89; punishment by flat of the sword, 93, 102; execution of generals, 95; general discussion of, 97–118; nature of in a revolutionary army, 97–101; corporal punishment in ancien régime, 102; *fautes contre la discipline,* 102, 104; disciplinary laws, 104–5; drunkenness, 108; sale of equipment, 108, 110, 116; animosity between line, volunteers, and *Fédérés,* 109–10, 114–15; role of examples in punishment, 115–17; theme in songs, 150; problem in winter of 1793–94, 236
Divertissant, 142
Dubois, Paul: assumes command, 16; at Fleurus, 202, 212
Dubois-Crancé, Edmond: reports to Convention on need for *amalgame,* 58, 59; on old attitude toward soldiers, 63; praise of revolutionary soldier, 64; on rights of soldiers, 99; political benefits of *amalgame,* 158; fraternity, 173; *élan* of revolutionary troops, 187
Dubouchet, Pierre: on inspiring songs, 147
Dufresse, Simon: and Lille political club, 155–56
Duhesmes, Philibert-Guillaume: led light infantry along the Sambre, 18; view that French fought only as skirmishers, 241, 265; reserve supporting skirmishers, 250, 257, 272; contradicted himself, 233, 269–70; condemned combat ability of the Nord, 233; use of line, 250, 251; on Hondschoote and Wattignies, 256; use of attack column, 256, 257, 260, 273; use of route column, 258; tactics of skirmishing natural to the French, 261; light infantry on the march, 272
Dumouriez, Charles François: foreign minister, 4; as Minister of War, 6, 221; *chassé-croisé,* 6; commander of Nord, 7–10 passim; armistice with Austrians, 11, 78; treason of, 11, 85; on rights of soldiers, 64; caused government to fear treason of officers, 59, 78–79, 162; on desertion, 110, 112; complained of pillage, 113–14; soldiers attending political clubs, 121; influence over *Argus,* 123; treason as impetus to journal distribution, 124; attacked in journals, 139; troop comment on treason, 158; confidence in bayonet assault, 192; training at Maude, 222; at Jemappes, 223; at Neerwinden, 226; on integrating new levies, 228; effect of winter campaign, 236; use of column and line at Jemappes, 250–51, 255; Argonne campaign, 255; concern with *petite guerre,* 279; mentioned, 3, 19, 67, 82, 191; treason mentioned, 94, 100, 119, 120, 131, 153, 168
Dunkirk: besieged, 13; Nord garrison, 220, 230; as allied objective, 227
Duplaisset: on dispatching skirmishers, 267
Duquesnoy, Ernest: purge of officers, 83; orders *Rougyff,* 129

Eblé, Jean: soldiers and political clubs, 155
Eckelsbecke, engagement at: skirmishers, 273
Ecole de Mars: received songbooks, 146
Élan: as theme in ancien régime and revolu-

tion, 186–89; and morale, 192; exaggeration by Convention, 192; rhetoric of, 214; and tactics, 282
Election of officers: described, 73, 74, 89; problems created by, 89, 100
Elie, Jacob-Job: routed at Beaumont, 14; reliance upon *élan*, 192; use of line, 249
Embrigadement, 57–58
Emigration of officers, 4, 69–72, 81
Ernouf, Jean-Augustin: chief of staff to Jourdan, 14; on constant combat along the Sambre, 237
Erquelinnes, combat at: 18
Esprit de corps: as indoctrination, 27; in combat effectiveness theory, 29–30; in revolutionary army, 171–72, 181; of horse artillery, 212, 214; development after 1794, 285; mentioned, 25, 38
Executive Council: and military courts, 104; creation and description, 125; mentioned, 161. *See also Commissaires du conseil exécutif*

Famars, Camp de: first fight at, 11; second fight at, 12; use of bayonet at, 189; Nord concentration at, 229; evacuation of, 230; mentioned, 6, 191, 221
Fêtes: as elements of political education, 120–21, 151–53
Fête de la Fédération, 1792: 120
Fête de l'unite, 152
Federations, 120
Federalism, 161
Federalists, 138
Fédérés: called up by Legislative Assembly, 51; as a disciplinary problem, 98, 109; mentioned, 122
Ferrand, Jean-Henri-Becays: seige of Valenciennes, 12; commander of Nord right, 15; interim commander of Nord, 15; relief of Landrecies, 16
Feuille du salut public: subscription and distribution, 127–30 passim
Flers, Louis-Charles, marquis de: commander of Hollande, 10
Fleurus, battle of: described, 18; musketry at, 189; defensive action, 191; cavalry at, 202, 203; artillery at, 212; ability of troops at, 219, 239; mentioned, 284
Fourcade, Pascal-Thomas: publisher of *Antifédéraliste*, 129
Foy, Maximilien: on importance of bayonet, 192; artillery school, 208–9

Fraternity: theme of revolutionary press, 138, 172–73; theme of revolutionary song, 149, 172–73; theme of *fêtes*, 153, 173
Fraud and Liberty, 157
Frederick the Great: concern with desertion, 265
French Army: size 1716–94, 44, 48, 53, 60; social composition 1716–94, 44–49, 60–61; 1st Ainse, 110, 228; 1st Butte des Moulins, 224; 1st Cavalry, 196, 198; 11th Cavalry, 200; 15th Cavalry, 199; 20th Chasseurs à cheval, 199; Chasseurs de la Meuse, 266; 7th Dragoons, 198; 1st Haute Marne, 224–25; 1st Haute Vienne, 213; 9th Hussars, 198; 172nd (demi-brigade) Infantry, 258; 1st (regiment) Infantry, 228; 56th (regiment) Infantry, 248; 104th (regiment) Infantry, 224; 3rd Nord, 256; 3rd Paris, 224; 5th Paris, 212, 213, 226, 266; 10th Paris, 248; 2nd Pas de Calais, 112; 1st Seine-et-Oise, 228; 9th Seine-et-Oise, 256. *See also Levèe en masse;* Levy of 300,000; Volunteers of 1791; Volunteers of 1792
Fréron, Louis-Stanislas, 123
Fricasse, Jacques: good self-opinion of, 169–70; on amalgamation *fête*, 173; stories of patriotic deaths, 173, 175; training, 225; constant combat on the Sambre, 237; use of line at Grand-Reng, 250; detaching skirmishers, 267
Fromentin, Jacques-Pierre: at Cateau-Cambrésis, 15; criticized by Jourdan, 90; forms battalion column, 260
Furia francese, 186
Furnes: pillage at, 114–15; use of line at, 249
Fuzier, Louis: detachment of skirmishers, 267

Gaius Gracchus, 157
Gavrelle, Camp de: training at, 232
Gay de Vernon, Louis: on animosity between line and volunteers, 109; seasoning troops by combat, 232
Gervais: on songs, 142; greasing the marmite, 167; enlisted with a friend, 168; training, 323n5
Ghivelde, 230
Gillet, Pierre: goodness of common soldiers, 66; replacement of Sistrières, 157; on incorporation of *levèe en masse*, 238
Girardon, Pierre: on patriotic death, 175–76
Girondists, 123, 161

Goguet, Jacques-Gilles: attack on Cateau-Chambrésis, 15; assassinated by troops, 16, 109
Gossec, François: and National Institute of Music, 146
Gouffroy, Armand: publisher of *Rougyff,* 129
Gougelot, Jean-Florimond: use of line at Furnes, 249
Goupilleau, Philippe-Charles: on need for cavalry, 196
Gournay: publisher of *Journal militaire,* 129
Gouvion-Saint-Cyr, Laurent, comte: on troop performance, 239
Grand-Pré, combat at: French maneuver at, 248
Grand-Reng, combat at: described, 18; good performance of French troops, 239; use of line at, 250, 251; use of column at, 256; use of square at, 260
Great Fear: and creation of the National Guard, 49–50
Gribeauval, Jean-Baptiste: artillery system, 205–6, 210, 283
Gudin: training order, 233
Guibert, Jacques: on citizen soldiers, 44; on common soldiers, 63; praise of *arme blanche,* 187; relationship with Dumouriez, 250
Guiot, Florent: journal distribution problems, 135; against radicals in Lille, 156; on importance of political journals, 162; on poor quality of cavalry equipment, 199

Harville, Louis-Auguste, comte de: at Jemappes, 9
Hébert, Jacques: against aristocratic officers, 82; influence on the Ministry of War, 84; relationship with Celliez, 85; arrest, 126; praise of Jesus, 138; attacked in journals, 138; subsidies from Ministry of War, 137; support of song, 144, 149–50; egalitarianism, 149; mentioned, 135, 161
Hecq, 230
Helmer, John: on primary group cohesion, 54–55
Hentz, Charles: against radicals at Lille, 156
Hondschoote, battle of: described, 13; cavalry, 198, 202, 211; infantry at, 234; columns at, 256, 257; as a battle of skirmishers, 268, 272, 273; mentioned, 188, 219, 233, 280
Horse artillery. *See* Artillery

Houchard, Jean-Nicolas: takes command of Nord, 12, 232; Hondschoote, 13; relieved, 13–14, 81; goodness of soldiers, 77; caused government to fear officers, 78; called traitor, 85; proclamation against drunkenness, 108; attacked in journals, 139; favored bayonet attack, 189; complains of state of Nord, 232; divisional organization, 233; his Instructions, 233, 267, 269, 271–72, 274–75; use of line, 250; use of column, 256; on route column, 258; detachment of skirmishers, 267, 269, 274–75; concern for *petite guerre,* 271–72, 279; skirmishers at Tourcoing, 273; mentioned, 199
Housset, Pierre: used certificate of civism, 87
"Hymne à la fraternité," 144

Incorporation: of *levée en masse,* 58–59; and *amalgame,* 59; threat to regionalism, 171; and primary group cohesion, 171; method of getting recruits from depot, 324*n*34; mentioned, 236
Indoctrination: general theory, 27
Initial motivation: theory, 26–27; in French army, 177–78
Infantry: social composition of French infantry, 45, 46–47; tactics, 185–93 passim, 241–78, 279–86 passim; training, 216–40
Instruction de M. Noailles: description, 217; volunteer battalions sent a copy, 222
Interest: and French revolutionary soldier, 21–23; compliance theory, 23–25
Isoré, Jacques: suspended officers, 85; on desertion, 112; and political club of Lille, 155–56

Jacobin, club and party: petition favoring *levée en masse,* 56; opposing aristocratic officers, 82; recommended troops attend club meetings, 121; Valenciennes club, 123; news of in journals, 137; Jacobin centralism, 138; and T. Rousseau, 145; military clubs associated with, 153; views of infantry tactics, 244, 246; mentioned, 90, 121, 122, 161, 188
Janowitz, Morris: on primary group cohesion, 31
Jardon, Henry-Antoine: at Mouscron, 16
Jarry, Antoine-Anatole: on Celliez, 85
Jemappes, Battle of: description, 9; old

battle cries at, 172; cavalry at, 202; artillery at, 211; performance of French troops at, 223; casualties at, 224; use of line at, 249; use of columns at, 254, 255; mentioned, 111, 188, 218
Joliclerc, François: willingness to die for Patrie, 175
Jomini, Henry: on pikemen, 190
Jourdan, Jean-Baptiste: at Linselles, 13; refused to pursue enemy, 14, 236; at Wattignies, 14, 211; takes command of Nord, 14; relieved of command, 15, 83; receives command of Moselle, 16; leads Moselle to Sambre, 18; evaluation, 19; critical of Fromentin, 90; at Fleurus, 191; for integration of *levée en masse,* 235; training in Nord, 236, 237; led attacking column at Hondschoote, 256, 257; concern for *petite guerre,* 279; mentioned, 15
Journal des hommes libres: purchase and distribution, 126–32 passim, 135; message, 137; purpose, 137; on government care of soldiers and families, 180; mentioned, 147, 148
Journal militaire: purchase and distribution, 127–30 passim; in print after Thermidor, 146; mentioned, 136
Journal de la Montagne: Custine frustrated distribution, 80; purchase and distribution, 126–34 passim; format and message, 137; attacked Brissot, 138; suspicious of generals, 139; T. Rousseau wrote for it, 145; mentioned, 148
Journal universel: purchase and distribution, 126–35 passim; format and message, 137
Journals, political: general discussion, 124–40; rationale for distribution of, 124–25; agents responsible for distribution, 125–26; purchase of subscriptions, 126–30; distribution to troops, 130–36; message of, 136–40; public reading of, 136; criticism of Church, 138; read in *ordinaire,* 168; distribution of, 312n32
Julian: publisher of *Antifédéraliste,* 129
Justice. *See* Military justice

Kellermann, François: at Valmy, 9, 211, 222; on tactical ability of French troops, 233
Kilmaine, Charles-Edouard Jennings de: interim commander of Nord, 12; on lack of cavalry, 203; on need for horse artillery, 210; on drilling troops, 231; abandoned Camp de César, 232
Kléber, Jean-Baptiste: replaced Balland, 16; on conduct of generals with troops, 95; on use of line and column, 246–47; advocates attacks, 253; maneuvered in attack column at Charleroi, 257–58; at Grand-Reng, 260; Instructions say little about light infantry, 269; on march protection, 272; concern with *petite guerre,* 279; Kléber's Instructions and Schérer, 326n6; mentioned, 258

La Barre, André de: complained of cavalry weapons, 199
La Bourdonnaye, Anne-François, comte de: commands Nord, 10; asked Convention to send Representatives to front, 85; complained of unarmed battalions, 225
La Capelle, engagement at: use of columns at, 257
Lacoste, Élie: declared local *levée en masse* in Nord, 55; authorized club to remove military officers, 86, 154
Ladré: composer and singer, 142
Lafayette, Marie-Paul Motier, marquis de: received command of Centre, 4; *chassé-croisé,* 6; attempted coup, 7, 122; went over to Austrians, 7, 67; ordered *embrigadement,* 57; aroused suspicion of government against officers, 78; traitor, 85; condemned flat of sword, 102; declared crying "we are betrayed" a crime, 106; criticized for laxness, 113; threat posed by, 162; and training, 222; claimed to have originated skirmishers, 269; mentioned, 3, 79, 82, 285
Lahure, Joseph: concerning Luckner's advance into Belgium, 221
Lake: at Linselles, 13
Lamarche, François Joseph Drouet: interim commander of Nord, 11; leaves Ferrand at Valenciennes, 12
Lamarlière, Antoine-Nicolas Colier, comte de: Custine backed him for Lille post, 80; relations with Lille club, 155; drilled troops, 229
Lamorlière, Alexis Magallon, comte de: command of Rhin, 6
Landrécies: seige of, 15, 16; political club in, 154

Lannoy, engagement at: skirmishers used bayonets, 273
Last Judgment of the Kings, the, 157
Latour-Foissac, François-Philippe: reported animosity between line and volunteers, 189
Lauerma, Matti: on foot artillery, 92–95; on political character of battalion guns, 205; on concentration artillery, 211
Lavalette, Louis: and Lille political club, 155–56
Laveaux, Charles: editor of *Journal de la Montagne,* 126; criticized Vincent, 126; suspicious of generals, 139
Laws. *See* Military justice
Leadership: in combat effectiveness theory, 38; among revolutionary officers, 87–96
Le Bas, Philippe: and revolutionary justice, 107, 115; rigorous disciplinarian, 107
Le Blaton, combat at: artillery there, 211; French assault, 255
Le Bon, Joseph: and revolutionary justice, 107; ordered song published, 145; had troops of actors, 158; suspicious of cavalry, 194–95
Leclaire, Theodore-François: at Esquelbecque, 13, 273; on skill of French troops, 223; troops at Grand-Pré, 248; on use of line, 248, 250, 251; use of column attacks, 255, 256; use of skirmishers, 273
Le Couturier: on lack of need for light infantry regulations, 268–69
Lefebvre, François-Joseph: use of artillery at Fleurus, 212
Legislative Assembly: calls up Volunteers of 1792, 6; votes command of Nord to Dumouriez, 7; proclaims country in danger, 7, 51; expands line army, 48; calls up fédérés, 51; calls up Volunteers of 1791 and 1792, 51–52; sets procedure for election of officers, 72; military penal code of 1791, 99; reform of military justice, 103; dispatched representatives, 106; created Provisional Executive Council, 125; praise of pike, 190; ordered Volunteers of 1791 to join the line, 219; ordered army to form camps of instruction, 219; orders Noailles *Instructions* sent to volunteer battalions, 222; mentioned, 100
Legrand, Antoine: on desertion, 111; documents Rhin court cases, 115
Lenoble, 266
Leplus: French skill at Pont-à-Chin, 238–39
Le Quesnoy: besieged, 13; allied objective, 227
Le Roy, Claude: volunteered for ancien régime army, 61–62
Le Tourneur, Charles-François: purged aristocratic officers, 85; complains about seniority, 89; troops well trained, 233
Le Vaneur: troops well trained, 233
Levasseur, René: backed revolutionary theater, 157–58
Levée en masse: carried out early in Nord, 55–56; voted by Convention, 56; description and composition, 56–57; incorporation into Nord, 58–59, 234, 235; desertion in, 112; initial motivation, 177; need for training, 219; yield for Nord, 234–35; impact on unit capacity, 238; mentioned, 49
Levy of 30,000: for cavalry, 54
Levy of 300,000: decreed by Convention, 10; description and composition, 53–54; incorporation of, 58, 227; initial motivation, 177; arrived at Nord, 219
Light artillery. *See* Artillery
Light infantry. *See* Skirmishers
Lille: military tribunal at, 113; soldiers in Lille political club, 154–55; controversy surrounding club, 155–56; as allied objective, 227
Line, regiments. *See* French army
Line, tactical formation: use at Cambrai, 232; use of at Abbaye d'Orval, 234; Colin on use of, 241–42; and discipline, 242; general characteristics, 243; general discussion of, 244–51; against cavalry, 259; table listing instances of use of, 287–89; ragged order in, 326n7; at Neerwinden, 326–27n12; mentioned, 191, 193
Linselles, combat at: 13
Little, Roger: on buddy relationships and cohesion, 32
Louis XIV, 11, 190
Louis XV, 43, 169, 170
Louis XVI: flight of, 3, 4, 50, 69, 219; and Brunswick Manifesto, 7; bland address to troops, 122; mentioned, 63, 120, 138
Louvain, Battle of: 11, 78, 98, 226
Luckner, Nicolas, baron: commander of Rhin, 4; received command of Nord, 6; "La Marseillaise" dedicated to, 6; and *chassé-croisé,* 6; assessment of, 6; guillotined, 14; and training, 221; advised by

Dumouriez to use columns, 255

MacDonald, Etienne-Jacques: brigade commander in Nord, 16; at Mouscron, 16; maneuver at Pont-à-Chin, 248; attacked in line at Menin, 251; use of close order infantry to support skirmishers, 275
Mack, Karl Leiberich, baron: plans allied advance 1794, 17; dealing with Dumouriez, 78; on French weakness when deploying, 260
Madeleine, Camp de la, 229, 230
Maestricht, siege of: 10
Marat, Jean-Paul: as publisher of *Publiciste*, 129
Marceau, François-Severin: at Fleurus, 212
Maréchal, Sylvain: playwright and composer, 157
Marie Antoinette: vilified in journals, 138
Marmite: and cooking in the *ordinaire*, 165, 316n3; supplied to Nord, 166; greasing the marmite, 167
Marquant, François: calls Lafayette lax, 113; takes oath, 174–75
"Marseillaise": composed in honor of Luckner, 6; sung at *fêtes*, 151, 152; capacity to inspire troops, 162; mentioned, 147, 174, 192
Marshal, S. L. A.: defines morale, 26; on primary group cohesion, 31; on isolation of the battlefield, 263
Martin, Marc: on *journaux des armés*, 122; on *Argus*, 123
Maubeuge: besieged, 14; troubles in political club, 156, 157; training, 220, 230, 233; allied objective 1793, 227; Nord concentration there 1793, 229; columns at siege of, 257; use of light infantry in sortie, 272–73
Maude, Camp de: Dumouriez at, 6; size, 222
Melletier, François: activities, party allegience, and goals as publisher of *Argus*, 122–24
Méhul, Etienne-Nicolas: with National Institute of Music, 146
Menin: combat at, 13; taken by French, 16; use of line at, 251; French skirmishers at siege of, 274
Mercier, Louis-Sebastien, 123
Mesnil-Durand, François-Jean: advocate of *arme blanche* and columns, 187

Meunier, Hugues-Alexandre-Joseph: emphasized bayonet, 189; as trainer, 219, 246; training camp at Cambrai, 231–32; his "Changements," 246; criticized Schauenburg, 246; emphasized passage of defiles, 248; on refinement of *Règlement du 1791*, 253; on deployment of attack column, 254; suggested square, 259; on detaching skirmishers, 267; emphasized columns and skirmishers, 276
Michaud, Pierre-Antoine: division commander in Nord, 16
Michon, Georges: on military code of 12 May 1793, 104
Milice: description of, 45; resistance to, 45; parallel with Levy of 300,00, 53; recruitment of, 62
Military justice: general theory, 36–38; description of justice system in the French revolutionary army, 97–118
Ministry of War: as agent of surveillance and purge of officers, 84–86; eliminated by Committee of Public Safety, 90; desired harmony in camps, 100; insists laws be read to troops, 105; fourth bureau for military justice and political education, 118; and campaign of political education, 125–26; distribution of journals, 135; Hébertist character of, 137; and distribution of songbooks, 143, 145; and *fêtes*, 152; and political clubs, 153; experimented with pikes, 191; accused skirmishers of wasting ammunition, 264; mentioned, 119, 147, 159, 160
Miranda, Francisco de: commander of Nord, 10; at Neerwinden, 10, 226
Mireur, François: described certificate of civism, 87; willingness to die for country, 175, 176
Montesquieu, Charles Louis de Secondat, baron de: ideal of citizen soldier, 44; climate and national character, 186
Morale: defined, 23; theoretical discussion, 26–30
Moreau, Jean-Victor: divisional commander in Nord, 16; at Tourcoing, 17; on time to train, 238; support of skirmishers, 257; mentioned, 188
Moskos, Charles: on primary group cohesion, 32, 34
Motivation: defined, 23; motivational system, theoretical discussion, 26–36; moti-

vation of the French revolutionary army, 177–82
"Mourir pour la patrie," 147
Mouscron, engagement at: described, 16; skirmishers at, 273–74, 275
Musique à l'usage des fêtes nationales, 146
Mutinies, 120

Naett: publisher of *Batave,* 129
National Assembly: authorized army of 157,000 in 1791, 4; called up Volunteers of 1791, 4, 50; and citizen soldier ideal, 44; abolished venality of commissions, 69; laws on soldiers' political clubs, 99, 121; reforms of military justice system, 102–3; economy measures, 196; created artillery as separate arm, 203; created horse artillery, 204; mentioned, 187, 216
National Constituent Assembly. *See* National Assembly
National Convention: Levy of 300,000, 10, 53; declared war on England and Dutch Netherlands, 10; the treason of Dumouriez, 11; creates Sambre-et-Meuse, 18; adopts conscription, 44; Levy of 30,000 for cavalry, 54; raised troops to fight in the Vendé, 54, 229; Hérault plan, 55; *levée en masse,* 56, 234, 235; *amalgame,* 58, 59; new laws on officer selection, 74–75, 80, 90; held officers' families as hostages in 1793, 74, 79; declared the Terror, 82; stand on relationship between officers and men, 94; laws on military justice and discipline, 100–101, 103–5, 106, 108; authorized soldiers to marry, 108–9; limited numbers of women in camps, 109; established *Bulletin,* 122; seen as ultimate legitimate authority, 124; sent Representatives on Mission to the Nord, 125; distribution of journals, 136; praised in journals, 137, 139; dispatched decrees to be read in armies, 140–41; songs sung at, 142; exaggerated the value of *élan,* 192; passed laws to increase the size of cavalry forces, 195–96; laws to provide horses and equipment for cavalry, 197–98; increased size of horse artillery, 204; mentioned, 90, 119, 147, 161, 187, 192
National Guard: source of Volunteers of 1791, 4; created, 49, 120; as a source of officers, 72; Parisian National Guard musicians, 145–46; artillery added to its infantry battalions, 204; mentioned, 224. *See also* Volunteers of 1791; Volunteers of 1792
National Institute of Music: founded, 144; work of, 145–46
Neerwinden, Battle of: described, 10; use of bayonet at, 189; cavalry at, 202; artillery at, 211; performance of French troops at, 226; use of line at, 249, 326–27*n*12; lack of column at, 254; mentioned, 78, 98, 113, 191, 198, 218, 219, 225, 232, 258
Nicknames: and political education, 158
Noël, Gabriel: cooking in the *ordinaire,* 167; singing in the *ordinaire,* 168
Normative compliance: defined, 24–25; determines motivational system, 26; and notion of appreciation, 28; and discipline, 36–37; and French skirmishers, 262; and French motivation, 283

Oaths: taken by soldiers at *fêtes,* 152, 153; oaths to die the patriotic death, 174–75
Officers: composition, reliability, and competence of the French officer corps, 67–96; selection, promotion, and social composition of line officer corps to 1793, 68–73; laws on selection and promotion of officers, 73, 74, 75; selection, promotion, and composition of Volunteers' officer corps, 73–74; literacy, 75, 77; composition of officer corps in 1794, 75–77; patriotism of officers, 77; surveillance and purge of the officer corps, 77–87; competence of revolutionary officers, 88–91; schools for training officers, 91; field examinations for artillery officers, 91; relationships between officers and men, 91–96; desire for *sans-culotte* officers, 96; government fear that officers might manipulate esprit de corps, 181; age and quality of cavalry officers, 200–201
Officers of fortune: defined, 68
Officier de police: creation and function, 104
O'Moran, Jacques: used attack columns at Le Blaton, 255
Orders of the day: concerning distribution of journals, 131, 312*n*32; set revolutionary passwords, 158; stipulated training at Maubeuge, 233; stipulated that *Règlement du service de campagne* was to be distributed and followed, 166
Ordinaire: reading of political journals, 136;

general discussion, 163–77; structures and practices of the *ordinaire,* 164–69; relationships and standards within the *ordinaire,* 169–77; set standards, 182; *ordinaire* and motivation, 283; cooking in the *ordinaire,* 167, 316*n*3

Ordre mixte, 258

Osté, 258

Otto, Rudolph: at Tourcoing, 17

Pache, Jean-Nicolas: orders concerning distribution of the *Bulletin,* 122

Palis: wrote "Credo of the Good Soldier," 176

Paret, Peter: on light infantry, 265, 268, 274

Passwords: as elements of political education, 158

Patriotic death: myth of, as an index of group standards, 173–76

Patriotic Songs Sung at Lille, 144

Patriotism: of officers, 77; as a theme in political journals, 139; as a theme of revolutionary songs, 147–48; as a theme in *fêtes,* 153; impact of campaign of political education on, 162; and troop motivation, 178–80; and combat motivation of revolutionary troops, 282

Payan, Claude-François: publisher of *Antifédéraliste,* 129

Penal codes: of 30 Sept. 1791, 103; of 12 May 1793, 103–4. *See also* Military justice

Père Duchesne: praised Hérault plan, 55; deliveries frustrated by Custine, 80; praised by Celliez, 85; advocated equality between officers and men, 94; purchase and distribution, 126–35 passim, 143–44; format and message, 137; attack on Brissot, 138; praise of common soldier, 140; counterfeit, 141; Hébert did not include songs in it, 149; mentioned, 147

Petite guerre, 279–80

Peyssard, J.-P.-C.: declared local *levée en masse* in Nord, 55; gave political club right to remove officers from command, 86

Pichegru, Jean-Charles: took command of Nord, 15; split Nord into two commands, 15; left Souham in charge of advance into Flanders, 16; appointed inspectors to survey training, 237

Pike: in song, 150; resurrection of, 186, 189–91

Pillage: discussed as a disciplinary problem, 113–15; mentioned, 98–112 passim

Pion des Loches: training as an artillery officer, 209

Poland: allies concerned with, 3, 19

Political clubs: denunciation of officers, 86; petitioned Convention on use of *tu,* 94; right of soldiers to attend, 99; National Assembly outlawed formation of soldiers' clubs, 121; as an influence upon troops, 121–22; Rochambeau against clubs, 121; Sijas requests clubs watch the postal service to facilitate distribution of journals, 135; singing songs in, 142; purchase of songbooks, 143; clubs as a force in political education, 153–57

Political education: campaign begun in response to Dumouriez's treason, 79; influences before April 1793, 120–24; public ceremonies and *fêtes* as political education, 120–21, 151–53; political journals as a medium of political education, 124–40; agents of political education, 125–26, 312*n*32; other printed tracts, 140–41; song as a medium of political education, 141–50; political clubs as agents of political education, 153–57; revolutionary theater as a medium of political education, 157–58, 315*n*95; impact of political education, 159–62; as a factor in troop motivation, 282–83; in all revolutionary armies, 284–85

Poncet: formed units into battalion squares, 260

Pont-à-Chin, combat at; good performance of French troops, 238–39, 248

Popular societies. *See* Political clubs

Postal service: problems in distribution of journals, 135

Précis historique de l'infanterie légère, 269

Prévôt des maréchaux: decided punishment on the march, 101

Prieur de la Marne: on Vendé levy, 55

Primary group cohesion: importance of, 23, 163; group as a source of loyalty, 25; general theoretical discussion, 30–35; Smith's definition of the function of, 31; and combat motivation, 36; *ordinaire* as the French primary group, 163, 168, 182; cohesion dependent on standards as well as structures, 169; cohesion in French revolutionary army, 182; cohesion and desertion, 317*n*15

Projet d'un ordre français en tactique, 187
Prostitutes: with Nord, 109
Public ceremonies. *See Fêtes*
Publiciste de la Révolution française: purchase and distribution, 127–32 passim

Quartering: of *ordinaire,* 165

Raffet, Denis-Auguste, 239
Règlement concernant l'exercise et les manoeuvres de l'infanterie du 1er août 1791: formal character of, 217; used and modified at Cambrai, 232; patterns of musketry in, 242; passage of lines in, 248; relaxation of alignment in, 250; columns detailed in, 252–55, 327n19; square, 259, 260; deals with skirmishers on the march, 271; little on skirmishers in general, 268, 269; mentioned, 256, 283
Règlement concernant le service intérieur de l'infanterie: defined *ordinaire,* 164
Règiment provisoire: on skirmishers, 115
Representatives on Mission: empowered to make promotions, 75; role in surveillance and purge of officers, 85–86; empowered to appoint officers, 90; evaluated officers as part of *amalgame,* 90–91; highest authority at the front, 97; role in the imposition of discipline, 101, 106–8, 115, 236; duties defined by National Convention, 106–7; activities related to purchase and distribution of journals, 122, 125; concern for political education, 124; as agents of Convention and Committee of Public Safety, 125; bought songbooks, 143; initiated local *fêtes,* 152; and revolutionary theater, 157–58; reported patriotism of troops, 178; complained of system of buying horses, 196; detailed to requisition horses, 197; report on state of infantry and cavalry in Nord, 198–99; insist Dampierre attack, 227; visit Camp de la Madeleine, 229; proclaimed early *levée en masse* in Nord, 234; an *amalgame,* 236; report on zeal of recruits in drill, 239; mentioned, 11, 18, 98, 101
Républicain française: purchase and distribution, 129–30
Requisitionnaires: arrived in autumn, 234; incorporation of, 235; impact on unit capacity, 238; mentioned, 111, 236. *See also Levée en masse*

Rêveries of Marshal de Saxe, 187
Revolutionary tribunals: reorganized by Convention, 82
Rexpoede, engagement at: described, 13; use of line at, 250
Reynier, Jean-Louis: claimed Mouscron fought entirely *en tirailleurs,* 274
Richard, Joseph-Charles: on spirit of French troops, 192
Rifle: as a skirmisher's weapon, 263–65
Robert, chief of the Brigands, 158
Robespierre, Maximillien: on active citizens and National Guard, 50; on citizen soldiers, 64; attacked in *Soirée de camp,* 137, 138; Bricard's reaction to his fall, 139; his report distributed, 141; fearful of esprit de corps, 181; fall of, 285; mentioned, 86, 130
Rochambeau, Jean-Baptiste de Vimeur, comte de: made commander of Nord, 4; resigns, 6; against troops going to clubs, 121; commanded military divisions along northern frontier, 219; labored to train Nord, 220; resisted order to fight, 221; mentioned, 3, 19
Rolland: on need to bring up new battalions to increase size of army, 224; in charge of Sedan depot, 228, 324n34
Roncq, engagement at: skirmishers used bayonets, 273; Delaporte describes action there, 276–77
Ronsin, Charles-Philippe: on influence of clubs in Nord and Pas-de-Calais, 155
Rougyff: purchase and distribution, 129–32; praised the role of song, 147
Rousseau, Jean-Jacques: on citizen soldier, 44, 64
Rousseau, Thomas: received subsidy from Bouchotte, 143; sent at least 100,000 songbooks to army, 144; work as a songwriter, 145; his view of the function of song, 147; patriotic theme in his songs, 148; theme of equality in his songs, 149

Saint-Germain, Charles L., comte de: on low quality of common soldiers, 63; reform of the purchase system, 68; flat of the sword punishment, 93, 106
St.-Just, Antoine-Louis: cashiered a lieutenant-colonel, 86; rigorous disciplinarian as Representative on Mission, 107; ordered courts to judge "revolutionarily," 107–8, 115

Saint-Quentin: streets renamed, 65
Sans-culottes: Coburg promised to become one, 14; the soldier as an armed sans-culottes, 66, 159, 175, 185; notion of a sans-culotte general, 80, 90; and the use of the tu form, 94; need for sans-culotte officers, 96; the soldier as a model sans-culotte, 116, 140, 150; sans-culotte direct democracy not a theme in journals, 138; praise of as a theme in journals, 138; misguided by generals, 139; and the bayonet, 189; trust in, 192; mentioned, 172, 186
Sarette: work as founder of National Institute of Music, 145–46
Sautai, Maurice: on number of cavalry in 1794, 196; on low quality of cavalry officers, 201; Fleurus as a turning point in cavalry development, 203
Saxe, Maurice de: praise of the attack, 187; mentioned, 188
Scharnhorst, Gerhard von: test of fusils and rifles, 264; on effect of French skirmishers, 274; on unconscious nature of the French doctrine, 279
Schauenbourg, Alexis, comte de: as a source for Colin, 246; proponent of the line, 246; his training system, 284
Schérer, Berthélemy: his tactical instructions, 253–54; present at the drafting of Kléber's Instruction, 326n6
Scott, Samuel F.: his works on army composition, 44; peasant participation in military service, 45; on erosion of artillery personnel, 208
Sections of Paris: demanded exclusion of aristocratic officers, 82; printed songs, 144
Sedan: troubles in political society, 157; as a replacement depot, 228
Ségur decree: provisions described, 69
Self-interest: relationship to combat effectiveness, 25; and primary group cohesion, 31–32, 182; and combat motivation, 36
Semestres: leaves of French officers, 62
Seniority: selection of officers on the basis of, 69, 72, 74, 75, 76, 88, 89; produced old officers, 88–89; Committee of Public Safety emphasized, 90
Serrat: on recruiting Volunteers of 1792, 52
Seruzier: on horse artillery, 212
Servan, Joseph: author of Le soldat citoyen, 44; praise of pike, 190
Seven Years' War: artillery in, 210

Shils, Edward: on primary group cohesion, 31
Sijas, Prosper: headed fourth division of Ministry of War, 126; measures taken to insure better delivery of political journals to armies, 135; concerning Maubeuge political club, 156
Sistrières, Michel-François: replaced by Charbonnier, 90; controlled Sedan political club, 157; marched in line at Abbaye d'Orval, 234; on importance of light infantry units, 266
Skirmishers (or light infantry or tirailleurs): in cult of the bayonet, 186; and artillery, 213, 214; training, 217, 232; no detailed regulations for French light infantry, 217, 268–69, 272; French fought only as skirmishers in 1793, 233, 241; and initiative, 242; characteristics of skirmish tactics, 243, 268–77; dash of skirmishers, 244; lack of control over skirmishers, 246; Colin on skirmishers, 246; close order troops used in support of skirmishers, 249–50, 257; general discussion of French light infantry forces and tactics, 261–77; character of light infantry forces, 262–68; and normative compliance, 262–63; used against enemy artillery, 262, 274; advantages and disadvantages of, 262; specialist and non-specialist light infantry forces, 265–68, 279; in support of troops in close order, 274–77; and the march, 280; in battle, 280–81; tables concerning the use of, 291–98; mentioned, 191, 193, 243
Smith, M. B.: defined function of primary group cohesion, 31
Soirée de camp: created, 129; purchase and distribution of, 126–30 passim; format and message, 137; used against Robespierre, 138; on patriotism, 139; songs in, 142, 144; explained why French fought, 160
Soissons: camp at, 225
Soland: used line in retreat, 248
Soldat citoyen, le: by Servan, 44
Soldier, attitudes toward: ancien régime condemnation of common soldier, 61–63; revolutionary praise of the soldier, 63–66, 77, 140, 150, 162, 178–80
Songs: general discussion of song as a medium of political education, 141–50; French love of song, 141–43; purchase

and distribution of, 143–45; songwriters and subsidies, 145–47; message of the songs, 147–50; singing together in the *ordinaire*, 168

Souham, Joseph: divisional commander under Pichegru, 16; leads advance into West Flanders, 16; victorious at Mouscron, 16; at Tourcoing, 17, 18; evaluation of, 19; on training in winter of 1793–94, 237, 238; on importance of tents, 166; stated camping equipment in adequate supply, 166; on invincibility of French on the attack, 188; ordered attack in line at Menin, 251

Square: general character of, 243, 244; French forms of the square, 258–59; use in battle, 259–60; as a sign of tactical maturity, 260; as an element in a flexible system, 260; table detailing the use of, 291

Substitutes: in Volunteers of 1792, 52; allowed in Levy of 300,000, 53

Sustaining motivation: theoretical discussion, 35–36; in the French army, 178; and training in the Nord, 283

Tactical combat strength: theoretical discussion, 38–40

Tactical system: theoretical discussion, 37

Tactics: cavalry tactics, 201–3; general discussion of artillery tactics, 209–12; light artillery tactics, 212–13; tactics of battalion artillery, 213–14; close order infantry tactics of the revolutionary army, 241–60; the line, 244–51; the columns, 251–58; the square, 258–60; open order infantry tactics, 268–77; general discussion, 278–82

Tactique et la discipline dans les armées de la Révolution, la: by Colin, 246

Teil, Joseph du: theories regarding artillery tactics, 210

Tents: importance of, 166; supplies of, 166; role in life of *ordinaire*, 167–68

Terror: proclaimed by the National Convention, 82; effect on military justice, 104–5; and *armées révolutionnaires*, 235; mentioned, 284, 285

Theater: role in campaign of political education, 157–58; as a school of morals and patriotism, 315n95

Théâtre de la République, 148

Thermidor: overthrow of Robespierre, 83, 130, 284

Thiébault, Paul Charles: described his unit of Volunteers of 1792, 52; on dangers of being a general, 81; on his incompetent captain, 89; complained of *fédérés*, 109; description of artillery and infantry, 211; on training of his battalion, 224; on French tactics at Le Blaton, 255; mentioned, 90

Tilleul, combat at: 14

Tirage au sort: to raise milice, 62

Tirailleurs. See Skirmishers

Tondeur, Joseph: kept *livret de route* with songs, 150; song he recorded as evidence of patriotic death, 174

Tourcoing, Battle of: described, 17; as defensive engagement, 191; cavalry at, 202; artillery at, 212; ability of troops at, 219; earlier engagement at Tourcoing fought entirely *en tirailleurs*, 273; mentioned, 19, 238

Tournai, Battle of: described, 17; good performance of French troops there, 238–39, 248; use of route column in earlier engagement at Tournai, 258

Training: training of cavalry, 200; training of artillery, 207, 208–9; general discussion of infantry training in Nord, 216–40; course of instruction and time required for, 217–18, 323n5; training to November 1792, 219–23; from November 1792 to March 1793, 223–26; from April 1793 to October 1793, 226–34; from October 1793 to June 1794, 234–40; exposing troops to small actions as part of training, 220, 222, 232, 238, 279, 324–25n47; belief that skirmishers needed little formal training, 261

Tribunaux criminels militaires, 104, 105

Tribunaux de police corectionnelle: established, 103; abolished, 103; reestablished, 104–5

Troisvilles, combat at: described, 16; use of line at, 249, 260

Trompette de l'armée du Nord, 122

Tu: use of, between officers and men, 94; decree ordering the use of, 141

Turgot, Anne-Robert-Jacques: on *tirage au sort*, 62

Uniforms: as symbols of loyalty in political education, 83, 158

Va-de-bon-coeur: narrator in *Soirée de camp*, 137, 142

Valcour: editor of *Soirée de camp*, 129

Valence, Jean-Baptiste de Timbrune, comte de: receives command of Ardennes, 9, 10

Valenciennes: siege of, 11, 12; political club of, 121; site of training camp, 220; as allied objective, 227; Nord garrison in 1793, 230

Vallière, Jean-Florent de: artillery system of, 205–6

Valmy, Battle of: described, 9; artillery at, 211; mentioned, 111

Vandamme, Dominique-Joseph: brigade commander under Pichegru, 16; defends Courtrai, 17; at Tourcoing, 17, 191; on inspired French soldier, 188; on using small actions to train troops, 238; on French skirmishers at Menin, 274; use of skirmishers at Courtrai, 275

Varin: role in controversy with Custine over distribution of journals, 134; on reading of journals by troops, 136; report on drill at Camp de César, 230

Vatar: editor of *Journal des hommes libres*, 126

Vendée rebellion: 20,000 men raise to fight against it, 54–55; condemned in political journals, 138; troops taken from Nord to fight it, 229; mentioned, 11, 161, 284

Vézu, Claude: controlled Maubeuge political club, 156; reported decimated condition of 3rd Paris, 224

Vidalin: on lack of horses in Nord, 199

Vincent, François-Nicolas: demanded extermination of aristocracy, 82; influential at Ministry of War, 84; criticized by Laveaux, 126; claimed postal service was responsible for delays in distribution of journals, 135; mentioned, 125

Volunteers of 1791: called up, social composition, description, 49–51; reach Nord, 51; formed separate battalions, 57; percent of army in 1794, 60; composition of officer corps, 73; percent of its officers in officer corps of 1794, 75; could leave after one campaign, 111; desertion among, 111, 112; initial motivation of, 177; need for training, 218; in Dumouriez's army, 226; received replacements in 1793, 228; *levée en masse* as replacements for, 235; mentioned, 219

Volunteers of 1792: called up by Legislative Assembly, 6; called up, social composition, description, 51–53; as percent of army in 1794, 60; composition of officer corps, 73–74; percent of its officers in officer corps of 1794, 75; thought they could leave after one campaign, 111; initial motivation of, 177; with Dumouriez, 223, 226; at Neerwinden, 226; moved up to fill gaps in spring 1793, 224, 227; training of, 224; role in early 1793, 225; received replacements, 228; *levée en masse* as replacements for, 235; mentioned, 219

Voltaire: view of *arme blanche*, 186–87

Walmoden, Johan Ludwig: at Hondschoote, 13

Wattignies, Battle of: described, 14; use of bayonet attacks at, 189, 276; cavalry at, 202; artillery at, 211; infantry at, 211, 234; need to apply tactics applied there, 232; use of line at, 248; column attacks at, 256; mentioned, 188, 215, 236, 280

Werwick: seized by French, 16

Wimpffen, Félix de: argued army must have different code and rights, 99; on time necessary to train troops, 216

Women with the army: in headquarters of Nord, 93; crackdown of numbers of, 95; seen as a disciplinary problem, 98, 108–9; washerwomen allowed for each battalion, 165

York, duke of: commanded English forces in Belgium, 12; at Dunkirk, 12; at Tourcoing, 17

Ypres, seige of: 18

Zucotte, engagement at: 275